# ALL
# OR
# NOTHING

## ALSO BY SIMON SPENCE

*The Stone Roses: War and Peace*

*When the Screaming Stops: The Dark History of the Bay City Rollers*

*Staying Alive: The Disco Inferno of the Bee Gees*

*Happy Mondays: Excess All Areas*

*Just Can't Get Enough: The Making of Depeche Mode*

*Still Breathing: True Adventures of the Donnelly Brothers*

*Immediate Records: Lets You In*

*Stoned: Andrew Loog Oldham (Interviews and Research)*

*2Stoned: Andrew Loog Oldham (Interviews and Research)*

*Rolling Stoned: Andrew Loog Oldham (Interviews and Research)*

*Rock Stars at Home (Contributor)*

*Mr Big: Don Arden (Interviews and Research)*

*Night Fever: Club Writing in The Face, 1980–1997 (Contributor)*

# ALL OR NOTHING

## THE AUTHORISED STORY
## OF STEVE MARRIOTT

### SIMON SPENCE

**OMNIBUS PRESS**

London / New York / Paris / Sydney / Copenhagen / Berlin / Madrid / Tokyo

Copyright © 2021, 2023 Omnibus Press
(A division of the Wise Music Group
14–15 Berners Street, London, W1T 3LJ)

Cover designed by Paul Tippett
Picture research by the author

ISBN 978-1-7876-0184-0
PB ISBN 978-1-9158-4120-9

Every effort has been made to trace the copyright holders of the photographs in this book but one or two were unreachable. We would be grateful if the photographers concerned would contact us.

A catalogue record for this book is available from the British Library.

Printed in the Czech Republic

www.omnibuspress.com

To Shirley

'I got a packet in my pocket, it's full of racket, let's go and rock it.'
Steve Marriott

*More praise for* Steve Marriott

Steve Marriott was one of the best British rock singers of all time.
Roger Daltrey, The Who

I wanted to be Steve Marriott.
Robert Plant, Led Zeppelin

I loved Stevie Marriott, what a great voice and guitar player... one of
my favourites.
Keith Richards, The Rolling Stones

Simply an amazing talent... he was his own meter, tethered by nothing.
Bob Dylan

Very short but long on big ideas: Steve Marriott was the best vocalist
that this country has ever produced.
David Bowie

He could sound like a pixie with the sweetest pipes. He could have led
children off a cliff with that side of his voice. And then he could bray
like a donkey, gale force and the power of his voice would turn your
skin to ice.
Mick Jagger, The Rolling Stones

The greatest British singer of all time. The most talented person I've ever
known.
Peter Frampton

The greatest frontman ever. Steve Marriott was unbelievable, an
inspiration.
Paul Stanley, KISS

I loved Stevie, just a fantastic singer. But he pissed off everyone around
him.
Paul Rodgers, Free and Bad Company

When he died, a part of me died too.
Ozzy Osbourne, Black Sabbath

Steve Marriott is one of Britain's great white soul voices... and his cockney music hall vocals paved the way for musicians like Bowie and the Pistols to sing in hometown accents while also influencing people like myself to write in their local dialect. A towering cultural icon.
Irvine Welsh

He was something else.
Steve Perry, Journey

He is the guy ... it's so obvious I'm a Steve Marriott rip-off.
Chris Robinson, The Black Crowes

He was a huge figure in my life.
Martin Freeman, *The Hobbit*, *The Office*, *Sherlock*, *Fargo*

One of the greatest vocalists and a powerhouse of a performer. It's so sad that he's not with us anymore.
Gary Kemp, Spandau Ballet

One of my heroes. Steve's voice was the perfect combination of soul and blues.
Bryan Adams

Steve Marriott's voice is as sweet and soulful as Otis or Aretha.
Bobby Gillespie, Primal Scream

One of the greats.
Paul Weller

He had everything it took.
Nik Cohn

# CONTENTS

# FOREWORD

There have been a number of books written about my old friend and brother in arms Steve Marriott. Some have been well researched and some have not been researched at all; they have been based on hearsay or untruths that have pervaded Steve's life since he passed away, almost thirty years ago, in such dreadful circumstances on 20 April 1991.

I agreed to partake in Simon Spence's book *All Or Nothing* so that the truth, whether it be good or bad, could be told. Steve's family have all contributed for the same reason. We have all stayed close ever since he left us, and we have all watched as people who claimed to be close to Steve, but never knew him, have profited from his awful death.

When I first met Steve, he was a very kind man who did everything he could to help me improve as a drummer. He taught me more about music than anyone else. He had the best record collection I have ever seen. He also introduced me to another up-and-coming young musician who was looking to form a band of his own: Peter Frampton.

We went on to play together in Humble Pie, now considered one of the best live bands from the early to mid-1970s. I continued to work with Steve on and off up until five years before he died. No musician, dead or alive, worked with him more than me. We spent many years together, through the best of times and through some of his worst.

This book covers both sides of Steve's life and career. Everyone who was an important part of Steve's life has had their say in this book. His son and rightful heir to his musical legacy Toby Marriott said it best: 'If you were a genuinely close friend you would inevitably have fallen out with him at some point.' Steve was hard wired to be confrontational with anyone who disagreed with him, but, having said that, he always respected those who did stand up to him. He hated yes men, arse-lickers or sycophants.

What I will say is this: Steve was the greatest white blues singer this country has ever produced, and he was one of the finest songwriters (especially in partnership with Ronnie Lane). At their best, the Marriott/ Lane partnership could easily be compared to Lennon/McCartney or Jagger/Richards, they were *that* good. *Ogdens' Nut Gone Flake* by the Small Faces is the only British concept album, from the 1960s, to come close to *Sgt. Pepper's Lonely Hearts Club Band*.

So what went wrong? I had a front row seat to it all. As a drummer I saw him at his best from my drum stool, which literally was 'The Best Seat in the House'. In my humble opinion, he was the victim of the two-pronged evil twins of cocaine psychosis and untreated alcoholism.

Had he taken the path of so many of his contemporaries and got clean and sober, I truly believe he would still be with us today, making great music and being happy in his own skin. Sadly, his party lifestyle continued. To quote a simple line from Danny DeVito, 'The choices we make dictate the life we lead.' Steve chose the wrong path and look what happened.

The truth is in this book. As they say, sometimes the truth hurts, but it is here for all to see, and nothing in these pages stops me, and all of us, from loving him in spite of himself. He was a one off, the like of which we shall never see again. His influence on the generations that followed him was momentous. They made some great music – from Oasis to the Black Crowes, from Paul Weller to Bryan Adams – but there will only ever be one Steve Marriott.

Jerry Shirley
2020

# AUTHOR NOTE

This book has the authorisation of Steve Marriott's family – his sister, his first two wives and his children – the backing of his bandmates in the Small Faces and Humble Pie *and* a contribution from the manager of Marriott's estate (whose sole beneficiary is Marriott's third and final wife), a rare triumvirate, unique in print. It is not, however, a hagiography, far from it. As well as his successes, Steve Marriott's many failings are dealt with in coruscating detail. It is a messy work, a mass of recollections, incomplete in many ways, but it is as close to the truth as you will ever read. The format of oral biography does away with author subjectivity and makes for an honest, often brutal form of storytelling, especially when dealing with the shadier side of Marriott's life; the gangsters, addictions, immorality and those long-held suspicions over his untimely death.

*All Or Nothing* is drawn from 125 interviews with those who knew Marriott best: wives, children, lovers, bandmates, family, friends, producers, managers, associates, contemporaries, road managers, record label executives and journalists. Included in the list are scores of people who have never told their story before, certainly not as candidly. It is a work that explodes the myth of not just Marriott but of rock'n'roll – insightful, gossipy, engrossing, frightening and stickily intimate. Here is the man in full, warts and halos, on stage, in studios, backrooms, bedrooms and dark holes.

Unless stated, the following were interviewed by the author (★denotes interviews conducted by the author during his research for Andrew Loog Oldham's autobiographies *Stoned* and *2Stoned*): Keith Altham★, Dee Anthony courtesy Chris Welch, David Arden, Don Arden, P. P. Arnold courtesy Pete Mitchell, Lesley Ashcroft courtesy Mick Taylor, Kofi Baker, Mark Ballew, Paul Banes, Lionel Bart★, David Bowie courtesy

AUTHOR NOTE

VH1, Mick Brigden, Elkie Brooks courtesy Robson Publishing, Joe Brown courtesy unknown, Mel Bush, Rob Caiger, Tony Calder★, Ron Chimes courtesy Andy Neil, George Chkiantz★, Keith Christopher, Dave Clarke, Chris Clements, Dave 'Clem' Clempson courtesy Dan Muise, B. J. Cole, Mel Collins, Don Craine, Dan Crewe★, Roger Daltrey courtesy Blink Publishing, Phil DeHavilland, Jenny Dearden, Graham Dee, Jeff Dexter courtesy Andy Neil, Martin Druyan, Jeff Edmans, John 'Rhino' Edwards, Allen Ellett courtesy Paolo Hewitt, Steve Ellis, Mick Eve, Marianne Faithfull courtesy Little, Brown, Mark Fenwick, Venetta Fields, Anton Fig, Malcolm Forrester★, David Foster, Sally Foulger courtesy unknown, Peter Frampton courtesy Dan Muise, Jerry Shirley and Iain McGonigal, Chris France, Bob Garcia, Victor Gersten, Craig Goetsch, Sammy Hagar courtesy It Books, Jim Hannibal, Bill Hibbler, Simon 'Honeyboy' Hickling, Tim Hinkley, Dallas Hodge, Hugh Janes, Glyn Johns courtesy Plume Publishing, John Paul Jones★, Kenney Jones (also various sources including Blink Publishing courtesy Kenney Jones), Ron King courtesy I Did It My Way blog, Simon Kirke, David Krebs, Ronnie Lane courtesy various sources, Claudia Lennear, James Leverton, Christine Lore, Kenny Lynch★, Gary Lyons, Gered Mankowitz★, Bill Marriott courtesy Len Brown, Kath Marriott courtesy Dan Muise, Mollie Marriott, Toby Marriott, Kay Mateus Dos Anjos (née Marriott) courtesy Dan Muise and Jerry Shirley, Pam Marriott Land, Ian McLagan courtesy various sources including Sidgwick & Jackson and Andy Neil, Ken Mewis★, Zoot Money, Richard Newman, Billy Nicholls courtesy The Strange Brew podcast, Dale Ockerman, Alan O'Duffy, Laurie O'Leary courtesy Paolo Hewitt, Andrew Loog Oldham, Jimmy Page courtesy unknown, Stephen Parsons, Gregory Phillips courtesy Andrew Loog Oldham, Manon Piercey, Eddie Piller, Gary 'Diz' Putnam, Marge Raymond, Craig Rhind, Rick Richards, Greg Ridley courtesy Dan Muise, Bobby Rio, Sir Tony Robinson, Steve Rowland, Elliot Saltzman, Brian Shaw, Jerry Shirley, David Skinner★, John Skinner, Sheila Smith courtesy various sources, Colin Spaull, Sue Tacker courtesy Andy Neil, Shel Talmy, Bobby Tench courtesy of Dan Muise, Denis Thompson, Pete Townshend★, Val Weedon, Chris Welch, Mark Wheeller, Peter Whitehead★, Alan 'Sticky' Wicket, Vicky Wickham courtesy unknown, Fallon Williams III, Rick Wills (also courtesy unknown), Jimmy Winston courtesy Mark Paytress, Richie Wise, Larry Yaskiel, Brian Young. The selected Steve Marriott quotes are taken from a variety of sources.

# INTRODUCTION

Steve Marriott was a freak of nature, a little man, just over five foot tall, with the hugest of soul voices and the most overwhelming of personalities. He was a show-off, a loudmouth, a child star, a pop star and a rock star, a drunk and a drug addict. He was lovable, kind, funny and charismatic but could also be vicious, belligerent, reckless, violent, sadistic, quite evil (especially when alcohol was involved). Above all he was a performer.

In the sixties he led the Small Faces, Mod icons famed for hits such as 'Whatcha Gonna Do About It', 'All Or Nothing' and 'Lazy Sunday'. In the seventies he became an American rock god fronting the unstoppable Humble Pie, whose vocal-shredding heavy metal guitar anthems such as 'I Don't Need No Doctor' and '30 Days In The Hole' saw them endlessly sell out arenas and stadiums and spawn a host of imitators. It did him little good. He left both bands virtually penniless, worn out by the age of 30, with a troubled soul, a headful of demons, unable to grow up or take any responsibility for himself; a boy-man who blamed his worse behaviour – cracking his wife's cheekbone, wrecking hotels, spitting at bandmates and record label executives, squandering countless opportunities and millions of pounds (the list is long) – on a bizarre alter ego, a bald-headed wrestler called Melvin, familiar to all who toured and lived with him. And on Melvin's tail; regret, tears and self-hatred.

His mistrust of the music industry and his appetite for self-sabotage is legend and, perhaps, here we can cut him a little slack: his songs and affairs were looked after by some of the industry's most notorious and terrifying figures – Don Arden, Dee Anthony, Tony Calder and Andrew Loog Oldham – all tough, sharp, unsentimental and mobbed up. Marriott never could recover from his perceived mistreatment at their hands, and yet, he chose them all, drawn to their underworld braggadocio and inviting soft, warm bosoms. And each, initially at least, gave him the affection he craved, but he was worked hard, sold easily and ultimately left with little more than a debilitating cocaine psychosis and alcohol problems. His financial ruin – at times he had little but the clothes he stood up in – was pitiful.

On Marriott's long downward trajectory, senior (and less so) English crime figures and high-ranking members of the American Mafia pervaded his life. His close links to the Krays stretched back to the sixties and from the mid-seventies until his death he was informally managed by Laurie O'Leary, Ronnie Kray's best pal and a senior Kray business associate. In America his contractual problems saw him negotiating with infamous Mafioso figures such as Carmine 'Wassel' DeNoia and Joe Pagano. And yet, perhaps the most controversial figure in Marriott's later years was his third wife, Toni Poulton.

They married in 1989, less than two years before his tragic death in a house fire. He was 42; she was 28, a foul-mouthed Essex livewire, the former girlfriend of a Chas & Dave roadie, a heavy drinker and drug user and the subject of a hugely successful, anti-drink-drive stage play *Too Much Punch For Judy*. The play relayed a horrific 1983 car crash that saw her elder sister decapitated while Poulton, drunk behind the wheel, escaped with minor injuries. Many, including Marriott's close family and friends, felt the marriage was ill conceived, the volatile relationship doing little to becalm the inner demons of either husband or wife. Divorce was already being spoken about when Marriott died and it is easy to understand why many of those closest to him feel Poulton's standing as the sole beneficiary of Marriott's estate is an insult to Marriott's four, now adult, children. In 1994, she received a five-year jail sentence after a second fatal car crash, again drunk at the wheel, causing the death of a 21-year-old woman, incredibly only a few hundred yards away from the scene of her sister's death.

The cruel circumstances of Marriott's own horrific death – battling alcoholism and drug addiction but on the verge of a tantalising comeback – lend a degree of sympathy to a man who was so often his own worst enemy, a willing participant in his own demise, who refused to compromise, who beat and cheated on all his wives and was careless in fatherhood; a liar, insecure, immature, angry, selfish and needy. Maybe, had he lived, he would have changed, mellowed, wised up, kicked the drink and drugs. Many thought he had undiagnosed issues from a traumatic childhood, the result of an overbearing mother, or that his short attention span and personality defects were caused by a chemical imbalance in the brain, while others blame the old familiars – the booze and drugs and the fame that came too soon when he was just a boy of 13. Often it's said he never recovered from the failure of his first marriage to model Jenny Dearden. Andrew Loog Oldham, Marriott's manager and record label boss during the Small Faces' most successful years, offers a blunter version of his life. 'Steve was a criminal opportunist,' he says. 'Always went to the highest bidder. Then lay down and bitched about it. Steve could outhustle both Don and me. Eventually he outhustled himself.'

Maybe he was just the real thing, a rocker – undiluted, uncompromising, cursed and unrepentant, unforgiving – the type that comes around every once in a while, a Jerry Lee Lewis, or a Chuck Berry, even a Hank Williams, the product of a philosophy that runs, boy, hell, you got to live it if you want to make it, you can't fake it, got to live it. Even now, given the tarnish and indignity he heaped upon himself, Marriott continues to shine among his British contemporaries, breathes a rarefied air amongst the greatest who ever lived, as a singer, songwriter, guitarist and keyboard player. Many of his songs still stand as classics, his live performances legend. He cannot be imitated; can never be forgotten. Not for nothing was he first choice as the frontman for Led Zeppelin, wanted by Keith Richards to replace Brian Jones in the Stones, considered for AC/DC, Bad Company and Guns N' Roses and rated by artists as diverse as Jimi Hendrix, John Cale, The Four Tops, Mark Hollis, Johnny Depp, Paul Weller, Aerosmith, KISS, Alice Cooper, Ozzy Osbourne and Oasis – to name just a few. It is often remarked it took two men to replace him when he left the Small Faces, Rod Stewart and Ronnie Wood.

This books pays full tribute to Marriott's supernatural talent and fully explores his musical inspirations: the reader is encouraged to listen or re-listen to the wonderful R&B, country, rock'n'roll, soul and blues music he treasured, to share his deep knowledge and exquisite taste. It also illuminates a side less often seen, behind the cockney swagger, beyond the salaciousness and the heart-breaking ache of his performing life, a man, real and ragged, a humble cook, generous friend, broad intellect, sentimental soul, caring brother, just and unpretentious, proudly working class, compassionate, animal lover, shy and unsure of himself, a joker – always quick to laugh, especially at himself – wistful, romantic, a loving son, father, nephew.

It is, simply put, a celebration, a vain attempt to capture what fuelled Marriott's drive, commitment, determination, ambition and indefatigability. An exploration of the pain at his core, the devil-may-care attitude he fostered, and his true force and pure spirit. It answers, why, for all his faults, he was truly loved, even by those he hurt most. It is a rich portrait, with revealing stories of his family life, childhood stardom, early musical career and fame with the Small Faces and Humble Pie. It also covers – for the first time – his long years in exile, first in Santa Cruz, then New York and finally Atlanta, and his low-key return to London in the eighties, homeless, penniless, unwell, refusing to work for anything but cash in hand, churning out hundreds of low-key pub and club gigs a year. It is a bewildering life; one of raw talent gone to waste, of magnificent highs and stomach-churning lows – heart attacks, turned backs, cocaine, heroin, pills, brandy, crack, ulcers, blood, sweat, tears, abandoned recordings, punch-ups, jail cells and tax bills – the story of a boy and a man who never stopped, a real-life road runner.

And finally, ultimately, for here is the great controversy, for the first time, Marriott's tragic death is given proper examination. The coroner said it was carbon monoxide poisoning due to smoke inhalation – his bed, the police said, had caught fire either from a lit cigarette or a candle after cocaine, Valium and booze had rendered him unconscious. His family has questions about the timeline and events surrounding that fatal night. *All Or Nothing* attempts to tie up so many nagging loose ends, unravel the rumours and shine a little light into the murk of Marriott's final days.

# CHAPTER 1

# **Consider Yourself**

**Sir Tony Robinson:** He was very hyperactive. Certainly if he had been at school today, he wouldn't necessarily have gone to special school but there would have a been a teacher who would have appreciated he was showing some signs of anti-social behaviour and he would have been helped in a way he wasn't back then. But maybe that would have inhibited the person he became. Maybe he was the best Steve Marriott he could possibly have been and that included the downfall.

**Sheila Smith [Née Devo, Aunt]:** He was a very, very, naughty boy. In fact he was wicked sometimes. He was a difficult child and he and [his mother] Kath did not get on because he was headstrong. So he would come round [to see us] because he needed a bit of comfort. He and I always got on well and he got on well with my husband, David [Smith, a cameraman who frequently worked in America]. Kath would be on the phone crying about the latest bit of naughtiness. I was his aunty and I hope I was good to him but I had to give him a ticking off sometimes. He upset his mother so much.

*Pre-adolescence, known examples of Marriott's bad behaviour included incidents such as putting manure through neighbours' letterboxes, stealing milk bottles from doorsteps and alarming neighbours with fake screams about his mother and father fighting. He'd also been seriously injured when a firework exploded in his face. The strangest episode involved him pouring tarmac over the local milkman's horse, distressing the animal and causing chaos.*

**Kay Marriott [Sister]:** He'd insist we all played cricket as a family and he had to bat but when he was bowled or caught out he'd refuse to give the bat to anyone else. When Mum told him no one was going to play with him anymore unless he behaved, he'd angrily throw the bat away and storm off. Half an hour later, he'd stroll back acting as if nothing had happened. 'Who wants to play cricket,' he'd shout, 'I'll bat first.'

*Marriott's mother Kathleen was an attractive woman, quite glamorous, extroverted, forceful, sometimes a bit over the top. Her husband, Bill, was the opposite, a small, quiet, unassuming man who kept himself to himself. It was clear who was the household's dominant figure. Aunt Sheila was Kath's younger sister, a sympathetic figure in Marriott's early life and instrumental in his burgeoning professional career. She was the subject of his very first attempt at songwriting, 'Sheila My Dear', and she had bought Marriott his first puppy when he was 11 in 1958. They listened to the radio together, the Spike Milligan/Peter Sellers/Harry Secombe comedy vehicle* The Goon Show *being a favourite of both. Crucially Sheila was the family's link to fame and showbusiness, assisting the well-known impresario (and former singing star) Jack Hylton, who produced light entertainment shows for TV, managed radio, film and theatre productions and organised Royal Command Performances. By contrast, Marriott's mother held down a full-time job at the Tate & Lyle sugar factory in the heavy industrial district of the Port of London in the East End.*

**Sir Tony Robinson:** Steve was 13 when I met him. I knew him as Stephen. I was the understudy to the Artful Dodger [in West End musical *Oliver!*] and Steve came in as my understudy about two or three months after the show had started [*Oliver!* opened on 30 June 1960]. They realised it was going to be this mega hit [becoming the most successful musical ever to be mounted on a West End stage], so they hired this new tranche of boys that included Steve [to back the original cast of pubescent boys who, due to their age, were subject to working restrictions]. When I went on as the Artful Dodger, Steve played my part in the chorus; the rest of the time he would just be sitting around in the dressing room weeks at a time with the other understudies. Later on, when I left the show [after nine months, approximately March 1961], Steve and his lot would have been on every night but as far as I recall he never played the Artful Dodger. He would have taken my role as part of the cheeky cockney chorus: first half [he'd have been] one of the workhouse boys, second half part of Fagin's gang. The one thing I remember about that time is we were always tired, always squabbling and bickering. You'd never get a 12- or 13-year-old boy these days travelling up to the West End to do eight shows a week… not finishing until ten past ten, getting home at 11 p.m.

**Kath Marriott [Mum, 1926–2015]:** Steve would have loved to have played the Artful Dodger and, if he hadn't been so cheeky and so rude, he would have got the part easily. But he didn't like the matron [whose role was to educate the child performers in lieu of them missing school] because she was posh and she didn't like him because she thought he was cocky and disrupted her boys.

**Steve Marriott:** My mum and dad almost forced me into acting. I certainly didn't feel like I had any say in the matter.

**Kath Marriott:** We had just come back from holiday and had a picture of Steve with the guitar we had bought him. It was nearly as big as him, cost us £10. Bill brought the paper home [the *Daily Sketch*, where he worked as a printer, was running ads for auditions for boys to appear in *Oliver!*, 'no experience required'], and he said, 'Send in that picture of him with the guitar just for a laugh and see what happens.' All right. Not dreaming that anything would. And, the next we heard, he had to go to an audition in the West End, to the New Theatre [where *Oliver!* was being staged] in St Martin's Lane. He was dreadful with nerves. He was nearly sick with worry and then he would walk out on stage and you wouldn't believe it was the same person. He was the only one accepted on the spot. And I was so proud.

*The base requirements for the stage role were boys with a reasonable voice who were small, cute and looked younger than their years. Stephen Peter Marriott – to give him his full name – had always been a small boy ever since being born prematurely on 30 January 1947, weighing just four pounds four ounces and suffering from jaundice. Kath, to emphasise the point, made Marriott wear shorts to the audition. He sang two numbers, 'Who's Sorry Now' by Connie Francis and 'Oh Boy' by Buddy Holly's Crickets, both huge UK hits in 1958.*

3

*Prior to the* Oliver! *audition Marriott had entered a couple of 'talent shows' while the family holidayed, as they did every summer, often joined by Aunt Sheila, in Jaywick Sands, Clacton-on-Sea, Essex, a popular destination of choice for many Londoners. They would hire a holiday bungalow, hit the beach, see concerts on the pier, play in amusement arcades or take trips on the pleasure boats. Bill had bought Marriott a ukulele in 1958 and that year he had used it to score first prize in the holiday resort's 'Uncle Ken's Music and Talent Show', organised near the sea wall. It was a bit of seaside shtick that rivalled the Punch and Judy puppet show on the beach in popularity, a family business, with Ken's wife taking the money and his two children aiding the musical proceedings. If the talent that day was a bit lacking, the two children would jump up from the crowd and play the piano or sing. Marriott won with his take on George Gershwin's popular and much-recorded 'Summertime' and the following year he won again with a rendition of the comedic 'Little White Bull' (a 1959 Top 10 for Tommy Steele, written by* Oliver! *creator Lionel Bart).*

**Kath Marriott:** We never knew anything about it until he came back with the first prize. My husband showed him how to play the ukulele and he entertained everybody with that. He loved it. But he progressed to the guitar. A friend of ours who played in a Hawaiian band on the BBC showed him chords. Once he understood the concept of it, you couldn't teach him anymore because he didn't want to know. He wanted to do it his way. And he just went on from there. Never had a lesson after that.

**Sheila Smith [Née Devo]:** When the social club closed we would go back to Strone Road for sandwiches and coffee, Steve would be up waiting for us, guitar in hand, Bill would get on the piano and they would all sing songs.

*Strone Road was maternal Grandma Kathleen's home in Manor Park, a residential area in suburban east London, almost fifteen miles from the heart of the city. It was where Marriott spent the first thirteen years of his life. The large two-storey terrace house had been split into an upstairs and downstairs flat, the latter, with garden and cellar, home to Marriott and family. Grandma Kathleen doted on the young Marriott, taking him to see popular films 'up West' (central London).*

4

**Toby Marriott [Son]:** Steve's nan was great. She was born in India. Her mother hung herself when she was young and the father sent her and her sister back to London, where she went to a convent school. Steve would often tell people that he had Mongolian in him due to this. Unfortunately, through modern DNA science, I can confirm this isn't true. Apparently, she was really happy-go-lucky and she partied – danced, listened to music. She could have been the one who turned Steve on to music. She was a wild lady and because of her lifestyle I don't think she was around her children much when they were growing up. That's why my nan [Kath] had to look after her sisters [growing up]. I think that's where Kath might have got the uptightness because she had to grow up sooner than she should have.

**Steve Marriott:** It was my dad [who got me interested in music]. He was pub pianist and that meant he got his drinks for free. He used to be invited to parties because he could play about thirty songs right off the bat. I'd go to sleep listening to it… singing, stomping and dancing. Everyone was happy. It instilled in me that music was happy.

**Kath Marriott:** Steve loved the family singalongs. It was typical pub playing. We made our own entertainment, which most families did. Everybody had a piano. And everybody sort of tried to play a tune, sang or danced [Kath played piano]. Some were good and some were hopeless. It would be a full house: my daughter [another Kathleen, shortened to Kay, she was five years younger than Marriott], my mother and my [step]father, my sisters. They were always here.

**Kay Marriott:** I was born into it. My brother was the one who entertained. I was the introvert. He was the extrovert. He was very mischievous, very cheeky and very protective toward me. He didn't have a shy bone in his body. We fought like hell. We punched each other's lights out. We were a normal brother and sister. Hated each other at home. Loved each other to bits. If anyone said something about him, I'd go mad. If anyone said something about me, he'd go mad. If he liked you, he loved you. He'd give you anything. But if he didn't like you, there was no two ways and that was it.

*Music was Marriott's passion. He had sought out Lonnie Donegan, so-called 'King of Skiffle', Britain's first and most successful pre-Beatles rock star, who had a huge string of hits from 1955 to 1960, at his home address. Marriott said he came away disappointed to find the man not all that off stage, exuding none of the star appeal he expected. The first record he bought was the 1959 No 1 by Britain's best answer to Elvis yet, Cliff Richard & The Shadows' 'Travellin' Light'. In a fury with something Marriott had done, his mum smashed the 7-inch on his head, breaking it. While at the rough-and-ready local Manor Park secondary, Sandringham Road, which he attended from age 11 to 14, Marriott claimed to have formed his first bands. He said they played Buddy Holly or Cliff Richard cover versions in local coffee bars and at the local cinema on Saturday mornings. His sister recalls he wore fake Buddy Holly glasses and was nicknamed Buddy Marriott. One classmate at Sandringham Road recalled Steve as a bully, a 'real hard case' and a 'pent-up' loner.*

**Kath Marriott:** At [Sandringham Road] school the teachers used to leave him to do what he wanted. If he wanted to hang outside the window, as he invariably did, they would leave him. If he wanted to jump on the milk float and ride around the playground they would let him. Otherwise he would just disrupt the whole class. As soon as they had exams and they had to study Steve would swot up for a fortnight and then be in the top ten. He didn't do anything for a year and then pass his exams. It used to drive the teachers mad.

**Bill Marriott [Dad, 1912–1996]:** We went to see his teacher on open evening and she said, there's only one thing I can say about Steve. He's unique. A woman down the street where we lived was a fortune-teller and she told us he would get right to the top in his profession and that we wouldn't have to worry about him.

**Steve Marriott:** I couldn't concentrate and ended up more or less being expelled. For burning the school down! It was an accident. I got bored during a lesson and we were mucking about and I dropped a lighted match through a hole on the floor. If I had stayed at Sandringham I would have ended up in prison, no doubt about it.

*The fire, which was said to have destroyed a large portion of the old Victorian school building, was one of several Marriott stories relating to his childhood that*

6

*he exaggerated for effect. It made good copy in his Small Faces days to suggest he had burned his school down, emphasising his rebel qualities. However, it simply, as his sister confirmed to this author, never happened. There was a lit match, a bit of smoke in a classroom and Marriott got detention.*

**Kath Marriott:** He put a match in between the cracks and there was a bit of smoke and that was it. He's rather like his father. It's how he told a story. His father told a very good story. And each time they told it, they added a little bit on to it. And it got completely out of hand. They just glorified it a bit.

**Sir Tony Robinson:** I really had a love/hate relationship with Steve. One minute he'd be my best buddy ever, the next he'd heap scorn and derision on me. He made me cry more than once but I loved the fact he was frightened of no one. I was rather respectful of my seniors, Steve never was. We would spend time together at weekends. Steve modelled himself very much on the 1950s London geezer, even as a 13-year-old. He was not really from the East End but he liked to see himself as quite tough, a wide boy, a chatty boy, very much a cockney boy. My parents came from Hackney and we talked in a similar kind of way and about similar things but there was a big divide between us – my dad had got quite a good administrative job which had allowed us to move out into a semi-detached house in [north London suburb] South Woodford. My family was lower middle class, there was a respectability about us that Steve didn't have and was really quite suspicious of… it coloured our relationship. It was a class thing but the irony was you couldn't get a Rizla paper between us as far as our families were concerned.

*Marriott's family, mum and dad and little sister Kay, moved to a new three-bed Manor Park council flat in 1961, shortly after Marriott started to bring in a healthy weekly wage from* Oliver! *The flat was on the third storey of one of a small number of a four-storey blocks that formed part of a purpose-built estate. Close to the Essex border, Manor Park was a nondescript area (there was no Tube station) with the busy Romford Road running through its heart and fringed by the busy North Circular Road, a poor relation to the larger close-by commuter suburbs of Ilford, Romford and East Ham.*

**Manon Piercey [Girlfriend, and mother to Mollie]:** They were new blocks of flats, a little cul-de-sac, and he was in the one opposite me. We used to wave at each other through our windows, point down and we'd meet downstairs. He was in *Oliver!* We went out together when I was about 14 and he was 15 and that fizzled out and then we went out together again. We were always friends. I loved him from the first minute I saw him: he was really different to everybody else. He was so kind, very generous, a good friend.

*Mum Kath was 34 and now worked as a receptionist at a photography studio in Holborn in London's West End (she had also briefly worked as a bookbinder). She was originally from north London, the eldest of three sisters. Her father was a fishmonger, violent and abusive, her mother a chambermaid. The marriage broke down. Kath had moved to Manor Park when she was 10, left education with few, if any, qualifications and had married Bill, who was fourteen years her senior, when she was 17 in 1943.*

**Mollie Marriott [Daughter]:** His mum was not a nice lady. When I was a teenager I was told a story about Dad when he was 7 or 8. He had a pet chicken that he adored; it was like a dog for him. He had this really close bond with the chicken and he was naughty, nothing out of the ordinary for a 7-year-old, and she killed the chicken and she made Dad pluck it and eat it. Brutal. It blows my mind. As an adult he was the most troubled soul and had some serious mental battles, demons, and it goes back to his childhood, 100 per cent.

*Here was another story embellished by Marriott in later life, seemingly to illicit sympathy. The family kept a vicious rooster that attacked all and sundry, including neighbours, but somehow had grown attached to Marriott. It was slaughtered by a visiting butcher and eaten for a Marriott Christmas dinner – at a time when such meat was hard to come by. It is true that an early ambition of Marriott's was to work with animals, perhaps as a vet.*

**Kath Marriott:** He hatched a little duck. He saw these boys had rifled a nest and he brought this egg home. He was 10. This little duck followed him everywhere. We put him in a big cardboard box. And at nighttime he would jump up until he got out of this box and went to sleep with Steve. Another time he brought a baby owl home that had been abandoned.

*Bill, almost 50, was a thwarted artist. He was also the eldest of three siblings. He kept in touch with his brother Alf who had moved to Manchester. His father had been a taxi driver while his mother had died when he was 18. As a child he had won a scholarship to attend the prestigious Royal Academy of Art, but after leaving he had only managed to land what must have been a succession of frustrating low-paid, low-skilled jobs. When he married Kathleen he was in the Navy. Soon after he lost an eye in an accident and was subsequently demobbed. In the late forties when Marriott was an infant Bill had opened a fish stall, Bill's Eels, outside the Ruskin Arms pub (where the Small Faces would initially rehearse) in Manor Park, selling jellied eels and whelks. A doomed attempt to launch a more concrete enterprise, a pie and mash shop, ate up the remainder of his disability money from the Navy. He'd held down his job as printer for the* Daily Sketch, *a populist tabloid with a one million circulation, based on the famous Fleet Street, since the mid-fifties. He and Marriott frequently fought.*

**Jerry Shirley [Humble Pie]:** I never quite understood where he and his dad were at: when I knew him, his dad worshipped Steve and everything he did. However, Steve apparently had a bit of a rough go of it as a young man with his father. His father was quite tough on him. But then again Steve was such a little bugger he probably needed it. Knowing what I know about Steve, it wouldn't surprise me if his parents had been somewhat heavy-handed with him as a youngster because he was a handful. I am not condoning that behaviour, it's just the way it was done back then in many families.

**Kath Marriott:** He never realised how much his father loved him.

**Jenny Dearden [First wife]:** His relationship with his parents was extremely complex. His relationship with his mother was difficult and he always said she broke a bowl over his head at some point. He, himself, was difficult and complex. He had that hyper, hyper energy. His dad was rather silent. His mother was much more outgoing.

**Manon Piercey:** Bill was very browbeaten by Kath. She was the boss and she was not nice to Bill. She was always putting him down. He was very quiet but he was a very funny man. He'd hardly say anything, he'd hardly get a chance, but when he did say something it was really funny.

He was a good piano player and I think Steve got his music from him. But they weren't close as father and son, they really weren't.

*Fights between father and self-willed son could be brutal and grew increasingly violent as Marriott entered his teenage years. His mum more often directed her ire at Marriott's sister, Kay.*

**Kay Marriott:** My dad would never ever lay a finger on me and he didn't to his dying day. My mum seemed to chastise me. She'd give me a slap, she'd punish me and I'd get cuddles off my dad, which Steve was always a bit jealous about. But in that day and age it was old school, you didn't sit and cuddle a boy.

**Toby Marriott:** I lived with Kath and Bill for the majority of my childhood. Growing up with Bill I could always tell that Steve – they got along but Dad had this frustration with Bill because he was so quiet and reserved. Sometimes I think my dad tested that. Nothing nasty, never attacked him but you could kind of tell that maybe Steve wanted his dad to be a bit more demonstrative or dominating. Bill was very talented, used to play in pubs on the piano but he was very different to Dad, he was very reserved and moralistic, a very decent man. My nan could be very firm and very outspoken – if she smelled bullshit she would speak up – and sometimes that would piss people off. She's definitely where Dad got his edginess from. But I'm not sure about some of the stories. Forcing Steve to eat his chicken? They never did anything like that to me. I didn't see any cruelty from them. I always heard Steve had a duck and he was holding it and a cat or dog jumped up and crushed it by accident. I don't know about him having to eat it... If she was cruel to Steve I don't think he would have been around much in her life. He definitely wouldn't have bought them [his parents] a house [in the early seventies] and looked after them. For me, Kath was a great woman. She took me in and raised me for about six years. She could be bossy toward Bill but no more than any other married couple. They were good people. She was well-to-do, well-spoken, a little posh. I know Dad used to hate that sometimes. He'd say there's nothing worse than an East End snob, not that she was snobby but she kept her house clean [and later on] tended her rose garden. But I think he adored his mother. They did fall out here and there. When I was 9, they didn't speak for about six months. That was over a bicycle of mine he'd given away that she got really angry about but 80 per cent of the people you've interviewed have fallen out with him at one time. To not fall out with Steve you didn't really know him. My nan could be a little possessive of Steve and she was possessive of me, thank God she was because I needed that in my life when I was a kid. And she was one of the few that did stand up to him and I think he might have liked that but sometimes he didn't. She was very down to earth, she didn't come across as fame hungry – I don't get that at all. I never saw that. I don't think she had aspirations to be famous at all. Some of the things Dad said about them were probably exaggerated, something he was known to do from time to time. I know burning down the school was an exaggeration. Nan always told me he didn't do that. He just happened to be outside the school at the time.

**Sir Tony Robinson:** Every Sunday I went to Manor Park to visit him. I don't remember his dad. It was his mum who dominated. I never got the feeling that he didn't love his mum but I did get the feeling they had a very robust relationship... it was certainly more *EastEnders* than *Downton Abbey*. They were always rowing and they'd say terrible things to each other. We never really used to play in his house, we always went out. We'd go down to Ilford to Valentines Park [supposedly inspiration for the Small Faces hit 'Itchycoo Park'], which was run-down and boarded up, and one time he'd got some super-strength untipped cigarettes for us to try. He had a magnetic and seductive air. There was a layer of us [schoolboy actors] who were streetwise, extrovert, had some talent, were confident in auditions, didn't feel out of place on a stage and they were the ones you always tended to meet at auditions and who would get the parts. Steve was one of those who stood out. Dennis Waterman [future *Minder*, *The Sweeney* and *New Tricks* TV star] was around at that time. He was another who stood out.

**Kath Marriott:** He could completely overwhelm some people and they couldn't handle it. If somebody upset him, then he would put them down all the time. And he would be serious. He was unique. You didn't have kids like that then. He was so different.

**Sir Tony Robinson:** Even though he was younger than me [by six months] he did intimidate me. He said he would teach me guitar and I said, 'I don't have a guitar.' He said, 'Well, give me £5 and I'll go buy you one.' That was a huge amount of money for the time but we were earning huge amounts. I was earning £10 a week [in *Oliver!*] and Steve was earning £8 a week. I gave him the £5 on a Monday and on the Friday he brought in this red and yellow, really quite small, musical instrument. I was so intimidated I didn't complain or anything. I took it home and my dad said they cost £1 in Woolworths and not only that but it's not even a guitar, it's a ukulele, and this one wobbles, the neck is loose. When I took it back in to Steve and said I want my money back, he said 'Why?' And then he said it's supposed to wobble like that... it's a Hawaiian ukulele and it goes 'Wah! Wah!' when you move the neck backwards and forwards and that's why it's so expensive. I kept it and he taught me the basic three chords and that was all. I was so humiliated. That epitomised my relationship with Steve. When I started growing a little moustache, he started calling me 'Moustachio' and all the other kids started calling me that. It felt so cruel, but there was also something about him that was lovable, people did warm to him even though he could be so horrible.

*Marriott got his first taste of publicity while appearing in* Oliver! *In early 1961, he featured in the local paper, the* Stratford Express, *as the 'shaggy-haired 14-year-old who leaves his neat council home every evening to join London's worst gang of juvenile cut-throats'. The article described him as 'pocket-sized' and suggested he liked swimming, billiards, table tennis and English but hated maths. 'I want to go on stage when I leave school,' Marriott said, adding that he was putting aside a third of his weekly* Oliver! *wage to buy a new guitar.*

**Kath Marriott:** When he left *Oliver!* after a year he had stars in his eyes. He wanted to be in showbusiness.

**Mollie Marriott:** For Nan [Kath], Steve was the goose who laid the golden egg, big time. He wasn't fame hungry. My nan was fame hungry.

**Christine Lore [Friend]:** *Oliver!* is when he realised he was special and until that day he was the most insecure kid, he would do the most stupid crazy things to get attention. Bad attention is better than none at all. He told me, 'I was always doing crazy things.' He burned his schoolhouse down. He told me his mum and dad would lock him in the coal cellar. His father used to knock him around. I said, 'You've been traumatised, you need to talk this out with professionals.' His problems started with his parents. It was sick some of the things that happened – that whole cockney way of thinking after the war, there was rationing but the dad can still go get drunk at the pub every night. Kath played it all down when Pam [Marriott's second wife and Lore's friend] brought it up. I don't think Bill liked Steve being a success in *Oliver!* He liked the money but not the premise of how it was coming in. Steve was the family cash cow. Steve got his self-confidence from the love of the audience – that's when he felt like something, felt wanted, and when that happened his parents couldn't have control over him anymore. He was free... that was his ticket.

**Tim Hinkley [Scrubbers' sessions]:** The rumours are his parents used to lock him in the coal cellar when he was naughty and those old coal cellars weren't very pleasant, they were dark and dank. There was a round disc in the pavement the coal man would lift and pour the coal down and you could access it through the basement.

*Again, this is another childhood story Marriott stretched and worked to his own ends. He and his sister Kay were sometimes locked in the cellar at Strone Road as punishment for misbehaviour but it was not the terrifying hole he later recalled. It was lit and they would be shut down there for relatively brief periods, as a form of 'naughty step'. As an adult Marriott would become notorious for bending the truth to his own ends, his remembrances of childhood traumas used to perhaps excuse flaws in his own behaviour or draw kindness from the listener.*

**Laurie O'Leary [Marriott manager]:** You'll hear stories about his relationship with his parents but the gospel truth is he that he loved them.

*The sole creator of* Oliver! *was Lionel Bart. He would undoubtedly have left an impression on the young Marriott. Bart was big in pop as well as theatre, having started out as a songwriter for cheeky cockney rocker Tommy Steele ('Rock With The Caveman', 1956) and gone on to pen hits for Cliff Richard ('Living Doll', 1959), Marty Wilde, Adam Faith and many more. 'I used to have something in the Top 10 every week for about four years,' he said. 'I could see the market in those days. I could suss out which performer needed what song a couple of months in advance: it was rather like writing for a character in a play.' By the time* Oliver! *was launched, Bart had won nine Ivor Novello Awards.*

**Lionel Bart [1930–1999]:** With Tommy [Steele] I did quite a bit of Brit rock, which went on to be something I did more of. Ray Davies did more of, Ian Dury did more of, Stevie Marriott did more of. It's what I call cockney rock, street stuff. Steve was in *Oliver!* He was one of my Artful Dodgers. He was one of the best Artful Dodgers I had.

**Sir Tony Robinson:** Lionel Bart made a huge impression. He had that very East End Jewish charming patter and I'd never seen anyone wear Italian suits or Robin Hood hats. We all started wearing Robin Hood hats, all about four foot six, wearing these hats because Lionel wore them and the Rat Pack wore them, so ridiculous… and we would have big dark glasses from Woolworths and aqua filters, these white filters you stuck your fag in… we would all walk about with very broad smoking gestures. And he smelled of scent. Every man I knew before that smelled of fags and sweat.

**Paul Banes [Immediate Records]:** Steve and Lionel Bart were very close.

**Christine Lore:** Lionel and Steve had ups and downs. In the seventies, Lionel told me Steve was not one for taking direction in life or in a play… and I think he had a crush on Steve as well.

**Sheila Smith [Née Devo]:** When Bill and Kath realised he had an awful lot of talent, they thought he ought to go to an acting school. So I approached the people at the [world-renowned and prestigious] Italia Conti [acting] school because I used to deal with them through work. [At the Saturday morning audition Marriott was asked to recite Shakespeare and was offered a month trial and then a permanent place.] The deal was that we said we can't pay any fees. They said, 'Don't worry, we'll get him work and we'll take our fees from the work.' They were so convinced that he would be employed and they'd be able to get their money.

**Kath Marriott:** They said he was a natural and they wanted him. Sometimes it's taken that the mother is pushy. But I wasn't really. We always worried. Were always scared about the people he would meet. And the different environment. But he was able to take care of himself.

**Hugh Janes:** Steve and I were at Italia Conti stage school together. I joined in the September of 1958, when I was 11. Steve came along about a year and half later. We were the same age [both born January 1947]. He very much had that East End sound to his voice. That never changed. That's how he spoke all the time. I don't ever remember him doing a performance where he tried to modulate his voice. He was a rudimental actor, he just did it the way he did it... it was a very natural talent he had in terms of acting. The rest of us were trying to craft something. This school had had the likes of Noël Coward, Roger Livesey... the roughest it got was [cockney superstar crooner and actor] Anthony Newley.

**Steve Marriott:** I never really acted the whole time I was there. All the parts [I got] were cockney kids, which is what I was anyway.

**Manon Piercey:** He used to speak really nicely when he went to Italia Conti and then he realised they quite liked the 'cor blimey'... so he got into that but when we were at home he spoke normally. My mum used to call him Little Lord Fauntleroy. So he was acting and turning the cockney accent on a bit.

*Marriott's first booking with Italia Conti came when he appeared in the musical* Peter Pan *at London's West End Scala Theatre over the Christmas period of 1961. Jane Asher played Wendy and Anne Heywood was Peter Pan, with Marriott one of the Lost Boys supplied by Conti.*

**Sir Tony Robinson:** As child actors, we all went up for every job. Even if you'd played the lead in something three months ago you would still go up for a part that only had one or two lines. Conti sent them off to all sorts because the fees they paid [to attend the school] predominantly came from the jobs they got.

**Hugh Janes:** Steve was a nice-looking kid and his photographs always looked good; we all went to the same photographer, Angus McBean [who also photographed album sleeves for Cliff Richard and The Beatles]. There was a standard pose, looking slightly away from camera, you look a bit angelic, your hair is neatly combed... everything that Steve wasn't but it was all about the presentation.

**Sir Tony Robinson:** About two years after *Oliver!*, Steve and I were modelling for Fair Isle knitting patterns, on the cover showing what the finished article would look like. The photos were taken in the basement of the Raymond Revuebar in Soho. Steve was a snappy dresser and the cardigans and scarves looked great on him. He'd just sung the part of the Artful Dodger on a new budget LP of *Oliver!*

*The original* Oliver! *album had been released by Decca in 1960. This budget* Oliver! *album Marriott sang on was released in 1962 via World Record Club. The album's producer, Cyril Ornadel, told Marriott he was an 'absolute natural'. He sang lead on the songs 'Consider Yourself', 'Be Back Soon' and 'I'd Do Anything'.*

**Hugh Janes:** We made a film together called *Night Cargoes* [1962] that was made for the Children's Film Foundation to be shown at Saturday morning pictures. You made it as a normal feature-length film and they would cut it up into episodes and *Night Cargoes* was cut up into eight episodes. I played a young squire who had inherited a house after his father died and Steve played the stable boy. We were both on the picture for the entire period, eight weeks, and then there was a couple of weeks post-production. It was an adventure story for kids. There were smugglers using the land and we got captured because we were going to reveal where they stored all their illegal products. There was a lot of horse riding but Steve was a hopeless rider. When I knew I was doing the film I did a crash course. Steve didn't bother and he'd be like a sack of potatoes bouncing around. One of the locations was Frensham Ponds in Surrey and we used to take the horses at lunchtime and go for a ride along the beach there... we became really close. He had a very volatile relationship with his mum. They would shout at each other. Steve always had that slightly belligerent side, not fighting but very determined to do things his way. I went round to his place quite often, just a regular flat, everything nice. We played music, talked.

**Colin Spaull:** Conti's was opposite the stage door of the Windmill Theatre, [notorious for] the nudes on stage with their feathers. It was an amazing place to go to school, right in the middle of theatre-land. Stevie, Hugh and I would visit the music shops, Boosey & Hawkes, and get slung out because we were making too much noise on the drums or double bass. We'd go to the 2i's coffee bar, wander up Berwick Street, go for coffee at Le Macabre, go get burger and chips. We were naive, innocent, met a few ladies of the night who told us to come back when we had more money and were older. We were all over the girls; the hormones were all over the place, trying to look over into the girls' dressing rooms. And with girls outside school it was great, they'd ask, 'Oh, what do you do?' 'I'm making a film with Peter Sellers.' But there were no drugs. We never even dabbled. Stevie was very likeable, genuine nice bloke, one of the lads, up for anything. I loved him as a mate. We had a lot in common. We were both working class. I'm a cockney, a south London boy. He got quite a bit of work. He was in *Citizen James* [BBC TV series – Marriott appearing in December 1961]; we might have done that together. There were a lot of people at Conti's who never worked and left after their four years and that was it. Not a lot did it… just a few of us. It was a tough business. When you went for auditions you were up against a lot of other young actors.

**Hugh Janes:** Colin was a couple of years older. When we started at Conti, Colin was already a bit of a star because he'd done quite a number of TV series. The school was on Archer Street [in Soho]. There was an instrument shop next door and all the musicians used to gather on the corner on Monday morning and the band organisers would come along and say, 'Okay, I'm looking for a trombonist, right you're playing Leeds Grand,' and they'd give them the docket and off they'd go. We'd watch that. The working girls had been moved off the street but they used to stand in the doorways and it was really exciting to talk to them… the slightly older boys would say, 'Oh, go talk to her, she likes you.' The [Berwick Street] market was nearby and we used to play football in a little park, although Steve wasn't really into sports. He used to bring a guitar into the school. There were lots of flamboyant kids at Conti. We'd do half the day on the acting, singing, dancing in mixed age groups and then half on the academic side in our year group. But it wasn't focused on academic studies. We did take O levels but I didn't get any, but what you got instead was an all-round theatre education and they taught us how to go to auditions, to have self-discipline.

**Colin Spaull:** We were really badly educated, to be honest. It didn't have a great reputation for turning out Einsteins. We had educational lessons in the morning until twelve and then have a wander around Soho and back at two. The rest of the day was devoted to theatre studies: dancing, singing, voice production, voice control, tap-dancing class, voiceover class, acting classes. They had kids from the age of 11 to 16 and then some older students attending drama lessons. In our acting classes there was about fifty kids [even now Italia Conti only has seventy-eight pupils aged 11–16, with some older boys aged up to 19]. A bit ahead of us was [*Are You Being Served?* and *EastEnders* TV actress] Wendy Richard.

**Hugh Janes:** Companies rang the school because they wanted kids. The Old Vic always used Italia Conti. Lots of kids would go off for auditions for *Oliver!* from the school. There were mass auditions every three months. After *Night Cargoes*, Steve and I did a couple of other TV shows together but he was already playing in the bands. Music was always his first interest. He always loved music, he was always playing music, singing. We'd go to see a lot of bands, mainly in small village halls as opposed to clubs in the West End. Steve would drag me off to see some band I'd never heard of. We were 14 or 15. He stayed with me, at my parents in Cheam, south London, so we'd go and see bands near me if Steve wasn't playing at the weekend.

**Jenny Dearden:** He left home when he was incredibly young.

**Manon Piercey:** He was hardly ever at home, unless his parents were out. He wasn't happy at home. His mother wasn't very nice to him. I think she wanted to be in showbusiness and she lived through him. She wanted to have the attention. He had so much talent. She was a bit jealous of him. She wasn't very loving.

*Conti's kept Marriott busy through 1962 and into early 1963. He scored a small part in the popular BBC children's comedy show* Mr Pastry's Progress *(for which he earned £13), a lead in an 'Afternoon Theatre' forty-five-minute BBC radio play,* Don't Get Caught, Freddie. *Marriott was Freddie Moore, a difficult boy and a problem to his headmaster. There was also a job reading the letters on Marjorie Proops' Radio Luxembourg Sunday night agony aunt show, a TV commercial for 1001 carpet cleaner, a repeating role as pop star Art Joyful on* Mrs Dale's Diary, *the first significant BBC radio serial drama, a few appearances on popular BBC Saturday night cops and robbers show* Dixon Of Dock Green *and a role (paying £18) in* William, *a BBC TV series based on the* Just William *books, starring Dennis Waterman as William Brown. Marriott also landed a prominent feature film role, second billing to future* Blow-Up *star David Hemmings, in the hackneyed but commercially successful music biz caper* Live It Up! *(released 1963). Marriott was the chirpy cockney drummer in an aspirant beat group led by Post Office messenger boy Hemmings. The film featured guest appearances from Gene Vincent and British oddball star Heinz, the bottle blond who had been in The Tornados when they scored a massive 1962 UK and US No 1 with instrumental 'Telstar'. Heinz was now a solo star, although really just a receptacle for the controlling record producer Joe Meek, who was musical director for* Live It Up! *There is a long-standing rumour, although no evidence, that Marriott recorded for Meek during this period. The Carnaby Street fashion king, John Stephen, and King's Road fashion queen, Mary Quant, supplied the clothes for the film.*

**Colin Spaull:** Stevie and I both got cast in a Boulting Brothers [renowned filmmakers famous for movies such as *Brighton Rock* and *Lucky Jim*] comedy film called *Heavens Above!* [also released 1963], starring Peter Sellers. We played brothers. I was a couple of years older than Stevie, so he played my younger brother. He'd have been about 15. We were very much typecast for the roles we were playing in that movie. We went on location and filmed in a field and between takes we would either play cricket or Steve would have his guitar with him and he'd sit on the steps of the caravan thing that was supposed to be where our family lived [in the film] and we'd have a singalong. We met Greg Phillips, who was also at Conti's, on the shoot. He was doing another picture on the next sound stage to us at Shepperton [Studios], *I Could Go On Singing* [1963], with Judy Garland and Dirk Bogarde [Sir Tony Robinson was an extra on the film and also knew Greg Phillips]. When we broke from our various film sets, we'd meet up and have lunch together at the studios. I was about 17 at the time and had a Vespa scooter and I was introduced by Greg to Judy Garland's daughter, this American girl, and I was quite taken with her, and I'd put her on the back of my scooter and we'd drive around the back lot together. It was Liza Minnelli.

**Hugh Janes:** Gregory Phillips was quite a popular boy. He was better looking than most of us and he did quite well. We were all playing school kids in this posh school for the Judy Garland film. Greg had got access to a scooter and we'd see him driving around with Judy Garland's daughter. We all thought, wow, he's got off with a star's daughter. We were 15 or 16. Greg could sing and dance... he was more of a wild boy than the rest of us.

**Gregory Phillips:** When I was 15, Steve Marriott was my best friend. We were always strumming guitars and singing stuff. I became very friendly with Judy [Garland] and more or less lived in her house. Her daughter Liza Minnelli introduced me to sex, not to mention vodka and fags. Through Judy I was hanging out with people like Sammy Davis Jr and Shirley Bassey. I was used to wearing handmade mohair three-piece suits with covered buttons, carrying a gold Dunhill lighter.

*In July 1963, Marriott released his debut single, 'Give Her My Regards', for Decca Records. The B-side was an original song by Marriott, 'Imaginary Love'.*

**Sheila Smith [Née Devo]:** One Saturday night Steve sat quietly and played a song he had just written called 'Imaginary Love'. I thought it was very good. I said to him, 'We have to do something, this is nice.' I said, 'What you do, Steve, is you go up to Denmark Street [Soho's infamous 'Tin Pan Alley'] with your guitar and you bang on the doors of the publishing houses and say, "I've got a song I would like you to hear."' He spent the day doing that and rang me from a phone box. No one was interested. I phoned my friend Lily who worked for Jack Hylton at the same time as I did. She made a couple of calls and I sent Steve to this office in Savile Row – it was Cliff Richard's agent. Steve got the Decca contract from that.

**Malcolm Forrester:** Steve and another young actor, Gregory Phillips, came in to see my boss Franklyn Boyd, when it was Belinda Music at 17 Savile Row.

*Belinda was primarily a publishing company, run by Freddy Bienstock, a Swiss American who had famously supplied hits for Elvis before setting up home in London. Among the acts Bienstock handled were Phil Spector, Cliff Richard and songwriter Kenny Lynch, who had written 'Give Her My Regards'. Boyd handled the production of Marriott's single, credited to Belinda Recordings. He was a former popular singer now in his late 30s, who had been instrumental in launching the solo career of Cliff Richard as his manager.*

**Steve Marriott:** Buddy has got to be the biggest influence of my youth. I used to run about the room wearing a pair of thick glasses, no glass in them, just the rims, and I had a tennis racquet to mime with. On 'Give Her My Regards' I was copying him – it was dire. It was a rotten record. I was still at Italia Conti when I recorded it.

**Gregory Phillips:** Steve made a record called 'Give Her My Regards' and he said to the company, 'I've got this mate of mine, who I'm at school with and he's a good singer and you know, how about him coming in and letting him make a record too?'

*Phillips would cut three singles for Pye, the first released in August 1963. Unlike Marriott, who only scored a few small music-press mentions with his debut single that disappeared quickly, Phillips appeared on leading pop TV shows* Thank Your Lucky Stars *and* Ready Steady Go!, *cast as a clean-cut, fresh-faced innocent.*

**Denis Thompson [Bandmate]:** I didn't play on 'Give Her My Regards'. That was in Steve's Buddy Holly days. When we hooked up with him and started playing together, that was one of the songs we did. There's a lot of disinformation out there about this period. I first met up with Steve in 1962. He was making some movies at the time we formed our band together: the first one was *Live It Up!* That's where we met Heinz. Then he did the movie with Peter Sellers. There was me and another guitar player, Johnny Herve, just messing around playing together with a drummer. We used to go to a coffee bar in Manor Park, owned by a wrestler, and above the coffee bar there was a dance hall where we played a couple of times and then this little guy came up and he asked, 'Can I sing a song with you guys?' We said, 'Yeah, okay.' It was Steve. He did a couple of Buddy Holly songs. Then he asked if he could join the band even though we didn't really consider ourselves a band. We said, 'Well, let's go find a bass player,' and we hooked up with a guy called Colin Fuller and started to play around Dagenham, Barking and East Ham. I was four years older than Steve. Colin was about my age and Johnny was a couple of years younger than me. Steve was really young when he joined the band, just 15. We did a couple of Buddy Holly songs and he also liked Bobby Vee, so we did things like 'Take Good Care Of My Baby' [Vee's 1961 No 1 American hit], all that stuff. We did some Cliff Richard songs as well. Then we started to do songs by American artists and then when The Beatles came out we did things like '[Twist And] Shout' like everybody else did and a couple of others… we gradually got away from the Buddy Holly. When we first got together we were doing The Shadows-type movements as well and eventually Steve said, 'Nah, let's not do that anymore, it doesn't look good.'

**Manon Piercey:** He used to sing with quite a sweet voice, he liked Buddy Holly, and one day he was about 16, and he said, 'I want to sing like Otis Redding, will you listen to me?' He knew I would tell him the truth. We went in his block of flats and he stayed at the bottom of the stairwell and I went upstairs to the top and he sang with that voice and I was just blown away. I went, 'Oh my God!' And he said, 'Is it bad?' I went, 'No, it's amazing'… and the neighbours came out and said, 'Steve, shut up.' I'm glad he asked me because if someone had said, 'Oh no, don't like that,' he would never have done it again. He didn't like being rejected like that. He didn't like criticism. His hair was long then and everybody had short hair so he stood out a mile, and he was small, really small, and local lads would say things, pick on him, call him 'puny' and things like that.

**Hugh Janes:** The first band I saw him in was Steve Marriott & The Moonlites. He had a fantastic voice. It really was an amazing instrument. He was mixing acting and bands. He was a natural performer, a natural frontman, he had a natural performing style right from the beginning; he did a whip thing with his upper body, it would dip as he played guitar, his foot was always jumping around. The thing with the finger in the ear, he did that, and he was already using the 'Come on children' phrase… [from James Brown's 'Night Train']. He'd often wear dark glasses and he played big guitars, he wasn't a Fender man. With the bands, he was always chopping and changing musicians. He was fairly uncompromising. There was this volatility to him, but that's what partly made him such a charismatic frontman. It was the same if you were his friend. There was always that danger he could cut you off, that something else would take his interest. You'd go along to see his bands and some nights it'd be, 'Oh, my great mates are in tonight. Hello boys, I'm going to sing this one for you,' and then you'd go have beers. Other nights you'd trudge across London to see him in some dive and he'd go, 'Oh, what you doing here?' It was a strange relationship. I think there was a large side of Steve that wanted you to stay loyal so he could come and go a bit. Colin [Spaull] and I used to go to all Steve's gigs. He'd come into Conti with LPs by people you'd never heard of… it was blues music, he was mad on it, Bobby Bland and Ray Charles. We progressed to going to the West End clubs; he took me to see The Yardbirds at the Marquee.

**David Arden [Jet Records, son of future Marriott manager Don Arden]:** I got to Italia Conti just before my 12th birthday [September 1962, when the school had moved from Soho to Landor Road in Clapham North]. Stevie and another guy tried to initiate me by putting my head down the toilet and pulling the chain. I was as tough as him, so it didn't happen. There were some real tough nuts there… there was a kid, Francis Larkin, real East End. Francis was outside *Oliver!* and saw Lionel and said, 'Here, I could fackin' do that, them poofs in there, I can sing, I can dance.' Lionel said, 'Well come on in and have a go.' He was useless. So Lionel said, 'You need a bit of training, but if you really want to do this I'll send you to school for a year,' and he paid for Francis to come to Conti for a year. Stevie and I got on well despite our age difference: I was four years younger. I got him tickets for one of the shows my dad was promoting, the Little Richard one. He was there for my first two or three terms [at Conti] and then he left. We [the Arden family] used to have a little house in Birchington-on-Sea, close to Margate, and we went to Dreamland in the school holidays and we watched *Heavens Above!* and I went, 'Bloody hell, that's Steve Marriott.'

**Hugh Janes:** The school acted as an agency so they would take 10 per cent [of any acting jobs pupils got]. We all had Post Office accounts in our own names. They would hold one third of your money after they deducted their 10 per cent and would put it in these PO accounts. The rest was sent to our parents. When we left at 16, they gave us our PO book in our own names, which was great because you suddenly got this lump of money. It was very sensible because they knew that when you got to 16, 17, if you'd been successful as a child, you were going to have a difficult time in that transition [to getting adult roles]. Steve and I would both have been 16 in the summer of 1963 but I seem to think we may have left in early 1964. Once you did, you then had to find an agent, get your own jobs... it became more difficult. You'd just be thrown to the wall [after leaving school].

**David Arden:** Ruth Conti [principal of the school] never liked Steve. He was a bit coarse for her. Steve at school was like Steve all his life, he never changed: you never really knew Steve. Nobody really knew him. He wanted to be a toughie, always loved to be around the tough guys. He was not the kind of guy who made friends easily. On the one hand he was kind of bolshie, one of the Jack the Lads of the school, along with Greg Phillips and a couple of other guys, but he also had his own little world, out there, and he used to skip off most of the lessons so you'd never see him in class doing singing or dancing... usually he'd wind up in the pub next door.

**Denis Thompson:** He did a follow-up to *Live It Up!* [called *Be My Guest*, released 1965, more dated music/caper gruel, starring again as the chirpy cockney drummer in David Hemmings' accident-happy beat group. This time Jerry Lee Lewis was a guest star]. I used to go with him to the film set. He couldn't drive so I used to drive him there. That's why we were billed as Steve Marriott & The Moonlites because his name was a little bit known.

*Gregory Phillips was also progressing with his career. He cut a George Harrison song as a single, but was becoming disillusioned with the way he was being presented.*

24

**Gregory Phillips:** I did not want to be the dork in the dinner jacket. The only relief was hanging out and smoking dope with Steve Marriott.

*Phillips said he'd been introduced to dope by a gay singer called Nicky Scott who took him down to Brighton to meet 'a circle of theatricals, mostly gay, who lived down there'. He named Terence Rattigan, Robin Maugham and Lionel Bart. 'I took to the weed like a duck to water,' he said.*

**Steve Marriott:** I was starting to turn Mod when I was still living at home, when I was 15, trying to be an individual and having terrible rows with my dad for looking like a poof. It was a case of all my mates were Mods and I was a Mod. Like, we'd take a pill, stay up all night. It was the Scene club until midnight, then the Flamingo for the all-nighter. It was being sick in alleyways, ruining the jacket you just paid an arm and a leg for. I just thought everything was marvellous, just goofing around, getting stoned, meeting chicks. My average week consisted of playing in groups about twice, drifting around clubs about four times and meeting various chicks in offices about twice. I had a lot of opposition from my parents about what I wanted to do. I got in a lot of rows.

**Kath Marriott:** He was a little outlandish [at the time]. His white trousers, you never saw boys in white trousers. And his jazzy jackets, lovely jackets. You had to be brave to walk out and wear them because everyone else was in dark suits and short hair. Bill adored Steve but they could never get it right. Steve always thought his father was ashamed of him. If they went to the pub for a drink, his father would say, 'Are you going to sort your hair out?' And Steve would get narky and say, 'No, I bloody ain't.' See, it was Bill's Victorian upbringing. He wanted Steve to have a short back and sides and of course Steve would have none of it.

**Denis Thompson:** Steve was a very volatile young man. He had lots of run-ins with his parents. They did not want him to be in the music business, they wanted him to be in the acting business. There was a lot of tension between them. They were pushing the acting. They had big plans for him, especially after the Peter Sellers movie – he got a lot of compliments from the people on that cast, including from Peter Sellers. The big argument was to do with some manager, or agent, coming in to become his manager, or agent, in the film industry and Steve wasn't interested, he didn't want to. He didn't like being in the movies. He thought it was stupid. He disliked acting.

**Manon Piercey:** He loved his music. He just wanted to sing. He wasn't that keen on acting.

**Steve Marriott:** My parents were dead keen on the acting thing and I was doing pretty well. They couldn't see why it wasn't enough for me. I had a big thing about groups, always had been dead keen on music. For me, acting wasn't absorbing, it was boring, all that hanging about.

**Denis Thompson:** One day over at my house, Steve asked my mum and dad if he could come and live with us. My parents said fine, we had a spare room. He came and lived with us in Barking for two or three months and then made up with his parents and went back again. A lot of that was to do with his sister, Kay. He really thought a lot about his little sister, he was really fond of her.

**Mollie Marriott:** Kay and Steve had a close relationship, but I don't think she was that close to her mum… when you grow up in a traumatic household the siblings do tend to become close.

*Marriott suggested in this period he also stayed on the sofa of British blues godfather Alexis Korner and sang at the legendary Ealing blues club with Korner's resident band, Alexis Korner's Blues Incorporated.*

**Kath Marriott:** One time he came home, he'd been away for a week. He was only about 16 and he said to me, 'You never asked me to come back.' I said, 'I never asked you to go.' It was awful… he'd go to his aunties or his friends. Since getting the part in *Oliver!*, he'd gone from good to better. He stayed [at Italia Conti] until he was 17. He went to an audition at the National Theatre [their production of the Laurence Olivier-directed *Hamlet* starring Peter O'Toole] and told me he failed. Then a fortnight later we got a phone call to ask why Stephen hadn't turned up at the theatre. [The play opened at the Old Vic in October 1963 and Marriott was reputed to have secured a year's work in the touring production.] 'But he failed,' said Bill. 'No, he didn't, we're waiting for him.' That's when I realised that pop had taken over his life.

He had presence [on stage]. And I think, if nothing more, he got that from his acting time. He had the talent. But those three, four years gave him the ability to know how to use the stage and how to manipulate it.

**Sir Tony Robinson:** The cut and thrust of being a child actor, among these strong personalities, you could argue, informed everything he did as a frontman. He was a performer. There's something self-conscious about Steve [as a singer]; it's not faux or phoney but it is performance.

**Sheila Smith [Née Devo]:** It was very sad for all of us. I was upset because I thought there are so many pop people and he is just going down the same road as them. I really thought he was naturally gifted as an actor.

**Steve Marriott:** I was doing well and my parents were badly brought down when I started getting interested in groups, going out on the road and not living at home. But drama school did me good. It gave me confidence. It gave me front.

# CHAPTER 2

# You Really Got A Hold On Me

**Denis Thompson:** We were playing in Bournemouth [September 1963. Marriott is 16], top of the bill. Supporting us was Zoot Money and [future BBC Radio 1 DJ] Tony Blackburn & The Rovers. Steve walked on the stage and said, 'I'm sorry there's been a big misunderstanding, they've advertised us as Steve Marriott & The Moonlites and I've got to tell you we're not Steve Marriott & The Moonlites, we are Steve Wolverhampton & The Wanderers'... everyone was quiet for a moment until they got what he meant. It was a jab at Tony Blackburn and Blackburn [who was four years older than Steve] was not very happy at all. When we finished he came up and gave Steve a mouthful. Colin Fuller, our bassist, who was a tough guy, got in between them. Steve used to do a whole different bunch of stupid things like that. Sometimes we'd be on stage, halfway through a song, and he'd just walk off and walk into the crowd with the mic and sit down on the chair and continue. When we'd drive into a town we were going to be playing he would find a telephone box and find a name and [crank] call somebody. He'd say he was from the electric company and they were on the way to shut off the electricity. If we were walking down the street, he'd walk out into the middle of the street singing. With The Moonlites, when we were starting out, he was just a singer who stood out front – he didn't play guitar but he played an absolutely brilliant harmonica. Then one day he surprised us by turning up and playing the guitar and then he learned to play piano very quickly and then drums – he did a little drumming when he did *Live It Up!* the movie. He was so musically talented that it didn't take him any time at all to learn how to play an instrument. His girlfriend Adrienne Posta [from Italia Conti] used to sometimes come to practice.

*Posta, almost two years younger than Marriott, born March 1949, released her debut single, 'Only 15', for Decca Records, in December 1963.*

**Hugh Janes:** Adrienne Posta was quite East End. She often used to play cockney parts, working-class girls [finding a degree of fame with roles in films from the late sixties to the late seventies, such as *Up The Junction* and *Adventures Of A Taxi Driver*]. She was a year younger than us at Conti. We all quite fancied her. She was small, petite, pretty.

**Kath Marriott:** I didn't like her at all. Very cheeky, terribly spoilt girl.

**Denis Thompson:** It never blossomed into anything. We played in Watford and he met a girl called Jennifer or Jenny and he went out with her for some time. Steve had started to listen to the blues a lot more and he wanted to play bluesy music [the set now including Ray Charles' 'Talkin' 'Bout You' and R&B standard 'Route 66', covered by Chuck Berry and the aspiring Rolling Stones]. The first drummer left and we got a fellow [from Dagenham] named Tony McIntyre [RIP] who was really good [McIntyre stuck with Marriott through the Moonlites, Frantics and Moments]. He ended up dating a Miss England. Then this guy turned up while we were playing and he wanted to be our manager. His name was Tony Calder. He started getting us gigs all over the country. We were very popular. We didn't have records out, but we'd shock people when we told them the places we'd played. When we went to play the Cavern [in Liverpool], Steve went into a hardware store and got some lipstick kind of stuff and put things all over the side of the van, stuff like 'We Love You Steve' and then we drove to the Cavern with the van like that.

**Tony Calder [1943–2018]:** I was DJing the Saturday afternoon session at Ilford Palais and this kid comes up and says, 'Hello, I'm Steve Marriott, I'm a singer.' He wanted to play the records and I thought he looked the part so I had him come down every Saturday afternoon and help out. Steve had a problem with his height, as any short person does [Marriott was approximately five foot two].

*Calder had recently left a promising job at Decca Records, as Sales and Marketing trainee, finding the regimented attitude of the older generation of men running the major corporation frustratingly stiff and closed off to the appeal of modern pop music. As well as DJing, Calder had started a press relations company with clients including The Mojos, Swinging Blue Jeans, The Searchers and The Undertakers. He was also involved in the early promotion of The Beatles.*

**Paul Banes:** Tony was Steve's full-time manager. He got Steve on the circuit in London that all the bands were playing. The Stones were down in Richmond, Steve was more West End and East End pubs. Vocally Steve was fantastic, which was why he could adapt to playing all those blues tracks. 'Got My Mojo Working' [popularised by Muddy Waters in 1957] was right up his street. When Tony was DJing at the Ilford Palais dancehall I was his assistant, opening and closing the set. Monday nights were just records. We always hear about the Flamingo and the Scene in London but the Mecca dance halls early on were where the music started to change and get more Mod. [Ian] 'Sammy' Samwell [1937–2003, former Shadow and writer of Cliff Richard & The Shadows' hit 'Move It'] was [DJing] down in Purley [Orchid Ballroom, also owned by Mecca]. The Mecca Lyceum [where Samwell also DJed] in the West End was open at lunchtime, and that was attracting thousands of Mods. Tony Calder was in the middle of all this, he was getting the promo records [cuts he played ahead of their release] because everyone knew he was proactive on the circuit. We played stuff no one else did, which is why people like Steve came down, to discover music they couldn't hear on the radio. We went from nothing to 2,500 people on a Monday night at the Ilford Palais; it was becoming the hub of the Mods along with the Tottenham Royal, where Dave Clark played. Sandie Shaw, who lived down the road, would come and dance at Ilford Palais.

**Denis Thompson:** One day Calder came to our practice room, which was in a movie house in Manor Park, and he asked, 'Would you be willing to be [popular actor/singer] Jess Conrad's backing band for a few months?' and Steve said, 'Yeah, okay, we'll do that.' A couple of weeks later Jess came to practise and we learned all the songs he wanted to do and we went out and backed him. Jess made a comment to me and Colin one day about Steve, 'You know, we get up there on the stage and I have to sing knowing that the guy standing behind me [Marriott] singing back-up should be the one up front singing.' Next, Tony Calder brought Tony Meehan [1943–2005, former drummer from The Shadows who was now a producer at Decca] to one of our practices. Meehan wanted to make a record with us. He wanted us to do 'Move It', the old Cliff Richard hit. He asked us to learn it and play it and we did. That's where we came up with the name The Frantics. That was Tony Meehan's name for us. He said we did a frantic version of 'Move It' – 'You need to call yourselves The Frantics.' We changed our name to Steve Marriott & The Frantics. On the day we were going to record it, I was in Paris and I had to fly home to do my part. We did that and another song and they hawked it around but it never did anything. I think it came out in Malaysia or somewhere but it didn't do anything and eventually the band broke up. [Drummer] Tony McIntyre stayed with Steve, they were good friends, but Johnny and I went to play with Bobby Cristo & The Rebels but I kept in touch with Steve. We always had a good relationship.

We got arrested together once. I had a Bedford van and one time he wanted to move some stuff from where he was living and the cops pulled us over. Where did I get the van? I said it's my van but I had no proof. They put Steve and me in a police car and drove us to Barking police station and put us in a cell. Steve had his harmonica with him. All of a sudden he started playing some jailhouse blues and the two cops came back and stood outside the cell and just listened. After three or four songs, they clapped. Then they left and ten minutes later they came back with another two cops and they said, 'Let's hear some more,' and Steve did a bit more. My father showed up with the paperwork and they said, 'Okay you can go now, sorry you had to spend this time here but we really enjoyed having you.' About three years ago I got in touch with Toby, Steve's son, and I started to tell him that story, and he goes, 'Yes, I know, my dad told me all about it, as a matter of fact I've still got that harmonica.'

*Marriott continued under the name of The Frantics, sometimes billed as Steve Marriott & The Frantic Ones. The set was said to include two songs from The Beatles' 1963 debut album, 'I Saw Her Standing There' and Arthur Alexander's 1962 soul ballad 'Anna (Go To Him)', later revived by Marriott for Humble Pie's 1974 album, Thunderbox, plus 'Love Potion No. 9', a Leiber/Stoller song that was a minor 1959 hit for American R&B/doo-wop group The Clovers. John Weider, from Shepherd's Bush, was 16, a couple of months younger than Marriott, when he joined The Frantics. He was a Royal College of Music graduate (violin) who had already played lead guitar with Tony Meehan's hugely successful post-Shadows duo, Jet Harris & Tony Meehan.*

**John Weider:** My involvement with Steve was very brief. It only lasted a few months. The group was called Steve Marriott's Frantics. We did some rehearsals, played a few small gigs around London and we also played at Queens Park Rangers' football ground, at half-time. My father got us the gig, arranged it. He was a chef and he wanted to manage the group. We didn't do any recordings while I was with the band. Tony Meehan may have been the hook-up or I could have met Steve in the Gioconda [café] on Denmark Street. I'd go down there a lot to buy sheet music. Steve had a good voice and he was very ambitious, and a little bit flash. He attracted people to him because he had such an outgoing personality. He wasn't one to be told what to do.

*After The Frantics, Weider would go on to replace guitarist Mick Green in Johnny Kidd & The Pirates before joining The Animals in 1966. He also briefly played with Jimmy Winston's post-Small Faces outfit, Winston's Fumbs. The Frantics name would soon be retired as Marriott, alongside Calder, was drawn into the orbit of The Rolling Stones.*

**Tony Calder:** I was actually with Steve when I first met Andrew Loog Oldham under the lamplight on the corner of Poland Street and Great Marlborough Street [in Soho].

**Andrew Loog Oldham:** As I marched past Great Marlborough Street Magistrates' Court, I thought I saw somebody I recognised. It was Tony Calder... Calder had under his wing a young London artist, Steve Marriott, whom he'd just accompanied while the cockney tyke pleaded 'fair cop' to a petty offence.

*The nature of the offence Marriott was said to have committed is unknown. Oldham was The Rolling Stones' 19-year-old manager and producer. He and Calder quickly became inseparable and would remain so for the remainder of the sixties, with a complicated friendship that survived a lifetime. They shared a similar anarchic attitude.*

**Tony Calder:** Our attitude towards the business was fuck 'em all, they were all old men, they were sad.

*Initially the two agreed to form a new independent promotions company they called Image. It would soon be representing, alongside Calder's clients and the Stones, Herman's Hermits, Gene Pitney, Marianne Faithfull, Phil Spector, The Hollies, Georgie Fame and many others. Calder would become Oldham's right-hand man in many other aspects of the teenage Stones' Svengali's burgeoning career. One of their first collaborations was to record and promote a second Adrienne Posta single on Decca, 'Shang A Doo Lang', written to order by Jagger/Richards for Oldham, who produced the single. Released in March 1964, it was at the launch party for the single that Oldham discovered Marianne Faithfull, becoming her manager and swiftly producing her debut single 'As Tears Go By', a Jagger/Richards/Oldham song, released June 1964. Oldham formed a short-lived company with Lionel Bart called Forward Music to fund Faithfull's early recordings and Marriott also cut a demo for Forward called 'Don't Touch Me (I Might Like It)' written by Bart. 'Lionel in Ben E. King mood,' said Oldham.*

**Tony Calder:** Initially, Andrew had Peter Meaden around, poor fucker. Then he got rid of him. Peter kept falling off the chair, he was always out of it.

*Meaden, a sharp, influential, face-about-town, briefly involved himself as a surrogate manager as Marriott assembled a new band, suggesting they dress in military-style clothes. Meaden had energy and ideas to spare and became the force behind The Who, changing their name for a few months to The High Numbers and writing both sides of their debut single, 'I'm The Face'/'Zoot Suit', released July 1964.*

**Steve Marriott:** Peter Meaden – a great mate of mine. He kitted The Who out, dressed them Mod...

**Pete Townshend:** When I met Peter [Meaden] I was 18, he was 20 I suppose. He was kind out of control already. He was still really quite brilliant but a bit pilled out. He tended to babble his ideas. That condition, high energy, equacious, tumbling, he was a real holder of court. It was starting to get somewhat incomprehensible; he was using his own private language almost. The language he used about the Mods, which has passed into mythology, the words 'face', 'ticket', 'number', he was the only person I ever heard using it...

**Keith Altham:** Steve Marriott was like an office boy [for Tony Calder]; he came in delivering something for Tony when I was at *NME*. Steve was about 16 or 17, cheeky character. Sat on the edge of the desk chatting about the band he was forming. He'd come deliberately, Tony had told him to get in there, talk to journalists. He was saying, 'I know I'm going to be a big star'; he talked twenty-four to the dozen. He said, 'Tony told me to come and talk to you because he said you might be useful.' All [the music] journalists used to hang out together in those days, we all used to go to De Hems and a place called Brew Master over Leicester Square, close to the *NME* offices. Peter Jones [*Record Mirror*] would come up there, Penny Valentine [*Disc*]...

*In March 1964, Record Mirror reported four record labels were interested in signing Marriott and that he had been offered the lead in a new, unnamed, musical play. The following week the same magazine announced 'I Cried' was scheduled to be Marriott's second solo single. This was hype, hope, not reality: Image. The aching soul ballad, written by James Brown and Bobby Byrd, had been a minor 1963 hit for future Motown star Tammi Terrell and the song's chord progression would be reused for Brown's 1966 hit 'It's A Man's Man's Man's World'. In the same issue of Record Mirror there was a gossip about a possible romance between Marriott and Adrienne Posta.*

**Paul Banes:** One night Steve, Tony and I ended up in the Wimpy bar at Ilford Station and Tony said we've got to find a [new] name for the band and we called it Steve Marriott's Moments. Tony didn't put the band together though; Steve changed the pieces in the band as he went along. It was a four-piece. The music they played was called R&B but it was more blues, the same as every band in London, covering Muddy

Waters, Howlin' Wolf... all the bands were influenced by Alexis Korner and Cyril Davis playing blues. Steve was no different.

**Denis Thompson:** The trouble with that band was he was way younger than the guys in The Moments and he was actually too good for them. The keyboard player lived just around the corner from me in Barking. Colin Green, a guitar player, was around quite a bit with The Moments – he jumped around the bands a lot, never settled. Kenny Rowe [who had been in The Frantics] played bass. He had done some standing in for Colin Fuller during The Moonlites when Colin was sick a couple of times. I was with Kenny in Bobby Cristo & The Rebels and when Kenny left to go to The Moments I took over on bass. Kenny started his career with Tony Rivers & The Castaways. He was a terrific singer too.

**Steve Marriott:** They were older than me and all were better musicians than me. All I did was fuck about on piano, play a bit of harmonica and sing.

*Manor Park-born Allen Ellett claimed to have played piano with The Moments (he was also in The Frantics) on a wage of around £30 a week. He had worked with early Brit rock'n'roll singer Jackie Lynton and via Peter Meaden had contributed piano to The High Numbers – on record and on stage. He also played with The Nashville Teens when they backed Jerry Lee Lewis for his 'Live' At The Star-Club, Hamburg album recorded in April 1964. He recalled The Moments rehearsing at Manor Park's Essoldo cinema (closed in September 1963 and converted into a bingo hall) and upstairs at the Ruskin Arms pub in Manor Park, with a set including several Chuck Berry songs that he said Marriott would ad lib over, often with words pertaining to the band members, 'Zip-A-Dee-Doo-Dah', a Walt Disney film tune cut by Bob B. Soxx & The Blue Jeans for Phil Spector in 1962 and Jerry Lee Lewis's early 1964 single 'I'm On Fire'. Ellett recalled he also wrote a song with Marriott called 'A Touch Of Blue'. The Moments' set list was also known to include: 'Please, Please, Please' by James Brown (released 1956, the signature song of James Brown & The Famous Flames), Smokey Robinson & The Miracles' 1962 US Top 10 'You Really Got A Hold On Me' (which would also be regularly covered by the Small Faces), Ben E. King's 1961 US Top 10 'Stand By Me' (another*

*Leiber/Stoller written song), and The Animals' 1964 single 'House Of The Rising Sun'.*

**Paul Banes:** Tony put on a Moments gig at the Ilford Palais [April 1964, one of their first gigs]. We also put on The Who and Georgie Fame. Apart from Dave Clark up in Tottenham there were no live bands playing the Mecca dance halls, just the orchestras. To have an R&B band playing was unheard of. We saw a lot of Steve but not really the band members. We saw his girlfriend [Adrienne Posta] quite a bit because she got on stage and sang with him [duetting on an encore of 'Twist And Shout', a chart hit for the Isley Brothers in 1962 and popularised for a white audience by The Beatles, who covered it on their debut album. Written by Bert Berns and Phil Medley, Marriott later produced a version of the song for The Blackberries].

**Manon Piercey:** He did a gig in Dagenham and it was packed. When he came out, because he looked so different to everybody else, these big guys at the front started taking the mickey. So he sang with a little choirboy voice, a whisper, the beginning of 'House Of The Rising Sun', pretending to shake as if he was nervous and they all laughed and shouted, 'Yeah, rubbish.' And then he belted it out. You have never seen faces change so quick. They all went 'Wow', cheered, and after the gig they apologised.

*The Moments – often billed as Steve Marriott's Moments – played over eighty gigs in 1964, mostly one-night stands in small clubs around various districts of London, and the south of England, sometimes playing out of town in support of name acts such as Gene Vincent, Mose Allison, Billy J. Kramer, The Hollies, Freddie & The Dreamers and The Kinks. There were also gigs at influential London venues such the Crawdaddy club in Richmond, Soho's Flamingo club (supporting acts such as Zoot Money, the Graham Bond Organisation and The Cheynes) and at Oxford Street's 100 Club supporting Mod band The Action. Significantly, as the formation of the Small Faces creeps nearer, in July 1964, The Moments played a pub in Rainham, east London, alongside The Outcasts, who featured 18-year-old Ronnie Lane on guitar. Denis Thompson recalled Marriott taking him to the Rainham pub on another night to check out The Outcasts, who he clearly rated. The Moments also played The Who stronghold, the*

*Goldhawk Rooms in Shepherd's Bush, and had regular headlining shows at the Attic Club in Hounslow (after initially playing there in support of The Animals).*

**Allen Ellett:** We travelled down to Camborne in Cornwall to play a gig in the local skating rink. We hadn't taken the piano and in the quest to find one we went into a church. There was a funeral taking place but Steve just walked in wearing his leather jacket and leather cap and had the cheek to ask the vicar, 'Can we borrow your piano?' We went from there to the local cinema where an elderly woman rather stupidly told Steve that she had a piano at home that he could borrow. She lived near the top of a hill. We got there and loaded the piano in the back, and as we started to move away the piano fell out of the van and started to roll down the hill. We eventually got it to the gig. Then, at the end of the gig, Steve sold the piano to the guy at the skating rink. He was a lovable rogue really and definitely a bit of a tea leaf. I remember going to the BBC studios with him once and we nicked a professional microphone complete with stand. He could also be very cruel with his tongue. If he passed somebody in the street with a disability he would wind the window down and give it the whole spastic bit. But he had something about him; he could walk on stage or into a room and command attention without doing anything. Sometimes when he was lugging equipment from the van he would wear an old pair of jeans with rips in the knee. One night in Sheffield we were running late and Steve just went on stage with these jeans. We returned to the same venue about a month later and there were dozens of fans in jeans with rips at the knee.

**Denis Thompson:** The Moments made a huge, huge mistake when they recorded [a version of The Kinks' August 1964 UK No 1 single] 'You Really Got Me' [as a single for World Artists, an American company attempting to usurp The Kinks' American release of the song. A promo of The Moments' version was circulated around October 1964 but was quickly abandoned as The Kinks took the song into the American Top 10]. When I first heard The Moments' take on it, I laughed my head off. I called him up and said, 'What in the hell was that all about?' And he said we wanted to try to make it as different as we could from what The Kinks had done. I said, 'I don't understand.' It was one of the worst things he ever did, the way he tried to sing it. If he had just used his proper voice he would have been okay with it but that fake whatever it was he was trying to put on was way out of character. I think it was the influence of the guitar player and bass player. When I'd go to The Moments' practices now and again they were not very sociable.

**Steve Marriott:** The Moments were a great band [the B-side to 'You Really Got Me' goes some way to backing up that claim: an original recording of 'Money Money', written by The Tornados writer and session guitarist Alan Caddy and singer-songwriter Don Charles].

**Denis Thompson:** Eventually the guitar player in The Moments told Steve they didn't want him in the band anymore. Steve was very prone to doing off-the-wall things and he could also, when he was on stage, kind of be anti-audience and say stuff that was not really good. I know The Moments were very disturbed by all that and they just said he was too young. He didn't get on well with Kenny Rowe.

**Steve Marriott:** Aside from demos [versions of Leadbelly's 'Good Morning Blues' and 'You'll Never Get Away From Me', a Stephen Sondheim song first performed by Tony Bennett in the late fifties have surfaced], nothing was really happening so they got despondent and kicked me out to get a better singer, another boy, who was five years older than me. I don't really blame them.

**Denis Thompson:** When The Moments kind of ceased to be, Bobby Cristo took over the singing with a couple of guys in the band and got in a couple of other players.

**Bobby Rio aka Bobby Cristo [real name Bobby McKellar]:** I replaced Steve as singer in The Moments. I was about 21, just singing with a little amateur band. I lived in Manor Park as a youngster and ended up in Barking. The guys – my old lead guitarist Johnny Herve, Kenny Rowe on bass and Tony McIntyre on drums – threw him out the group. They didn't like him, didn't want to be with him anymore. It's hard work – five or six hours in the back of a van – it only takes one winding everyone up. I know they didn't like the type of music Steve wanted to do. Kenny liked Tony Orlando, Bobby Darin... he liked harmonies, Kenny's a very good harmony singer, very high voice. They looked upon Steve as a screamer rather than singer. I had already met Steve in Manor Park. He was friends with [future Jimi Hendrix Experience drummer] Mitch Mitchell, they'd been in the *Live It Up!* film together with Heinz. I'd used Mitch in my little band. When I joined The Moments, some of the venues wouldn't accept us because Steve wasn't there, one in Dartford and one in Dagenham, they'd already billed it as Steve Marriott & The Moments. We changed our name from The Moments to The Rebels. I recorded [for Joe Meek] 'The Other Side Of The Track' under the name Bobby Cristo & The Rebels [released by Decca, June 1964] and then after that I changed my name to Bobby Rio [and continuing to record for Meek].

*Marriott scratched around for openings, and would put together his own version of The Moments to capitalise on the reputation he and the band had created for themselves. Tony Calder was no longer fully committed. In June 1964, Oldham and the Stones had scored their first No 1 single, 'It's All Over Now'. The band's debut album, released in April, had also gone to No 1. Oldham was involved in recording a number of other acts too, such as Gene Pitney. Calder was heavily involved in plans to release the sexualised slow blues number 'Little Red Rooster', recorded originally by Howlin' Wolf, as the Stones' next single (released in November 1964, it also went to No 1). He had also now taken over from Oldham as full-time manager of Marianne Faithfull, who was working on a follow-up to the Top 10 success of 'As Tears Go By'.*

**Steve Marriott:** I'd hang out in the Gioconda [café]. If people wanted demos made they'd say, 'Can anybody plays drums?' We'd put our hand up immediately for anything. It was at least a few quid in your pocket. That's why a lot of us used to hang out there. I'd do anything: drums, vocals, harmonica, backing vocals, guitar, bass, anything. I don't really remember any of the things I worked on – most of it was foul! There were some good writers around and they favoured me for singing their demos... publisher's demos, not recordings.

*In October 1964 Marriott voiced a demo of song called 'Show That Girl A Good Time' in The Rolling Stones' favoured London studio, Regent Sound, located on Tin Pan Alley. It was written by Barry Mason, who'd written songs for Kiki Dee, The Warriors and The Merseybeats.*

**Don Craine:** Marriott used to come and see us [The Downliners Sect] over the island [Eel Pie Island, where Craine's band played the hallowed Ealing Club, established in 1962 by Alexis Korner, Cyril Davis and Art Wood, and said to be the birthplace of British blues], when he had Steve Marriott's Moments. They were really popular at the Attic in Hounslow. I liked them, they were a terrific little band, had a feel, bit Mod. Then, in late 1964, I sacked our harmonica player and Steve turned up for the job. He wanted to be our harmonica player. We were quite big round Hounslow and Eel Pie Island, that's where the R&B was happening. He came round my house to audition, he just rang up, 'Where are you?', got the bus and was here in twenty minutes. He played and he was terrific and a really great character, full of life. He was a little different [to other young R&B/blues players on the scene], pure showbiz right from the start. I knew he wasn't going to just be happy being the harmonica player, he was going to be passing through, you could see it a mile off, he wanted more and we knew that so we turned him down. It was the same as Rod Stewart, who sang with us a few times, another good harp player. The star quality with Steve was obvious, some people have got it; whether that was him or he kicked into gear before I opened the door, who knows? There was no point in us having him, he was too big for the job as a harmonica player, we'd have become his backing group. He was heading places, he wanted to be a big star and he was going to be. He had magic and that impish quality that lets little boys get away with shit.

*In December, Marriott was reduced to entering the Ilford Palais talent contest – Calder no longer DJed there – and took first prize singing the 'House Of The Rising Sun'. The same month he performed at the West End club the Starlite, advertised as The Moments but essentially solo, backed by The Quotations, whose debut single was produced by Ian Samwell and whose guitarist was Graham Dee.*

**Graham Dee:** I was freelancing all over on sessions. We all went in the Gioconda and got all our messages there. I showed Steve his first few chords and licks on guitar because he was a singer, harmonica and keyboard player. He played a Vox Continental organ when I worked with him on gigs [as The Moments], a very good performer, tremendous, had a lot in him, very naturally gifted man. We did soul and

R&B stuff. He could be a little bit moody but for an English white boy singing soul he was a bit special. He was an ambitious guy, knew what he wanted, he was never a slouch. He was about four years younger than me at the time. I was on guitar when Steve played with Elkie Brooks at the Starlite club. It was a private thing for Cilla Black's birthday but she wasn't there. In the audience there was Phil May from The Pretty Things, Twinkle [the 16-year-old whose debut single 'Terry' had been a Top 5 hit for Decca] and John Lennon, sitting at a little table down the front. I was on stage with a pianist, and Tom Jones, Elkie and Steve Marriott all singing together.

*Elkie Brooks was a month shy of being two years older than Marriott. She was heavily associated with fellow Mancunian Don Arden, who had persuaded her to adopt her stage name, dropping her original surname of Bookbinder.*

**Elkie Brooks:** I was introduced to Steve in 1964 by my manager Ian Samwell [who was now writing for Dusty Springfield]. I liked him immediately. I thought he was a very natural musician. He would quite often come up to my flat and we would just jam together; we had some great evenings and I was fond of him, in a completely non-romantic way. He was like my little brother and when I say little I mean it, because he was so tiny, he only came up to my shoulder and I'm not exactly tall. I was five foot three and he was only about five foot! I got on extremely well with him, and he deserved to do really well.

*Brooks often played the Starlite, owned by Maurice King (RIP) who had made his name on the supper-club circuit in the north of England. King took a shine to Marriott and was interested in bringing him into his Capable Management stable. King was also in the process of signing The Walker Brothers. He was strongly suspected of having underworld links. Scott Walker would look back and refer to him as 'Boris' as in 'Karloff' or simply as 'The Monster'. The other acts he managed included Van Morrison (whose contract would soon end up in the hands of the Mafia) and Shirley Bassey. By now Marriott's Post Office account was empty.*

**Denis Thompson:** Steve started working in a music shop [January 1965, the J60 Music Bar, Manor Park] and Ronnie [Lane] came in one day and they got talking and started to form the Small Faces with

Jimmy Winston on keyboards. Jimmy used to be in The Moments. When I heard they were getting together I didn't think Steve was going to play anything, I just thought he was going to be the singer but he turned out to be the lead guitarist too.

**Kenney Jones:** Ronnie was playing a Gretsch guitar and he said he would prefer to play bass. So I said, 'All right, let's go up the shop where I bought my drum kit.' It was a Saturday morning and in there was a real cocky little guy. I wandered over to this drum kit and started to play, Ronnie plugged in and started plonking away and Steve picked up a guitar and suddenly the three of us were playing, annoying the other people in the shop. We just sort of clicked right away. Steve was really friendly and a real ball of fun. I recognised his face straight away... I'd seen him in those films.

**Steve Marriott:** I worked there weekends. It was great working in a music shop because you meet other musicians. I knew where the good guitars were; even if they were cheaper some were better than others. So if I saw someone I liked, I said, 'Don't buy that, let me take you round the back and have a look at this.' That's what happened with Ronnie. He'd come in with his father to get a new bass guitar. We got on immediately, having seen each other before when The Moments played with The Outcasts. He was singing and playing guitar at the time and he was ever so good. So we kind of respected each other from a distance. We went back to my house and stayed up all night listening to blues records.

**Ronnie Lane:** He had some great records, Stax, Motown, American R&B records, James Brown, Otis Redding and all these great black singers. So I said, 'Why don't you take my guitar and I'll take the bass and we'll start a group'... he was very enthusiastic. I liked him.

*Ronnie Lane, born April 1946, was nine months older than the 18-year-old Marriott. The Outcasts had recently fallen out and the Lane faction had transmogrified into The Muleskinners, with 16-year-old Kenney Jones, born September 1948, on drums. They had a regular gig in a Bermondsey pub in south-east London.*

**Kenney Jones:** Steve came down to one of our gigs in Bermondsey and him and Ronnie got paralytic…

**Ronnie Lane:** We started drinking whiskies. First time I'd really drunk any and there was this false sense of bravado going on about how much we could put back. In the end we got totally pissed.

**Kenney Jones:** We said to the audience that night, 'We've got this very special guest for you,' winding them up, thinking they would all know Steve Marriott, which, of course, nobody did. Steve got up with us, sang a song and then he brought the house down with his Jerry Lee Lewis routine on the upright piano. He was jumping up and down on top of it…

**Steve Marriott:** I smashed the piano up or something… I was banging the shit out of it.

**Ronnie Lane:** So we all got the bullet and of course my name was shit because I'd brought this character down the pub and blown a really good gig.

**Ron Chimes:** When Ronnie and Kenney got together with Steve they asked [Muleskinners guitarist] Terry Newman to carry on with them but Terry refused. I don't think he liked the direction they wanted to go in. He eventually joined us [The Outcasts] and so did [Muleskinners singer] George Cambridge. Steve and Ronnie just clicked because they were both tiny little blokes with a similar sense of humour.

**Steve Marriott:** I got up the nose of the singer [in The Muleskinners]. I started to take over because I can't help it. I'm an overwhelming kind of guy and that's something I have to live with. Anyway, we got on George's tits so much, especially me, that we decided to form a band and I decided to learn to play guitar properly if Ronnie would play bass. Ronnie lost his job at Selmer's [Selmer's Electronic Ltd] about the same time because he was trying to get me a free PA. It was for The Moments, the band I was with. I found Jimmy Winston. Jimmy played with me in The Moments. He was a regular at the J60. His parents had the Ruskin Arms, great pub. He was proficient on guitar, more so than me. I didn't even have a guitar. Jimmy had an organ too, and a van... which was the big thing. He used to fight a lot, over chicks... he was always scuffling.

*Jimmy Winston's real name was Jimmy Langwith. He was almost 22, born April 1943, changed to 1945 by future Small Faces manager Don Arden, and had just left drama school where he'd picked up small parts in TV ads, films such as* Two Left Feet *(1963) and TV dramas such as the BBC crime series* Silent Evidence *(1963). He often acted as compère and sang with the resident pub band at the Ruskin Arms. Marriott sometimes sat in on harmonica with them.*

**Jimmy Winston:** I really wanted to be an actor. I was over in the Ruskin Arms singing one night, probably a few Beatles songs, and Steve came in with Ronnie Lane. Steve wanted to get up and play a bit of a harmonica. He played a bit and then we got chatting over a few beers. I was an out-and-out guitarist but Steve had already geared himself up for that... what they needed was a keyboard player. I'd never played keyboard so it was a case of finding what you needed for initial songs. It wasn't elaborate. On certain tracks I used to play guitar anyway, especially the ones I used to sing. Steve was learning the guitar. He wasn't a good guitarist. Everyone was slightly raw. My energy was with Steve really. He was similar to me in a way. He had a lot of drive, lots of attitude and lots of things he wanted to do. Ronnie and Kenney were slower, they hadn't been out there doing so much. Steve and me had both been at it a few years to find something to carve into a career and our energies were higher. We fascinated one another. He had this high gravelly growl that wasn't easy to do without losing pitch. With that, he could lift a song, give it heart and soul. He'd listened to Ray Charles. He'd watched Chuck Berry. He knew what it took. In his mind he was James Brown. He studied how they'd perform on stage and, when you do that to the extent that Steve did, it just rubs off on you. It was a lifestyle thing too.

*Winston had his own small house in Stratford, in the East End of London. Lane and Marriott stayed there often, smoking 'spliff after spliff' and listening to records. One key album Winston introduced Marriott to was Charles Mingus's experimental jazz opus* Oh Yeah *(released 1962). It included a track called 'Wham Bam Thank You Ma'am', a title Marriott would later steal.*

**Steve Marriott:** You've got to realise we were formed out of error. We couldn't get anyone to join the group. The name put them off. I was sitting in the Gioconda trying to tout for guitarists. They'd say, 'What's the name of the group?' because in those days it was a heavy thing. I'd say, whispering, 'The Small Faces', and they'd go, 'Fuck off, you've got to be joking.' It embarrassed them, so in the end I thought, fuck it, I'll play guitar. I knew my way around it but I wasn't proficient at it. We were not trying to make it... it was just to have a laugh. I was living in Loughton with Mick O'Sullivan [who later lived at the band's shared house in Pimlico, co-wrote the track 'Green Circles' and is said to have been the inspiration for 'Here Come The Nice'] and his friends from acting school and Ronnie would sleep there sometimes, and when Kenney would come over we'd have a little play... the equipment was at the house. Kenney's playing at the time wasn't too clever at all. Up until that time, I was used to playing with older people, more experienced musicians.

*If, as Pete Townshend asserted, Peter Meaden was the only person using terms such as 'face' in referencing Mod hierarchy, it would have been Meaden who inspired Marriott to choose the name. He told a different story.*

**Steve Marriott:** The term 'face' was a top Mod, a face about town, a respected chap! The name came from a girl called Annabelle I knew from Chelsea. I didn't know many from Chelsea but I knew this one! Any way she signed the hire purchase for my [Marshall] amplifier. We were trying to think of a name and she said, 'Call yourself the Small Faces,' because she said we were all little... it was great for us because it fitted with us wanting to be 'faces' anyway.

*Elsewhere the girl who came up the name, Small Faces, has been written as Annie or Annabella, said to work at pirate radio station Radio London; although Loog Oldham also had an 'attractive young girl-Friday' called Annabelle Smith working at his office. It has also been suggested she was Jimmy Winston's girlfriend with a flat in Kensington, where Marriott would go to smoke dope and listen to music. The band rehearsed either in the hall upstairs at the Ruskin Arms, where Winston's mum, who died in 1967 of cancer, fed the penniless hopefuls, or at the Starlite club, described in a Walker Brothers biography as 'a sordidly glamorous fleapit frequented by celebrities and gangsters like the Krays', where Maurice King continued to court Marriott. It was via King that the Small Faces travelled north to perform in Manchester, where their van was used by local villains in a leather shop robbery – the band members each receiving a free leather coat as their corner.*

**Kenney Jones:** Everyone knew the Krays. They were related to me. The East End was a small community and the music going on there was small... no doubt Steve and the Krays' paths had crossed before. It wouldn't surprise me if Steve rehearsed at Esmeralda's Barn [the Krays' Knightsbridge nightclub-cum-gambling-den that ran from 1960 to 1963]; probably did. With Maurice King... it was just everyone asked favours of the Krays. If you were a bit of a hood yourself, you wanted to know the Krays. People went out of their way to meet the Krays but our paths never crossed with the Krays in terms of the Small Faces.

**Steve Marriott:** We [the Small Faces] had done some rehearsals at the Starlite club that Maurice King used to own off Oxford Street. King was interested in me at the time so I'd asked him if we could use his place. King might have been managing Elkie Brooks because she used to be there a lot. I used to get up and sing with her sometimes.

**Kenney Jones:** Steve had a lot more street smarts than either Ronnie or me. With Steve as our guide Ronnie and I soon became acquainted with places like the 100 Club on Oxford Street and the Gioconda. Steve's ability spurred Ronnie and I on... but perhaps most important during those initial sessions was his attitude. He took being in a band far more seriously than those we'd been playing with... Steve's inherent drive pushed us to another level.

*Between the informal get-togethers with Lane, Jones and Winston, Marriott continued to hustle himself and The Moments, finding a proficient new band to back him on select dates.*

**Chris Clements:** Steve actually approached us [The Checkpoints] and said he needed to fulfil some gigs that were pending [as The Moments]. We did various venues in Essex, around the Basildon area. He had no guitar, he would use our lead guitarist's red Fender Strat. This was in 1965, he was with us for a couple of months. We rehearsed at the

Kentish Drovers in the Old Kent Road in south London. He got us to learn James Brown numbers. When we rehearsed with him, he almost spoke the words of the song, rather than sang the words. He was listening to us, making sure we got the backing right. But when we did the first gig with him, out came this fantastic soul voice; we all looked at each other, and our mouths fell open! His harmonica playing was also excellent. Our transport at that time was a converted ambulance, and Steve would always sit up front with the owner/driver, a man in his early 50s, rather than sit in the back talking to us. He seemed to me to be a bit of a loner. Even when I had a conversation with him, he always seemed to be looking past me, as though in a hurry to be somewhere else. One of the songs we did with him was 'Tell Me What I Say', which was a [1963] Ray Charles song.

*It was announced that there would be a second Marriott solo single released in March 1965, Andrew Loog Oldham having produced him singing a cover of 'Tell Me (You're Coming Back To Me)', the only Jagger/Richards original included on the debut Stones album. It was unclear when, or even if, the track had been cut. Marriott had certainly been around during recording sessions made by Oldham's quasi-grandiose, extremely punky musical side project, The Andrew Oldham Orchestra. This was essentially a multitude of young hip session musicians such as Jimmy Page and John Paul Jones and various Stones and hired string players blasting through Oldham's favourite tunes of the day in hazy, impromptu sessions with Oldham conducting (as well as contributing a few originals). The first Oldham album had been a tribute to his strong friendship with Lionel Bart, the self-explanatory* Plays Lionel Bart's Maggie May *– versions of the songs from Bart's 1964 musical about a Liverpool prostitute. A second album, released in 1964,* 16 Hip Hits, *had riffed on Dylan, Spector, The Beatles, plus the tabloid-headline-grabbing Mod phenomenon, following the 1964 mass brawls between Mods and rockers, notably the so-called 'Battle of Brighton Beach' (Oldham songs included 'The Rise Of The Brighton Surf' and 'Theme For A Mod's Summer Night Dream'). A third Orchestra album, released in 1965,* East Meets West, *was a sign of Oldham's and the Stones' growing focus on the States, with one side devoted to the hits of The Four Seasons (East Coast) and the other the hits of the Beach Boys (West Coast). Having said all that, 'Tell Me (You're Coming Back To Me)', just like 'I Cried', was ultimately never released and was 'withdrawn'.*

47

*The options were narrowing for the ambitious Marriott. The Moments' name was fading, the Small Faces going nowhere, and his only income the Saturday job at the music shop. His parents nagged him into taking a job as a dishwasher at the famous West End tea shop Lyons' Corner House (alongside Ronnie Lane). He was soon sacked. He auditioned to become singer in two new groups. At Soho's La Discotheque he tried out for a role in London R&B band Manish Boys, their debut single a cover of Bobby Bland's 'I Pity The Fool', released March 1965. The single was produced by The Who and Kinks producer Shel Talmy and featured Jimmy Page on guitar. The band was notable for having David Bowie as lead singer. At the time they were considering hiring an additional singer but soon split up. In March, Marriott auditioned to become lead singer with The Lower Third, a vacancy ultimately taken by David Bowie. At the Gioconda, The Lower Third were commonly referred to as 'The Lower Turd'. Marriott, however, became pals with Bowie, who was also just turned 18, and with another member of the band, Stuart Took, who had produced a fanzine dedicate to Marriott and The Moments and who now helped arrange the first hesitant Small Faces gigs at local youth clubs.*

**David Bowie:** The late but still irrepressible Stevie Marriott and I were quite close buddies. Steve was very short but long on big ideas. [Adopting exaggerated cockney accent] 'I've got this idea,' he'd say, over eggs and bacon [at the Gioconda]. 'Why don't we form like this R&B duo and call ourselves David & Goliath. You be David.' At the time I was messing about with a kind of knock-off Muddy Waters band called the Manish Boys. One night he came up to me in the dressing room and he said, 'I've got my mates Ronnie and Kenney together and we're going to form a band.' 'Yeah?' 'Well, what we're going to do is get these really big amplifiers and this enormous drum kit, kind of like The Who, y'know, but we're going be really, really little. We're going to call ourselves the Small Faces.' Well it worked out in a major way.

**Kenney Jones:** Bowie played with us on several occasions, in Ilford and other places. I thought of him as the unofficial fifth member of the band and if he hadn't primarily been a singer I'm convinced he would have joined.

# CHAPTER 3

# Whatcha Gonna Do About It

**David Arden:** The Old Man's story was that when Stevie came to the office with the Small Faces he said, 'Please tell Mr Arden I used to go to school with his son, David.' That's how it all started according to Dad.

**Don Arden [1926–2007]:** When the two boys, Ronnie Lane and Steve, first came to see me, they were living in the park [Marriott claimed he was living in Finsbury Park in a mud hut]. They came not just begging for me to be their manager but begging for some food, which I politely paid for. I'm giving you the cold hard facts because it's easier to pick up that way. They came to me at ten o'clock in the morning, they stank the office out, they hadn't washed for days, they had shit in their trousers, the stink was just unbelievable, the girls in the office objected. We had to bring in the cleaners to get rid of the smell. Steve had a mother that worked, earned very good money, and she might turn around and say she loved her son but she's a fucking liar... you don't put your son to sleep in the park if you love him. Steve told me he'd gone to school with David, so I phoned David up, he was still at Italia Conti, and he said, 'Oh yeah, I know him, give him a chance, Dad.' I arranged for them to audition for me and I sent them out to one of the shops [on Carnaby Street] and they came back with clean trousers. Stevie kept his mouth shut and got clothes as quick as he possibly could, he was embarrassed – the other one was too ignorant to be embarrassed.

*Arden was a concert promoter and Gene Vincent's manager. From the mid-fifties he had promoted the very best rock'n'roll music the UK had ever seen, handling tours by Chuck Berry, Carl Perkins, Jerry Lee Lewis, Sam Cooke, Little*

*Richard, Bo Diddley, Brenda Lee, The Shirelles, Duane Eddy, Ray Charles, Fats Domino and The Everly Brothers, among many others. His steering of the wayward Vincent was almost devotional and in direct contrast to the tough guy image he projected. In the post-Beatles period he had begun to reshape his operations and involved himself with bands such as The Nashville Teens, whose 1964 single 'Tobacco Road' had been a Top 10 hit for Decca, and The Animals, promoting their breakthrough 1964 No 1, 'House Of The Rising Sun'.*

**Steve Marriott:** A chick from Don Arden's office spotted us, his secretary. She just happened to be around. I'd seen her before at the Starlite club. She asked for my number. I was staying in Loughton and we didn't have a phone. They got hold of my mother, who I called once a week... I knew about Don Arden because I'd see his name on blues posters. He used to bring over Jimmy Reed and John Lee Hooker, so I was very impressed with that. Then [Arden's close associate, often mistaken for an enforcer] Pat [Patrick] Meehan came down to see us at the Cavern [in the Town club in Leicester Square, where the Small Faces had organised for themselves a short-lived Saturday night residency].

**Ronnie Lane:** We were all very excited because he'd had Gene Vincent. The Cavern was beneath a church. We played there for three or four weeks and even though we were kind of busking we got very popular. It was a chaotic lesson in bullshitting the audience. Fuck, we had some front! We used to take about an hour and a half to play four numbers [including their own 'Come On Children', destined for the band's debut album, and a cover of 'You Are My Sunshine', a song also performed by Ray Charles and Ike & Tina Turner, among many others]. Steve had my Gretsch off me and he only knew about three chords and I'd only just bought this bass and we used to bullshit our way through. But he had such a lot of front. Steve did, that's how we got away with it.

**Jimmy Winston:** It was a lot bluff, there were only about five songs, and we'd do different variations of those. You'd play it back to front and then play it again differently. We did 'You Need Loving' [the band's take on Willie Dixon's 'You Need Love', recorded by Muddy Waters, also included on their debut album], all the raw ones... they are like a jam that has become a song... it was a bit soul, a bit underground. We got uptight if people thought we were a pop band.

**Steve Marriott:** The Cavern was one of the nicest places we had played, curtain, nice high stage. Ronnie got a blackboard and drew a picture of a Mod in a parka with 'The Small Faces' painted on the back, like it was on Kenney's kit, which Ronnie also painted. We put it outside the gig and it brought all these Mods in [free tickets had also been distributed to nearby hang-outs, shops and clubs]. We got the following straight away down at the Cavern because we were Mods. We had a lot of energy and a little bit of flair. It was a very cultish thing. We thought we'd invented words like 'spliff'... we used to score the stuff off the Jamaicans. We had a song called 'Pass The Spliff' and another song called [originally] 'E To D' [later cut as 'E Too D' for their debut album] that was just that, E to D, two chords, a two-chord song. At the time The Who were playing down the road at the Marquee [The Who's breakthrough 1965 Tuesday night residency]. They were a bit Moddy but I hadn't studied them and they hadn't heard of us. Kit Lambert [co-manager of The Who] came down to see us at one gig and got a lot of flack from The Who, because he was going to take us on at one point.

**Pete Townshend:** When the Small Faces arrived, they'd picked up on the mythology or something had happened, but they were using the term 'faces' to describe themselves.

**Roger Daltrey:** We were the Mod band. We were the hot ticket at a hot club 'up West'. Until the Small Faces came up and spoilt it, bless them. They were real East End Mods, and Steve Marriott, in my opinion, was one of the greatest rock-soul singers we've ever had.

**Don Arden:** I auditioned them in Margate [the Dreamland Centre; Marriott had played there in 1964 with The Moments], where we had a summer home, on a Sunday night. They were fantastic. They had an image of their own. They looked like four little Oliver Twists, street urchins, four half-grown kids. And when they opened up the sound was so powerful. Those two things together: that was the impact. That's the way it hit me. I thought, they can't fail. I knew they were going to be big stars.

**David Arden:** Three years after meeting Steve, I'm at Dreamland and I'm watching the Small Faces with Dad. We saw the gig and went home and then there was a call. Bill's [Arden's road manager, Bill Corbett] on the phone, 'They're not paying us.' The Old Man's gone back there, told the main heavy what he's going to do with him, and his brother and his sister, his granny and his grandad, which is the way he'd terrify people, with his mouth more than his fists, and everything got sorted. Stevie loved it. He told this story about how the Old Man had wiped out four of the biggest guys around, smashed their heads in, cut their goolies off, shotgun in their mouths… to Steve that was fantastic. It was his shtick. Stevie loved having the Old Man around because he loved tough guys… guys who other guys would look up to and be in awe of. That was always his scene. In the seventies there was Dee Anthony and Laurie O'Leary looked after him at the end of his career. Laurie used to look after the Krays, used to run the Charlie Kray agency. Some boys just like gangster pals. Stevie was one of those.

*On 10 June 1965 the Small Faces (with parental consent required for the under-21s, Jones, Marriott and Lane) signed to Arden's Contemporary company, entitling him to 25 per cent of all their earnings. They were put on a £20-a-week wage. There would also be a less-publicised £20-a-week 'allowance' paid to each band member's set of parents, ostensibly to cover their food, accommodation, laundry. In August 1965 Kath and Bill went to Ibiza on holiday, not Jaywick Sands.*

**Steve Marriott:** We thought we'd go with whoever offers the most dough. Look, you go into it with your eyes open and as far as I was concerned it was better than living on brown sauce rolls. At least we had £20 a week guaranteed. In those days it was great: you could hold your head up with your mum and dad.

**Don Arden:** I found them, recorded them, released their record and got them in the Top 10, all in six weeks. The song I had on my shelf, two of the guys that worked for me, for £25 a week, Brian Potter and Ian 'Sammy' Samwell, they wrote 'Whatcha Gonna Do About It'. We tried it about twenty times and couldn't get any artists to take it and on this occasion I insisted because I considered the boys had a great image but I didn't think they knew a good song from a bad song, so I fucking told them to keep their mouth shut – 'You're going to do this song and this guy's going record it for you.' I admit I bullied them into doing it but it doesn't matter because I was proved right.

**Graham Dee:** I shared a flat in Clapham with the drummer in The Quotations, Brian Potter, who co-wrote 'Whatcha Gonna Do About It'. There was a pretty girl who rented a room in our flat who worked for Don. I think it might have been her who tipped off Don's office about Steve. Steve used to come over either to see her and have the odd lesson off me on guitar, or the other way round. Don had given Brian [Potter] a job. He worked in the office. I was booked by Ian 'Sammy' Samwell [to play on the 'Whatcha Gonna Do About It' session]. We did three or four tracks. Steve said to me, we tried to get [then leading session guitarist] Jimmy Page but he was busy, so I was second choice. I did two sessions for 'Whatcha Gonna Do About It', one at IBC and one at Pye. Ian Samwell was producing both sessions. Sammy used to go over to America a lot and get ideas from over there, the black music he loved, and then he'd come over here and write something similar ahead of the American release [Doris Troy's single, 'What'cha Gonna Do About It', was released by Atlantic Records in 1964]. I've got a feeling Tony [McIntyre] was drumming on the first session and Kenney was on the second. I played the riff in the background, it was similar to Lonnie Mack's 'Memphis'... that was the groove in those days... a lot of tracks had that... 'Hi-Heel Sneakers' by Tommy Tucker... Steve was doing the bar chords. Plonk [Ronnie Lane] was on the session. I often wondered what would have happened had I not been six foot three and a half.

**Steve Marriott:** We loved 'Whatcha Gonna Do About It'. It was a total nick of [Solomon Burke's] 'Everybody Needs Somebody To Love' but so what? It was a good record just the same. I was proud of the guitar part, my first solo on record.

**Jerry Shirley:** Jimi [Hendrix] told Clem [Humble Pie guitarist Dave Clempson] that the guitar solo on 'Whatcha Gonna Do About It' was his all-time favourite.

*The Velvet Underground's John Cale was another fan of Marriott's raw feedback-drenched guitar part on the Small Faces' debut single. At the time Marriott said he admired three guitar players – Dave Davies, Eric Clapton and Pete Townshend – 'and the easiest of those styles for me to follow was Pete Townshend, so I did'. The single was to be released by Decca Records as Arden already had a deal in place with Dick Rowe, the head of A&R at Decca (who had also signed The Rolling Stones), that stipulated all his Contemporary acts were offered to the company as a first option. Nonetheless he had offered the Small Faces to his friend Andrew Loog Oldham first. Oldham had worked for Arden as publicist circa 1962 and Arden had included the early Stones on an Everly Brothers tour in 1963. Oldham would coin the affectionate moniker 'the Don Corleone of Pop' to describe Arden and was considered one of the family. Oldham, with Tony Calder, had recently started their own independent record label, Immediate, a significant milestone in the British music business. Among their early releases was a record by Marriott's pal Gregory Phillips.*

**Don Arden:** Stevie knew Tony Calder. Andrew [Loog Oldham] didn't see the commerciality in them, he turned them down, he didn't want to know.

**Tony Calder:** I think the physical height of the band put them in a situation where on TV no one took them seriously. They were seen as more of a comedy act.

**Don Arden:** I paid for 'Whatcha Gonna Do About It' to be a hit. Never was even a sign of a denial. Not even when the police came to see me at the office. I told them exactly what happened. I had guys who worked for the music papers who did the charts and they were being paid peanuts so they came by my office once a week and I gave them money, more than they were earning in their jobs. I paid them to see that those boys [the Small Faces] were put in a position that allowed their music to flourish. Only if you've got a record that's moving up, only if that record has proven that it's on its way, that it's a winner, then drop the money. You know why? It saves you four, five weeks. So maybe the first week we'd automatically gone near the Top 30, well there's no surprise if they go from say No 30 to the Top 10. I also had a team of cheeky little bastards that went out into all of the districts of England and approached housewives and offered them money, £10 a week, to go and buy these records. They'd hold on to them and we'd go round the next week and pick them up and we sent those records to all the DJs we knew. When the people from the charts phoned up [the shops] and said what's your best sellers, the guy would say, 'Oh, we're doing great today – somebody came in and they wanted ten of these records.'

**Steve Marriott:** Ronnie and I used to go in and order a dozen of our own records at a time. Very suspect. They had promotional pictures and people used to look at us and say, 'Hold on a minute.' We had a list of stores that Don's office had supplied so we did that but only for about two days – we got tired of it. After it charted the rest of the machinery went to work.

**Don Arden:** I also gave people money to get them a TV show and on the radio. This wasn't just some little idea; I had it all worked out. I could phone up anybody you care to mention in the BBC and say, 'Fellas, I want this group on *Top Of The Pops*, I want them to do this show, that show,' whatever show was available, all I had to do was ask. Who was there that could top me on that one? I used to phone up *Ready Steady Go!* to get artists on television, just bosh like that – all through the fact that I was the number one promoter in Europe. I admit I was a little flamboyant at the time.

**David Arden:** There's no ifs, ands or buts about it: Dad made the band. The hustle and the bustle. I was running the errands, running the £250 to 'uncle' Phil Solomon for the week's airplay on Radio Caroline.

*The Small Faces performed on a spin-off of ITV pop show* Thank Your Lucky Stars *before 'Whatcha Gonna Do About It' was released in August 1965 and appeared on* TOTP *three times to promote the single, initially when it charted at No 27. They also appeared on* RSG! *'He is quite a one, he's a real little Mod,' said host Cathy McGowan as Marriott left the stage to dance with girls in the audience. Fellow host Vicki Wickham was likewise impressed.*

**Vicki Wickham:** I remember him being a little sweetheart, a cheeky little kid. Cathy McGowan and I loved him. If we liked somebody we could book them whenever we wanted and the Small Faces were perfect for *RSG!* They were a Mod group, they were cute, they had great music, they were right up our street.

**Kenney Jones:** Thanks to his training as an actor, Marriott was the expert when it came to TV miming. If you look at footage of him, he's invariably looking away from the camera during the intro, seconds before the vocal cuts in. He gives the impression that he's smiling at the rest of us, relaxed and enjoying himself. In fact, what he's doing is making sure he doesn't miss his cue. Once he's picked up the words, he turns back to camera looking like he's been singing all along.

*'Whatcha Gonna Do About It' peaked at No 14 in the UK charts.*

**Jimmy Winston:** Once the first record became a hit we became more conscious of the whole Mod image. There was Don Arden saying things like, 'Come on boys, dress the part and make me lots of money.' Up until Don it was a lot rawer, like The Who.

**David Arden:** The Old Man always stressed: if you were a star or going to be a star you had to have the threads, as Stevie would call it. There were two shops on Carnaby Street the Small Faces used to go in and drain of absolutely everything in their size. John Stephen's, which was beneath the Old Man's office, and the other one on the corner, Harry [Fenton]...

**Jeff Dexter [Club DJ]:** Don handed me a wad of notes to kit them out. They were like kids in a sweet shop but their style was all wrong. I said, 'You can't have stripes and checks together,' but 'Sammy' Samwell said, 'Think about it: they look like little clowns and people will recognise them.' I went back to Don's office and told him I thought they looked horrendous but that it was unusual. So I asked him, 'How do you want to package them, looking good or unusual?' Don thought about it and said, 'Fuck it, stick with unusual.'

**Steve Marriott:** I think to establish ourselves in the very early stages, clothes can really set an image for you... really work for you. We used to get laughed at, wolf whistles from geezers on building sites. My old man didn't like it all. It's nice to be different – well, that's the way I felt about it.

**Don Arden:** It was all my idea with the clothes, all my idea. Everything about the clothes is me. I was the first agent to set up offices in Carnaby Street. Why do you think I went to fucking Carnaby Street? I didn't need a suit. I didn't need to buy myself some fancy shoes. I was the best-dressed man in the business. I was the guy who could go up and say, 'Now, if you want to work for me, get fucking dressed.' They didn't go in and get these suits off the peg: those guys in those shops altered everything until they fitted to perfection... finished off beautiful... the Faces looked a million dollars. All the tradespeople on Carnaby Street loved me. There were six stores. They'd had a good show to start off with and then they'd started to fade and now they were dying. They were fighting for existence in Carnaby Street, there was no queues. When I came on the scene I brought the boys in and we made them. The Small Faces advertised the clothes and we get a cut of the sales. Everyone started to dress like the Small Faces, there were impersonations of a kind.

**Ronnie Lane:** We were like bunch of old women at a jumble sale, when we walked into a shop; some of the stuff we never even wore. We'd get home and think, what did I buy that for? We lived on the road and all the expenses were paid for. In actual fact, we often had money left over from that twenty quid [a week's wage], and we were out of our boxes most of the time. In the beginning when I trusted him I thought Don was a wonderful guy.

**Kenney Jones:** Don became like a father figure. We all liked him. He had faith in the band and he guided us. He worked hard on our behalf and he thought big. He used every trick he knew to make us a success. He introduced us to a friend of his called Ron King, owner of the booking agency Galaxy Entertainment. I only discovered later Don had a slice of the Galaxy action. Like Arden, Ron was a larger than life character. He travelled around in a chauffeur-driven Rolls shadowed by a Land Rover stuffed with four heavies.

*Ron Kingsnorth was 31. His colourful criminal past included shoplifting, ram-raiding, housebreaking, pickpocketing, illegal gambling, odd jobs for the Krays and prison. His first rock'n'roll club was in Romford and he expanded to running many other London clubs, including the Pigalle in Piccadilly. He started Galaxy in the early sixties and was now booking gigs for fifty or more groups, including Amen Corner, who he also managed.*

**Ron Kingsnorth:** I liked Don, we clicked immediately and when he asked me if I wanted to be an agent for some of his groups I immediately agreed. I knew ours would be an interesting match. The first 'official' Galaxy Entertainment office was a small, dump of an office in Oxford Street... when Don was offered the whole top floor of an office in Carnaby Street he asked me if I'd be interested in sharing the level with him. I got to know Don very well. He was ruthless, crass and he could scream and vent with very little concern or cause but he didn't have it in him to be physically violent. If violence were required to solve a situation he'd call on others, mainly me, to do the work for him. The music industry, as I knew it, was a cut-throat world during the sixties.

**Steve Marriott:** We did a gig for Ron and he wouldn't pay us. He said, 'You were too loud.' Our own agent wouldn't pay us. We thought, what have we got ourselves into?

*From late August 1965, Galaxy took whatever bookings they could get for the Small Faces, all over England in apparent random sequence. Invariably the group played two short performances per night at any venue they were booked into. The band's repertoire expanded to include covers of 'Jump Back' by Rufus Thomas, 'Think' and 'Night Train' by James Brown, Timi Yuro's 'What's A Matter Baby', 'Baby Don't You Do It' by Marvin Gaye, 'Shake' by Sam Cooke (sung by Lane and included on the band's debut album), 'Plum Nellie' by Booker T. & The M.G.'s and Jimmy Reed's 'Baby What You Want Me To Do'.*

**Steve Marriott:** We used to do a cover and then say, fuck that, listen to the original, it's much better.

*The band travelled in a van bought and driven by Jimmy Winston's brother Derek, who took 10 per cent of any gig money for this service. Winston's parents had also sorted out the group a fan club, managed by Fran Piller, whose husband ran the betting shop next door to the Ruskin Arms.*

**Eddie Piller:** My mum and dad were friends with Jimmy's mum and dad even though they were more of an age of the Small Faces. When the Small Faces started kicking off Mr and Mrs Langwith asked my mum if she would look after the correspondence and she did that for a while. She wrote newsletters for the fans, sent pictures… but after a while it got too big and in the end she complained to Don that she was spending a substantial amount of money paying for the post herself… this was after Jimmy had been kicked out. Before that I think Mr and Mrs Langwith paid for the cost of the fan club out of the bar takings in the pub. She asked Mr Arden for some expenses and he just said, 'No, fuck off,' and it was taken in-house.

**Jimmy Winston:** I'd go in and get the money for the gigs and pay my brother and then the rest of the band got grumpy about it. I started to get into conflicts with them. Steve was starting to have moans and groans. I was stuck in the middle. Things were going quite well and all of a sudden you've got a problem. Don also saw this 10 per cent for the van as 10 per cent of his money, so you're finding yourself a having a row… and it was becoming a drag.

**Don Arden:** Ronnie Lane never considered anything that was done for him and on his own he would have been absolutely nothing. Yet the first thing he did after the hit record came out was demand that the keyboard player be replaced. He was the nicest one in the group, his father and mother really looked after him [Winston was driving a flash, soft-top Triumph TR4, that cost over £1,000 new – out of the price bracket of the wages he received from Arden]. I never got over the fact that Ronnie pointed the finger at him when he thought the time was right, [saying,] 'I can't play with him, he's no fucking good.' I asked, 'Why don't you give him a chance? We've only just started, you're in the charts, you're stars, give him a fucking break. He was with you when you were struggling to get a gig, he gave you the use of his brother's van, at least talk to him, see if he can do things right for you.' He didn't want to know, so they just kicked him out. Ronnie Lane was an evil little man; he really was a shithouse. He was wallowing in success. It was a dirty, filthy trick. The guy they kicked out was ten times better than this Scottish cunt they got in [Ian McLagan]. I took him [Jimmy Winston] on as a solo artist but I didn't have any success with him.

**Jimmy Winston:** Steve said, 'This is just not going to work, get yourself another band and we'll record you.' He gave me an alternative... I was disappointed, angry and let down. It was always going to happen because I was older and edgier than Ronnie and Kenney. That made it harder for me to put up with Steve's moods. He was a great talent but awkward at times.

**David Arden:** Steve could do anything he liked... and he always wanted to work with the best. His favourite word was, 'Oh, yeah man, cool, that's cool,' even at school... fucking cool, he always had to be cool and the best... and he didn't think Jimmy was up to the job, plain and simple. We tried to look after Jimmy down the years.

**Steve Marriott:** Jimmy went off his rocker every now and then, plus we didn't get on too well personally... so it was decided by the three of us Jimmy should go. It was due to a lot of little things... we weren't even speaking so it was silly to continue. He got very moody. He actually used to call himself James Moody before he started using the Winston. But James Moody gives you a picture of the guy: collar up, coat on, shades...

**Ronnie Lane:** Jimmy was a bighead and I don't think Steve could take it anymore.

*Winston's last show with the group was in Stockport, Greater Manchester, on 31 October 1965. The next day Arden contacted Ian McLagan and asked him to come to his Carnaby Street office. McLagan was 20 (born April 1945, although he became younger for the press), an art school dropout who had buzzed about the Stones' early scene with his blues band Muleskinners (not the same band Lane/Jones had been in). They had released a single in late 1964, a cover of 'Back Door Man' by Howlin' Wolf, and acted as backing band, during UK visits, to Howlin' Wolf, Sonny Boy Williamson and Little Walter. He had recently joined, as Hammond organ player, jazzy, pop blues band Boz People (fronted by Boz Burrell, a future Marriott musical collaborator), who had backed*

*The Byrds during their debut tour in August 1965 but thus far failed to secure a recording contract.*

**Steve Marriott:** Don met him first for a bit and then we met him later on in the afternoon, shook hands, kitted him out with some gear in Carnaby Street, got his barnet cut... I couldn't believe it. Here's a guy standing right in front of us who is already one of the boys.

**Ian McLagan:** When I met the other Faces it was like looking at a mirror. I couldn't believe it. It was about the first time I've ever counted myself lucky to be small. Steve was larger than life. A cartoon of a person. Whenever he said something funny he'd scream with laughter before you could properly grasp what it was he'd said that was so funny. It was exhausting trying to keep up. He was probably the most electric person I ever met. It was never boring being with him.

**Steve Marriott:** The first thing we ran through together was Booker T.'s 'Comin' Home' [McLagan, similar to Marriott, was a major fan of Booker T. & The M.G.'s and the band also jammed on other Booker T. tracks, such as 'Jelly Bread', 'Green Onions' and 'Plum Nellie']. I didn't like to expect too much but I was really knocked back; the Hammond really slew me, he was so good.

**Kenney Jones:** It released me and we started to swing. Mac's arrival also freed Steve and Ronnie. The band felt complete.

**Steve Marriott:** Kenney really opened up. It was a different drummer – he just got better and better. It really was an eye-opener and there was no looking back, every song we did swung like Hanratty [James Hanratty, the A6 murderer, was one of the final six to be executed by hanging in 1962 before capital punishment was abolished].

*McLagan, however, was not initially required to play organ. His first job was to mime Winston's guitar parts to promote the band's second single, 'I've Got Mine', on kids' TV show* Crackerjack *and on RSG! Released in November 1965, the song was written by Marriott, Jones, Winston and Lane and produced by Ian Samwell. The single was supposed to coincide with the opening of a feature film the band guest-starred in,* Dateline Diamonds, *a schlocky B-movie about an explosives expert who blackmails a pop group manager into using a pirate radio ship to smuggle stolen gems. The Small Faces, with Winston, appeared miming to 'I've Got Mine' towards the end of the film. Unfortunately the film's release was delayed until spring 1966 and, despite good reviews, the single failed to chart.*

**Val Weedon:** In his book Mac wrote about a receptionist who gave him a hard time when he came to be interviewed by Don about joining the band. Well, that was me! He got the timing a bit wrong: I didn't start with Don until Mac was in the band [Weedon joined the office in March 1966, aged just 15, working for Arden and for 16-year-old Pauline Corcoran, who now ran the Small Faces fan club]. He said that he found out later that it was because I was going out with Jimmy Winston. I'd never told anyone about my relationship with Jimmy... we hung about a lot and I did go out with him briefly but I thought it was all a big secret. Pauline said I used to treat him [McLagan] rotten, push him out the way when he came up the office. I would have been quite loyal to Jimmy because I was an original fan, a fan from the beginning... and I knew he was really upset about being chucked out the band. The conflict [in the band] was more Ronnie and Jimmy. Pauline said Ronnie and Jimmy had fisticuffs in the office arguing over women. Steve was the one who was really friends with Jimmy and Jimmy was a bit of a show-off, a bit flash but they'd got this huge fame quite quickly, why wouldn't that go to your head? He loved being in the limelight at that time and he would compete with Steve on stage and show off and that would get up Ronnie's nose and Steve was probably talked around.

*Galaxy continued to work the band hard. The final six months of 1965 saw them play approximately 100 shows. In 1966 they would play 280 shows, on top of an estimated 40 UK and European TV appearances. 'Strike while the iron is hot,' Arden said.*

**Ian McLagan:** We were taking a lot of [speed] pills to keep going, and smoking dope to relax... but when we got a chance to work, no one in that band said no. It was like, 'Yes!' We were all going faster than anyone could possibly handle. We'd take as much work as we could possibly get. We were out of it all the time. We were like a soul band that would jam on stage and Steve would go into these raps throwing in

James Brown lines, Ray Charles lines, Steve would be flying. We all would. There was a lot of freeform stuff going on but basically we were just playing behind Steve's voice.

*The days of travelling in the back of Jimmy Winston's brother's van, sweaty socks and steamy windows was over. Roadies now took the band's gear to gigs in a separate van while Arden arranged for the four band members to travel in style.*

**Don Arden:** I got them a brand-new Jag [Mark 10 Jaguar] to travel in and this guy to look after them and be their chauffeur [and bodyguard]. He'd been away from The Beatles for four weeks, somebody tipped me off he was a looking for a job and I grabbed him; he was six foot six [and sixteen stone]. They were as safe as houses, there was no point me getting a normal size guy for them – because they were midgets, they had to have somebody that protected them.

**David Arden:** Bill Corbett, The Beatles' ex-driver [and ex-boxer]… he was lovely, old Bill. He would come in and report, 'Oh, they're smoking that fucking gear, Don. I can't drive home at night because my eyes are running.' He used to report everything to the Old Man. And Dad was horrified because he used to think smoking dope was like taking heroin, he didn't know the difference… just drugs! The Old Man genuinely didn't know the difference in those days… he was always dead against it… he just thought it was the worst thing in the world… same as booze.

**Ian McLagan:** Bill was stoned the whole time and he used to complain, 'You little bastards, drug addicts, not like The Beatles.' We used to put up a blanket in the back [of the car] and we'd be in the back smoking, and Kenney would be in the front with Bill. Kenney was a pill-popper but he didn't smoke dope like we did. We had one of those little record players in the car. 'Rescue Me' by Fontella Bass was Steve's favourite for a while. He used to play it over and over.

**David Arden:** As well as the clothes and the car, the Old Man always said a star had to live in a nice place. He got them a beautiful place [four-bed, four-storey Victorian townhouse] in Pimlico [central London, bordering Belgravia, noted for its garden squares and Regency architecture] with a maid to clean their clothes so they'd always look presentable.

*The band moved into the house in late December 1965.*

**Don Arden:** I put them in a mansion house fit for the young Prince of Wales. It was in the most expensive part of London. I wanted them to be all together so the group would get stronger. I got them this German maid who woke them up, gave them breakfast every day. Wherever they were, they had to come back and have lunch in the house, and no matter where they were they came in no later than eight o'clock and had their dinner prepared by the maid.

**Ian McLagan:** As soon as we looked it over we knew this was our party house. Steve typically had chosen the biggest bedroom at the top of the house. Steve's contribution [to the furnishings when moving in] was to bring some black Afghani, some Rizla papers and Mick O'Sullivan, a pal of his from Loughton. He was supposed to be an actor... he could roll a decent joint and pour a fair glass of brandy, as long as he didn't have to pay for it. He was permanently unemployed and became little more than a ligger and freeloader, but it was handy to have someone in the house while we were out of town. We were four very lucky, very happy guys... we had nothing to do but have fun. We had girls everywhere... everything was perfect. Downstairs in the dining room we had a piano. In the sitting room we had our guitars.

**Ronnie Lane:** Pimlico was a complete mind-blaster.

**Hugh Janes:** Pimlico was crazy. Steve never washed any of his clothes and he'd only wear something once. He'd get ten shirts in the same design, just different colours... there was this pile of this stuff, incredible: beautiful leather jackets, trousers, everything [Marriott bragged of a camel-hair coat that had set him back £400].

**Colin Spaull:** There was a huge pile in his room. I asked, 'What the bloody hell are all those doing there, Stevie?' He said, 'I buy them from Carnaby Street and I only wear them once and I can't be bothered to wash so I throw them in the corner, help yourself.' So I did and I came away with shirts, sweaters.

**David Arden:** They were very young, just kids, and all the Small Faces apart from Kenney were very generous people. All their mates, the hangers-on, got stuff too – the Old Man used to hate it.

**Hugh Janes:** All the Mod gear Colin and I had was Steve's stuff he'd worn once. It was insanity. The place was one non-stop party. One room was set aside for a giant Scalextric set... during the daytime there would always be dozens of girls outside and of course certain hand-picked ones invited in. Other pop stars of the day, such as Georgie Fame and Marianne Faithfull [and Eric Burdon and Steve Winwood], would be seen there regularly.

**Steve Marriott:** I remember Marianne screaming a lot. Sometimes there'd be so many people there I would have to go in the toilet and write.

**Ian McLagan:** We turned quite a few people on with our legendary hash brownies... even experienced smokers like Georgie Fame were surprised at how stoned they could be hours after they left our place.

**Kenney Jones:** You never knew who you might bump into. *The Avengers* actress Honor Blackman lived a door down... Mick Jagger, Paul McCartney, John Lennon would be there having a smoke, trying out new songs... McCartney was a big, big fan [of the Small Faces]. All the Beatles were great fans [of ours], they thought we were stunning... they gave us a lot of encouragement and Steve and Ronnie advice on what to do, how to cope.

**Kath Marriott:** When they moved into that house, they loved the freedom but their looks changed so much during that time [lots of spots from all the speed, booze and hashish and late nights]. I could tell they were overworking. Being a pop star wasn't all a giggle. The group was so busy and successful yet they never seemed to have any money. Even my mother who worked in the Co-op used to give Steve two quid on the quiet. She'd say, 'I'm not going to do it anymore,' but he'd go to the door and I'd hear her say, 'There you are, son.' When Bill would say, 'Watch your money,' Steve would say, 'Dad, I play and I write – we pay other people to do that.'

**Bill Marriott:** Steve reckoned Arden was a good manager but I didn't like him very much. I don't like managers very much and I told Arden so. I said to him I had never met a straight manager yet and suddenly I got a couple of big chaps behind me, so I kept my mouth shut.

*Marriott and the band wanted more control over their music. Chiefly they felt they wanted to work with a young engineer called Glyn Johns who they had met in IBC studios, where Samwell produced their singles and was now producing album sessions. Johns, born 1942, was also a singer, with three singles released in 1965 – all produced by Tony Meehan. His latest had been released on Calder and Oldham's Immediate Records. As an engineer he was also working with Georgie Fame, The Pretty Things and, most expediently for his career, The Rolling Stones, at the behest of Oldham. The Stones had released two albums in 1965 and both had been No 1s in the UK and America. They had also chalked up three massive No 1 singles that year, including 'Satisfaction'.*

**Don Arden:** After the first smash hit they said they didn't want to perform with Ian 'Sammy' Samwell anymore because they were ungrateful bastards. He cried his fucking eyes out. There was nothing I could do about it. He couldn't believe that they'd turned on him. I found out that they were now very friendly with a man who hated me called Glyn Johns. He used to boast that he was going to be in the studio with Mick Jagger and that the Stones thought he was the greatest find of the century... all that bilge. I arranged to have him picked up. I had to stop him. He was such an arrogant bastard.

*It is likely Johns bad-mouthed Arden. In his own telling, he was approached at Olympic Studios, Oldham's latest favoured London recording studio, by Reg 'The Butcher' King, who was Oldham's psychotic driver-cum-bodyguard, and then ushered outside to a car where a short, stocky man who apparently had been a professional wrestler levelled a sawn-off shotgun at his legs. It was a warning from Arden that if he ever mentioned the Arden name again it would not matter where he was or what he was doing, Arden would find Johns and shoot him and his family. Arden recalls the frightener going down a little differently.*

**Don Arden:** I got these three gentlemen to walk in [to Olympic] and while one of the guys was talking to Mick Jagger the other two picked up this cunt [Johns] and said, 'We've been asked to tell you Mr Arden sent us and he wants you to spend the night on the tree outside.' They picked him up and took him about a mile from the studio and tied him to a tree and they left him there all night. He never ever got over it. That was one of the reasons why the Small Faces decided eventually they were going to leave me because they wanted this guy to produce them. I said, 'What's this man [Samwell] done to you? He's given you a fantastic hit, you snotty-nosed little bastards'... it was disgusting: the two people that helped get them stardom [Samwell and Winston], they threw away.

# CHAPTER 4

# Sha-La-La-La-Lee

**Don Arden:** I rammed 'Sha-La-La-La-Lee' down their throats: they hated it. It wasn't just a hit. It was a massive hit. Whenever I've heavied any of the boys in the studio I've always won the day, I've never failed yet. To a lot of people 'Sha-La-La-La-Lee' sounded corny and it most probably was but I heard it in my mind with the boys, I knew that most probably they were the only ones that would make it a hit. Kenny Lynch [who co-wrote the song with the legendary Mort Shuman] was a pal of mine. [Lynch had also, coincidentally, written Marriott's debut single in 1963, 'Give Her My Regards'.]

**Kenny Lynch [1938–2019]:** Me and Mort were songwriting partners. I had replaced [his previous partner] Doc Pomus [Shuman and Pomus had written 'His Latest Flame' and 'Viva Las Vegas' for Elvis, as well as 'A Teenager In Love', 'Save The Last Dance For Me', 'Can't Get Used To Losing You', 'Sweets For My Sweet' and a host of other classics]. Don phoned me up, and said, 'I've got this group that are really good.' It wasn't the Small Faces. It was for Amen Corner. He said, 'I want a song like "Doo Wah Diddy Diddy" [written by Jeff Barry and Ellie Greenwich and originally cut by The Exciters in 1963, the song had been a huge 1964 No 1 in the UK and US for Manfred Mann]; I don't want none of that clever shit you and Mort write.' We wrote 'Sha-La-La-La-Lee' in five minutes exactly. [Note: in early 1965, Manfred Mann had hit UK No 3 with a song titled 'Sha La La', originally performed by The Shirelles in 1964.] Mort said, 'That's the biggest piece of crap I've ever heard.' I said, 'I couldn't agree more, but it's what they want.' He said, 'If they take it, put your name on it and give me half, I don't want my name on that song.' I took it to Don and he said, 'That's great, I want it for the Small Faces.'

**Steve Marriott:** I admired Mort Shuman for the work he had done with Elvis. I was totally knocked out by the fact that he performed it for us sitting at the piano. But what bugged me was Kenny Lynch... he was a fucking nuisance. He was a songwriter-cum-self-plugger. That's all he was there for, to sell his songs.

**Kenny Lynch:** They never wanted to do it. Don got one of my best pals, 'Sammy' Samwell, to produce it and, when I heard it, it sounded like [The] Dave Clark [Five] gone fucking mad. I said I am not letting this record out. [As songwriter] I could stop the song [being released] first time, can't stop it once it's been [put] out once. Don phoned me up and said, 'I spent £500 on that recording, they like it at Decca, what do you want to do with it to let it out?' I said I'll produce it. We went into a studio by the side of West End Lane station [Decca's own studio in West Hampstead] and we spent five hours on the bloody intro alone. Don never came to the studio. I said, 'Stevie, are you sure you're in the right key?' He said, 'Yeah, positive.' Five more hours and the backing track's finished and Stevie goes down to sing it. He says, 'It's too high for me to do the harmony.' I said, 'I asked you that six hours ago!' So I do all the harmonies on it, all the high falsetto stuff. I gave it to Don on the Friday morning, on Tuesday the record was out and the next Friday it was at No 1 and stayed there for two weeks. I phoned Mort up and said, 'You know that song we wrote?' 'Fuck that song,' he said. I said, 'It's No 1, they rush-released it.' He said, 'You did put my name on it, didn't you?'

*Released in late January 1966, 'Sha-La-La-La-Lee' became the band's first Top 5 single, peaking at No 3 in the UK. It radically transformed the appeal of the Small Faces. The catchy song, the four small band members' cute looks, the unusual colourful clothes meant they were suddenly the stuff of pre-teenage and young teenage girls' dreams, no longer the tough R&B band they imagined themselves as. Spotting Marriott at the Scotch of St James club, blues singer Long John Baldry, a musician Marriott admired (his band Steampacket also featured Julie Driscoll and Rod Stewart), declared, 'It's Steve Marriott, soul singer,' then in a silly high-pitched voice started to sing 'Sha-La-La-La-Lee'. Marriott was mortified.*

**Kenney Jones:** We had a cute look. We were all small and incredibly young. Without knowing it, we were four Justin Biebers. It would piss us off when we went to see bands we considered rock or blues – people like Georgie Fame, The Yardbirds and Zoot Money – because that was how we saw ourselves.

**Ronnie Lane:** We was teenyboppers! It was weird, very weird… to have thousands of chicks screaming, and if they got hold of you, they'd tear you to pieces, man. It was quite violent.

*There were reports of hasty finales at Small Faces gigs due to struggles between staff and screaming girls. At one show at Streatham Ice Rink fans invaded the stage, knocking Marriott unconscious and dislocating Jones's shoulder. Marriott described another gig for a magazine as 'a deafening wall of shouts and screams and hundreds of people clawing at the stage', and then 'the whole crowd came screaming at us. We just ran over the back of the stage, amps were going down, wires tripped us up.' He described how after the venue manager calmed the crowd the band returned to the stage: 'We did a few more numbers and everyone seemed to be okay but when we got to "Sha-La-La-La-Lee" they all went mad, they got up and came after us again. We finished up pretty sharpish and ran off.'*

**Kath Marriott:** They used to go hysterical. It was quite frightening. And all I could see were the veins on Steve's neck standing out because he was giving it his all and you couldn't hear him because of the screaming. I used to get quite concerned when the bouncers were being unkind to the girls because they were quite rough. My mother [Steve's nan] was so thrilled. Really, really thrilled. She went to most of the shows. And my stepfather used to go with cotton balls in his ears. He couldn't stand the noise but he had to see him perform. Everybody was proud and very supportive. And there always used to be about ten of the family there.

**Kay Marriott:** I was looking with so much pride. And love. And also with horror and fright. I got very frightened at the concerts and my parents did too because they would just surge. My father [Bill] used to get up in the aisle and try to barricade the girls off. You couldn't hear the band sing for the screaming and the yelling and you've got girls passing out in aisles and seats next to you.

**Ronnie Lane:** After the hit record we never heard ourselves again on stage... it was all screaming all the time. It was just curtains up, wiggle your arse and a lot of screaming.

**Steve Marriott:** We'd go out and it was a shambles every night, I'd be playing one key, or one song, Mac would be playing another, Ronnie would be playing another, and every night it was like that, and every hit record we had made it worse, because we'd have to drop something else we liked [the band's set now included 'Ooh Poo Pah Doo', an R&B hit for Jessie Hill in 1960, covered by Etta James in 1963 and later covered by Wilson Pickett and Ike & Tina Turner] to fit it in. We became pop stars and we never really wanted to be. It was mad. To see these screaming little girls getting hurt in a crush... and to not be able to hear us sing or play, we just wanted to go home.

**Kenney Jones:** Girls would sit in front of the stage and diddle themselves... it never went away... it haunted us.

**Ian McLagan:** We saw it lots, girls down in the front row fiddling with themselves and the smell was overwhelming... it was horrible. These were pubescent girls, 11, 12, 14. We used to play two twenty-minute slots. We'd play a few minutes and then someone would break through the barrier and it would get out of control and we'd have to quit.

*Demand for the band from TV, radio and particularly the teen magazines, skyrocketed. Both Marriott's mum and sister helped out in the office dealing with the sackfuls of fan mail – and now there was extra promotion to do in Europe, as 'Sha-La-La-La-Lee' charted in Germany and the Netherlands, more miming on TV, interviews, photo shoots and chaotic twenty-minute live sets.*

**Kenney Jones:** Steve was even more nervous of flying than I was and would grab my leg in a vice-like grip whenever we hit an air pocket... an overnight stay with Marriott was no bed of roses. He'd be so hyper after a gig, stalking around, talking incessantly, asking if I'd mind him bringing a girl back that it drove me nuts... in Berlin we jumped straight in a taxi at the airport, passing war-damaged churches and buildings with Marriott going, 'Fucking hell, we missed that one. Oh shit, we should have flattened that one...' The taxi driver chucked us out. Marriott was always doing daft stuff like that. On another occasion he decided to introduce us as Nazi war criminals... from the word go he'd always been bonkers in our company and over time he began to show that side of himself more openly. We'd be giving a press conference, or on TV, and for no reason whatsoever he'd suddenly start blowing raspberries or pulling daft faces. He loved attention.

*A new Small Faces hit – to mime to on TV or attempt to play live – arrived in May 1966. 'Hey Girl' was the first band single that bore the songwriting credit Marriott/Lane, a partnership that echoed, on paper at least, the ones of Lennon/McCartney and Jagger/Richards.*

**Keith Altham:** Steve was the boiler room of the Small Faces. He did all the hard work and although the idea of the Marriott/Lane partnership was a clever one it was never anywhere near 50/50. It was Steve who supplied the backbone to all the hits. When he took new songs into the studio the rest of the band would chip in with ideas – even Mac and Kenney – but Steve always had the last word. Even Ronnie's ideas would have to be bloody good for Steve to accept them.

**Kath Marriott:** I said to him, 'Why is it both your names, Steve?' He said, 'Without Ronnie's help keeping me awake and being there I wouldn't do half of it. He keeps me going.'

*'Hey Girl' was also, for the first time, a Small Faces track where the production was credited to Don Arden.*

**David Arden:** In his mind Dad was always a producer, he was an artist himself and he loved it when his artists did great. For him that was like he was doing great and he wanted to be a part of it... he saw himself as like a film producer... he put everybody together.

*The single peaked at UK No 10.*

**Steve Marriott:** It was a turning point. Don allowed us to continue writing our own material and we knew we could deliver. Both me and Ron knew as soon as we heard 'Sha-La-La-La-Lee' that it was a hit and in those days hit singles mattered, so 'Hey Girl' was an extension of that.

It was very single-minded. We weren't worried about albums. In those days albums were done in three days.

*The band's debut album,* Small Faces, *was also released in May 1966. It peaked at UK No 3. Marriott had co-written (with various band members, including Winston) six of the twelve songs. The album was put together from several sessions, many featuring Jimmy Winston, and production was credited to Kenny Lynch, Ian Samwell and Don Arden. The album included 'Sha-La-La-La-Lee' and two other Kenny Lynch-penned songs − 'You'd Better Believe it', co-written with Jerry Ragovoy, and 'Sorry She's Mine'. The latter song was also used as Jimmy Winston's debut solo single, released by Decca in June 1966.*

**Kenny Lynch:** I helped the Faces a lot in the studio. I was very tight with them until they said, 'You write the songs, we work them out with you, we want half the songwriting [publishing] dough.' I shook their hand, said, 'I write the songs, I don't get money for producing, so fuck you.'

*The promotional treadmill started up again apace. Marriott was now a pin-up.*

**Keith Altham:** Steve was a natural clothes horse, unusual for a guy of his height. In 1966 Steve was really up for the male modelling lark. It paid a good fee and got your face on the front cover. There would be a really cool pic of Steve and down the page it would say things like, 'Shoes from Ravel, £19', 'Trousers from Lord John', and so on. Although it was good fun the problem was it didn't help Steve's desire later on to be taken seriously.

*Arden worked the pop angle hard: went for stunts such as having the band posing with baby alligators on leads, had them mobbed while miming outside Lord John's on Carnaby Street, took them to get their own specially designed suits with Dougie Millings, The Beatles' tailor, who had designed famous collarless suits for the mop tops, and planted stories about the band scoring film roles alongside Brigitte Bardot and Jayne Mansfield. He began to insist the band get more prominent slots on TV programmes such as* Thank Your Lucky Stars *and* Top Of The Pops, *refusing to let them appear if they had to open proceedings. The band were regularly photographed and interviewed at their Pimlico address and the house became a honeypot for teen girl fans and was even burgled (with records and clothes stolen).*

**Val Weedon:** Don encouraged it all... all part of the hype... the girls were constantly knocking on the door [at the Pimlico house] and shouting through the letterbox. I think one fan sent Steve a puppy... and the band adopted it.

**Steve Marriott:** Sometimes it's annoying but you get used to it. It's worse during the holidays. One girl just stood out there all day crying! Nobody had done anything to her. I suppose it was her way of saying she likes us.

**Kenney Jones:** We regularly discovered extremely personal messages scrawled in lipstick on our cars and front door.

*The heavy workload, demands and realities of teen pop fame, internal conflict over the band's musical direction, plus prodigious drug intake and now heavy boozing, began to have an impact, particularly on the slight and unstable Marriott. His pal Gregory Phillips was a good source of strong grass and had introduced the highly potent, and potentially dangerous, central nervous system stimulant methedrine (methamphetamine) to the party. It came in the form of liquid in a glass ampoule.*

**Ian McLagan:** One Friday we started off with an appearance on *RSG!* at ATV studios in Wembley, drove to the Princess club in Birmingham, played there, drove across town to the Domino Club, played there too, then drove on to a hotel in Manchester, where we did a double the next night.

**Steve Marriott:** Doing TV can be a real drag. Glamour in TV? It doesn't exist. You get in about 11 a.m. and then wait around for your call – maybe for hours. Then you rehearse it for about an hour, over and over again, the actual broadcast is over before you know it. We were playing Leeds one night and we had to record a Simon Dee backing track in London. We flew down to London, recorded the track and were then driven back to Glasgow for the night's performance. When you're travelling around all the time you just lose all resistance, and you just crack up. You don't have time to sleep, except in the car, and that's hard enough. It can get on top of you.

*It is impossible to say what triggered Marriott's spectacular collapse while performing on RSG! – exhaustion, anxiety, drugs, alcohol, or a combination thereof.*

**Vicki Wickham:** He passed out in the studio. We were all concerned, thought he had flu or something, and it was only then did someone say, 'Oh, you know he's taken too much...' whatever it was.

*Several lives dates had to be cancelled.*

**Denis Thompson:** The next morning he called me asked me to come over to his house and we sat around... he was overworked, strung out, not in good shape. We decided to take a walk into Manor Park... people were stopping to get his autograph and stuff. I was asking, 'Don't you have a car now?' He said, 'No, I can't afford anything like that.' I said, 'What do you mean?' He said, 'Only get £20 a week.' That was stupid. I was making much more than that [playing with Tony Jackson & The Vibrations].

**Kenney Jones:** We were playing every night of the week – doing things like double gigs – so we complained and he [Arden] gave us £60 a week.

*The average weekly UK wage in the UK in 1966 was £15 a week.*

**Steve Marriott:** I kept asking for time off but I never got it. When my weight dropped to ninety-four pounds [under seven stone] I realised that I was quite possibly in the process of killing myself.

**Tony Calder:** I don't think Steve ever got to grips with the fact that he was famous. When people come out and they want to touch you and get a piece of you and you're 19, it's not like acting in the theatre or being in a TV studio. It's real life, it's your life and if you don't like it you've got big problems.

**Bill Marriott:** Steve hated the big star thing. He would walk around the corner to avoid the crowds. He wanted to mix with ordinary kids. It was difficult when he went back to the East End and met his little mates that he knew before he was a star. They treated him like a god and he said, 'I don't want that, they're my friends and I don't want to be a big star.' I liked him for that. He was never toffee-nosed or big-headed.

**Kath Marriott:** His mates did treat him differently. They were very shy and didn't know what to say. He used to say, 'I wish they would just be normal.' I said, 'They can't,' and he shouted back, 'But I'm the same.'

**Steve Marriott:** [Fame] alters your whole way of life and looking at things. The worst part is when you start believing the glowing reports about yourself in the papers. I went through a stage like that when 'Sha-La-La-La-Lee' was high in the charts. I soon got over it, but I feel ashamed to think that I ever thought I was someone special.

*There was one further pressure on the 19-year-old Marriott when a 15-year-old fan, Sally Foulger, informed him she was pregnant with his child, and in June 1966 she gave birth to his daughter.*

**Val Weedon:** Pauline [Corcoran] told me he came to her and cried on her shoulder, really sobbed... scared, didn't know what to do. Then he went and spoke to Don, and Don said, 'Don't worry, I'll sort it,' and Pauline thought Don was maybe going to sort an abortion but the next thing Steve came in the office with cigars celebrating that he'd got this daughter... slap on the back and all that, he was obviously chuffed.

**Kenney Jones:** It was all kept fairly quiet. It was like a flash in the pan – happened so quick and then forgotten about. Ronnie got accused of the same thing but it wasn't his child... lots of girls were doing it, saying [to pop stars] you're the father. It was a thing that happened at the time.

**Sally Foulger [RIP]:** At first everything was fabulous but it didn't stay like that. The trouble was that as Steve became more popular he gradually became more sensitive. I couldn't understand why his personality and temperament had changed so drastically. I just couldn't see how one day he could be so nice and the next day so horrible.

**Lesley Ashcroft [Daughter]:** Sally filed a paternity suit, naming Steve as my father; however, after lots of publicity, she decided to drop it and have me adopted. So at 15 months old I went to a National Children's Home in Surrey and was luckily adopted at about 18 months old. When I found my mother again at age 18, she told me who my father was. Sally was just 16 when she had me and I consider myself very lucky not to have been one of the many flushed into the sewage system after a hot bath and a bottle of gin! Steve apparently knew about me and once rang Sally to get her to bring me round so he could see me. However, it was about 1 a.m., so Sally decided to stay at home. He certainly wasn't ready to get tied to a bird with a kid! I remember looking through her [my mother's] photo album [when I found her again] and seeing photos of her with The Who and the Stones. I think she was a bit of a groupie. She certainly had some stories.

**Val Weedon:** The rumour was the mother was not of a good nature, she was a bit of a drug addict and so that's why Lesley was put up for adoption... and Steve took a step back and didn't really have anything to do with it... he switched off from it.

*In June 1966, Marriott was also offered his first opportunity to escape the teenybop lifestyle. Jimmy Page had left Immediate Records, where he was employed as a staff producer, and wanted Marriott to front a supergroup he was putting together with Jeff Beck of The Yardbirds and John Entwistle and Keith Moon of The Who. It would be a chance to return to his pure, R&B roots.*

**Jimmy Page:** It was going to be Led Zeppelin, yeah. Not Led Zeppelin as a name; the name came afterwards. Moony wanted to get out of The Who and so did John Entwistle... when it came down to getting hold of a singer, it was either going to be Steve Winwood or Steve Marriott. Finally it came down to Marriott. He was contacted; Keith [Moon] approached Steve. That filtered back to Don Arden and the reply came back: 'How would you like to have a group with no fingers, boys?' Or words to that effect. So the idea was dropped because of Marriott's commitment to the Small Faces. [Page instead joined The Yardbirds on bass before switching to lead guitar.]

**Steve Marriott:** Page wanted to form a group and asked me to come with them. I was very tempted but I said, 'Nah, that's bullshit.'

*Marriott's mood seemed to darken. In July, at the National Jazz & Blues Festival at Royal Windsor Racecourse, with 30,000 in attendance, he flew into a rage and stormed off stage when hooligans pelted the band with cans as they trotted out their pop hits. The glad-handing and fake bonhomie that made pop go round nauseated him, as did the respect for smarmy BBC producers, TV directors and DJs. He caused trouble for Arden when he accosted the producer of* Top Of The Pops.

**Steve Marriott:** I thought he [Johnny Stewart] was leaving the show and this other guy was taking over. Anyway, we had done our bit and this producer comes into the bar and he was doing this thing of, 'That was wonderful, lads – it was a gas, it was wild.' He was really full of shit. I knew he did it with everyone whether he liked you or not. So I turned around and said, 'You're a cunt, a real two-faced cunt.' And he wasn't leaving the show at all.

**Val Weedon:** Steve was impulsive and he couldn't sit still, he was hyperactive... a bit scatty, moved from one thing to the other... a bit erratic. He didn't seem to be the sort of person who'd plan things, just moved through naturally. There was no pretence. He wanted to grow as an artist, do more. He was the one who would come up the office much more than the others... often have meetings with Don. I got the impression he was this gentle soul but he was passionate about what he was doing, he really felt those songs. He had this foolish side as well, but Don loved Steve. Don does have that bad image amongst Small Faces fans and people slag him off but he put a lot of effort in as well...

**David Arden:** The Old Man knew if you were a great artist you were potty as well, a nutter, and he'd take it off you, like with Gene Vincent. If he thought you were ordinary you couldn't get away with it. Steve and I became good buddies and he gave me my first joint. We were in IBC doing [a version of Del Shannon's] 'Runaway' [as the group began cutting tracks for second album, scheduled for November 1966 release] that the Old Man was singing on, and a few other tracks, and I was doing handclaps. Steve had just left Pimlico and got his own place, this brilliant apartment in Knightsbridge, a mews. He invited me back to his apartment and gave me a joint to smoke. I was out of me tree, three in the morning the Old Man's banging on the door looking for me… furious.

*On top of the methamphetamine, weed and brandy, LSD now became part of the band's daily diet. The drug had been introduced to them by Beatles manager Brian Epstein at a party at their Pimlico house. A drop of liquid LSD was placed on a slice of orange and ingested. Marriott's initial reaction to the drug was not positive.*

**Ian McLagan:** Ronnie and I had the best time but Steve was having a bad reaction and went to bed not knowing what was going on. He'd arranged to catch an early train to Manchester the next morning to spend a few days with his new girlfriend at her parents' place. He was not what I'd call a particularly balanced person and he was rarely relaxed, and in the same way acid can lead you to the heights of illuminations and wonder it can also take you down to the depths of your darkest fears… he returned the next day after arguing with her parents and dumping her. He'd only wanted to get laid, not married.

*Sue Oliver was an important girl in Marriott's life, not least because she inspired him to write one of his greatest songs 'All Or Nothing', clearly about wanting sex with her ("If I could have the other half of you"). She was from the northern industrial town of Oldham, on the outskirts of Manchester. They had met at a Small Faces show in the city in late 1965. She was working the cloakroom and had ambitions to become a model. They had been dating for eight months and enjoyed horse riding together. Via Oliver's father, Marriott had bought a horse, which he called Petite Visage (French for 'Small Face'). Marriott must have asked Oliver to marry him because they had become engaged. 'Lovely girl, but the mother was there all the time,' said Kath Marriott.*

**Steve Marriott:** 'All Or Nothing' was obscene... I mean, I own up to that one. That was a groove. It even got me going.

*Released in August 1966, as the band's fifth single, 'All Or Nothing' became the Small Faces' first UK No 1. Again, the record was produced by Don Arden and credited to the songwriting partnership of Marriott/Lane. Marriott explained how the band had recorded the song.*

**Steve Marriott:** We were in the studio doing two songs, one of them mine, one of them Plonk's [Lane's]. Don didn't like the sound of either of them and we hadn't got anything else. We could see he was fed up. So Plonk said, 'Play him that tune you were working out.' So I just played him an idea I had. The organ hadn't played it, the drum hadn't played it, the bass hadn't played it but I'd thought about it, so I let him hear it. He liked it so we rewrote it on the spot. Don gave us two bits of paper and we wrote the lyrics in half an hour. It was all at an LP session and the song wasn't even on the agenda. We can't have a go at Don because he turned out to be right. The record has been accepted far more than others... [it's] the first proper thing we've done, instead of all that Mickey Mouse stuff like 'Sha-La-La-La-Lee' and 'Hey Girl'...

**Chris Welch:** I first met Steve when 'All Or Nothing' was a huge hit [to write a September 1966 *Melody Maker* front-cover story on the band]. They were the dominant pop band everyone was talking about. I interviewed him at Lime Grove BBC TV studios, *Top Of The Pops*, backstage in the dressing room and he was really hyperactive. There was a young girl pop magazine reporter, and she had a tape recorder and she said, 'Introduce yourself, say where you come from and what you play,' and all the band screamed, 'Get 'em off!', and then they took the mickey mercilessly. I thought, God, I hope my interview isn't as bad as hers, and luckily they were a bit more sensible. Steve could be quite sensible. The others were playing around, clowning around. Steve sat and started to tell me about what he wanted to do – they were working on [future single] 'My Mind's Eye' and he started talking about production and songwriting, how they wanted to use different instruments... he took singing and songwriting, and his influences, very seriously despite the fact the Small Faces were regarded by a lot of people as a kind of teenybop band.

*'All Or Nothing', despite the sexual yearning of the lyrics and harder soul/R&B sound, did nothing to shake the band's image. In the UK the screaming girls were out in force at the endless one-nighters and package tour dates. Galaxy continued to cash in. The band's engagements included an agricultural show in the Somerset town of Shepton Mallet and a residency at Blackpool Pier. In Glasgow the band was mobbed, hair pulled out in chunks, clothes ripped off and Lane was knocked unconscious. At a personal appearance at a charity football match in Bradford, Yorkshire, the band's car was swarmed, girls' bodies crushed against the car windows, in tears, screaming. Many more got on the roof and it started to cave in.*

*While the band promoted 'All Or Nothing' in Europe, as it charted in Germany, the Netherlands and Sweden, Arden eyed America. He hoped the band might catch the tail end of the 'British Invasion' a phenomenon led by The Beatles and capitalised on by the Stones, Dave Clark Five, Herman's Hermits, The Kinks and The Animals. He struck an American deal with RCA, on behalf of the band, to release 'All Or Nothing' in the States. A series of promotional dates and guest performances in America were lined up. Arden was too late however – the band had turned against him and the cultural tide was shifting, with American sunshine rock bands such as The Lovin' Spoonful, The Association, The Rascals (whose American No 1 hit 'Good Lovin'' was added to the Small Faces' live show) and The Byrds beginning to influence the British bands. The Byrds had namechecked the Small Faces in 'Eight Miles High', their 1966 drug-inflected hit.*

*At this stage in his career, steering a rock band to world success was also beyond Arden, his limitations being keenly felt by Marriott and the band, who were beginning to rebel against his paternal treatment of them and question his financial handling of their accounts. All plans for American promotion were cancelled.*

**Ian McLagan:** We assumed the real money we were making on top of our weekly cash-in-hand was being looked after for us. We were young and inexperienced in business but we weren't stupid and we were beginning to see the kind of people we were dealing with... Don, Ron King and beady-eyed cold fish Patrick Meehan. Steve was the realist of the bunch. He always picked up more shirts than anyone else when we raided Carnaby Street, as if he was collecting his money in advance, in the form of clothes. Don had encouraged us all to call him Uncle Don. This allowed him to treat us like children.

**Kenney Jones:** [Originally] Don said, 'Okay, I'll give you £20 a week and you can have a percentage of the records plus a shopping account in every clothes shop in Carnaby Street.' Unbeknown to us, everything – travel, accommodation, promotion, clothes – was charged against record sales. We expected the people looking after us to look after our money like they said they would… and they didn't. Our main weakness was we trusted people. Don was lucky… when I went back to the East End and told my dad I thought the band was being screwed, I went to the loo and right behind comes one of my cousins, Billy Boy. He stood next to me and said, 'Your dad says you think your manager's screwing you.' I said, 'Don't worry about it.' He said, 'I'll go kill him, I'll knock the fuck out of him, I'll sort it out.' I didn't want anyone fighting my battles for me and I didn't want to be associated with the kind of hoods they were [Billy Boy worked for the Krays and other firms].

**David Arden:** Remember the Old Man would have been on a maximum 8 per cent from Decca [record royalties paid to Arden's Contemporary for licensing them the Small Faces hits], so he would pay the band [their 1.5 per cent] from that. It doesn't amount to much: and people forget the Small Faces' first album, the only album they did for Dad, only sold 30,000 units. People say it's terrible they were on £50 a week but they were only earning £200, £250, £300 top a night… they were living in Pimlico, all their parents are on £50 a week… there's all the clothes.

*It was estimated the band had, in 1966, spent £12,000 on clothes [over £200,000 in today's money].*

**Don Arden:** One of the Small Faces gimmicks was to throw their clothes out to the crowd at gigs. I said fine but I was never thrilled about that. We couldn't have gone on forever throwing suit jackets out. Yeah, the kids were killing each other to get a jacket, it's great, marvellous, but I was thinking money. My first idea was to maybe get handkerchiefs made so we could throw them out to the girls. Why I hesitated was it might have appeared to be a bit effeminate. The band all knew that I was studying what to throw out and I was on the verge of doing a deal with the six boys on Carnaby Street. We were going to get a percentage of their sales. Then I got the call to say the band was leaving me. I spoke to the boys on Carnaby Street and said 'Fellas, I'm out.'

*The news of the band's unhappiness with Arden spread quickly. Robert Stigwood, manager of the Bee Gees and the world's first so-called supergroup, heavy rock outfit Cream, was keen to sign the band, the first to try and bravely go up against the feared Arden. Stigwood had a surreptitious, late night meeting with the band at their house in Pimlico.*

**Ron King:** Don worked hard to get the Small Faces to the top of the charts but in no time they started to think that Don was ripping them off. The group decided to approach Robert Stigwood. Don heard about this 'betrayal' and phoned me. 'Stigwood's trying to poach the Small Faces and other bands,' he hollered at me and then added, 'there's also talk of him trying to nab Amen Corner [the band King managed]'. He was smart and knew this reference to the Amen Corner would fire me up. I immediately contacted one of my bouncers, Mad Tom, to organise a visit to Stigwood. A few days later Don, Mad Tom and I rocked up [to] Stigwood's office and barged straight in. Stigwood was sitting behind his desk looking stunned by this sudden intrusion. I told Mad Tom to stand by the door to make sure we wouldn't be interrupted by anyone, including Stigwood's secretary. As soon as we walked in Don started bellowing at him in his usual style, 'You fucking bastard, you're trying to poach my bands – throw him out of the fucking window, Ron.' Stigwood started pleading, 'I didn't, I didn't,' while I grabbed him from behind his desk, pinning him against the window frame. With one hand I opened the window and moved Stigwood over to it. Now, here's where the story changes from what's been written and recorded. The story goes that Don dangled Stigwood out of the window when in fact Don went nowhere near him at any stage. The reality was that I had Stigwood up against the open window with his upper body only slightly outside but at no time was he ever 'dangled' out of the window or in danger of being thrown out or dropped.

**Don Arden:** The Small Faces told me about Stigwood. I laughed because Stevie was saying, 'I think he's after my fucking arse' [Stigwood was gay]. Marriott loved me and whenever he saw me he used to run and land on my back and we used to fuck around in the street for half an hour... it was an entirely different world with him than with the rest of them. Ronnie loathed and detested me. I often used to think, are these snotty noses Jew haters? I wondered if they were brought up to do that. With Stigwood it was all choreographed. I walked into Stigwood's private office unannounced and I said, 'You must never ever do this again and if you do this is what's going to happen.' We had arranged, at this point, that I pick him up and take him to the balcony of his office. I said, 'You see that pavement down there...' and then what happened was the guys, behind my back, had arranged a joke on me. Their joke when I said, 'Next time, if there's a next time, you're going over,' they rushed forward and said, 'Fuck next time, we're going to sling him now.' So they took him out of my hands, picked him up and made out they were going to throw him over. He actually shit himself. He used to wear these big cowboy boots and it was squelching in his boots. The stink was terrifying. We left him there.

*Mad Tom, the enforcer, was also alleged to have grabbed McLagan by the throat when his protests against Arden grew too sharp. The band members' parents now stepped in.*

**David Arden:** Stevie Marriott's mum was winding everybody up, all the parents, and they wanted to know what was happening to the money, why they weren't getting more than £50. She was a bit of a hag and the Old Man did not like her at all. She was always on about, 'Why are our boys only on £50 a week?'

**Don Arden:** Marriott's mother kept calling and coming up. I had a summerhouse down Margate and she knew I had that place, I'd had it for seven fucking years, she used to come in and ask, 'When am I going to get my summerhouse?' It's amazing really how there wasn't a fucking murder there. To think that instead of looking up and saying, 'Thank god for this Jew bastard' – but there was nothing like that... I took those two guys from the gutter...

**Kenney Jones:** Steve's mum pushed him to be a child actor and wasn't that keen on him being in a band. She would always want him to be an actor and give up on this being a singer... when we had a hit record and started to be successful she changed her tune. She did get stuck in up the office; she was a very pushy lady like that. She was not exactly the leader of the parents, she probably went up the office a little more than my mum and dad would. She was checking on Steve basically. Steve's father was very quiet. His mum would be the mouthpiece.

**Kath Marriott:** I didn't like Don Arden. He showed my husband and the other fathers different papers with sums of money and it was ludicrous: £2 or £3 here, £50 there. And they were earning hundreds then. They had been going for a good year. And every two or three months they had a hit. And everywhere they went they were successful. And they were doing television shows. They were going to Germany one minute, back in England, back up north, all in one day! His father always warned him to watch what's going on and to stop signing things. Study it first. And Steve would always say the same thing, 'I pay people to look after things for me. Other than that, I don't understand a thing about it. I just hope that the people I'm paying can and do.' How can you argue with that?

**David Arden:** Anyway, the Old Man lost his cool and he shouldn't have said it... he's gone, 'Don't you think rather than worrying about how much money you're getting you should start acting like parents? You know what your boys are on, they're smoking dope,' and that was it...

**Don Arden:** I held a meeting with the parents. I requested it. The reason for the meeting was they'd been interviewed and they said, 'Oh, we're very worried, they're very tired, this fella Arden gives them too much work.' When they walked in I said let it be clearly understood the reason your sons are tired isn't because they are doing too many gigs, it is because at night they hold their own parties and they enjoy that [mimes sniffing up his nose] and they looked at each other and they didn't know what that was, no idea. I said there's all this and the young ladies who can't really make it home, and they make sure your sons don't sleep until seven in the morning. I wanted to tell them what the facts were but when they left they still didn't know what [again, mimes sniffing up his nose] was. And in those days it was heavy money [for drugs]. If they were being screwed, where did they get all that money for drugs? The Scottish boy who's been doing all the moaning [McLagan], he's told everybody that he took all this stuff. The parents left my office still saying that I was the most evil man in the world.

**Ian McLagan:** He fobbed them off... he said, 'Well, people in showbiz spend their money and they've spent theirs,' and they said, 'Well, that's not a good enough explanation.' Then he said, 'They're all on heroin,' and that shut them up. When they were all done crying, they left.

**Bill Marriott:** Steve had already come clean with us some time before and said he was smoking joints. We didn't like it but he said it was a social thing. He doesn't smoke them all the time but he goes to a party and they pass it round. The other parents didn't know and they were really shocked. The way Arden put it they were on drugs. Not that they are smoking a joint, which is very different. I said to Arden, 'That's all right, we know.' And that shocked him then.

**Kath Marriott:** When Steve first spoke about it, I was absolutely horrified and terribly upset. He said to me, 'Don't be frightened, there are books and things. Read about it and you'll realise smoking cigarettes and things like that are far more addictive.' At the time it was frightening. We had never dealt with it or heard about it. So that was worrying.

**Don Arden:** I hate to criticise someone else's parents but there was never any sincerity about any of them. The parents even denied I gave them money and you know why? It was because they didn't pay income tax. Do you know how ignorant they were? They knew nothing other than 'Where is the money? Where's the money?' Ronnie had his brother [Stan Lane] come round to see me, he was a lorry driver and I think he thought because he was a lorry driver that I was going to be frightened by him. He said, 'I've come here to talk to you about royalties.' I said, 'Get out, fuck off, get out.' He said, 'What if I don't want to go?' I said, 'I'll tell you, all the people who don't want to go get killed at this place.' I'd spoke to Ronnie while I had his brother waiting to see me and he said, 'Oh, I don't know anything about it, tell him to piss off.' So I did what he told me but I told him in my particular fashion... the boys knew how I spoke at that point. I said to Ronnie, 'Should I kill him?'

I'll never forget the receptionist's face when she told me this prick was here to see me and I asked what's he like. He's got a pair of filthy stinking trousers and a shirt that's never been cleaned and his hands – that's something I always look at – he had the hands of a dog. He was a dog.

**Andrew Loog Oldham:** By now it should be obvious that everyone in Don's universe had either been invited in and knew the rules of the house or else had invited themselves in and found themselves rather brutally unwanted and unneeded. The working-class suss and longing for financial security Don shared with the Small Faces led to their parents trying to kid a kidder. It was as if most of the boys' relatives had a bad case of Brian Jones disease – the compulsion to take with both hands what one should be grateful to accept with one. Double-dipping between band and their near and dear was frustratingly common, as each would claim not to know that the other had received funds that now must be given again to the petitioner at hand. While Don might have grudgingly admired their front, he resented what he sensed was an unjustifiable arrogance in their demands.

**Steve Marriott:** Our relationship was bad and it never really recovered after he was talking with our parents. But without Don Arden there would not have been a Small Faces. I think he managed us very well, money regardless. He put us over very well and opened a lot of doors. It's all very well to scream 'rip-off' and be bitter and belligerent; ain't no good to you. Without those people you'd never get anywhere.

# CHAPTER 5

# Itchycoo Park

**Don Arden:** Initially Brian Epstein was interested in the group. David Jacobs was my lawyer and he also represented Epstein. He was negotiating with me to take over the Small Faces. Over dinner Epstein asked if I'd be willing to help with Allen Klein. What he was saying was he wanted me to get rid of Klein because Klein was trying to steal The Beatles away [American music heavyweight Klein had already struck deals with Andrew Loog Oldham to become his business manager and secure shares in The Rolling Stones and Marianne Faithfull and with Mickie Most for The Animals and Herman's Hermits]. Epstein's contract was due to end with The Beatles [and it was well-known Klein wanted them]. The day that Epstein was supposed to come back to me to tell me how much he was going to pay for the Small Faces, David Jacobs told me he'd committed suicide. He said you won't see that in the paper but he decided he didn't want to live without The Beatles. It's very sad that you give up your life for a poxy group.

**Steve Marriott:** Me and Ronnie did a bit of teamwork on shopping for a new manager and agent. We flitted around a few different things. First we went to Chris Blackwell of Island, he said he'd love to but couldn't. He said, 'I can't run this company and keep Steve Winwood happy with his new band Traffic; I wouldn't be able to give you the time.'

*The band also approached Robert Wace, manager of The Kinks. In the meantime, Arden ploughed on with making sure they remained a viable commodity. He talked up a two-week Christmas run of shows at the*

*Hammersmith Odeon to coincide with the release of the band's second album. A sixth single, the LSD-tinged 'My Mind's Eye', was released in November 1966. It reached UK No 4.*

**Steve Marriott:** We'd presented a bunch of demos, left them in Arden's office and then we went out on the road and the next thing we knew it was out as a single. We hadn't really been asked about it. I think he took it straight from the tape of the demo. We hadn't finished with it and even if we had we wouldn't have wanted it as a single. Our reaction to him when that happened begins with a C and ends with a T.

**Don Arden:** Oh bollocks. So what?! So what?! It was as much my record as it was theirs. It belonged to me. I was paying 'em fucking royalties. I don't know what their thinking is. It's so difficult when you've got four guys rattling away all the time like old women, they were like four whores... 'and she said... and she said...'

*Despite issuing legal proceedings against Arden, seeking to free themselves from his control, the band promoted the single on TOTP and RSG! and continued to gig for Galaxy/Arden, including on a co-headlining English tour with The Hollies, where a stand-off over top billing grabbed a few headlines. 'We are better than the Small Faces,' said Hollies singer Graham Nash. 'What should you burn on Bonfire Night? Graham Nash,' replied Marriott. 'Don Arden even tried to make his point by using physical force,' said Hollies drummer Bobby Elliott.*

**Don Arden:** They sent me a letter written by their solicitor saying they had to leave me because they couldn't stand by and watch promoters getting beaten up. What could you say about that?! That was one of the excuses they used in the suit against me. Do you think you could get any lower than that? I'll tell you what happened: it was about six months before they decided to look for new management and Steve called me at one o'clock in the morning, said the promoters won't pay and they won't give us back our equipment that was brand new, cost almost £20,000, a small fortune. They'd been performing and this heavy had told them to fuck off. It happened all the time and most managers would never ever get the boys their money back if they were knocked. Maybe they'd sue them but nothing would come of it because they'd just go bankrupt the next week. Well, in those days I moved fast. We walked into this place at 2 a.m. and we were twelve-handed. There was about four or five of them and I saw this heavy with the bag of money. I walked up to him and asked, 'How did you do tonight?' He said, 'Oh, we stormed them.' I said, 'Listen, my boys were booked to get £1,000.' He said, 'Oh, I didn't know,' and I knew he didn't. This guy was just one of the heavies that worked there for the boss on a Saturday night. I said, 'Well, fucking hard lines because we not only want our money, we want what's in that bag, over and above, we're taking it all.' He said, 'What do you mean?' I said, 'I mean, you're dead. Do you want to leave a note? Have you got a son? Have you got a wife?' There was about £2,500 in the bag. The guy had no chance. I called Stevie over and said this is your figure tonight and I counted it out and we gave him the two and half, and one of their men made a go of it, brave guy – he attacked us and when we finished with him he was unrecognisable. I do think that was one of my mistakes because he was battered to near the end of the road. We left him on the floor... and, of course, we took all our equipment and put it in the van and the Small Faces put their arms around me and they kissed me and we all drove away laughing. I could have gone down for GBH. So when I got this letter from their solicitor... what did they think I was going to do at two in the morning? They knew I was coming in with heavies but they said I was helping destroy their career by beating up promoters. When I saw that statement, it took me weeks to get over it. I couldn't ever. In that situation, I don't care what anybody says, you're risking your life... at two in the morning, going up against thugs that don't give a shit. I think I was stupid but I did it. I did it because I loved it, I'll be honest with you, but nevertheless I didn't do it so these people I'm trying to help can use it as an excuse to fuck me over.

*The band's solicitor was Victor Gersten. Their accountant, Don Bettis, who had begun to act for the band after striking up a relationship with Marriott's parents, recommended him to them. Bettis ran a youth club in the East End that was partly financed by the Krays.*

**Victor Gersten [1931–2019]:** I did two significant things: they had made an agreement with someone called Langwith [Jimmy Winston's brother Derek] that they would pay a proportion of their earnings forever for using him as a roadie and everyone thought they were earning huge amounts of money and so he sued them for his portion. I defended the action on the basis the contract had been made with people under 21 and I won that action and the agreement was declared to be void. I also wrote letters saying they didn't want Arden to be their manager anymore. The band felt they had been robbed but they had never had a decent set of accounts. I started an action for account... someone running a business can be made to produce accounts. I sued Arden, two of his companies, and quite early on in the proceedings we got an order for a small amount of money he agreed he owed. He was forced to pay that and then he put the two companies into liquidation... and so there was no point proceeding in the action for account.

*Arden argued he had insufficient funds to cover the £4,000 the court had ordered him to pay the band and proposed a monthly sum of £250. He paid two instalments and abruptly ceased payments.*

**David Arden:** There was about £2,800 due to them in royalties and the Old Man didn't have it at the time and he said he'd pay them off this much per whatever. Gersten wasn't having it. You can't threaten the Old Man because his reaction is, 'Fuck you.' He said, 'Right, you can't wait for the money, bollocks,' and he put the company into liquidation for £2,800. It was to the Old Man's own detriment, the biggest mistake of his life. The only person who really lost was the Old Man – he lost all rights to the material [the band had recorded for Contemporary] as it all went into the hands of the liquidator... the official receiver. The Old Man never got a penny more. Decca don't pay anyone but the official receiver. But in those days we didn't know how long these things would possibly go on earning. It was in the charts and gone, that was it.

**Don Arden:** It was the first black mark on my name. Gersten did everything in his power to destroy me by saying I was the most dangerous man in the world, I'm a thief, I'm a this, I'm a the other. Gersten should have been murdered. I had the Small Faces on one small company, Contemporary, there was nothing else in it. We only had one album, that's all we had. I was talking to them [about it] but we never made the second album. That's why the whole thing was ludicrous about me taking all the money because it was in the days of if you did 29,000 albums you were a big man. We did do some healthy figures for the singles but what do you think we collected for singles in those days? We didn't get rich. I think the first one, maybe we did half a million [sales], then there was a couple of them that did fifty, sixty thousand and then 'Sha-La-La-La-Lee' was bang on target... money-wise that one did it.

**Victor Gersten:** I was very angry about it; this ability to refuse to produce a set of accounts, have the business wound up. I don't know for sure what happened to the copyrights of the songs [the assets of the companies put into liquidation] but I felt Arden somehow managed to squirrel these things away to the States. I met [investigative journalist] Paul Foot at a party and told him this story and then *Private Eye* got to work on Arden [resulting in an infamous Paul Foot attack on Arden in a *Private Eye* article entitled 'The Jungle of Arden']. As I've got older, however, my opinion of Don has changed, softened slightly. When you had difficult kids like the Small Faces maybe you needed someone like Don to control them. But basically I found him displeasing. Free of Arden, they were then being chased by various people who wanted to manage them, particularly a very, very pushy American bunch who sent some young lawyer over to sign them up [Eric Kronfeld, who worked with Allen Klein]. They were so pushy... I just didn't like them. I asked around about managers and ultimately I introduced them to the Grade Organisation and Tito Burns. Arden thought I got money from the Grade Organisation. I didn't. They initially got on very well but quickly it became not a good gel. The people at the Grade Organisation were used to dealing with people like Dusty Springfield, not stroppy kids like the Small Faces.

**Val Weedon:** There was an atmosphere in the office. I was backward and forward delivering legal letters to some lawyer over near Bond Street. Patrick Meehan delighted in sending me. It was November 7, my birthday, I was 16, Kenney and Ronnie had come up to the office and were in conference with Don, and I was given this letter to deliver to Harold Davison's office in Lower Regent Street.

*There followed a sequence of events that remain slightly murky, said to include the exchange of huge sums of cash in brown paper bags. In December 1966 the press announced that Harold Davison (1922–2011), who was a key part of the respectable but staid showbiz establishment elite, the Grade Organisation, had paid Arden a fee of £12,000 to take over as the band's manager and agent. Under this arrangement Tito Burns (1921–2010), the deputy managing director of Harold Davison Ltd, was to act as the band's main agent/personal representative. Burns was an old-school, showbiz promoter/agent/manager. He had replaced Franklyn Boyd as manager of Cliff Richard and had handled tours by Bob Dylan, Dusty Springfield, The Searchers and the Stones before selling his agency to the Grade Organisation for £250,000.*

**Don Arden:** Harold and I knew each other since I was in my early 20s. Harold's claim to fame was he represented Frank Sinatra in the UK and Europe. He was an impresario, he wasn't just a promoter or an agent, he did everything. From Sinatra he went to Sammy Davis [also Count Basie and Duke Ellington]. In that kind of music he excelled to such an extent that nobody could really bother fighting him. He and I had done a lot of things together. I sold the Small Faces recording contract and the management contract to Harold. I was happy about the whole thing because I said if they want to go, let them go and in the meantime I'd come away with £50,000. Harold said, 'Well, here's your cheque, love,' gave me a kiss on one cheek and maybe at the end of the week we'd gone out to dinner and it was 'any time, any time'… meaning, any time you want a cheque call me. That was his attitude. But Harold couldn't stand the Small Faces, he used to phone me up every day; I had to tell Val to tell him I was out.

**Steve Marriott:** We didn't get out of the contract with Don. It was sold to Harold Davison. We were sold – that's what it felt like, pounds of flesh. Like a cattle market.

*Kenney Jones claimed the fee paid to Arden by Davison was actually £20,000 and that Arden also took an extra £5,000 earmarked for the band. Under the new arrangement the Small Faces, the press were informed, would continue to record for Contemporary – and to the public it was business as usual – the band appearing on the traditional end-of-year TOTP performing two tracks: 'All Or Nothing' and 'Sha-La-La-La-Lee'. The band, however, did not warm to Tito Burns. McLagan called him a creep. Marriott detested his music biz smarm and complained quickly about an early 1967, thirty-date tour Burns booked the band on, a joint-headline package with Roy Orbison. 'A right cock-up from the*

93

start, with the beehived barnet brigade down one side of the theatre and all these Mods on the other,' Marriott said.

Concurrent to the Arden/Davison sale, Marriott had begun working with Andrew Loog Oldham. 'I really dig Andrew Oldham,' Marriott told the press. 'He's too much. On a scene of his very own and it's great.' Oldham wanted to record Marriott/Lane songs with his Immediate Records acts and invited Marriott to Olympic Studios, located in Barnes, south-west London, where engineer Glyn Johns now virtually worked in-house. In late 1966, Chris Farlowe cut a version of the Marriott/Lane song 'My Way Of Giving' for a new single. Upon release (in January 1967), the single was credited as being produced by Mick Jagger (who, alongside Keith Richards, was a staff producer at Immediate) but Marriott and Ronnie Lane were both heavily involved in the recording – 'a crazy session', said Farlowe. Similar fun was had as Immediate pop duo Twice As Much cut a Marriott/Lane/O'Sullivan track, 'Green Circles', as a possible future single. Marriott took more control at Olympic, producing another Marriott/Lane song '(Tell Me) Have You Ever Seen Me' (its LSD-inspired lyrics mentioned hearing flowers breathing) with a young teen band he had decided to help out called The Little People. The track would become their debut Immediate single, albeit after Oldham renamed the group Apostolic Intervention. The band's 15-year-old drummer, Jerry Shirley, would join Marriott in Humble Pie in a few years.

**Jerry Shirley:** We just approached Steve on the street. He was dressed immaculately in a tailor-made Dougie Millings suit, double-breasted waistcoat, black silk mohair trousers and white trainers. Plus he smelled like a million bucks. Then we went back to his place in Knightsbridge and got really stoned. As The Little People we had opened up a couple of shows for the Small Faces. There were a bunch of sessions done at Olympic with Eddie Kramer or Glyn Johns as the engineer. I was playing on something that Steve was doing as part of this possible Andrew Loog Oldham Orchestra thing and I looked up and there was Jimi Hendrix. Steve was like showing me off, check this guy out. All Steve wanted to do back then was work, work, work. It was scary to be around him sometimes, he was that good. His singing, his keyboard playing, was amazing, his rhythm playing second to none. The man possessed limitless energy and when he added an abundant amount of liquid methedrine to that, there was no stopping him. To coax Glyn Johns to the session Steve would tell him it was for the Small Faces and then spike Glyn's tea with methedrine. So, even as Glyn was throwing his usual hissy fit about being conned into working with a bunch of unknown reprobates like us, he would inexplicably start to see the absolute sense in it! Ronnie was a bit distant. I think he had some resentment about us coming in and recording one of their songs. He left halfway through the session.

**Glyn Johns:** Steve was a bolshie little bugger. I never really liked him very much. I got on all right with him but he was cocky. He was obviously very insecure and he had a huge ego but he wouldn't have been the artist he was without it. Ronnie and Steve were very different characters. Marriott had more energy and was more determined to do what he wanted to do with his music. He was far more openly aggressive than Ronnie and that came out in his music and the way he played his guitar. Ronnie was much more of a romantic, a bit of a softie really... but he had an unpleasant side too.

**Ian McLagan:** After Steve died I spoke to Glyn Johns and he said, 'Yeah, he's a fucking cunt. I hated him.' That's a bit sharp. I didn't hate him. He was just too much.

**Kenney Jones:** He had ideas and he would piss Glyn off, everyone was tired, wanted to go home. Steve would want to stay because he had drugs to keep him awake. Glyn would say fuck it, stay with the tape op then.

**Victor Gersten:** They had got friendly with The Rolling Stones guy [Andrew Loog Oldham] at Immediate Records. I spent quite a lot of time in their New Oxford Street premises but I never met the druggie in charge, he rarely appeared. I had more to do with Tony Calder. They were very cheeky – they had renamed the whole building Immediate House and they always had a Rolls-Royce with darkened windows outside. Immediate had their own lawyers and I stopped acting for the Small Faces... but those lawyers made terrible contracts for them.

*The Small Faces escaped Harold Davison and signed to Andrew Loog Oldham as their manager. Davison and the Grade Organisation would stay as agents for the band, the unpopular Burns replaced by a younger man, Barry Dickens. There was also one other significant change. The band would no longer record for Decca/Contemporary and instead sign up to Immediate Records.*

**Don Arden:** Harold sold the recording contract and the management contract to Immediate. Tony Calder says, 'Oh, yes, we bought the record contract for £25,000 [over £425,000 in today's money] from Don, delivered it to him in a brown paper bag because he needed cash at the time.' Tony Calder is full of shit. First of all, if he ever bought anything, it was on behalf of Immediate; if he ever did anything it was on behalf of [Andrew Loog] Oldham really. He was a bullshitter, all the time. I never liked him and I never trusted him.

**Tony Calder:** I got a call one day from Don Arden. He said, 'Do you want to buy the Small Faces? I've got to sell the contract. I need the money; I need £30,000 in a brown paper bag by tomorrow lunchtime, here's the contracts, they'd love you to manage them.' I said, 'But they're cold, Don, they've gone off the boil – you fucked them up.' He said, 'Well, this new record's not very good [the follow-up single to 'My Mind's Eye', called 'I Can't Make It'].' I said, 'What do Decca think of it?' 'Oh, they'll put anything out.' I said, 'Give me the paperwork.' He said, 'I want thirty grand.' I said, 'I'm not paying thirty grand, twenty grand.' We settled on twenty-five. I said, 'I'll read the paperwork and if it's okay we'll do it tomorrow.' He said, 'It's got to be in a brown paper bag.' I think Andrew [Loog Oldham] was in sleep treatment, by then I couldn't give a fuck what he was doing, I wanted Steve Marriott so badly. Andrew didn't even know this was going on. I just knew Steve Marriott wasn't a problem. I read the paperwork, I read the Decca contract and I read Don's contract [with the band]. They were signed with Contemporary. There was no contract direct [for the band] with Decca. Don had a contract with Decca, there was no artists inducement letter. I said draw up the paperwork, transfer Don's contract, fuck the other one. I couldn't wait for the morning to come so I could get the £25,000 to Don. We signed the deal. I found Andrew and said I've signed the Small Faces, we paid £25,000. He said, 'Where did you get the money?' I said, 'I got it from EMI [the UK and European distributors of Immediate Records].' He said, 'What are we going to do about Decca?' I said, 'They're not signed. We're going to give this piece of shit ['I Can't Make It'] to Decca.' So wherever he was he turned up and listened to it and said, 'Yeah, I agree, get rid of it.' I think ['I Can't Make It'] had already been half delivered to Decca.

*Oldham's recollection is as follows: Allen Klein wired him the money for the Small Faces, he put £25,000 in a brown paper bag and gave it to Arden, who was then happy to induce a breach of contract with Decca, allowing the Small Faces to sign with Immediate.*

**Ken Mewis:** I was in my office [at Immediate – Mewis was head of promotions] at seven o'clock one night while Andrew and Tony were at the Dorchester with [Allen] Klein when a huge guy entered, sent by Don Arden to collect from Andrew and Tony. That they weren't there made no difference, he'd had his instructions, which were to wait with a Saturday night special dangerously close to my knees. He said he hoped my bosses would show because he quite liked me and didn't want to kneecap me. An hour or so of frantic phone calls and an agreement was apparently reached. Another Arden employee arrived to say everything was all right.

**Tony Calder:** I sent the contracts girl to the house in Pimlico to sign the contract and she came back and said, 'There's your piece of paper and never ask me to deal with that band again.' She said, 'I went to the house and there was marijuana smoke everywhere. I go to the upstairs bedroom, knock on the door and the first thing that Steve Marriott says to me is, "Do you fancy a shag?"'

*NME called the Immediate/Small Faces deal 'one of the most important label changes this year'. The £25,000 was a colossal amount to pay for a group, equalling the industry's largest ever advance, which EMI, the UK's most powerful major label, had recently put up to sign The Yardbirds in a hotly contested bidding war. In industry terms the deal firmly established Immediate Records as a significant force, when previously it could have been perceived as a hobby horse for the Stones' young millionaire manager, with its smorgasbord of hip and esoteric singles by acts such as Nico, John Mayall and Twice As Much and sprees of outlandish music press adverts and provocative statements.*

*Oldham and Calder created Immediate in response to the stultifying nature of the British record industry of the era. In aping American independent record labels, it directly challenged the business model and attitudes of the major labels such as Decca and EMI. Stealing the Small Faces away from Decca was perhaps Immediate's greatest achievement at the time – certainly in terms of long-term cultural impact, signalling a very real changing of the guard in the British music business. While the label had already scored a couple of UK No 1 singles – 'Hang On Sloopy' by The McCoys (1965) and Chris Farlowe's 'Out Of Time' (1966, a Jagger/Richards cover produced by Mick Jagger) – they had not yet established a major act.*

**Ian McLagan:** Steve knew Andrew and he knew the Stones… he took it to be a foregone conclusion that we'd sign with Immediate. His mind was made up as soon as Andrew agreed to meet us. To him anybody who smoked dope like he did had to be cool. Andrew was a raver all right, and had amazing style… a breath of fresh air. He encouraged us to get it together ourselves but was very involved, always interested in us and the songs. We couldn't believe it. You mean we get paid? We get to do what we want? We get treated nice? What's the catch?

**Steve Marriott:** I liked Andrew's flair… we all did. He had a lot of style.

*As well as signing to Immediate Records, the band signed a publishing contract with Immediate Music. Previously the band's self-penned songs had been placed in the hands of a variety of publishers, often with links to Arden, who, for instance, controlled the lucrative publishing on Marriott/Lane's biggest hit, 'All Or Nothing'.*

**Tony Calder:** We set up the Small Faces with their own publishing company called Avakak, a name Steve chose. They were getting 75 per cent of the gross [on their song publishing] and we were left with 25 per cent. We set Immediate Music companies up in most territories around the world; we used to handle it [abroad] for 5 per cent or 10 per cent, so 90 per cent came back to England and was then split 75/25. In terms of record royalties, the Small Faces were on 5 per cent [at Immediate], which was the highest royalty anybody was paid at that time on Immediate [Kenney Jones recalls the deal being 7 per cent for UK and 6 per cent for overseas, plus an increase in the band's weekly wage]. Anything that came in was charged to them. If they rang up and said,

'We want a block of hash that'll cost 300 quid,' you put it down for tip to driver; if an act rings up and says, 'I want a helicopter to the Isle of Wight Festival,' and it flies over the Isle of Wight Festival and he says it's muddy, I don't want to land, fly back again, you put it down as TV promo… £900.

**Paul Banes:** I keep seeing things about Immediate [Banes was general manager] short-changing the Small Faces. One of the fairest things we did for the band was something Andrew had already done with the Stones – he'd set up their own publishing companies so from day one they co-owned their own songs. In comparison, The Beatles, when they signed to [publisher] Dick James, didn't co-own Northern Songs. Avakak meant 'have a shit', very East End. In terms of record royalties, Immediate was only getting 12 per cent [from distributor EMI] so more than a third of what we were getting was going to the band. Bands at major labels were on 2 per cent, divided by however many were in the band… that's the real world. We looked after the artist at Immediate and the administration was always above board.

*In late February 1966, Marriott became national, rather than just music press, news, appearing on the front pages of both the* Daily Mirror *and* Daily Sketch *after being arrested on suspicion of drug possession. The police had stopped a cab he had been travelling in late at night. He was with his new girlfriend, Mick Jagger's former fiancée, Chrissie Shrimpton. Finding tablets and a hypodermic needle on Shrimpton, Marriott's flat in Kensington was searched – it was surprisingly drug-free. Shrimpton was considered the bigger news item. Her sister was the world-famous model Jean Shrimpton and the break-up of her long-term relationship with Jagger had been heavily publicised. Marianne Faithfull had become the famous new woman in Jagger's life, with Shrimpton said to have recently attempted suicide.*

**Gregory Phillips:** Chrissie was desperate and Camilla, Andrew's [Loog Oldham] secretary, persuaded me to bring her together with Steve. They got it on, but it turned out to be a disastrous relationship. Chrissie was off her head and still infatuated with Mick.

*Shrimpton nicknamed Marriott 'Peter', as in Peter Pan, because he was so small, while she made him call her 'Wendy'.*

**Steve Marriott:** I'd seen her a lot in the office at Immediate. I always thought she was beautiful. We all fancied her a bit. We did a gig that New Year's, maybe at the Albert Hall [1966, a charity event for the recent Aberfan disaster] and she was there but I didn't know it. I went back to my home and Greg Phillips brought her round and she flung herself at me. It was great! It was terrific. I don't know what she was on but go ahead! It was probably a rebound thing. I don't know... the papers went mad about it [the relationship], load of articles.

But I'd [actually] known Marianne Faithfull before Mick. I'd been the first one to leave Pimlico, got a little flat around the corner and one night they all rang me up and said, 'Marianne is here looking for you.' They had heard she had a fancy for me... so I went round and she had gone. She left a little note saying, 'Come to my house.' Acid had just come out and it was really strong, in brown lysergic bottles. So we all had a bit on a biscuit and went steaming over there. There were all these moody actors and actresses... she looked like the biggest ugliest tart I had ever seen in my life, the acid had hit... great big jam tart lips... The Miracles record 'Ooh Baby Baby' was on and she kept sliding over to me whispering the words into my ear. I was getting paranoid and was looking for a way out and she was getting the hump. It was a disaster... so I ran away from that and she got it on with Mick.

*Marriott's arrest was considered to be part of a coordinated crackdown by police on high-profile and flagrantly pro-drug pop stars. The stridently anti-establishment Stones were considered public enemy number one and Jagger and Richards had recently been busted in a police raid at Richards' home. Marriott told the press he had never taken drugs in his life and he was released without charge.*

**Steve Marriott:** They busted me just because I'm a name. As far as I'm concerned there should be a distinction between hash and pot and hard drugs. If you read any dictionary they are not even classified as drugs. Pills are a bad scene and so are hard drugs. The only thing against hash and pot is that people can say they are a stepping stone to hard drugs but that's only because the public are under the impression it's all the same thing. Why don't newspapers wake up and give people the facts?

*Decca Records released the Small Faces seventh single, 'I Can't Make It', in March 1967. It was written and produced by Marriott and Lane for Immediate Productions. The band promoted it with a live performance on the hugely popular* Morecambe & Wise *variety TV show.*

**Steve Marriott:** It was a bad time for us. I thought, oh great, it's going to be a hit ['I Can't Make It' entered the charts at No 26], but because Decca had all but dropped the option, the next week it had gone.

*In April, Immediate released The Apostolic Intervention single '(Tell Me) Have You Ever Seen Me'. Marriott appeared on stage with the band to help promote the record, guesting on a cover of his favourite slow blues song, 'Five Long Years' by Eddie Boyd, which Muddy Waters had made his own.*

**Steve Marriott:** I wanted to call The Apostolic Intervention The Nice... Andrew said, 'You're not calling them that, that's a stupid name.' And then he went and called P. P. Arnold's backing band The Nice...

**Ian McLagan:** When we were stoned we were 'nice' and Steve would sign autographs with a snigger, 'it's nice to be nice'. He loved to shout 'Nice!' at the top of his voice just to be able to say it out loud, 'I'm stoned out of my tiny mind, it's totally illegal and you can't do a fucking thing about it.'

**Steven Inglis:** At Immediate, come three o'clock in the afternoon, [Andrew Loog Oldham's] chauffeur Eddie would come and join me [Immediate head of graphic design] and mass-produce joints for Andrew. He would roll twenty or thirty joints and pack them up in cigarette packets and that's what Andrew would go out with for the evening. In those days they could send you to jail for fifteen years for marijuana.

*The band was now firmly ensconced in Olympic, mixing with myriad Immediate acts and associated songwriters and producers. These included Cat Stevens, who had penned 'The First Cut Is The Deepest' for P. P. Arnold (released as her debut solo single by Immediate in May 1967 with Kenney Jones playing on the session). Arnold had toured the UK as backing vocalist with Ike & Tina Turner in 1966 and stayed in London at the request of Mick Jagger, who had intended to record her for Immediate. Manfred Mann singer and songwriter Mike D'Abo wrote 'Handbags And Gladrags' for Chris Farlowe and 'Little Miss Understood' for new Immediate act Rod Stewart (his only Immediate single). Kenney Jones played on the session.*

**Kenney Jones:** Olympic became our home from home, we could come and go as we pleased, almost living there for up to a week at a time. We stopped playing as many gigs. There was no pressure, we had a lot more time to try things out. We also had the good fortune to work with Glyn Johns as an engineer and he progressed with sound, more tape machines... more toys... one of the greatest sounds I've heard is in the early Olympic Studios.

**Steve Marriott:** I would have a bed in there [Olympic] if I could. It was a good move [signing to Immediate]. It was such a big family thing, all helping out at each other's recording sessions. There were only about four or five acts on the label, admittedly all charting, but only a handful of people were responsible for it all, so everyone got to know each other very well. They wanted us involved with all their artists, wanted us to produce for artists, write for artists.

*Marriott now moved home to be closer to Olympic. The* Daily Sketch *reported he had been asked to leave his flat in Knightsbridge after complaints about late night noise. He had moved to a flat in Marylebone but also been asked to leave.*

**Steve Marriott:** Cilla Black lives underneath and you'd think she'd understand but she has been complaining most. I'm sorry I make so much noise but I'm really only having fun. The guy who owns the place came and said, 'No noise after midnight,' and I'm paying £40 a week. It's a joke.

**Ian McLagan:** Steve didn't stay long in one place. He could never keep the noise down, he always played his sounds and guitar at full volume, and when he laughed he laughed like a drain. He liked to have people around him, liggers or otherwise, but he'd rather have bad company than none at all. There was Mick [O'Sullivan] and then a geezer called Ron [surname unknown] appeared, amusing but rather slippery, he found an ancient Bentley for Steve to buy... and drove him around in that.

**Paul Banes:** Steve went to live down in Chiswick [west London] and he could walk to Olympic [in Barnes] from there. Andrew and Tony gave the Small Faces an open book, get in the studio and do it. Olympic was the hub for everything that was going down. We did a Christmas record with the whole of Immediate... everyone was on it... and they all sang on it and Steve wrote it. Pat [P. P. Arnold] was going out with Steve at the time. You'd knock on the door at Pat's [house] and Steve would come out the door. We were very close with Donovan, he was working with the Small Faces in the studio.

**P. P. Arnold:** Steve and I lived round the corner from one another, just off Baker Street [in Marylebone]. Jimi Hendrix and Mick Jagger also lived close by. We used to hang out, Steve and I were always jamming. There were plans afoot for Steve and Chris [Farlowe] to do an album together. During 1967, Chris Farlowe was Steve's favourite singer in the whole wide world. Steve thought he was the greatest thing England had ever produced. Immediate was my family. We were all kids, really young. We were all fascinated by Andrew. He was our Svengali. We all worshipped Andrew. Steve was fabulous. We hit it off straight away. We were the same height, the same age. He loved my voice and I loved him, he was so soulful. He was a hyper-high-energy individual and a beautiful sensitive soul. I was the new black girl on the block; I'd been an Ikette, which was hot stuff then. I was soulful, Steve was soulful – it was natural we'd connect.

*In June, the Small Faces released their keenly anticipated debut single for Immediate, the Marriott/Lane-written 'Here Come The Nice'. Marriott, alongside Lane, was credited as producer.*

**Tony Calder:** We couldn't wait to get it out. A drug song on Immediate!

*Despite the climate – the high-profile Jagger/Richards drug trial was about to begin and now Brian Jones had become the latest pop star to be arrested on drug charges – the single was heavily played on BBC Radio and the band promoted it on a variety of TV shows, including their twentieth appearance on* TOTP. *As a side note: Marianne Faithfull hid out with Marriott at his new Chiswick home on the first day of the Jagger/Richards trial – 27 June. They took acid together. Jagger and Richards got long jail sentences: four months and a year respectively.*

**Ian McLagan:** 'Here Come The Nice' was really pushing it. Steve was pushing it to the extremes… the title came from the Lord Buckley track 'Here Comes The Nazz' [from American stand-up Buckley's 1955 album *Euphoria*]. 'The Nazz' meant Jesus, and Steve used it… the nice, a dealer, basically. Here comes the man who gets you high, a friend… it was obvious what the song was about… a methedrine dealer.

**Kenney Jones:** Mick O'Sullivan was what you might term a 'friend' of the band. He was a mate of Steve's, lived in my room at Pimlico. He wasn't a roadie… he hung around, helped out, ran errands, made things happen. As Steve sang in 'Here Come The Nice', his song about Mick, "He knows what I want, he's got what I need, he's always there when I need some speed". For uppers, downers, weed and LSD, Mick was the man. He was part of our lives for some time. He was a great laugh.

*'Here Come The Nice' peaked at UK No 12 and was a minor hit in Germany and the Netherlands. Like Arden, Immediate was not opposed to chart fixing.*

**Ken Mewis:** Immediate had their own methods of promotion. About a week after I started there I opened a cupboard looking for stationery and out fell a thousand copies of the Stones' [late 1966 single] 'Have You Seen Your Mother, [Baby, Standing In The Shadow?]', all neatly bagged from retail outlets throughout England. We had lists of the chart shops and either sent teams out buying or used locally established teams throughout the country. A few bent dealers were easier. We just sent money. We also sent money to chart compilers. We used [name withheld], who for £200 would guarantee Top 50 providing the record had sufficient potential and credibility. He was very honest. He refused a couple of too-obvious hypes. Even records by our top acts that would definitely go Top 20 still got the £200 insurance, if only to expedite their chart rise. Fan clubs also helped, particularly the Small Faces fan club. The newsletters would tell the fans where to buy the single.

*The Small Faces' debut album on Immediate was also released in June. It was a rushed, incomplete work that would not have appeared had Immediate succeeded with an injunction served on Decca to prevent them releasing, in June, a cash-in Small Faces compilation album,* From The Beginning. *The Immediate album was an attempt to nullify the Decca release, which featured the band's early hits plus material they had recorded as a planned second album for Arden, including Don Covay's minor 1964 hit 'Come Back And Take This Hurt Off Me'. It peaked at UK No 17. The Immediate album was launched with a heavy print ad campaign – 'Whichever way you look at it, there are only four Small Faces. But there is just one Small Faces LP. It's on Immediate.' It featured two tracks also included on the Decca album, the Small Faces' own takes on '(Tell Me) Have You Ever Seen Me' and 'My Way Of Giving'. The rest of the album was made up chiefly of new tracks written by Marriott/Lane, recorded at ad hoc sessions at Olympic over the past few months. One, 'Get Yourself Together', had also been cut with Adrienne Posta on vocals for a potential single release. Marriott/Lane were credited as producers on the album. It was a surprise to see Lane take lead vocals on five of the fourteen songs. 'Here Come The Nice' was not included on the album and no further singles were released from it. Nonetheless the album peaked at UK No 12, becoming Immediate's best-selling album to date, allowing the label to boast of having beaten Decca in the battle of the albums.*

**Paul Banes:** I was the third oldest when I started at Immediate and I was 20. Immediate were miles in front of everybody else, the attitude, the rapport we had with the artists. The Immediate staff was tight and dedicated, we buckled down to do the work. When a record went in at No 1 we were all happy, and it just stuck a couple of fingers up at the people down the road. That's what it was all about! The staff wasn't making a fortune. Everybody used to chip in. We'd systematically do a mail-out to the fan clubs, Small Faces, whatever. Everybody would be there until midnight, sticking bits of paper into envelopes. Tony would nip round the Wimpy Bar and buy us all Wimpy and chips.

*In July, the Small Faces were a key part of Immediate's first European radio, press and TV promotional tour (a second similar tour took place in October). Alongside Chris Farlowe, P. P. Arnold and Twice As Much, they travelled through Germany, France, the Netherlands, Belgium, Luxembourg, Sweden, Austria, Switzerland and Italy, meeting the press, pressing the flesh, playing on TV shows and appearing on radio. EMI, Immediate's distributor, had offices in each country and, as well as forging contacts with the media, the plan was to make contact with EMI reps in each territory in the hope of ensuring Immediate releases got priority promotion in the future. It was the sort of long-term planning rarely associated with Immediate and served not only the label well but helped coalesce the entire breadth of EMI's European music business operations.*

**Tony Calder:** Our whole thing was to promote in Europe with junkets. I remember one conference where Steve got the needle with this German guy and started on about the war. This was the biggest German press crew [in physical size] I have ever seen. They were all big fellas and he's coming up trying to hit them. Ronnie says, 'What the fuck are you doing?' And Steve goes, 'This one tried to kill my father.' So Ronnie joined in. It was hysterical.

**David Skinner [Twice As Much]:** The sallies into Europe were very funny. It was sort of flower power and one big binge. It wasn't a very responsible time. There was a lot of laughter. It was a loon... just this sort of drug- and alcohol-ridden haze of music and great times. You used to do a lot of miming in Europe, you basically mimed to your single or your hit... that was it, you were on for about three minutes. So people tended to be very out of it, didn't have to actually sing or do anything, just sort of look all right. As long you could unstick your mouth it was all right.

**Ken Mewis:** Mike Leckebusch, the producer and director of Europe's top [TV] pop show [Germany's *Beat-Club*], was introduced by Immediate to substances and subsequently wanted a monthly delivery. He knew I needed a reason to visit Bremen and what better reason than to take an Immediate act over for his TV show? So between 1967 and 1969 we always had acts on *Beat-Club* [the Small Faces appeared four times on the show in 1967].

**Paul Banes:** None of the Small Faces liked flying; you'd be waiting at Heathrow with your fingers crossed, hoping they'd turn up. Steve, more than anybody else, hated it. Trying to get Steve on an aeroplane was difficult.

**P. P. Arnold:** I've held his hand and tried to keep him together on so many flights. He really hated it.

*In London, Marriott was a frequent visitor to the Immediate offices, smoking, joking and occasionally working.*

**Billy Nicholls:** I'd be in my office at Immediate [as a staff songwriter] most days between nine to five and Steve would often pop in around lunchtime and play new songs to me on an acoustic guitar. He was very prolific. He came in with a very rough sketch of a song and within literally sixty minutes he wrote 'I'm Only Dreaming' ['Itchycoo Park' B-side]. The song was credited to Marriott and Lane but there was no Ronnie input at all.

**Tony Calder:** Records are what Steve liked. Records. He didn't like bands as such. He just heard records he liked. He would come into the office raving about a record and then about a week later he would play us a new song of his and I would say, 'That sounds like that record you were playing last week.' 'No it doesn't,' he would shoot back. End of conversation. But it did. Next door to Immediate was [Beatles publisher] Dick James Music, where Caleb Quaye and Reg [Dwight, better known as Elton John] used to work. So, many a Friday afternoon Reg would come in, 'I've just got twenty quid from Dick, boys. We can go to [Italian restaurant] Verbanella and eat.' Steve would pump us up for twenty quid and they'd all be down the Verbanella on a Friday afternoon, and of course out would come the wine and they'd all get pissed.

*Calder was the first person Marriott called to hear a new song the band had recorded, the era-defining 'Itchycoo Park'.*

**Tony Calder**: I got a phone call from Steve one night, two in the morning. He says, 'You've got to hear this song, it's a smash.' He says, 'Where's Andy?' Steve always called Andrew 'Andy'. He said, 'Do yourself a favour, get hold of him, it's got phasing on it.' I said, 'What the fuck's that?' He said, 'There's a tape op here [at Olympic Studios], George Chkiantz, and he's done something amazing.' I went straight to Olympic and, when I heard the song ['Itchycoo Park'], I heard a No 1...

to me it was a great pop record; the consequences of it being another drug song came later. I got hold of Andrew, he was moaning. I said get your fucking arse down here now. In comes the zombie – even he could hear it.

*Phasing was an audio effect where a listener hears a 'swoosh' or jet plane sweeping effect created by mixing two identical signals but with one slightly delayed, causing shifting harmonics. It is sometimes referred to as flanging. 'Itchycoo Park' made the effect world-famous.*

**Steve Marriott:** I did this radio interview and one of the questions was, 'How did you get the effects on "Itchycoo Park"?' It was live and I said, 'I pissed on the tape...' I'm laughing my head off until I realised I was the only one laughing.

**George Chkiantz:** I first tried out on phasing on P. P. Arnold's 'First Cut Is The Deepest'. The one thing that was characteristic of Steve Marriott was he'd always push that twenty minutes beyond which you could not go, so you wound up hating him. You just couldn't stay awake any longer and he'd say, 'Just do a backing vocal, another mix...' If you had an all-night session with Marriott you were not going to get out until they'd already set up the studio for the next batch of musicians. You could not get him out of the studio, he just loved it in there. He wanted to get every penny out of what was, after all, an expensive thing. Andrew was in and out of Olympic all the time, with the Small Faces and P. P. Arnold, doing demos. The Small Faces were in at the same time the Stones were recording their new album [*Their Satanic Majesties Request*, their own psychedelic response to The Beatles' May 1967 album *Sgt. Pepper's*], and Olympic became the nightclub that was open after all the others closed, we got the bloody lot, the whole scene of hangers-on, sometimes fifty people. Olympic lost an inordinate number of headphones. I think Bill [Wyman] sang on one of the Small Faces tracks or they sang on some of The Rolling Stones stuff. [Marriott sang on *Satanic Majesties* track 'In Another Land' and it was rumoured he had co-written and recorded songs with Jagger.]

**Paul Banes:** 'Itchycoo Park' blew the whole thing up. They wrote about what they saw around them. 'Itchycoo Park' was a place he used to go down to in Manor Park, and itchycoo is the stuff that falls off the plane trees, which, when we were kids, we'd stick down the back of your shirt because it itched.

**Steve Marriott:** I used to take the piss as much as I could. 'Itchycoo Park' is a piss-take because we were never too hippy-trippy. Ronnie came to me and had the melody of the first part [lifted from the hymn 'God Be In My Head'] and the chorus, and I thought up the middle eight...

**Ronnie Lane:** Andrew had a lot of influence over us because we were very impressionable and he was very moody. He would swan around in his shades and his limousine and he was quite amusing really. He had this camp humour and that's when we started to do these little cameos like 'Itchycoo Park'. Had Andrew known it at the time [that his personality was inspiring the band], of course, he would have probably have demanded a royalty payment.

*The band shot an innovative promotional film to promote the single with acclaimed director Peter Whitehead (1937–2019), who had shot the pioneering 1965 on-the-road documentary film with the Stones, Charlie Is My Darling. Whitehead had already shot a similar promotional clip with the Small Faces for the track 'Get Yourself Together' in the wake of Marriott's February drug bust. It saw Marriott kicking a police helmet down the street. For 'Itchycoo Park' the band were filmed in Chiswick Park, with Marriott decked out in cartoonish kaftan and painted plimsolls. Whitehead filmed the band again on Camber Sands beach in East Sussex.*

**Peter Whitehead:** That was a whole session Andrew set up. He said, 'Listen, the guys want to film in Camber Sands, we're all leaving on Friday at five in the morning.' It was Small Faces, P. P. Arnold, Twice As Much. We just set off. I was sitting in the back of Andrew's Rolls-Royce with him and Tony. By the time we got to Camber Sands we were stoned. I couldn't see through the fucking camera. I think the idea was to film 'Itchycoo Park' as the dawn was breaking. There was no time at 7 a.m. to get the instruments together so we stuck them all in the sand and started filming. The whole thing, as far as I was concerned, was a total catastrophe. By the time I got back and stuck it all together, none of us thought it was terribly good, and it was never properly finished. It was shown to all the salesmen [at EMI sales conferences]. I don't think you could have got two more madder people than Andrew and Tony at the time. You went in the office, which was opulent and kitsch, and it was thick with smoke and other things. There were always crazy people around.

**Tony Calder:** We were tripping our heads off at Camber Sands. We didn't have a licence to film there and some little guy, a Mr Plod from the beach, started giving us an argument. I'm telling him to fuck off and Marriott is saying, 'Okay Tone, we'll do it in the sea. We'll hold back the waves, like Jesus.' All day he just kept saying, 'I'm the nazz, man.'

*Scheduled for release in early August 1967, 'Itchycoo Park's "I got high" and "we'll get high" chorus refrain led the BBC to ban the record. There was also reference in the lyric to "blow my mind".*

**Tony Calder:** It was Monday morning and I came in early to the office. Marriott was sitting there. I said, 'What are you doing?' He said, 'They've banned the record.' I looked at him. 'When did you last go to bed?' 'Couple of nights ago.' So we scammed up the story together... and got the ban lifted.

**Ken Mewis:** I had to convince radio producers "I got high" was a reference to swings in the park where they played as kids.

*'Itchycoo Park' peaked at UK No 3 and – testament to the success of the Immediate European promo tour – hit No 17 in German and No 3 in the Netherlands. The band promoted the single across Europe and gigged sporadically in the UK, still playing two twenty-minute sets per night to screaming teen girl fans. The set now included a cover of The Beatles' 'Paperback Writer', The Supremes' 'Love Is Here And Now You're Gone' and The Ronettes' 'Be My Baby'. The constant attention of the teen girl fans led to Marriott complaining of feeling like he was 'in The Monkees'.*

**Steve Marriott:** Quite honestly, I couldn't care if we were dropped by the kids and died as a group tomorrow. As long as we carried on making good records – that's all I care about. When we started I used to love

A very volatile relationship, domineering mum Kath and the belligerent – 'very, very naughty' –13-year-old Marriott, at the zoo, 1960.

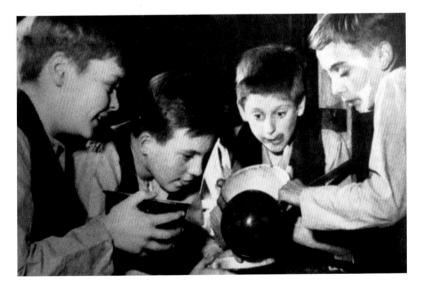

Understudy to Sir Tony Robinson, Marriott as part of the cheeky cockney chorus in hit musical *Oliver!* A workhouse boy and one of Fagin's gang but never the Artful Dodger on the West End stage, 1960.

Publicity shot taken for the famed Italia Conti acting school, an 'angelic look' that did not reflect the reality of 15-year-old Marriott, 1962. The photo is 'everything that he wasn't,' according to a pal. GEMS/REDFERNS

The only known surviving photo of Marriott's first semi-professional band, Steve Marriott & The Moonlites, 1962. Marriott on the far right. 'We used to do Shadows-type movements,' says guitarist Denis Thompson (left). COURTESY DENIS THOMPSON

Steve Marriott's Frantics preparing to perform during half-time at the Queens Park Rangers football ground, 1963. The gig was arranged by the father of guitarist John Weider (second left), who can be seen in the background. COURTESY JOHN WEIDER

Starring in *Be My Guest*, the follow-up to successful music/caper film hit *Live It Up!* Shot in 1963 but not released until 1965. 'He thought it was stupid,' says a friend. 'He disliked acting.'

'Steve had such a lot of front, that's how we got away with it in the early days,' according to Ronnie Lane. Small Faces with original member Jimmy Winston (centre, back), 1965. PICTORIAL PRESS LTD/ALAMY

'They look like little clowns but people will recognise them,' noted band songwriter and producer Ian 'Sammy' Samwell. Small Faces with Winston's replacement, Ian McLagan (right) in their shared London home, 1966. PICTORIAL PRESS LTD/ALAMY

A familiar Marriott live pose, finger in ear in an attempt to hear his own vocal on stage with 'thousands of hysterical teenage girls screaming', 1966. PICTORIAL PRESS LTD/ALAMY

With then fiancée Sue Oliver, who inspired 'All Or Nothing', the song's yearning sexual lyrics described as 'obscene' by Marriott, 1966.

With Small Faces manager and producer Don Arden in his Carnaby Street office, 1966. 'Without Don Arden there would not have been a Small Faces,' said Marriott.

A pin-up, 1966. 'Steve was a natural clothes horse,' says Keith Altham. 'He was really up for the male modelling lark. It paid a good fee and got your face on the front cover.'

PICTORIAL PRESS LTD/ALAMY

'We became pop stars and we never really wanted to be,' Steve Marriott, 1966.

PICTORIAL PRESS LTD/ALAMY

New management and new record label: Andrew Loog Oldham and Tony Calder, co-founders of Immediate Records, pictured in 1965. Signing with Stones manager Oldham in 1967 expanded Marriott's creative scope. WILLIAM H. ALDEN/EVENING STANDARD/GETTY IMAGES.

With Immediate act Chris Farlowe, 1967. 'Steve thought he was the greatest thing England had ever produced,' says P. P. Arnold. KEYSTONE PRESS/ALAMY

On the move – noise complaints forcing his eviction from a flat in Kensington, 1967. 'Steve didn't stay in one place long,' said Ian McLagan. 'He played his sounds at full volume, laughed like a drain and liked to have people around.' MIRRORPIX

personal appearances but now I would rather be in the studio. As far as recording is concerned, the sky's the limit.

*Marriott's workaholic lifestyle – away from the Small Faces, he was involved in recordings on the* Supernatural Fairy Tales *album by Art (a band who would become Spooky Tooth and who featured future Humble Pie bassist Greg Ridley), guested on the Traffic album* Mr Fantasy, *played on sessions for a Del Shannon album (produced by Oldham) and worked with Immediate act P. P. Arnold (she cut a version of 'Itchycoo Park' with the Small Faces and he sang on her debut Immediate album) – and increasingly heavy drug and alcohol consumption caught up with him again and he collapsed, suffering from, reportedly, nervous exhaustion. The 20-year-old also admitted to suffering from jaundice (suggesting liver damage). His mother was deeply concerned for his health. He was also becoming increasingly prone to making impetuous decisions, displaying casual cruelty and beginning to harbour the kind of anti-music-business attitude he would in later life find cold comfort in. Future Humble Pie member Peter Frampton, at the time guitarist and singer in The Herd, recalled supporting the Small Faces in Paris and overhearing Marriott – to protests from Ronnie Lane – turning down an offer to support Jimi Hendrix on his early 1968 American tour. Marriott apparently stated, 'No fucking way, he should be opening for us.'*

**John 'Rhino' Edwards:** Andy Bown [of The Herd, who alongside Edwards is now a member of Status Quo] thought Steve was a real arsehole. He told me Steve used to throw money out the window and watch the people running to pick it up, going... 'Ah, look at them cunts.'

*It was a tempestuous time in sixties pop as the forerunners of what had been seen as a teen cultural revolution, chiefly The Beatles and the Stones, were now being talked about in broader terms as a more societal phenomenon. Marriott was not the only one feeling the strain. An increasingly fragile Brian Jones had been arrested again on drug possession and feared he would inevitably be handed a long jail sentence, especially after, in a highly charged atmosphere, the initial sentences for Jagger and Richards had now been dismissed on appeal.*

**Steve Marriott:** Brian Jones was on his way out and I was apparently considered as a possible replacement but I wouldn't have taken it. Later

I talked to Keith about it but back then Mick wouldn't have it. Keith would have liked it.

*Andrew Loog Oldham, still only 23, was perhaps suffering most, quitting his position as the Stones' manager and producer. Problems had been brewing between him and the group since the end of 1966 when, after years of heavy touring and increasing drug use, the astonishingly odd single 'Have You Seen Your Mother, Baby, Standing In The Shadow?' was deemed a flop. A successful early 1967 single, 'Let's Spend The Night Together', and album* Between The Buttons *had seemingly steered the band back on course, but the Jagger/Richards drug bust had caused further friction between the pair and manager. The strung-out, lackadaisical recording of* Satanic Majesties *had been the final straw for Oldham, who admitted he often felt suicidal, suffering from recurring bouts of depression. A psychiatrist diagnosed him as manic depressive and put him through a treatment of electro convulsive therapy. Oldham was also spending weekends at Hampstead's Bethanie Nursing Home, where he was administered with deep sleep treatment, put into a sort of coma for days, held down with a combination of barbiturates, sedatives and the latest psychotropic drugs on the market.*

**Keith Altham:** Oldham was a very good manager for the Stones but by the time he took on the Small Faces he was a truly fucked-up guy.

*Brian Jones staggered on. Marriott bounced back, in part dragging Oldham with him. Small Faces sessions at Olympic continued. There was still music – great music – to be made.*

**Billy Nicholls:** A songwriter called Jeremy Paul brought in [to Immediate] a song called 'Would You Believe' and I just loved it and so did Ronnie Lane and Steve Marriott and they said, 'Why don't we just go in and do it?' We had unlimited studio time. Andrew had Olympic block-booked. He was throwing so much money around. We just went in one night when the Small Faces were recording and did 'Would You Believe' [released as Nicholls' debut solo single in early 1968]. Steve was singing backing vocals. Andrew heard it and wanted to put his stamp on it. He put on the orchestra, lots of backing vocals, sped up vocals, all sorts of stuff… and then, once he finished it, he decided he wanted to do an album with me. Steve was involved in the album [*Would You Believe*]. He sang backing vocals on the track 'It Brings Me Down' and I asked him if he would help me on 'Girl From New York'. I thought it would be the Small Faces coming down but Steve brought in [drummer] Jerry Shirley and a [different] bass player, which was odd... the track turned out great but it felt a bit strange. Steve was obviously looking around at other musicians. You could say that was the start of Humble Pie. He played the most amazing guitar solo all the way through on 'Girl From New York' and then at the very end of the song he pulled the neck so hard to get what he wanted out of the guitar, it snapped... he snapped the neck in half. And he just went, 'Oh well, there you go'... typical Steve, wasn't really upset. But what he got out of it was fantastic. It was probably one of the best guitar solos he'd ever done.

*The engineer on the 'Would You Believe' single was the teenage Alan O'Duffy. He had come to the attention of Oldham while working at Pye Studios, where Oldham had recorded with the Stones, Twice As Much and Rod Stewart.*

**Alan O'Duffy:** The guy who came in to produce for Billy [Nicholls] was Stevie. Then Andrew came in and we did a bit of faffing around and I mixed it with Andrew. Steve was a lovely guy, Mr Enthusiasm. I compare him to Prince, in terms of his multi-skilled confidence as a musician, his talent, and in particular he's an outrageous singer, unbelievable, always blew me sideways. I think Steve was actually the drummer on 'Would You Believe', he was a fantastic drummer too. I also did [the original version of] 'Tin Soldier' [a Marriott/Lane song inspired by Marriott's reading of Hans Christian Andersen's fairy tales] with P. P. Arnold. It was a thing we were working on with P. P. Steve's interest was The Staple Singers, Edward Hawkins Singers, Otis Redding and the whole Stax catalogue... he tried in his life to emulate Mavis Staples and Aretha Franklin and Mahalia Jackson... he was trying to sing like them. A lot of those people came from an American Baptist gospel choir background so when P. P. walked in the door of Olympic to work with Steve he met someone who had a voice he loved to bits. He was in heaven, he was a fan of Pat Arnold big time.

**Steve Marriott:** We played 'Tin Soldier' for Pat Arnold and she freaked over it so much I thought I better hold back! It was just too good to let go. We later wrote her one called '(If You Think You're) Groovy' [released as a P. P. Arnold single by Immediate in early 1968 but also cut by the Small Faces].

**Kenney Jones:** I thought Steve and Ronnie were really kind to give '(If You Think You're) Groovy' to her because it could've been a big hit for the Small Faces. I played on it. Steve was in the booth with Glyn and Steve was trying to show the drummer how to play it... so I got on the kit and showed him. I'd never played the song before... in the end, I just played it. It wound up being the whole Small Faces on that cut. Steve was great in the studio. He wasn't overbearing. He was very confident. The greatest gift we had as a band was we all had a built-in telepathic feeling about each other. They never ever told me what to play. They knew I was going to come up with something good. I'd sing the songs we were working on to myself – my nickname was 'Shut Up Kenney' until I lost my temper one day. I'm only looking for the right fill to play! And they all got the message, big time. I did a lot of big band sessions and played with orchestras and it taught me how to play differently and I took that back to our sessions. I'll never forget Andrew Oldham saying to me, Kenney play it like you mean it... in other words, get in there, push yourself forward.

*The Small Faces cut their own version of 'Tin Soldier'. Produced by Marriott and Lane, it was released as a single by Immediate in December 1967. P. P. Arnold appeared with the band, singing backing vocals, as they promoted the song on TV, including a fondly remembered* Top Of The Pops *performance. The single failed to match the commercial success of 'Itchycoo Park', peaking at UK No 9, but is considered by many to be the band's finest moment.*

**Steve Marriott:** 'Tin Soldier' is the real us. 'Itchycoo Park' was really just a nice kind of send-up. We wanted to make a record that was really us. We can play this one live but we could never get the same effects on 'Itchycoo Park'.

**Ronnie Lane:** 'Tin Soldier' was primarily Steve's tune.

**P. P. Arnold:** Steve and I were lovers around the time of 'Tin Soldier' but he wrote it about Jenny... she was the love of Steve's life.

# CHAPTER 6

# Lazy Sunday

**Jenny Dearden:** I was brought up in Prestwich, Manchester. I used to go to the Left Wing [club] that became the [city's celebrated] Twisted Wheel [club]. They had people like John Lee Hooker, Sonny Boy Williamson play there, real blues. And then [aged 18] I moved to London to go to UCL [University College London, to study Philosophy with Psychology] but that didn't last at all. My friends in London were friends from Manchester, Mo McDermott [artist-designer, and model for David Hockney] and [celebrated fashion designer] Ossie Clark, who was a bit older than me. His very first commission was my sister's wedding dress. In London we used to go to clubs together and in the Cromwellian [club] I met Julie Driscoll and we became great friends. She was a secretary but had started to sing with a band, The Steampacket. It was through her that I met Rod Stewart and he became my very first boyfriend. At the time he was living at home with his mum and dad and playing acoustic guitar while working in his brother's picture framing shop in Archway. My relationship with Rod lasted for four and half years on and off, but during that time I did meet Steve who I knew was quite keen on me, but I was with Rod so nothing happened.

**Steve Marriott:** I'd tried every trick in the book to pull her and couldn't. So I wrote her that song ['Tin Soldier'] and she married me!

**Jenny Dearden:** Rod and I lived together for a while toward the end but that was disastrous. I wasn't very well and we split up. I went to work with Ossie and Alice [Pollock, a fellow designer] in [hip boutique] Quorum [on the King's Road]. Ossie had just joined Alice, who started

Quorum. I did some modelling. I was with the original model agency that [leading model agency] Models 1 sprang from called English Boy [co-founded by Pollock]. I was on the top of their head sheets, so I did a few things like the Harp adverts, but I wasn't a natural model, I was too introverted. During that time, Steve found out Rod and I had split up and he bombarded me basically. I did resist for a long time because I didn't want anything to do with the music business anymore. We were all somewhat overdoing it, doing a lot of substances, and I was quite ill. Steve continued to be persistent and he started to look after me. I later had to be rushed to hospital... I was in a ward, with a particularly nice lady opposite to chat to. After being in there for a couple of days, Steve arrived, announcing that he was taking me to a private room, demanded a wheelchair and wheeled me there himself. The nice lady recognised him and was thrilled when he went over and gave her a kiss. I think it must have been on that night that they were on *Top Of The Pops*, singing 'Tin Soldier', during which he embellished the lyrics with 'This is for you in your private room'. He then said, 'No strings, just come and stay with me in Chiswick,' where he had this little house, 'and I'll look after you.' People don't think of him in that way. This cheeky chappie cockney thing was very much his defence and an act... he was a lot more complex. I'm not saying he pondered advanced philosophical concepts but he was definitely more sophisticated than his image suggested.

*At Immediate, plans were being laid to finally launch the Small Faces in America. Oldham had struck a new distribution deal for the label with CBS, the giant American entertainment conglomerate whose recording arm handled such acts such as Janis Joplin, Bob Dylan, The Byrds and Simon & Garfunkel. CBS had paid Immediate a $100,000 advance for rights to the label's product in America and had released 'Here Come The Nice' as a market taster. Now, in early 1968, they put their full might behind promoting 'Itchycoo Park' as a single. There was talk of a February visit from the band with a possible appearance on the massive* Ed Sullivan Show. *CBS wanted the group to tour there as soon as possible. Immediate packaged a 'special' album, titled* There Are But Four Small Faces, *featuring the best of the band's Immediate debut album plus the recent hit singles, especially for American release.*

**Steve Marriott:** CBS is a good label to be on out there and we're very hopeful. That's where Andrew comes in again.

*'Itchycoo Park' climbed America's* Billboard *charts, selling over 300,000 copies to peak at No 16 (the single had sold about 250,000 in the UK and the same again in the rest of Europe). It went to No 1 in Canada. This was a more than promising start to the CBS/Immediate/Small Faces relationship. The band, however, incredibly, failed to appear in America themselves. In November 1967 Ian McLagan had been busted for drugs at Heathrow Airport, caught carrying eighty-five grammes of hashish, a sizeable block – almost three ounces. He was released on £1,500 bail after fifteen minutes in jail.*

**Ian McLagan:** Andrew paid my bail and I was in the Roller puffing on a joint before we left the police station car park... Steve thought it was a good laugh... but US Immigration told Andrew I shouldn't bother applying for a visa as I would never be allowed into the country.

*In court, McLagan, said to be earning £200 week, was lucky to be let off with a £50 fine. Why the Small Faces could not have visited America, at least for promotion, with or without a replacement for McLagan, is unclear. It was suggested Marriott had no appetite for the sort of transatlantic hop across and back that was routine for Oldham and many others. CBS were unimpressed by Immediate's excuse that the band's inability to promote themselves in America was due to 'unbelievable demand' for the group in Europe. The huge label had myriad other acts to work on, and ambitious president Clive Davis – the foremost executive in the American record industry – was juggling multi-million-dollar budgets with a keen eye on record division profits and CBS stock prices. With no act available to support the release and no immediate prospect of a tour, CBS put little effort into promoting the* There Are But Four Small Faces *album and it peaked at a disappointing No 178 in America. Calder, in particular, was left to rue the decision to sign to CBS. In allowing Oldham to make the deal, he had been forced to cancel a similar American distribution deal he'd made (and signed) with United Artists (UA), another large film/TV/music institution.*

**Tony Calder:** The deal with UA was done in three days: they paid the [advance] money [$50,000], they were going put 'Itchycoo Park' out. Andrew then came out of one of the sleep treatment centres in London, the Bethanie Nursing Home. He'd been in there a week, and went straight off to see Lou Adler in LA, bumped into Clive Davis and did the deal [with CBS] without even speaking to me. I didn't even know he was in LA. Well, we wanted to go with CBS because they were the ultimate [American] record company. So we went to United Artists and asked to get out the deal. Their lawyer screwed us. To get out of the deal we had to agree to pay back a quarter of a million dollars over three years with a debenture [United Artists would take over Immediate's publishing company, Immediate Music, if the money was not paid]. We paid the first year and then the second year got heavy. At CBS, Andrew upset Clive Davis [threatening to blow up the bus he infamously travelled to work on]. CBS can sit on records, they still do it today. If an American record label decides to work the record, they'll work the record. They can also go through the motions of making out they're working the record. If the president of the company doesn't call it a priority, you're dead. With United Artists we could have been top of the pile, who knows?

**Paul Banes:** We needed to do consistent sales in America, that's where the money was. The company could have easily run on the back of what we were selling everywhere else.

*One territory the Small Faces were able and willing to visit was Australia. 'Itchycoo Park' had gone to No 2 and 'Tin Soldier' to No 3 in the Australian charts. In part to escape the English winter and top up on suntans during Australia's summer season (as he had done previously with the Stones), Oldham organised, with Australian promoter Harry Miller, who had handled the Stones tours down under, a short fifteen-day tour of Australia and New Zealand. The Small Faces were to be supported by The Who (a single from The Who's latest album, Sell Out, 'I Can See For Miles', had peaked at No 20 in Australia – although it had gone Top 10 in America) and The Herd (who would ultimately pull out of the tour). Oldham and Calder would also accompany the band to Australia.*

*A subplot of the visit was to tighten up the under-rehearsed Small Faces (they had played approximately 180 shows in 1967, the majority before signing to Immediate and would play only eighty gigs in 1968) for live dates in the UK and, potentially, an American tour. Instead, it broke the group. Their thirty-minute set – featuring 'Sha-La-La-La-Lee', 'All Or Nothing', 'Itchycoo*

*Park', 'Tin Soldier' and two new covers, 'If I Were A Carpenter' (by Tim Hardin, a Top 10 hit for Bobby Darin in 1966, and also covered by Joan Baez, Johnny Cash and The Four Tops) and 'Every Little Bit Hurts' (a hit for Motown's Brenda Holloway in 1964 and covered by the Spencer Davis Group in 1965) – rarely ran smoothly. Marriott was chief wrecker. He was disgruntled with the band's sound amid stage and equipment issues in Sydney, and walked off, but not before verbally returning the crowd's hostility (coins were thrown at the stage). At another show, while playing organ, he threatened to beat up a fan flicking pieces of paper at him. In an attempt to replicate the effects on 'Itchycoo Park', he had the idea of taping the sounds of jets from a hotel roof on a portable cassette machine to play into a mic on stage. The result was disastrous: invariably it led to feedback and comedy, with the tape machine falling off the organ.*

**Ian McLagan:** The Who slaughtered us, really. We weren't a good band then.

**Kenney Jones:** We were flat and unprepared. Too much time in the studio, too much time miming hits on TV shows across Europe… the will to tour had been fading for a while, and it showed in our performances.

*It was agreed that The Who, who had been touring since their triumph at the 1967 Monterey Pop Festival, would close the shows. To compound Marriott's disgruntlement with events, the Australian press ridiculed the Small Faces, particular offence taken at the 'screaming of obscene four-letter words on stage' by Marriott. He was unrepentant. Asked at a press conference if McLagan was a drug addict, Marriott shouted, 'Leave it out, you cunt!' It was during this string of problematic gigs that Marriott first discussed leaving the Small Faces.*

**Tony Calder:** Steve said to me, 'I'm leaving the band.' He said he'd already spoken to Peter Frampton about forming a new band. I said, 'What do you mean?' He says, 'I'm not going on with that fucking arsehole Ronnie again, I'm not having that cunt nick my money anymore, he's never written a fucking song, he's only written one song, he's a fucking arsehole, he treats me like a piece of shit, I'm not finishing this fucking tour.' I said, 'You've got to finish it.' He said, 'Okay cunts, you have to stay with me.' That was the deal, we had to stay with him, because our [Calder and Oldham's] plan was we would arrive in Sydney and it'd be, whoa, is this really the New York of Australia? Okay, fine. 'Is everything okay, lads?' Lovely, off we go then, thank you… that was our idea. I remember going to Brisbane – it was awful. We arrive in Cairns or somewhere and there was all this press, and two German reporters. Someone says something to Steve and he says, 'How many people did your father kill? I bet he killed my father.' You can get away with that in Germany, but not in Australia.

**Steve Marriott:** Ronnie and I wrote 'Itchycoo Park' together; nigh on all the rest were written apart. I wrote 'Tin Soldier', 'Lazy Sunday', 'All Or Nothing'… I tended to write the hits, as it were.

*Off stage there was plenty of sun, sex (Kenney Jones recalled Marriott catching pubic lice), booze and drugs. One local support band was amazed to see Marriott with a big bag of grass, scarce in the country. Police were called after complaints of drinking and loutishness on one internal flight. Oldham was hospitalised by a bouncer at a show in Melbourne. Roger Daltrey called Australia a 'backwater' – 'like nowhere we'd ever seen: every building still had a tin roof'. Newspapers urged fans to boycott the concerts, describing the Small Faces as 'weedy, bumptious, arrogant, sulking, sneering' and 'dirty flea-ridden thieves'. The Australian prime minister, John Gorton, remarked: 'We never wanted you to come to Australia. You have behaved atrociously while you've been here, and we hope you never come back.'*

**Steve Marriott:** They called us dirty but I'd caught mange off my dogs… the trip was a total disaster. The police escorted us out of Australia. Every day seemed like a year. We never want to go back there again. The older generation had it in for us so much it nearly drove me round the twist.

*It was clear Marriott and Lane were growing apart. In Australia, Lane formed a close bond with Pete Townshend over a shared interest in exploring areas of spirituality such as Sufism (Islamic mysticism) and leading spiritual figures like Meher Baba, a master teacher who claimed he was God in human form. Marriott, in contrast, talked pinball with Townshend and ended up having a fight with The Who songwriter in a hotel corridor over a girl.*

**Ian McLagan:** After Ronnie took acid he found religion. First Buddhism. Then he found Meher Baba and went to India. There was some underlying aggro between Pete and Steve. It wasn't that they didn't get on but I think Steve was jealous of The Who's success and both being highly strung like racehorses something had to snap. Steve was always so hyperactive, you'd want to chin him now and then for his own good, but we weren't about to hit him. But, when Pete and Steve got into a scuffle in the hotel corridor in Melbourne, it almost got out of hand. Pete had him in an arm lock on the floor, but Steve wouldn't give in and Pete for his part was probably enjoying finally and physically putting him in his place. In the end nobody got hurt – just some feathers ruffled.

*The tour concluded in New Zealand. Marriott walked off stage again in Auckland, screaming, 'This fucking piano's out of tune,' and in Wellington he and Who drummer Keith Moon went on an infamous hotel-wrecking spree to celebrate Marriott's 21st birthday. 'This one ends with the police,' said Townshend, ducking out early.*

**Steve Marriott:** We let fly. Chairs, TVs, settees... mirrors, everything through the windows and over the balcony... portable record player, I threw over the balcony... me and Keith Moon destroyed the place, pissed as newts... we were drinking champagne, celebrating... I was hurting with laughter it was so funny at the time. I had a great idea [to get out of the blame]... let's say someone's broken into our room and complain about it. Terrible slags we were – terrible liars. They spent all day refurbishing the place, new French windows, everything... come the evening Keith comes up and says they've done a great job and immediately puts an ashtray through the French windows... and off it goes again... we didn't get away with it a second time... It was fun but we came away owing money...

*It cost Immediate a small fortune, not only to compensate for hotel damages but also to stop any further action being taken by New Zealand authorities. Oldham ended up losing around £10,000 on the tour.*

**Andrew Loog Oldham:** 'Itchycoo Park' had opened the door a bit for Immediate in America, despite the fact that Clive Davis, who was running our distributor, CBS, personally disliked me. And why not? The Small Faces at their best captured the zeitgeist as well or better than Yank purveyors of psychedelic pop like Cowsills and The Monkees. Unfortunately, the band never recovered from their imagined ill-treatment at the hands of Don Arden and Decca. At first, their demands seemed reasonable, at least by the artist-dominated standards of the late sixties: a house in the country to write in, a studio in town presided over by Glyn Johns, and all the hash they could smoke, eat or otherwise consume. Their conditions met, they promised to deliver a commercial masterpiece. And that they did. But unlike the Stones, who thrived on endless world tours, the Small Faces felt they'd paid their dues under Don's strict work ethic and refused to tour America. I disagreed and our relationship suffered... [the] gutter, scum-line, inbred, ungrateful midgets McLagan and Lane [ultimately] made my Small Faces experience much ado about all-or-nothing, while the calm and manners of Kenney and the loving madness of Steve made the journey worthwhile.

*Back in London, at the start of February 1968, Marriott doubled down in Olympic, experimenting with different musicians, including players from the London Philharmonic Orchestra, determined to finish the new Small Faces album. Recording sessions were interrupted by promotional engagements in Europe, as 'Tin Soldier' climbed the charts to reach No 7 in Germany and No 4 in the Netherlands. On one European TV show Marriott was asked if he believed in rock'n'roll. 'I just trod in some,' he replied. In April, Immediate released a new Small Faces single, their eleventh, 'Lazy Sunday', again written and produced by Marriott/Lane.*

**Steve Marriott:** I had an awful fight with Andrew when he said 'Lazy Sunday' was the single. It was an album track. It was me taking the piss... I did it for a laugh... it was this funny, jokey, novelty thing. We didn't want to release it as a single even though we virtually knew it would be a hit. We didn't want those gimmicky things to be a trademark. We'd just done 'Itchycoo Park', with the exaggerated cockney accent. I wanted [future *Ogdens' Nut Gone Flake* album track] 'Afterglow' [as the next single]. They [Immediate] knew 'Lazy Sunday' would make it, just like they knew 'Itchycoo Park' would. But we did them as one-off tracks... a spin-off thing for a giggle.

**Andrew Loog Oldham:** Blatant commercialism often scares the act. The Stones had initially regarded 'Satisfaction' as a bit of a gimmick.

**Kenney Jones:** For a while we had been growing increasingly frustrated, Steve perhaps most acutely. Whenever we bumped into people like Eric Clapton or Jeff Beck, guys who were playing heavier, rawer music, we'd be chatting with them, cracking jokes, laughing, being the Small Faces that everyone expected, but inwardly we were groaning, desperately wanting the equivalent of the musical recognition and respect they received. 'Lazy Sunday' all but ensured it was never going to happen. At the time I sensed there would be repercussions...

**Paul Banes:** When I first took 'Lazy Sunday' to the radio, there were no bells on it, no tweet tweet tweets, no 'Satisfaction' [riff]... Alan Freeman's programme director at the BBC said there was something missing. Andrew came up with the idea to put the [church] bells on [from the square in Barnes] and they came up with the idea to play with the comb and a piece of paper a little bit of 'Satisfaction' [as a tribute to Oldham's belief that the song was a national anthem à la 'Satisfaction']. It was Andrew who made it an even bigger record than what it was... but the whole song was typical Steve. He'd get up at lunchtime, start playing the music and the neighbours would knock on the wall.

*Marriott's yell of 'Fuck the neighbours' was disguised but still audible on the finished record.*

**Jenny Dearden:** Steve and I lived at Eyot Green in Chiswick. We had three dogs: Seamus, his Border Collie that we got from Shepherd's Bush Market, my black terrier Love, and Lucy, an Alsatian puppy, who we found in the window of a dingy pet shop on a tour of Steve's East End haunts. She was emaciated, had blood on her coat and was lying in the window – so irresistible. At the vet, it was discovered that she had distemper, as well as rickets and several parasite infections. Distemper is a viral disease, easily spread and often fatal, so, until the disease had been treated, she was not allowed outside as she was infectious. The same applied to Seamus and Love as they now could be carriers. Which is why, for around a month, they all had to use the balcony as a loo. We had a daily routine of much disinfectant but it was a difficult and smelly time. Despite that, the neighbours – the Hasselblads – were pretty tolerant, until Steve acquired studio-size Wharfedale speakers from Olympic. I was sympathetic at the time and even more so now. The adjoining walls were thin and the bass reverberations shook the house. We were not ideal neighbours. The Hasselblads are the ones he wrote 'Lazy Sunday' about as a sort of joke... and of course they [the band] were all furious when that was released. I've always thought that this was a pivotal moment – they had been determined to move towards heavier music, less pop, they wanted to be taken seriously as musicians. Steve was furious, as was Ronnie. I am almost 100 per cent sure that it was whilst they were out of the country in Australia that Immediate decided to release 'Lazy Sunday' as a single.

*'Lazy Sunday' was the Small Faces' biggest hit yet. The band appeared on TOTP three times as the single rose to No 2 in the UK, peaking at No 2 in Germany and No 1 in the Netherlands (and No 5 in Australia). There was a Peter Whitehead promo film and the usual performance on Beat-Club in Germany. In America, 'Itchycoo Park's follow-up 'Tin Soldier' had sold a disappointing 35,000 copies, peaking at No 73 (No 37 in Canada). CBS now reported back to Immediate that they were not convinced of the potential of 'Lazy Sunday' and were unsure when it would be released (when it was, without significant promotion, it peaked at No 114 in America and No 42 in Canada). It was clear now that as far as CBS were concerned the Small Faces had no chance of prospering in America.*

*Marriott had all but given up on the band too. The new album was incomplete. His musical tastes had changed. Psychedelic whimsy was replaced by the sound of heavy blues, powerful soul and American roots music. He was listening to Blood, Sweat & Tears, the heavy American jazz-rock band, admiring their powerful singer, David Clayton-Thomas, and tracks like 'Spinning Wheel' from the band's eponymous second album. Marriott also ate up debut albums from American roots rockers The Band (Music From The Big Pink) and from New Orleans singer/guitarist Dr John (the hybrid blues/swamp rock of GRIS-gris). Many other British musicians were making a similar journey and alongside the quest for writing earthier, heavier, more meaningful material came a geographical shift. Only the countryside was compatible with inspiring this new sort of music. Swinging central London – Soho, even the King's Road – was considered pop and the migration out to the nearby commuter-belt greenery was prevalent. In*

*Marriott's case, his dogs and loud music, hit record about neighbours, and the hassle from fans, made the move a prerequisite anyway. Lane, who, in April, married 21-year-old model, sitcom actress and pop act Susanna Hunt, was also keen to explore new ground. So was McLagan, who, in January, had married 20-year-old Sandy Sarjeant, an RSG! and Beat-Club dancer. Marriott became the third Small Face to marry when, in May 1968, he tied the knot with the 23-year-old Dearden at Kensington Registry Office.*

**Steve Marriott:** After I married Jenny some fan letters came that weren't so nice and others came with our records broken up and scratched... Oh, he's married, there's no chance for me. As if there was ever a chance. I mean, what's all that about?

**Kenney Jones:** They all married young. It was the environment we all grew up in. It was, you got to be like your old man, you've got to be a lorry driver and you've got to get married young.

**Jenny Dearden:** Jerome Cottage [famed for being the home of *Three Men In A Boat* writer, Jerome K. Jerome] was a beautiful, lovely house just outside Marlow in Buckinghamshire [now worth close to £2 million]. The rental had been finalised prior to Steve and I getting married and we were all (Ronnie and Sue, Mac and Sandy, and Steve and I) due to move down there imminently. Two days after our wedding, I was rushed to hospital, by ambulance, with severe abdominal pain. I had been feeling unwell but the symptoms suddenly escalated. At the time, prior to moving to Marlow and having left Chiswick, we had moved to Ronnie and Sue's in their rented mews house in Spear Mews, Earl's Court. It was small and quite cramped, especially as we had a lot of animals between us. Whilst I was in hospital, everyone else moved to Jerome Cottage. I was hospitalised for around ten days, being treated and investigated. The results were not definitive – I had begun taking a contraceptive pill that, it was decided, had inflamed/aggravated my system. Ironically, some of the tabloids got wind of my hospitalisation and implied that I had probably had a miscarriage – therefore, we had got married because I was pregnant.

The doctors allowed me out of hospital, saying that I had to rest and be careful. So, when I finally arrived at Jerome Cottage, I was not in great shape, exhausted and still quite unwell. This is why I stayed in bed and didn't appear much, at least for a while. As with any shared space, the dynamics of all living together proved to be tricky sometimes. Ronnie and Sue and Steve and I had lived together before and we all got on extremely well. Sue was her usual kind and caring self, helping look after me and generally holding everything together. What I would not normally share is the fact that, although Mac could be witty and amusing, he was well known for being chippy, angry and resentful. Understandably, it would obviously be difficult for him to deal with the fact that Steve and Ronnie were the 'creative' partnership and would often be sitting together working on songs. When we took the boats down the Thames, the same thing happened and this is when most of *Ogdens'* was written. So, despite the bucolic surroundings, there was sometimes a somewhat strained atmosphere. I don't think it's particularly helpful to the Steve story to diss Mac, or indeed anyone who is not around anymore. However, I have discussed with other people who knew all concerned and the general consensus is bemusement and sadness that Mac continued to talk about Steve with such unabated vitriol, even after Steve had died so horribly.

We were not in Jerome Cottage that long, a few months. The house was split in two and actually owned by these two old ladies who lived there but whom we very rarely saw. The only time they objected was when everyone had taken acid and they were playing music all night and Lyn Dobson, who was a wonderful flautist, played the flute in the garden. That's the only time they said anything: 'We thought the music was beautiful but could it please not be in the middle of the night?' Steve was very talented. He could pick up any instrument... he wanted a sitar so he went to this Indian family... and he learned to play it pretty quickly... it seemed to come naturally to him.

**Ian McLagan:** Generally we lived the life of Riley [in Marlow]... we had as nice time as possible without much money, working up songs. 'Speedy' Acquaye [1931–1993] came down a couple of times bringing herb [and his congas], and we jammed for hours in the woods. Mick Jagger came to visit. We lived quite peacefully together although there was bound to be more tension with the girls living there as well.

**Jenny Dearden:** The Small Faces were Mods and as the sixties were progressing, they were moving on from that. I knew the people [Nigel Waymouth, Sheila Cohen and John Pearse] who started Granny Takes A Trip [a so-called 'psychedelic boutique' in Chelsea] and I started getting Steve clothes from there... and in the end they all started getting clothes from there... so it changed the whole vibe. Being a Mod in the late sixties was not that cool anymore, you had to go more with what was happening on the King's Road.

*The house in the countryside, all the dope they could smoke, the increasingly hippy-ish threads, no hassles... and no album. Oldham and Calder needed the promised Small Faces album completed.*

**Kenney Jones:** Andrew suggested we take time out to clear our heads, in the hope of kindling inspiration, and hired each of us a motorboat [cabin cruisers] for a cruise down the Thames.

**Jenny Dearden:** We all went down the Thames in hired boats, with our dogs. Poor Seamus and Lucy. You could just hire these boats, get on them and drive away. It was very productive... Steve and Ronnie did a lot of writing. It was only a weekend but a huge amount happened. We had a lot of fun. Sue and I tried to keep it all together in a little galley [kitchen]. Mac and Sandy had a separate boat. There were a few disasters. Mac and Sandy's puppy fell into a lock and Steve rescued it. We were chugging along and I looked across and said that looks like Seamus on that boat and it was, he had jumped over. Mac rammed another boat driven by someone in a captain's hat, terribly grand.

**Steve Marriott:** It was a real gas. We hired this eight-berth boat and went upriver and directly we crunch into a nice quiet lock and we play the [Frank Zappa's American freak-rock band] Mothers Of Invention album full blast, ruin the peace of the countryside. We're quite destructive really...

**Ian McLagan:** Stop, have a smoke... have a drink and a play... we worked on songs like 'The Fly', 'The Journey', 'Happiness Stan' [that appeared on the new album], and then the idea evolved about having links between the songs. We talked to Spike Milligan originally [to provide a narrative voice] and he turned us down. It was Steve's idea to have him write and perform links between the songs. Someone suggested Stanley Unwin [the 'professor' of gobbledygook, who spoke his own language, Unwinese]. As soon as he spoke he had us all on the floor laughing. Steve was screaming with pain, banging on the sofa and begging him to stop.

**Steve Marriott:** We gave Stanley Unwin a glossary of hip terms to throw in with the cockneyisms. The album made us laugh – anything that made us laugh we liked. God knows how it worked but it did and I'm very proud of it. It was worth the year's work. We recorded backing tracks over and over...

**Pete Townshend:** *Ogdens' Nut Gone Flake* was a world-shaking record. When they first played it to me, the only material I'd heard to which it could be compared was concept pieces like *Pet Sounds* or *Sgt. Pepper's*. I was very jealous of their sound; they were becoming a real extraordinary sonic force to be reckoned with.

**Rod Stewart:** *Ogdens'* was a masterpiece.

*The sleeve would become as much of a talking point as the music; for the first time ever, an album was released in round, not square, packaging.*

**Tony Calder:** Everything Marriott did he did quickly because he had such a small attention span. He came in and said, 'Do you think we could do the sleeve like a tobacco tin? Can we do it like an Ogden's?' [Ogden's Tobacco were a huge Liverpool firm, noted for the innovative cigarette cards and tobacco tins, part of the Imperial Tobacco Group.] I said, 'Yeah, I'll have a word with them.'

**Ian McLagan:** Andrew got us delivered the actual Ogden's archives... and we had the real things in the Immediate offices. And we found Ogden's Nut Brown Flake, a rectangular tin, and Steve went, 'Oh!'... all the pictures, slogans, are all exactly the same, it's just we changed 'Nut Brown' to 'Nut Gone'. The round sleeve was Andrew's bright idea; the world's first round album cover would get us extra press.

**Ronnie Lane:** The album's title just came from us thinking, if it [marijuana] was legal, what would it be called…

**Kenney Jones:** We called it 'Nut Gone' because your nut's gone if you smoke the stuff.

**Paul Banes:** Steve and Ronnie made all the decisions. With all due respect to the other two, the Small Faces were the voices of Steve and Ronnie, end of story. The whole sleeve was put together in such a way that we needed a lot of authorisation [from Imperial Tobacco – there were plans to release special Small Faces edition smoking pipes and pipe tobacco]. Everybody said what a great idea. It took time and it took money. We actually invented the machine at the printers to make the sleeve around the world because there was no other machine [that] could do it. We used it twice [Immediate released the commentary of the 1968 European Cup Final between Benfica and Manchester United in a round sleeve made to look like a football]. The sleeve was a fantastic idea, that's what sold the record.

Ogdens' Nut Gone Flake, *the Small Faces third studio album proper, was released in late May 1968. Marriott and Lane had written the bulk of the twelve songs and were credited as producers. The album sold 20,000 copies on the first day of its release, entering the UK charts at No 9. Seven days later it was at No 1 and stayed there for six weeks, remaining in the Top 10 for nineteen weeks. The band showcased the album on one of the first editions of a new half-hour BBC 2 pop show,* Colour Me Pop, *with each show devoted to one act. Ken Mewis recalled bribing BBC personnel with electrical goods – a TV and fridge – to secure the booking. Immediate also promoted the album with controversial print adverts that bastardised the Lord's Prayer, creating yet more hubris around the album release. Ultimately, in a year that saw the release of the Stones'* Beggars Banquet, *The Beatles'* White Album *and Jimi Hendrix's* Electric Ladyland, Ogdens' Nut Gone Flake *would be voted 'the album of the year' by* NME, *with many other critics concurring.*

**Paul Banes:** But the sales figures weren't what you think. We did 90,000 in the UK. *Sgt. Pepper's* only did 150,000. We weren't talking about selling millions of records.

*In Europe Ogdens' was also a huge smash, selling an estimated 110,000 in Germany, but, predictably in America, the world's largest music market, it was a flop, reaching just No 159, selling just 25,000 (many said to be on import from the UK). CBS had also – to the increasing chagrin of Oldham and Calder – redesigned the album sleeve and released album track 'Mad John' as a single.*

**Paul Banes:** There was a bit of a screaming match.

*'Mad John' did nothing in America. The band would not be touring there, resigned now to the fact that unlike many of their contemporaries they would not be enjoying the fruits of American success. Instead they played a smattering of shows in Europe and a disappointing, small UK tour over the summer.*

**Steve Marriott:** We tried to do some of *Ogdens'* live and it sounded awful... we should have sussed it all out if we had only used our brains. We could have taken Stanley Unwin on tour with us, maybe a string section as well, and it would have been okay. But we didn't... at the time I couldn't see how we could follow *Ogdens'*. That's when I thought it's got to be over.

**Kenney Jones:** Nothing had changed. The girls were still screaming, ripping at our clothes. Not listening to the music. We were still a teenybop band. Even after *Ogdens'* we hadn't shaken off the image. The realisation began to sink in that we would never do so. Steve was incredibly fed up at that point. He hated us still being labelled as a pop band... everyone was deathly sick of the whole teenybop image.

*Marriott found it difficult to express a solution to the dissatisfaction he clearly felt toward the band. Jones thought that perhaps the huge success of Ogdens' had overwhelmed and exhausted him, and he was frightened of attempting to write its successor. Marriott's frustrations, and perhaps aspirations, were spelled out clearly when he insisted on releasing, as the follow-up to the band's biggest ever single, a song he had recorded on his own in the garden at Jerome Cottage on a cassette player! It was a sign of Oldham's increasing disinterest in events at Immediate that he allowed this to happen when all logic suggested 'Lazy Sunday' should be followed with another track from Ogdens' – 'Afterglow' or 'Song Of A Baker' had both been flagged up as potential singles. Instead, 'The Universal', a low-key acoustic strum-along, was readied for release.*

**Ian McLagan:** Steve was becoming more and more self-centred. I'm not even on 'The Universal'. He was moving away from us. I love Steve but he was a pain in the neck to be around. He was very, very intense, the most hyper guy I've ever met. He didn't need any leapers. He was always like that. I mean, you'd go to bed and it was like, whew! 'Lazy Sunday' embarrassed him but Steve was a music hall kind of guy, Lionel Bart's Artful Dodger, and in a way he was perfect for that. But he'd decided he wanted to be Jimi Hendrix, Pete Townshend and Muddy Waters.

**Steve Marriott:** 'The Universal', great song. I thought it was the best lyrics I ever wrote... just the word associations, the way it worked out. I needed all of ten minutes for it. I just woke up and thought, we are the universal – it was such a beautiful day, the sun was out, the wind was blowing... I wrote it about how I felt at that moment... and recorded it in my back garden. The dog was barking, you can hear my missus on there... *Ogdens'* was rather contrived, a metallic thing born out of living in the city. Living out here we are writing more country music with bottleneck and lots of acoustic guitar. To me, all those things like 'Lazy Sunday', 'Itchycoo Park' and *Ogdens' Nut Gone Flake* were all right in the terms of a good pop record but they were a substitute for anything with any kind of feeling. Those sort of songs eased the strain of thinking I've got to write something or sing something real good.

*Released in June 1968, 'The Universal' peaked at UK No 16. Reviews were mixed at best – one suggesting the song was 'an ill-timed catastrophe'. Marriott spoke of aiming for 'the most terrible production' and 'a really evil sound' and was forced to deny the song was a send-up of Don Partridge – the one-man-band novelty act, king of the buskers, who was in the charts with 'Blue Eyes' that month. He then cancelled all promotional TV and radio dates.*

**Tony Calder:** 'The Universal' was the end of the band. We had got them to a level where the pre-sale was big. We were coming off 'Lazy Sunday', a No 1 record, but the band wouldn't promote it. They didn't do the TV stuff plus radio didn't like it.

*The single sold disappointingly in Europe, reaching No 35 in Germany and No 12 in the Netherlands. It peaked at No 37 in Australia. Forget America.*

*It became clear now that Marriott was more than just unhappy with the image of the band. In a case of history repeating itself, he now felt the Small Faces' finances were being mismanaged. Immediate had told the band, due to excessive recording and living costs, they were £10,000 in debt.*

**Paul Banes:** No one was stitching them up, I can tell you that for a fact. I did all the royalty statements.

**Tony Calder:** The Small Faces were earning the money but they were always taking money, which we would put against their royalty account. One year we got a bill for dog food for 400 quid. If you've got a guy like Steve Marriott, he goes into a shop to buy a pair of shoes, he says, 'I like them, what other colours you got? Four other colours? Right, I'll have them all, sixty pairs, send the bill to the office.' So you get a bill for £1,500. So that's a charge on their royalty account. You book them a car to go up and down for a TV show, it gets back to London at midnight, the car is finally handed back at eight o'clock the next morning. They've used that car to go round every club, picked their parents up, dropped them off at work in the morning. What are we going to do; are we paying for that, no. You put that on their charge.

**Ian McLagan:** There were [big] bills from music stores [too]… we messed ourselves up. We got into the habit of living well and didn't want to change; we always used Daimler hire cars.

*Marriott thought that the contract Immediate had inherited from Arden was now coming to an end and began to agitate for a new record deal [and advance] – if not with Immediate than with one of a number of labels who would likely be interested in a band fresh from scoring a huge No 1 album.*

**Steve Marriott:** Immediate wanted us to re-sign and we wouldn't at the time. We wanted so much dough to re-sign…

**Ian McLagan:** Tony Calder told us we owed Immediate the money they paid to sign the band and we never got clear, so we never got money or royalties…

**Steve Marriott:** Immediate bought our contract for £25,000 and it was our thing to pay them back... then they pulled an option on us [an option clause written into the Small Faces/Immediate contract that gave Immediate the right to extend the length of their deal with the band] so they said we were still under contract. That was what the dispute was over. They didn't tell us they had an option.

*To placate Marriott, Immediate Music paid him a £10,000 advance on the publishing monies he was owed for the songs he had written and placed with Avakak/Immediate Music. McLagan and Jones were furious Marriott took the money when they felt it should have gone four ways.*

**Kenney Jones:** It was £12,000 not £10,000 and it went to Steve and Ronnie, being principal songwriters. That's when we were renegotiating [our contract] with Immediate. Mac and I were incredibly hurt we were left out of that advance because it was the Small Faces who got that advance not Steve and Ronnie, the Small Faces... and it was quite a lot of money in those days [the equivalent of £120,000]. It caused the first major argument we'd had as a band. We only found out after the deal was signed... the cash should have been split four ways. I left the Small Faces with £800 in my bank account.

**Ian McLagan:** Steve got a lump sum up front for his publishing [from Immediate Music] to buy a house but when I tried to get £800 as a deposit on a £8,000 Georgian double-fronted house on a couple of acres in Fyfield, Essex, I couldn't get it, there was no money there for me.

**Victor Gersten:** They weren't being paid and in the end I kicked up a row with Immediate and they then gave Steve Marriott £10,000, with which he bought the place out in Essex. I was instrumental in getting him that money.

*Marriott's new home was the secluded Beehive Cottage, Moreton, near Ongar, Essex, about twenty miles out from the north-east of London. A picture-book thatched cottage set in several acres, Marriott planned on building a recording studio in a large outbuilding there.*

**Steve Marriott:** I asked Andrew to lend me £1,200 so that I could finish off the completion of buying this [new] house and he said, 'Yeah, if you'll get the rest of the band to sign for two more years... and I can keep your publishing.' I said, 'Goddammit Andrew, I can't do that,' and [the Small Faces new booking agent] Arthur Howes lent it to me. We went with a thing [for management] called Shillingford Lamm – they owned a place in Marlow, where we were staying – they were an advertising firm making TV commercials and they said, 'We'll manage you.' We didn't know what to do, we were kind of lost.

**Ian McLagan:** We were basically fucked and we didn't have any money... we didn't have any idea what was going on... Andrew was our manager, our record company boss and our publisher *and* he was higher than we were.

*Arthur Howes, who had promoted British tours for Cliff Richard and The Beatles, had not lent Marriott the money for nothing – he mapped out a large-scale end-of-year European and UK tour for the Small Faces followed by tours of America, Japan and Australia in early 1969. In September 1968, the band went out on a handful of dates in UK with Canned Heat, whose 'On The Road Again' had been a Top 10 hit. The Small Faces had decided to try and augment their onstage sound with additional musicians, including 'Speedy' Acquaye on congas and trumpeter Eddie 'Tan Tan' Thornton.*

**Kenney Jones:** All of a sudden, we were fucking great. That sound, I would have liked to continue with.

**Ronnie Lane:** There was a half-assed attempt to present [ourselves with] Georgie Fame's brass section. So we got into it all right, but this turned out to be so bloody expensive and people were still screaming so we gave up on it.

**Jenny Dearden:** Once we arrived at Beehive, after a few months settling in, Ronnie and Sue moved in. There was the barn, the old stable, and it had to be converted to a certain extent... a bit of work was done and they moved in there. It was above the double garage... and that's what ultimately became the studio.

**Kenney Jones:** Beehive was bought with the publishing advance, and Ronnie got the raw end of the deal because in Beehive Cottage there was garage with a flat above it and Ronnie got that and Steve got the cottage.

**Sue Tacker:** We started converting the barn into our own home but that's when the falling out between Steve and Ronnie started. I guess Steve didn't give Ronnie enough credit in the writing and Ronnie not having a pushy personality… you could sense that there was an issue about who got the credit for what. They would have horrible arguments over that kind of stuff… they were very different personalities. Steve was very outgoing and flamboyant. Ronnie was more sensitive and inward, very deep and very caring.

**Jenny Dearden:** At the time you're in a bubble, but in retrospect Steve and Ronnie began to grow apart when Ronnie got into Meher Baba. That was Pete Townshend and Mike McInnerney, a graphic designer, and in the end Ronnie left Sue for Mike's wife, Kate… so that was the most terrible time. All these terrible things were happening. Ronnie was quite difficult too. There was all that about peace and love and let's rise above it all but both he and Steve were quite ambitious and had egos… and probably anyone who worked with Steve, inevitably, there would be niggles of resentment because Steve was such a big personality and had such a big voice so he got more attention whether he wanted it or not, and some of the time he did and some of the time he didn't.

# CHAPTER 7

# Natural Born Bugie

**Steve Marriott:** My mother phoned me and said, 'You didn't win your Battle Of The Giants [end of year poll in *Rave* magazine]. Whatever will happen?' Well the world won't end, for sure! Eighteen months ago I worried about the next move and the next day. Now I say, 'Great, man, let it come and we'll see.' It's fun not knowing what's going to happen. I used to think so hard about things that I felt my head was going to split! We've been through the phony scene of being the four little Mods for the public. We were just four ordinary geezers having to pretend we're pop stars. Now we've stopped pretending anything. We recorded rubbish like 'My Mind's Eye' because we knew it was commercial and it would sell. Now we can afford to do what we like.

*Marriott was increasingly doing as he pleased. In September, he'd got away from the screaming at Small Faces gigs and toured Scotland as a guest with the 40-year-old 'Godfather of British blues', Alexis Korner. Fans at these shows listened intently and applauded musicianship not bum wiggles.*

**Keith Altham:** This was miles away from the Small Faces... Steve's friendship and admiration for Alexis went a very long way towards him leaving the Small Faces.

*There was a growing apprehension among the Small Faces as a rumour spread that Marriott was considering forming a new band with The Herd's 18-year-old pop pin-up guitarist/singer Peter Frampton, who* Rave *magazine, in January 1968, had put on their cover, declaring 'This is the big pop face of 1968.' Marriott said he was only helping Frampton put a new heavier band together but it was clear he was also harbouring hopes Lane, Jones and McLagan might consider having The Herd man join the Small Faces. Marriott had been tipped off about Frampton's talent as a musician by Pete Townshend and taken the guitarist under his wing in mid-1968, using him as a guest musician on a July 1968 Skip Bifferty single, 'Man In Black', that he and Lane had produced for RCA Victor. Psych-rock beat band Skip Bifferty were managed by Don Arden (more of which shortly). Marriott had since made several derogatory references to The Herd, who had scored two major hits in 1967 with 'From The Underworld' and 'Paradise Lost', while praising Frampton, in the press. In October 1968, it was rumoured he had been involved in the production of a new Herd single, 'Sunshine Cottage', co-written by Peter Frampton, and Immediate had sounded out the viability of signing The Herd, with plans for Marriott to produce the band.*

**Steve Marriott:** When I heard him [Frampton] play I couldn't understand why he was in such a group. People only have to hear him play to know where he's at. I don't want to be rude to Pete or The Herd but he was in a Mickey Mouse band.

**Peter Frampton:** I was a huge Small Faces fan. Steve and Ronnie had long assumed the role of house producers [for the Small Faces and other Immediate acts at Olympic] and they saw in The Herd an ideal opportunity to further everyone's career. Anyway, we went along there and really hit it off with Steve and Ronnie.

**Steve Marriott:** He came over and he wanted advice on leaving The Herd. We were playing stuff he had never heard because he was a young boy... gave him a few joints, he didn't smoke them, and played him a few sounds. He'd never heard of Booker T. & The M.G.'s... it was like opening up a flower. I thought he was great.

*The move did not go down well with the Double-R Production, run by Steve Rowland and Ronnie Oppenheimer, who owned The Herd's recording contract via a deal with the band's managers and songwriters Ken Howard and Alan Blaikley – the team behind hugely successful novelty pop act Dave Dee, Dozy, Beaky, Mick & Tich.*

**Steve Rowland:** I had a problem with Peter Frampton: he didn't want to sing 'I Don't Want Our Loving To Die' [the band's biggest hit, released March 1968, reaching UK No 5]. I talked him into doing it. I said, 'You're the "Face of '68" and everybody's going to go mad for this track.' He didn't want to be out front singing the lead as if it was Peter Frampton & The Herd but finally he said okay and he was very good at it and that's the first time he ever sang on a record. He was a very good guitar player, very pretty boy, right in line to be a big star. At the same time he was very friendly with Steve Marriott, and The Herd, as a whole, were unhappy even though we gave them three hits. They wanted to be credible. What we were doing was too pop. They would complain, just whinging. It got worse as time went on. They didn't like what Howard and Blaikley were writing so they wrote 'Sunshine Cottage' [themselves], which didn't do anything.

**Peter Frampton:** I'd been pushed to the front in The Herd and had become a 'mini-sensation' but it wasn't the audience I craved. Steve told me I should do something else because I was wasting my time with The Herd. He said, 'I've got this drummer that every now and again, if Kenney's ill or something, we use called Jerry.' I met up with Jerry [Shirley] and we enjoyed working together and were soon looking for a bass player and guitarist.

**Jerry Shirley:** Steve introduced me to Peter because Peter wanted a drummer that sounded like Kenney Jones.

**Steve Rowland:** Peter was getting more and more aloof and he didn't want to be around the office after he met Marriott. When you're young and want to get someplace, and you're unhappy with what you're doing and you talk to somebody who's doing something you really want to do... and then that person says, 'Look, play your cards right, I can get you out of your deal, I'll get you into this, we can form a group.' It's a natural thing. I'm sure that's what happened. Andrew Oldham took the guys [The Herd] round in his car and told them what they were going to do. They were trying to get Peter out of his contract with us. Peter's parents got involved. I don't know what happened in the end... it was Ronnie Oppenheimer, my partner, and Andrew Oldham who did the deal for Peter to go with Steve. He did all the business side of it...

Ronnie wasn't a bad guy, he was a financier; after the situation with The Herd happened I couldn't stick with him, things started to get a little tense.

*On 12 October 1968, it was reported that police were investigating gunshots at Marriott's Beehive Cottage: shotgun pellets were dug out of a first floor bedroom window frame. There had been a similar incident two weeks earlier.*

**Jenny Dearden:** At the time, because of much paranoia, we suspected that we were being warned off talking to the *News of the World* relating to a major front-page exposé about Don Arden. Graham Bell [Skip Bifferty's vocalist] had been staying with us and he was a focal point of the article. On the other hand, we were regarded with some suspicion by the locals, especially the younger ones. I had to take one of our cats to the vet because he was peppered with air-gun pellets.

*The same month, Frampton joined the Small Faces on stage for gigs in Manchester and Essex. 'The Small Faces and The Herd are simply good friends,' Frampton told the press. 'I went to Manchester to see the group and I was persuaded to sit in with them.' Marriott added: 'Peter and I are good mates and we thought it would be a bit of a loon if he played with us that night.' These gigs were noted for their heavier rock sound on tracks such as 'Rollin' Over' (from Ogdens') and new Marriott song 'Wham Bam Thank You Mam' (the same title as Charles Mingus track on Oh Yeah and a phrase used by Dr John as a lyric in 'Mama Roux' on the GRIS-gris album).*

**Steve Marriott:** I played Ronnie 'Wham Bam Thank You Mam' and he said, 'Cor, it's a bit heavy, innit,' giving me the needle. I said, 'Of course it's fucking heavy'... we still recorded it and in a way it was getting into Humble Pie direction. I thought it was a good idea to get Peter Frampton in and have another guitarist, get a fresh start, and he was a very good guitarist, not for what he looked like, a pretty face, which was being put about, but because he was an excellent player. I just wasn't satisfied with my live playing. I'd lost something in the studio... forgotten how to do it live. It just seemed a great idea to have another guitarist, give me a chance to sing properly and maybe get us out of doing that same vein we were still in live since the day we started... the others were dead against it. The reaction was terrible. It just didn't go down well. Ronnie didn't want it. No one wanted it. We were beginning to hate the sight of one another, we rowed constantly over niggly little things...

**Ian McLagan:** Maybe Steve was already leaving... a lot of people used to think of us as being Steve Marriott's backing group. We tended to think so as well. Frampton sat in with the band a couple of times. I don't know what Steve wanted. Steve was like twenty miles ahead of you. That's when I first thought, well, Christ, I want to play live but not the way I feel about it now... We constantly had to shout him down because he often had bad ideas like this.

**Ronnie Lane:** I felt Peter Frampton was an intrusion and he was. Steve got frightened by many things. He was insecure about his talent, although I don't see why he should be. If anyone had a whole lot of talent, it was him.

**Kenney Jones:** I loved Peter Frampton when he played and sang but everyone was trying to rally round Steve, saying, 'Why? We don't need another singer, we're happy with you.' We were paying him a compliment but he was taking it the wrong way. He wanted another singer in there so he could concentrate on playing more lead guitar. We were all wanting to get better... but Steve was such an impatient guy it had to happen straight away, he was incredibly spoilt like that. We should have found a way to overcome those issues.

*After a few European gigs, and a handful of November UK tour dates with The Who, Arthur Brown and Joe Cocker, including at the Roundhouse in London, the Small Faces began recording for a proposed follow-up to Ogdens'. Other than 'Wham Bam Thank You Mam', there was precious little in the way of new, finished Marriott/Lane material. The band toyed with covers of two Tim Hardin songs, 'Red Balloon' and 'If I Were A Carpenter', The Band's 'Long Black Veil', Brenda Holloway's 'Every Little Bit Hurts', Lonnie Mack's 1963 classic 'Why?' (the original rated as one of the great rock'n'roll vocals) and Smokey Robinson & The Miracles' 'You Really Got A Hold On Me'.*

**Ian McLagan:** When we were doing those sessions at Olympic Steve was too pushy and I said, 'Fuck you, I'm leaving'... and the motherfucker got Nicky Hopkins in to play piano… he said he was sorry about anything he did or said to upset me, but if I did leave, I wasn't to worry as he could get Nicky any time I walked out… he was hard to live with and so hyperactive that sometimes in the studio he'd suggest an idea, ask you what you thought of it and then decide it was rubbish, all before you had a chance to say or do anything. It gave you no time to think for yourself and eventually it wore me out.

**Steve Marriott:** I was quite an overwhelming person both in the studio and out of it. If I didn't like the way someone was playing something I'd go and play it myself. So that was the vibe… They'd say, 'Well, you fucking play it,' and I would.

*These were the end days for the Small Faces. Also recording in Olympic, in December 1968, was Lamborghini-driving French rock'n'roll superstar Johnny Hallyday. He was making his twelfth studio album, Rivière… Ouvre Ton Lit, under the musical direction of his long-time guitarist, 24-year-old Mick Jones, and drummer Tommy Brown. The pair had often in the past enrolled the cream of English session players such as Jimmy Page and Big Jim Sullivan for Hallyday albums. Glyn Johns, who was involved in engineering the Hallyday sessions at Olympic, was also booked to complete the album in Paris. It was he who suggested taking the Small Faces to the city to back Hallyday.*

**Steve Marriott:** He offered us a lot of dough and we did his album and a few TVs [TV appearances]. I took Peter Frampton with me… it was the best we sounded. We unloaded some songs on him [Hallyday], songs from way back like 'That Man' [from 1967] and some new ones that I'd just begun to write which appeared on the first Humble Pie album, 'What You Will' and 'Buttermilk Boy'…

*The Hallyday album has since been voted by* Rolling Stone *magazine as the sixth best French rock album ever. Marriott/Lane were credited with three songs on the album: 'Amen', 'Réclamation' and 'Regarde Pour Moi'.*

**Steve Marriott:** I kept asking the others if Peter could stay because I thought he made great improvements to the band. Anyway, they all hated it and that was a big downer.

**Peter Frampton:** Steve intimated to me he'd like me to join the band. He'd been helping me put a band together with Jerry Shirley. The Herd by this time had finally collapsed. The Oldham/Calder thing had failed to work out.

**Glyn Johns:** A great argument happened and the shit hit the fan.

**Kenney Jones:** Peter was great in the studio, a joy to watch up close... but when Steve announced he was going to ask Peter to join the band, Ronnie and Mac went mad, refusing to even consider the idea.

*The band returned from Paris to play a New Year's Eve gig at London's Alexandra Palace.*

**Steve Marriott:** That was the night we'd come back from Paris. The gig was so bad. The sound was appalling. The whole set was diabolical. No one was looking at each other, they were in their own little universe, it was a shambles really. Alexis [Korner] got up to play, it was my idea but I didn't think it was going to be that much of a shambles... I thought, this is terrible, I slung my guitar down and walked off. It wasn't even finished... it was very unprofessional of me, I know, but I couldn't handle it. I just blew up.

**Jenny Dearden:** I didn't know what was happening, he never discussed it with me. He was very impulsive.

**Steve Marriott:** I thought, sod it. What am I doing? I've got to do something else myself. Frampton's unhappiness [with The Herd] made me feel I had to get out of the depressive rut I was getting into. You grow apart. You're talking about people living together from the ages of 17 to 22 and that's a growing up part of life.

**Kenney Jones:** Alexis was someone we looked up to, a British version of Muddy Waters, and we were honoured that he was willing to play with the band... but Steve asked Alexis to accompany us on absolutely the worst song imaginable, 'Lazy Sunday'... there was this almighty scream-up afterwards. Mac went mad. Steve just simply said he couldn't do it anymore. He felt we couldn't cross over from being a pop band into heavier music. I don't think any of us really forgave Steve. It hurt.

**Ronnie Lane:** It was a surprise to me when Steve said he was leaving. We were certainly in a lot of financial trouble... but I thought we were going to concentrate on getting out of that situation.

**Ian McLagan:** Steve wanted Peter in the band. We didn't. So he quit. He told us he was leaving there in the dressing room. Steve said he was forming a group with Peter. He felt, after 'Lazy Sunday', we were becoming a joke band. I was devastated but it was worse for Ronnie, his best friend and writing partner.

**Steve Marriott:** Ronnie lived in this barn at the back of me and that made it embarrassing. He was moving out but it took about three months, which was awful because there was all this bad feeling... he couldn't understand why I had to go. I don't think Ronnie believed me, as close as we were, he thought I was just pulling a moody. When he realised that I definitely did want out, he didn't talk to me for a long time...

**Jerry Shirley:** They had an advance from Immediate in both their names to buy Beehive and when Ronnie tried to get some compensation for it Steve just turned around and said, 'You'll get nothing, this was bought with money from the hits I wrote not we wrote.' Steve actually produced a PRS [Performing Right Society – a collecting body for publishing income; money is earned whenever a song is publicly performed, or recordings of songs are broadcast, streamed or played in public places in the UK and globally] that showed a list of all the hit songs they had. He underlined all the biggest hits, and said, 'I wrote these so you get nothing.'

**Peter Frampton:** 1 January 1969 – I was in Paris with Glyn Johns listening to a pre-release of Led Zeppelin's debut album. The phone rang. Steve said, 'I've just walked off stage and left the Small Faces, can I join your band?'

**Jerry Shirley:** My first reaction was, what about the Small Faces? I was a huge fan. But Marriott was adamant. Then he said, 'By the way, I've got a bass player, Greg Ridley, who wants to come with me.' He was the most respected bassist in all of England through Spooky Tooth, as far as American funk-style playing was concerned.

*Spooky Tooth had developed under the influence of Island Records boss Chris Blackwell from the ashes of the band Art, who Marriott had previously recorded with. When Art broke up, four of the five surviving members, including Greg Ridley, had joined forces with American Gary Wright and formed Spooky Tooth. They had recorded two albums with Stones, Blind Faith and Traffic producer Jimmy Miller for Island (that had failed to chart) and were on the bill at Alexandra Palace the night Marriott quit the Small Faces. Ridley was originally from Carlisle, Cumbria, in north-west England, just ten miles south of Scotland. Jerry Shirley called him 'tough but sweet'. He had dated Sandy Sarjeant before she married McLagan. He was older than Marriott by at least three years, possibly five – he was coy about his real birthdate, best placed at 1942.*

**Greg Ridley:** We were both pissed off. We'd realised we'd both reached a peak. Bitchiness had come into the various bands. Steve said, 'Do you want to join a band?' And I said, 'Yeah, I'm ready for a change.' With his energy... he was a real livewire and that's what got me interested. Spooky Tooth was a kind of a heavy, underground type of band, a band's band rather than a pop group.

**Steve Marriott:** It wasn't a planned thing. Greg said he wouldn't join unless I did. I'd literally formed the band for Peter. I wasn't involved beyond finding him the personnel. I thought it was going to be great so about two weeks later I rang Pete up and asked if I could join. There was a long silence and he said, 'I'll have to think about it.'

**Jenny Dearden:** Steve respected Greg. He was a macho Cumbrian, he was quite stable and he kept an eye on Steve.

*Frampton has suggested that, in this fractious period, Lane, Jones and McLagan backtracked and were prepared to acquiesce to Marriott's demands he join the Small Faces. It was too late, but McLagan was considered for Marriott's new line-up and even wrote a song with Frampton that would appear on Humble Pie's debut album. Contractually Marriott was forced to perform again with the Small Faces on a few German dates in January 1969. He was said to be in a foul mood, thrown out of one hotel after smashing a painting over a cleaning maid's head.*

*In February, as rumour swirled over Marriott's future, Tony Calder told the press, 'I have heard the rumour but I don't know whether the Faces are splitting yet. One minute they are getting on fine. The next they are talking about going their separate ways. I do know though that the other three are getting a bit uptight about the Peter Frampton thing.' Marriott said, 'How could I ever exist outside the band? And I'm not one for two-timing.' Frampton, Ridley, Shirley and Marriott were, however, already rehearsing – jamming on cover versions such The Band's 'We Can Talk' – and eager to make themselves public.*

**Peter Frampton:** We all enjoyed playing with one another. It was like being released from all our other bands. And it was like raw energy.

**Jerry Shirley:** Steve wanted us to be like The Band, where they're sharing vocals and playing musical chairs, instrument-wise. That's what we were trying to do in the beginning. Humble Pie was Steve's choice of name for the band. Island Records made a stab at it. So did Track Records. Andrew had the advantage of having Steve signed. So, if he wanted to be a bitch about it, he could have put his foot down and said, 'Well, you're signing with me anyway,' but he didn't approach it like that. He wasn't the enemy. He came up and stood at the plate and said, 'I want this, I want to do this.' There were other managers at the time [interested in the band]; Kit Lambert was one of them. Andrew just came up and said, 'I'll do this. However you want to do it, whenever you want to do it, let's go to bat.'

**Andrew Loog Oldham:** Tony Calder said to me one day, 'Pick a straw.' Then he explained we had a choice. We could either go with the three Faces – Kenney, Ronnie and Mac – wherever they were going to go with their lives or we could follow Stevie. I didn't regard it as a choice. Neither did Tony. Marriott was our man.

**Tony Calder:** For me, it was all about Steve. He had a heart of gold. He'd come into the office, 'Tone, I got to get a new guitar.' 'What happened to the last one?' 'I saw some bloke and I gave him my favourite guitar.' 'Why?' 'Because he didn't have one.'

**Steve Marriott:** I asked Andrew what he thought of me and Peter playing together because I was broke. We were all broke... and I couldn't get out of that contract. The accounts were still outstanding... we were left with bills we thought we'd paid off years ago. I told Andrew what I was doing, that I couldn't handle this [the Small Faces] anymore. I had a lot of pressure not to do it [quit the band] because it was not good in a business way.

**Peter Frampton:** The business and financial disasters that had precipitated the band's demise were still churning behind the scenes as Humble Pie got started.

**Jerry Shirley:** We were making £60 a week when we signed with Immediate. And that was big money back then [about £950 in today's money]. We got all the equipment we wanted. We got the road crew we wanted. We got the truck we wanted. We got all the recording time we wanted... you name it – we had it. It was the equivalent of an advance. If you add it all up, it amounted to quite a bit of money.

**Greg Ridley:** It was the first time I'd ever seen any money in my life through playing rock'n'roll.

*In March 1969, Immediate released a final Small Faces single, 'Afterglow Of Your Love' (from* Ogdens'*) and the Small Faces played a final show in Jersey. With no real support from the band or label, 'Afterglow' peaked at UK No 36, and Marriott officially announced the Small Faces split, saying he 'had to get away from being labelled a dirty pop group for teen screams'. In April, Humble Pie were unveiled via a front-page story in* Melody Maker *under the headline 'Pop Giants Supergroup: Steve Marriott–Peter Frampton Tie-Up'. It told how the pair, 'two of Britain's biggest pop idols', had been secretly rehearsing for weeks. Marriott said he was hoping to avoid the 'old pop star bit' with his new group and described the band's sound as 'strong-arm music'.*

**Chris Welch:** After that disastrous Alexandra Palace gig, it seemed like a rescue... from the ashes of two groups, a great idea. It was Andrew and Immediate's idea to call them a supergroup... there had been a huge development with heavy rock bands becoming popular, including Spooky Tooth, who were a well-respected band. Things seemed to move quickly... one minute it's all screaming teenyboppers and the next minute it's serious rock music.

*It was easy to forget Marriott had only just turned 22. Frampton celebrated his 19th birthday in April, Shirley his 17th in February. Ridley, the old man of the group, was still only 27.*

**Steve Marriott:** There was so much pressure. I was really at the point of mental breakdown. We wanted to come in the back door but the media wouldn't let us.

**Peter Frampton:** Steve was going through a period of dreadful self-doubt... he had even given up songwriting temporarily and in the beginning pushed me to the front. He just wanted to stand behind me and get really stoned and just play along.

**Jerry Shirley:** It was Peter's band, more so than it was Steve's, in the early days. Really Steve just wanted to see Greg and Peter shine more than himself.

**Jenny Dearden:** Steve had been burned so badly with the Small Faces and he'd obviously thought about it a lot and he said he didn't want to be the frontman anymore... and the music was much quieter, a lot of acoustic stuff, that's what he wanted to focus on, he wanted to explore that other side of himself that he hadn't been allowed to do prior to that. He didn't want to be this bombastic frontman with this loud amazing voice and he wanted to share the frontman position with Peter.

*Rehearsals took place at Magdalen Laver Village Hall in Ongar, close to Marriott's Beehive Cottage. Humble Pie also recorded material here, with a mobile studio and brass section, cutting a version of Ray Charles's 'Drown In My Own Tears'. There was talk now of Brian Jones, who had recently left the Stones, joining Humble Pie. Marriott and Jones shared a mutual friend in Alexis Korner.*

**Jerry Shirley:** Brian Jones was going to come down and jam with Humble Pie to see if he could join the band but he chose to go for a late night swim instead. Sad but true. [Jones drowned in the swimming pool at his home in July 1969, aged 27.]

*As work began in earnest on a debut album, Immediate booked Humble Pie time at Olympic and the relatively new Morgan Studios in north-west London, where Blind Faith, Free and Led Zeppelin all recorded.*

**Jerry Shirley:** We recorded all of the material for the first two albums within no more than two months. Oldham would be in the studio on a regular basis. Steve and Peter were determined to make the band as equal as possible in every way, especially in the songwriting.

**Peter Frampton:** We had limitless recording time. We were just forever recording. It was great. It was anything goes, when we first formed. We were almost too diversified to get a handle of what we did.

**Steve Marriott:** We did [debut album] *As Safe As Yesterday Is* and [second Humble Pie album] *Town And Country* before the first was released. Delays, delays… I don't know why.

*Marriott did know why. The Herd's production company, Double-R, had placed an injunction on Immediate to prevent them releasing any music featuring Frampton until they had settled on a figure to release Frampton from his contract with them. The legal wrangling went on for weeks. Immediate was now in perilous financial straits, due to profligate spending and Oldham's profound lack of interest in the label's current crop of groups, such as The Nice, Fleetwood Mac and Amen Corner. An overworked Calder was scrambling to attract new talent, discussing deals with Scott Walker and Status Quo, hoping to record his way out of trouble. Marriott, and Humble Pie, however, reignited a passion in Oldham and he fronted money from his own pocket to buy out Frampton's contract for a figure said to be $24,000 ($170,000 in today's money).*

**Peter Frampton:** I remember being bought and sold. I believe that Andrew had to buy me from Ronnie Oppenheimer.

**Tony Calder:** We had to buy Peter Frampton out of his contract for £30,000 or some ridiculous price.

*The injunction was lifted in August 1969. Oldham had chosen the song to lauch the band and Immediate had Humble Pie's debut single, 'Natural Born Bugie', ready for release. It was produced — as was all early-period Humble Pie — by 20-year-old Andy Johns, the younger brother of Glyn Johns, who had engineered for a succession of heavy rock acts such as Led Zeppelin, Blind Faith, Jethro Tull and Spooky Tooth. On the single, Frampton, Ridley and Marriott sang a verse each.*

**Jerry Shirley:** Andrew had a remarkable knack back then of spotting a hit single. The song was a throwaway that Steve came up with, a direct rip-off from [Chuck Berry's] 'Little Queenie'. He wanted to record it as a comedy song, with a bunch of Indian and Pakistani guys singing 'natural born woman' on the chorus in their heavy accents. He even went so far as to go out on the streets of Willesden [where Morgan Studios was located] and recruit a cross-section of the local Asian community and have them come to the studio to record the repeat chorus.

**Steve Marriott:** The single doesn't lay any schmaltz. People have said that they expected something a little more original from us, and there is some justification for that. The next one will be more original. But we never took the song that seriously. It just came to me, as I was sitting on the toilet playing my guitar. I literally wrote the words in ten minutes. They're nothing and the top line is rubbish. But the back track is great and that's more important to me than the vocal track. I've never been so excited about anything as I am about the group.

*The press campaign for Humble Pie was Immediate's biggest, most expensive ever, with full-page adverts in* Record Retailer, Rolling Stone, International Times, Oz, Black Dwarf *and* Time Out, *as well as special posters and window displays for the 140 shops in the WHSmith chain in the UK.*

**Ken Mewis:** Immediate spent huge amounts launching the band. We'd often book *NME* front pages [for adverts] at about £550 a time, they were great for our in-industry image and artists' egos, but the most extravagant was when we bought the front and back pages of the *NME* to launch Humble Pie – we just used a David Bailey photograph of the group with no ID copy or explanation.

*The group performed 'Natural Born Bugie' on* Top Of The Pops *as the single climbed up the charts, peaking at UK No 4.*

**Steve Ellis [Love Affair frontman]:** The story was they were all in the dressing room getting ready to go on and Peter got his hair tongs out and Marriott slapped him round the back of the head, 'You're not in a girlie band now.'

*The single was quickly followed by the band's debut album. It was ingeniously packaged by Immediate in a sleeve made to look as if it were a parcel, wrapped in brown packing paper, tied by string, with the album information written as the address and photos of the band, again by David Bailey, tucked away as mock postage stamps.*

**Steve Marriott:** Andrew had all these concepts for the album cover and I said, 'Fuck it, put it put on a brown paper bag and write Humble Pie on it with a pen.' So they did that and photographed it and that was the cover.

*The album featured a cover of American rock band Steppenwolf's 'Desperation' amongst five self-penned Marriott songs and two by Frampton (only the title track was a co-write between the pair). 'We've done our second album already and it has got a beautiful sound,' Marriott said helpfully while promoting the album, which peaked at a disappointing No 32 in the UK.*

**Jerry Shirley:** There was a lot of expectations but not a lot of record sales.

*The band debuted live at a boozy, Oldham-arranged, press launch/showcase at Ronnie Scott's jazz club in Soho (with Shirley's pal David Gilmour in the audience). With the plaudits flowing they next headed to Europe for festival shows and promotion. Marriott was back on Beat-Club as 'Natural Born Bugie' climbed the German charts to peak at No 20 (the single also reached the Top 10 in the Netherlands and Belgium). The band's early live shows were notable for their mix of gentle acoustic and amplified rock segments.*

**Greg Ridley:** Early on we started doing unplugged stuff, acoustics, sitting on stools, which you never saw. We tried to make it a bit more credible and let them know that we could all play our instruments and make good music without all the screaming. They would all scream at Steve and Peter.

**Jerry Shirley:** To intentionally take away the attention from little girls screaming at Peter because of The Herd, we tried to come off laidback, man. Start slow and easy and drift into this... we did that little acoustic thing just to try and throw them a curve. To calm them down, to force them to listen. We had a group motto which said that the one style musically that we want to develop is no style at all, just anything that we wanted to do.

**Steve Marriott:** We were trying all sorts of things. What we wanted to do was go from acoustic numbers to jazzier things to electric rock numbers and back again. We wanted to do everything we could do.

*Notable cover versions in the set included Dr John's 'I Walk On Gilded Splinters', Ray Charles's 'Hallelujah I Love Her So' and Etta James's 1968 Chess single B-side, 'I Worship The Ground You Walk On', sung solo by Marriott accompanying himself on acoustic guitar.*

**Chris Welch:** Andrew invited me to go to the Netherlands and Belgium with Humble Pie to see them debut their live show. We stayed at the very modern Esso Motor Hotel. The band were walking down to the restaurant and none of them had ties on and the head waiter said, 'I'm sorry you can't come in without a tie on,' and the band went back upstairs, took their shirts off and put ties on... so they were allowed in! Andrew and Steve were always locked in conversation, talking about plans for the band. We drove around in a great big white American Cadillac, chauffeur-driven. There was a bit of tension, the weather was lousy and they were worried about launching this new band and Peter said to me, 'Who's paying for all this?' Talking about the hotel and the big limo... The first gig was dreadful, they were [headlining] at this open-air festival in Bilzen, Belgium [Jazz and Pop Festival, 40,000 people in the crowd, with Deep Purple as main support], pouring with rain, full of Hells Angels. Deep People had tomatoes thrown at them but

Steve battled on, determined to put on a good show. They were much better at the Paradiso in Amsterdam [where they played two nights, now supporting Deep Purple], where everyone was smoking dope quite freely. They were a much heavier rockier band [than the Small Faces].

**Steve Marriott:** At the Paradiso, Andrew was carried out over the shoulder of his chauffeur, Eddie. That sort of sums up the road thing. It was just one big party.

*Promotional copies of a second single, 'The Sad Bag Of Shaky Jake', written by Marriott and taken from upcoming second album* Town And Country, *were sent out to record stations as the band prepared for their debut sell-out UK tour beginning in October. The band was to be supported by Marriott's old pal, David Bowie, who was scoring with his first hit, 'Space Oddity'. Their stage show was set to feature a huge polystyrene elephant that blew smoke from its backside, designed by Oldham's pal Sean Kenny, the revolutionary British theatrical stage designer who had made his name designing the pioneering stage set for* Oliver! *in 1960.*

**Jerry Shirley:** Oldham was very committed to being on the road with us. The other bands on Immediate he was bored with or weren't pulling his chain. He gave us his great big Rolls-Royce [Phantom V] to travel England in, with Eddie driving. That was our tour vehicle. We were still doing a lot of the acoustic stuff as a reaction to all that supergroup publicity. We were trying to say, 'Don't expect too much, give us a chance to grow, we haven't found our niche yet.'

**Steve Marriott:** My missus helped me with the whole changeover scene. You need someone who can give you advice and understands. If Humble Pie hadn't happened, I would have stayed on in the Small Faces, bringing everybody down. I never ever thought I would leave the Small Faces. I thought it would just go on forever. But it feels like Humble Pie has been together for years. I just want to be part of the band and do my job. I don't have to freak out anymore. I can relax and play music.

Town And Country *was released in November. 'A little more contrived but a lot more relaxed,' said Marriott in interviews. 'There's more clarity on it than the first. The first was not representative of what we are doing now. I am really pleased with the second album, much more than the first.' Marriott supplied four of the eleven songs, Frampton contributed two and there were debuts from Jerry Shirley and Greg Ridley and two collaborations between Marriott and the group members, plus a cover of Buddy Holly's 'Heartbeat'.*

*The album failed to chart in the UK, but Humble Pie and Oldham had their sights and hopes set on a far larger market. In November the band began a six-week college tour of America. Advance copies of 'Natural Born Bugie', renamed 'Natural Born Woman' for America, had started to receive airplay throughout the US and made the 'Up and Coming' chart of trade magazine Record World.*

**Jerry Shirley:** The term 'bugie' back then was consider derogatory... we didn't know it at the time but it had the same kind connotations as 'nigger'... we had no idea, we thought it was like 'boogie-woogie'.

*Oldham spent $15,000 on print advertising for the band in America, with elaborate eye-catching adverts in trade bible* Billboard, Cashbox *and* Record World. As Safe As Yesterday Is *picked up glowing reviews.* Billboard *praised 'a strong commercial package and underground-orientated numbers'.* Record World *described the album as 'Head-turning rock'n'roll, a very powerful smile, moving from heavy rock to country funk to poetic folk-jazz, Humble Pie display considerable talent and energy. Keep tabs on this set, they could be big.'*

**Jerry Shirley:** Humble Pie's primary concern, once we got the initial release of the records out in England, was just get to America. That was our total focus.

**Greg Ridley:** England's so small and you've already made your mark from the stuff you'd done before. With all the screams and things it was necessary for the band to have a breath of fresh air and a bigger market. We wanted to able to prove to ourselves that we could actually play and sing for real. Without the hype. To break the States, for an English band, you're doing very well...

*Switched-on American rock fans were keen to finally catch Marriott in the flesh. A new wave of English rock acts such as Blind Faith and Led Zeppelin had begun to draw huge audiences (and command large fees) in the country and*

*Humble Pie were being considered as part of that movement. In fact Led Zeppelin's latest single, their breakthrough hit 'Whole Lotta Love' (released November 1969), owed much to Marriott, being a rip-off of the Small Faces 1966 album track 'You Need Loving', which Marriott had initially taken from Muddy Waters. Robert Plant, the band's singer, had been a Small Faces devotee, and Jimmy Page was also keenly aware of the Small Faces song.*

**Steve Marriott:** I couldn't sing like Muddy Waters so it wasn't that much of a nick by me. I had to make up a lot of my own phrasing. I was a high range and Muddy was a low range so I had to figure out how to sing it. It was our opening number for all the years we were together [in the Small Faces]... after we broke up, they [Led Zeppelin] took it and revamped it. He [Robert Plant] sang it the same as me, phrased it the same as me, even the stops at the end were the same. They just put a different rhythm to it. I would hear it come on the radio while driving in America and I would think, go on my son, until one day I thought, fucking hell, that's us, the bastards. He took it note for note, word for word...

*Reviews of the band's live shows were overwhelmingly positive. A show at the packed Fillmore East in New York, supporting Butterfield Blues Band and Santana, was 'considered one of the happiest pop events of 1969' by influential trade weekly* Cashbox. *'Humble Pie are well on their way to innovative rock stardom... the act begins quietly with a solo song by Pete accompanying himself on acoustic guitar. Greg Ridley then sings his solo with Pete joining him as second guitarist. The non-electric segment ends with Steve singing lead on a Scottish folk song done in three-part harmony. A quick switch to amplification and the group is off on an extended jam of Dr John material, "I Walk On Gilded Splinters" and "Gris-Gris Gumbo Ya Ya". Humble Pie's presentation is much like [folk-rock supergroup] Crosby, Stills, Nash & Young, in that they both feature beautiful and intricate vocals in which different people take over the lead. The music moved from country to blues to real jazz and on to straight rock with an enviable fluidity. And Stevie's guitar work was frighteningly good (frightening because very few people in this country have heard of him). Given six months, with a national tour under its belt, Humble Pie will return to the Fillmore topping the bill.'*

**Steve Marriott:** It was hard work. We came in the back door and had to work our way up, like third on the bill, little dives, but watching great acts [such as] Santana when they first formed and Johnny Winter when he was first having a go. It's the best way we could have done it. We were being called a supergroup at the time and we'd had one hit, and we thought if we carry on like this, there's only one way for us to go and that's down... we literally went to America to break our bones and become a band.

**Paul Banes:** Everyone had been dying to see Steve Marriott. 'Itchycoo Park' sold 500,000 in America and this lad didn't want to get on an aeroplane to promote the record... he was almost a living legend before he got to America. But the tour introduced the band to what it would be like in America: a slog, it really was a slog...

**Jenny Dearden:** They were in New York and Steve rang me up freaking out, saying, 'There's all these girls on the floor of the hotel corridor [hoping to meet a band member], I don't know what to do'... he was almost in tears, he said, 'I can't handle it here.' Some guys would think, oh great, but he didn't like it at all. He wanted me to go out and I did in the end. We stayed in grotty hotels, one in San Francisco with the most hideous waterbed in it. There was no money. When they played the Whisky [a Go Go, in Los Angeles] they complained to Andrew [about the motel accommodation] and we ended up going over to Lou Adler's [Adler, famed for his handling of The Mamas & The Papas, Carole King and Cheech & Chong, among many others, was a close pal of Oldham's]. It was shortly after the Manson murders so the whole of LA had switched virtually overnight from being cool and peace and love to being complete paranoia and terror. [Oldham put the band up in the most exclusive hotel in LA, the Hyatt House on Sunset Boulevard.]

**Paul Banes:** I did the whole tour, going back to the [Immediate American] office in New York when I could. Six and a half weeks on the road with Humble Pie wasn't the easiest thing in the world as we were working on $8 each per day. We picked up the bills for the hotels and everything else. We played with Mountain in Boston, Santana at the Fillmore East [in New York] straight after Woodstock, amazing gig, Philadelphia with [the band] Chicago, a strange gig in Washington with

Neil Diamond, who had just come off 'Sweet Caroline'... we did a couple of gigs with the Moody Blues [Marriott renamed their 'Nights In White Satin' hit 'Tights That I've Shat In'].

**Jerry Shirley:** All the American bands we opened for [on the first tour] were in a class of their own. Chicago were stunning. When the Grateful Dead couldn't get out of Altamont [the Stones' disastrous 1969 free concert], we ended up playing our third show at the Fillmore West as headliners as we were the only band who could get there. At that time there were a number of great rock'n'roll clubs across America that were custom-built for live bands. You would usually play in one of them for two or three or four nights, with at least two shows per night.

**Paul Banes:** After we'd done the Fillmore [West] no one wanted to get back on a plane so we drove down from San Francisco to LA via Big Sur and when we arrived Andrew had already fixed up with Lou Adler to record two concerts [at the Whisky, for a proposed live album]. Andrew was on another planet at that time... he had this concoction he would drink, consommé soup and vodka. He would get out the tin of soup, heat it up, fill up the tin with vodka, tip that in and then we would go out.

*The band was due to play four nights at the Whisky, two shows a night. Dan Crewe, the brother and business partner of acclaimed writer and producer of The Four Seasons, Bob Crewe, was close to Oldham at the time.*

**Dan Crewe:** When Humble Pie were appearing at the Whisky and Oldham was recording them for a live album, he was in the control booth and he overdosed and passed out on the control panel. He was literally dead meat. I was scared to death, I thought he was going to die on me. I spent the next two hours with him draped around my shoulders walking up and down Sunset Boulevard, trying to keep him alive. Everyone knew Oldham by this point, they knew what a problem he was and he was a big problem. He was getting antagonistic in social situations, very apt to throwing tantrums and getting into fights. It was not the kind of thing you would eagerly get involved in.

*This was the end of the road for Immediate Records. The live Humble Pie album cut at the Whisky, featuring covers of The Yardbirds' 'For Your Love' and Johnny Kidd & The Pirates' 'Shakin' All Over', would subsequently be released circa 2002. The demise of the label was precipitated by a number of factors, but significant among them was Oldham's determination to see Humble Pie make it in America. He had spent close to $70,000 (almost $500,000 in today's money) on their American launch. Despite interest and lucrative offers from Atlantic and Bell Records, Immediate had manufactured, distributed and promoted Humble Pie's American single and album independently. Oldham had been forced into the move. He was locked in a lawsuit with CBS, who had, to his surprise, considering the lack of success the CBS/Immediate partnership had enjoyed during the previous two years, decided to exercise an option to extend their US rights to Immediate product for a third year.*

**Paul Banes:** Nobody would touch us because of this legal situation with CBS. Overnight, Oldham had come in and said, 'We're doing it ourselves, get on the phone, call all these independent distributors.' Oldham took out this amazing, quadruple-page spread for Humble Pie in *Billboard*, fucking unreal, the label looked great, the whole thing.

*In quick time, deals had been made with record pressing plants, ten of the biggest and most powerful independent distributors in the US and five independent promotion men (at a cost of $2,000 a month each). CBS, however, hit back, serving a legal action against Immediate and their independent distributors. Tens of thousands of the Humble Pie album Immediate had manufactured specifically for the American market were left to gather dust.*

**Paul Banes:** I came back from the tour [to the Immediate New York office]. I'd left Humble Pie at the airport in LA. It was five days before Christmas. Tony and Andrew are in the middle of a discussion. They told me to go take a walk. I go out and when I come back Tony says, 'We've broken up, I'm leaving, I'm going to Antigua for Christmas.' He explained, 'I'm keeping the house in Antigua, Andrew's keeping the house in Connecticut. Bye.'

**Tony Calder:** Andrew didn't want to listen to anybody. He just wanted to get rid of everything. He bought me out neatly within twenty-four hours. It was done privately; the money didn't come out of Immediate.

All the Immediate properties didn't come out of Immediate, they came out of the Stones' income.

*Oldham put Immediate into liquidation. United Artists were demanding the $175,000 they were owed under the 1967 debenture deal that had, ironically, been struck to allow Immediate to sign to CBS. Oldham's personal finances were in a disastrous shape – he was facing a $600,000 ($4 million in today's money) personal tax bill on his Stones income – and he was advised it was no longer viable for him to keep propping up Immediate with cash injections from his own pocket. In London there was a fire sale of his collection of cars, the Rolls, Aston Martin and others, as Oldham prepared for life in America as a British tax exile (concurrently, Mick Jagger and Keith Richards were also presented with tax bills they were unable to pay and also decided to become tax exiles). Oldham's final act of the sixties was to set Marriott free.*

**Jerry Shirley:** He did us the biggest favour that any single manager has ever done any band. As soon as he knew that Immediate was definitely going down, he said, 'Here, call Jerry Moss [A&M Records co-founder].' We said okay. Andrew said, 'You're not getting the point. Call Jerry Moss, he will sign you.' Andrew would have had the ability at that time to hang us up in all kinds of legalities; he didn't choose to. He chose to give us a career that he felt we deserved.

**Peter Frampton:** It was a very nice gesture. We would have been unable to make a record and he knew that. He was basically giving us our career...

**Steve Marriott:** Andrew was great about it. He just said, 'We're going under, mate.' He warned us all. He said, 'Get out now and sort yourselves out, I release you of your contract. Get other labels, I don't want any of you going down with the company.' He was a great bloke, a right old blagger, but underneath all the front he was a very nice man. He suggested ways of getting a record deal, which was very nice because I had no idea. We could have gone down with the company and wound up an asset to the liquidator.

## CHAPTER 8

# Big Black Dog

**Larry Yaskiel:** I signed Humble Pie to A&M. I was working for Pye Records in Germany when Jerry Moss came over to look for distributors for his A&M label. He said he was going to open up in England and if I fancied going back home he'd like to make me European director. They brought me in to sign rock'n'roll bands. A&M had all the middle-of-the-road stuff, which was their reputation, Herb Alpert & The Tijuana Brass, The Sandpipers, Sergio Mendes & Brasil '66, but they wanted to go into the rock'n'roll business. My first two major signing were The Humblebums, with Billy Connolly and Gerry Rafferty, and Supertramp, and then somebody said Andrew Loog Oldham and Tony Calder are hawking Humble Pie. So I spoke to A&M in America because this was going to be something expensive and they said, 'Go ahead, we'd like to sign them.'

*A&M, founded by Jerry Moss and Herb Alpert in 1962, was the world's largest independent record label and, alongside its famed easy listening acts such as Burt Bacharach and The Carpenters, they had, since the late sixties, begun to assemble an impressive repertoire of contemporary musicians, signing British acts Procol Harum, The Move, Spooky Tooth, Fairport Convention, Free, Cat Stevens and Joe Cocker. Their American roster was also developing, with acts such as Jimmy Cliff, Phil Ochs, Lee Michaels, Melvin Van Peebles, Gene Clark and The Flying Burrito Brothers all on board.*

*Yaskiel was invited to see Humble Pie rehearse at the 100 Club in Soho. He was surprised to find a rival record label executive present, in the form of Ahmet Ertegun, boss of Atlantic Records. Ertegun had been invited to consider signing the band by Chas Chandler, former manager of Jimi Hendrix, and a friend of Peter Frampton, who was jockeying to become Humble Pie's manager. Ertegun was keen: 'It's like having two Jimmy Pages in one band and a baby-making rhythm section that just don't quit, outstanding.'*

**Larry Yaskiel:** I knew Chas. We were good friends. I'd represented Hendrix in Germany. My wife and I used to go for walks in Regent's Park with Chas when his girlfriend was Lynsey de Paul [who Yaskiel signed to A&M]. Their argument was Atlantic have got Led Zeppelin, Jimi Hendrix and Cream and my argument was we haven't – 'You'll be number one with us, you'll be number four on their list.' This was something I wasn't used to, it was like playing poker, you had to work out what the other guy was holding. I said to Jerry [Moss], 'This is out of my league'… it went up from $350,000 to $400,000 and he said go ahead. But I never talked to Chas about it. I only spoke to Steve Marriott. I felt a great affinity to Steve. He was their spokesman. I liked him very much straight away. He had a great sense of humour. The deal was $400,000 [approximately $2.5 million in today's money and a 14 per cent royalty rate]. Each member of Humble Pie would get $100,000.

*Chandler urged the band to sign with Atlantic as he was due a cut of the deal. Humble Pie signed with A&M and, when Chandler began arguing for a cut of that deal too, Marriott dismissed him. Marriott then wasted little time spending a significant chunk of his portion of the A&M advance on a house for his parents at Stoneleigh, Sawbridgeworth, close to the historic market town of Bishop's Stortford in Hertfordshire, a thirty-minute drive from Beehive Cottage. After an early visit, to see if his parents had settled in, he joked that he thought he had made a mistake moving them out of London because Bill was now wearing a cravat and walking a spaniel. He had overstretched himself in the purchase of the house, and dipped into band funds to do so.*

**Jerry Shirley:** It was three advances, adding up to $400,000 – split over three years. It amounted to a yearly income of just over £14,000 each, which was, back then, slightly more than the prime minister was getting. Steve had his shit together and with a lot of help from his mates, especially Peter, he was on a mission. This period of the band's history was probably the happiest for many reasons but mostly because of Steve's frame of mind. Simply put, he was deeply in love with Jenny, he had almost single-handedly negotiated one of the biggest record deals ever done and he had done it without the help of an expensive manager; although, it has to be said his partner, Peter, did help him a lot with that. This was truly Steve's golden moment and to make it all the more special he was the nicest man you could care to meet. He had become very compassionate, understanding and just plain content for the first time in his life. Steve was at his absolute best during that period of his life.

**Jenny Dearden:** There were lovely moments with Steve. We had this time when we first moved to the cottage, he'd left the Small Faces and all that trauma... it was just us and our dogs and our cats... and we'd go for long walks and we'd smoke dope... and he used to sing me songs he'd written for me and it was a brief idyllic time before he got taken up by Dee Anthony.

*Yaskiel booked the band a month at Olympic with Glyn Johns as producer to record their first album for A&M. Johns was now producing Steve Miller, Family, a Stones live album, as well as engineering for acts such as Led Zeppelin, Bob Dylan and Joe Cocker.*

**Glyn Johns:** I'd known Peter for a long time and, although I wasn't overly fond of Steve Marriott, he was such a great artist, I agreed to produce Humble Pie.

**Peter Frampton:** Glyn got us all together and said, 'Look, you're too diversified. It's all very well that whatever somebody writes you record.' He said, 'I think what you have to do is look at your best points and make a meal of those.' The list of things we had was, Steve was one of the world's all-time greatest singers so he should be the singer. I was the lead guitarist that did a bit of singing. Greg was the bass player, did a little bit of singing. Jerry was the drummer. That was it. These were our jobs. Now let's make a record. It went over great with everyone. As far as I was concerned it was a necessary direction that we needed to take because no one could blast it out like Steve could on vocals. It was great sharing the vocals within a song with Steve but let's use our strongest assets, that's what Glyn was saying. That's what changed it for us.

**Larry Yaskiel:** Going with Glyn was something Steve came up with. There was an argument about one of the tracks on the album. Steve had written a song ['Theme from Skint (See You Later Liquidator)'] and the lyric was 'Tony Calder's digging holes'... Sometimes artists get it in their head that the people they're involved in have done them wrong... and he wrote it and there was going to be a lawsuit. Then Steve got stopped by the police and they found marijuana in the car... and he wrote a song [in fact, the song is credited to and sung by Jerry Shirley] about it ['Only A Roach'] for the album.

**Jerry Shirley:** Steve and I were on our way to his house one morning after an all-night session at Olympic. I was driving Steve's Alvis, a lovely old car and a major attention-grabber, gold with chromed wire wheels. Steve had just lit a large joint of some of the strongest hash we had seen for a while. As we pulled up to a set of lights I noticed a car in the rear-view mirror and two very suspicious-looking chaps getting out and heading in our direction.

*Marriott quickly stubbed the joint out and hid it, swallowing the large lump of hash in his pocket. The two policemen found the remainder of the joint and Marriott was charged with cannabis possession. The incident hit the papers. The police also visited Beehive during this period but having been tipped off by Greg Ridley, Jenny met them at the door with the home's barking dogs, explaining she had no control over them and that her husband was out. Recording on the album continued. Steel guitar player B. J. Cole, then unknown, now a hugely celebrated session player (and has worked with Elton John, Robert Plant and Depeche Mode), was used as guest.*

**B. J. Cole:** I did a lot of stuff for Humble Pie in the early days. They didn't really quite know what they were doing. I don't think they were thinking of it as a heavy blues rock band. It was more a country rock thing. When I entered the studio one day, Steve shouted down the talkback, 'Hey B. J.,' and nobody had called me that before. Up until then I was known as Brian, and he didn't know my initials were B. J. So after that the B. J. stuck. Who knows how he came up with that? Probably something rude. It was sort of where my career firmly established itself. I was lucky. For a pedal steel player to be asked to play on a band of that stature was pretty unheard of. The first song

I played on was 'Only A Roach'. I was hired exclusively for that and then they tried to think of other songs for me to play on, 'Theme From Skint', 'Sucking On The Sweet Vine'. I owe Steve a huge debt.

**Larry Yaskiel:** Herb Alpert was invited over for the Royal Command Performance at the London Palladium. While he was over he asked if we had anybody in the studio. Humble Pie were at Olympic and he asked, 'Would they mind if I visited?' I said, 'You're paying the bill for it, Herb'... I called up Steve and I said, 'Would you mind?' and he said, 'We'd love him to come down'... the next morning I called up Steve and said, 'How did it go?' He said, 'Oh, the guy was great, he was dressed just like we were... he had holes in his jeans just like we did, the only difference was his holes looked like they had been cut by a tailor'... that was the essence of Steve, summed it up in a nutshell: this multi-millionaire came in, he was one of the boys but one of the boys with the holes cut in jeans cut by a tailor.

*With the album complete, from April to June 1970 Humble Pie played a smattering of UK dates, mainly in universities, supporting acts such as Procol Harum and Mott The Hoople. A&M were keen to have the band tour America.*

**Larry Yaskiel:** Jerry Moss asked me to talk to them about doing a tour of America to coincide with the album release and I couldn't reach Steve on the phone. I sent him a telegram and he answered. I asked, 'What happened, why didn't you pick up the phone?' He said, 'I've run out of money, my phone's been cut off.' I said, 'But you just got $100,000'... and he had healthy publishing royalties coming in from some of his big Small Faces hits. I had sleepless nights worrying. When I told Jerry the reason I'd been unable to get hold of Steve, he said, 'It comes with the territory, get used to it.' A&M was extremely artist friendly and promotion conscious. But suddenly I'm stuck with problems that shouldn't have been my problem and it was because they didn't have a manager. I told A&M America this and they went out and they scouted out the duo of Dee Anthony and Frank Barsalona. Frank was the heavy agent and Dee was the heavy manager. They came over to London to hear Pie and we booked the band in at the Marquee so they could listen to this heavy rock band... of course they took it into their heads they wanted to be different, so everybody was sitting on bean bags and they played an acoustic set. Dee Anthony was managing at that time a very heavy American rock band called The J. Geils Band. I said to Dee, 'That's not them, really'... but that's the kind of thing they did, Steve Marriott's sense of humour... here they are without a manager, they've got one of the heaviest managers in the business coming to see them and, instead of playing rock'n'roll, he's playing acoustic... but that went through. Once Dee Anthony took over I wasn't involved in any of their day-to-day stuff.

**Jerry Shirley:** Greg [Ridley] had recommended that we hire his old chum, Danny Farnham, who had been Spooky Tooth's road manager. Once Danny was on board he suggested that we contact Dee Anthony, the American manager [Island Record boss] Chris Blackwell used for what was called 'service management' when one of Chris's acts went over to America. We had no idea how lucky we were at the time to have picked Dee and Frank as our representatives, for the single reason that we never heard another word about the bust [Marriott's arrest] as far as it affected our ability to acquire work visas for America. It was as if it just went away.

*Born Anthony D'Addario, Dee Anthony was in his 40s, an Italian American from the Bronx, short, stout, very tenacious. He had served in the US Navy, in the submarine force, during the Second World War, then performed in cabaret clubs 'miming to records – I'd do Al Jolson in blackface and do the whole trip', before making his name in the music business as personal manager to crooner Tony Bennett, a fellow Italian American, between 1949 and 1962. 'In those days you had one artist really and you were personal manager, you were road manager, you'd do everything, run the lights, everything,' he said. Other acts he managed in this period were in a similar vein, easy on the ear, jazzy and popular, names such as Buddy Greco, George Maharis, The Four Lads and Erroll Garner. In the mid-sixties he travelled to London and hooked up with several emerging rock acts. In 1968, with his brother Bill, he founded Bandana Enterprises, providing 'service management' for a percentage for a score of English bands such as The Troggs, The Spencer Davis Group, Traffic, Ten Years After, Jethro Tull, Joe Cocker, Spooky Tooth and Emerson, Lake & Palmer. He helped the bands establish themselves on the lucrative US circuit – for example, securing Ten Years After and Cocker high-profile slots at the Woodstock festival in 1969. Anthony was currently overseeing the release of Cocker's* Mad Dogs &

Englishmen, *a live double album that was heading to US No 2. He also was the manager of Detroit rockers the MC5 and Boston's The J. Geils Band, who he had signed to Atlantic with a debut album about to drop. He would take 20 per cent as manager of Humble Pie.*

**Dee Anthony [1926–2009]:** I came in [to rock music] at a very strange time. The bubblegum groups, like the 1910 Fruit Gum Co. were in, and Frank Barsalona was booking Freddie & The Dreamers. I was part of a group called International Management Combine, where we serviced groups that came through to America and, in 1967, I tied in with Island Artists, with Chris Blackwell, for The Spencer Davis Group. They did Traffic, and I had them too. Then came [Chrysalis Records boss] Chris Wright – and I took over Chrysalis in the States, and had Ten Years After. The English managers had never been to America, they didn't know the lay of the land, and I knew all that. I started my own company, Bandana, representing the Chrysalis Agency and Island Artists. But Frank Barsalona told me, stay in management. And he helped me originally to get started that way. He was an agent, struggling too at first, in transition from bubblegum to rock. That's why Frank and I had a very good rapport. The only partnership we've got is our friendship, and the ability to look at a group and work together on it. We've hit on quite a few groups together, where they've scored heavily, so we must be doing something right. I like challenges. Humble Pie was a challenge because they were obviously rejected by everyone. There was a big push here [in the UK]. Supergroup. And nothing happened. And I can't tell you how many people said you're crazy when I took them on. If the talent is there, the thing to do is give the artists confidence. I don't believe in the attitude of shouting, 'Today, we're the biggest band in the world.' They should build up, always growing, and never peaking.

**Jenny Dearden:** Dee apparently had somewhat tenuous connections to the New York Mafia. They were all terribly impressed by him, completely overwhelmed. He was this big, hearty, funny guy, charming, and he had that physique that commands instant respect. He was very egocentric. It was a father figure for Steve... Dee was an American version of Don basically.

165

**Jerry Shirley:** Dee was the hottest manager in the business at the time for our type of rock'n'roll band. He had all, or part of, the management of all of these great groups. He had his finger into everybody's pie. And he brought with him a truly great agent, Frank Barsalona. They were two of the funniest guys we'd ever met and were so sure of themselves. With Dee and Frank it wasn't if you were going to make it, it was when. It was incredibly fashionable in the early seventies to be mobbed-up. Bill Anthony [who was 38 in 1970 to Dee's 44] was the good guy in all of it, wonderful man and always did his level best to do everything right, the younger brother, good-looking Italian man, always had a dark tan… carried his reflector everywhere with him. They were a great double act. Bill was Frank Sinatra's roadie for a while and they were both on the road with Tony Bennett. Tony Bennett and Dee grew up together. Dee had Tony Bennett stories. He had Frank Sinatra stories. This was fascinating stuff… Sinatra was still a big star… and he had stories about all that other side of life, this Sicilian thing and this Mafia thing.

**Keith Altham:** Dee Anthony certainly smacked of Mafia to me. He even liked to boast about it sometimes. He was a clever, powerful man. His way of handling his artists was to give them whatever they wanted. 'You want more girls? Drugs? Bigger houses. Have them.' They don't find out until later that the money was a loan and they've got to repay it, and they're mortgaged to the hilt.

*Humble Pie's debut A&M album,* Humble Pie, *was launched in July 1970 with a London show at the Roundhouse with MC5 supporting. The album was a tight eight-song affair featuring a cover version of 'I'm Ready' by Willie Dixon and three group compositions including 'One-Eyed Trouser-Snake Rumba' and 'Red Light Mama, Red Hot!' with lyrics by Marriott. The album failed to chart but had its admirers. Ray Davies named it his album of the week in the press. There were no singles lifted from the record; instead a stand-alone single, 'Big Black Dog', was released, with Humble Pie credited as writers and Immediate Music listed as publishers. It again featured Marriott, Ridley and Frampton sharing the vocals, a verse each.*

*In interviews to promote the album, Marriott was said to have 'virtually finished with drink and accessories [drugs], preferring cups of tea and the fresh air'. Shirley commented: 'He's much calmer now, different. He's changed, but not that much... he's more himself. He doesn't get moods, he's just back into being the real Steve.' Marriott talked up the music. 'I think it's the best thing I've ever been involved in. What I'm knocked out about is the clarity, that's down to Glyn Johns, the engineer. It's not just a thin sound to get the clarity, he gets a nice loud sound at the same time. I'll stand up for this album to anyone any day of the week.' Humble Pie performed 'Big Black Dog' on* Top Of The Pops *in August. Marriott, however, sabotaged the broadcast of the performance.*

**Jerry Shirley:** Larry [Yaskiel] had got us a spot on *Top Of The Pops*. It was a period when they'd gone to taping performances and dropping them in the following week. They did these live interviews at the same time. We recorded our spot with 'Big Black Dog' and it was set to go the following week but they put us on a live interview with Tony Blackburn and Steve came up with this idea of each of us calling him by another famous DJ's name and coming up with the same answer. Whatever he'd ask us we'd say, 'Dunno, ask our manager.' He'd ask a question and so we'd say, 'Oh, hello Dave Lee Travis. Dunno, ask my manager.' Each one of us did that and we completely embarrassed him in front of fourteen million people, biggest watched TV show of its type. He flew at us afterwards, made the big mistake of coming up to Greg Ridley screaming at him. A consequence was they never aired 'Big Black Dog' the following week. He got the BBC to pull it. And not only did we not get 'Big Black Dog' on *Top Of The Pops*, the BBC radio stations stopped playing it too... that was it, any chance it had, which I think was a pretty good one, was ruined there and then.

**Steve Marriott:** Every time I spoke to him I would call him a different name – I'd call him Simon, Eamonn or any other DJ's name but never his own. Anyway, I wanted to give him a cabbage to let him know what I thought of him. So I'm calling him all these different names and at the same time he's holding this cabbage and doesn't quite know why he's got it. It hasn't dawned on him yet and as it slowly dawns on him what a cunt he looks holding this cabbage he went mad and offered me outside, he's shouting and all his make-up is running. He was shouting, 'You little cunt, you'll never work at the BBC again.' I was crying with laughter.

**Larry Yaskiel:** 'Big Black Dog' almost happened. It nibbled at the Top 20 for a couple of weeks. That was a major problem: we couldn't get a hit single, we could never ever get a song that was like a 'Natural Born Bugie'.

*The* Humble Pie *album failed to chart in the UK and did little to boost the band's popularity in their home country, where they continued to struggle to attract a live following.*

**Chris Welch:** When they started I don't think they quite knew what their policy was going to be, they were trying out more gentle country tunes, acoustic numbers, a little bit self-indulgent. I'd seen them in London live and they were playing too many slow tunes, at the Country Club in Hampstead [May 1970], Steve was in a bad mood, hardly anyone was there, maybe twenty people, and he was swearing a lot... Peter was not happy about that.

*There were American dates on the horizon, Dee Anthony and Frank Barsalona having lined up an American tour beginning in September. The band kicked back and all took on session work. Frampton worked with soul singer Doris Troy and on George Harrison's album* All Things Must Pass. *Jerry Shirley worked with The Who bassist John Entwistle and former Pink Floyd frontman Syd Barrett on his two solo albums,* The Madcap Laughs *and* Barrett. *Marriott kicked ideas around with Alexis Korner. Korner and his wife Bobbi had become good pals to Marriott and Jenny – 'like aunty and uncle really', she said. 'They'd come and see us quite often.' Marriott also guested at a gig at the Marquee club with B. J. Cole's band, Cochise, and would feature as guest vocalist on their second album,* Swallow Tales, *released in 1971.*

**B. J. Cole:** Before Led Zeppelin, [manager] Peter Grant had attempted to put together a country rock band, an English Flying Burrito Brothers, and I was involved with that. It didn't quite gel but Cochise came out of it. Our bass player Rick [Wills] knew Steve and Jerry Shirley and he got Steve in to do backing vocals on a [Buddy Holly] song called 'Love's Made A Fool Of You'. He completely upstages everybody. It's a great Steve Marriott vocal on that. Cochise had a similar sound to early Humble Pie. That part of the music business was very small and everybody knew everybody. [Jenny Dearden was pals with David

Gilmour, who had replaced Syd Barrett in Pink Floyd. She had met him in the late sixties when he drove the delivery van at Quorum.]

**Rick Wills:** Steve was absolutely in his prime. He looked fantastic. He hardly drank. He and Jenny were living an idealistic life in a thatched cottage in the country. He had it all: the voice, the look, the writing ability...

**Jenny Dearden:** But he could be quite the little shit as well. He would go off and meet people and I'd be left in the country. It doesn't mean if you're living with somebody and they're writing romantic songs about you that they're behaving quite like that in real life. Steve hated me going out for modelling jobs, he invariably would cause a terrible argument and have me in tears. Huge dramas every time. It was a long way to London and I hadn't passed my driving test so I'd get a cab up. The last thing I did was for the *Observer* and in the end I thought, what am I doing? It's misery. I was doing it less and less and, in the end, I thought, there's no point at all. He thought the photographers were going to want to get off with me – very, very jealous and insecure about that. His self-esteem was not high; in normal social situations he couldn't communicate at all with people. I got persuaded to go to a party at [antiques dealer and collector] Christopher Gibbs's on Cheyne Walk in Chelsea and Steve sat in the corner and couldn't cope at all. Any musicians around, he would have been able to latch on to them. We didn't stay. He got paranoid, he felt undereducated. So we stayed mainly in the country and the only time we would come up to London was maybe if his friends were playing at Olympic or when occasionally we went to clubs.

*From September until the end of year, with only a few weeks off, Dee Anthony had the band in America on the road. It was when things began to change for Humble Pie.*

**Bob Garcia:** A&M was a family company, and everything was 24/7 for what we [Garcia was A&M director of publicity and director of artist relations] thought were the right reasons. Humble Pie were a priority for us. Greg was incredibly friendly and open, so was Jerry. Everybody called Jerry 'the accountant' and 'the scheduler'. He was the only one you could talk business with. He carried some sort of attaché case [more of which later]. Stephen and Peter were not as friendly and not as open and welcoming... but that changed as I got to know them. At first Steve was the one out of the band who was the street guy, whether that was real or not I don't know, and then we had a long conversation one night at a J. Geils gig in Long Beach about how I had started as a boy soprano and ended up for two seasons at the Metropolitan Opera in New York ... he really warmed up after that. But with Steve he seemed to be able to switch the role on and off. While I was on the road with him, doing a promotional event, radio stations, there was that strutting, cock of the English walk thing, not this shy, retiring, professional little guy that, every once in a while, you had a conversation with.

*Humble Pie played similar clubs and dance halls to the ones they had during their first American tour – the Boston Tea Party, the Electric Factory in Philadelphia, Fillmore East and Fillmore West and the Whisky a Go Go – more often than not as support to bigger bands such as Mountain, Mungo Jerry, James Gang, Derek & The Dominos, Savoy Brown, Ry Cooder and Edward Bear. The gigs were booked through Frank Barsalona's Premier Talent, who took 15 per cent of the band's fees, which were low at approximately $500–$1,000 per gig. At the Whisky something of the old Marriott re-emerged when he threw a 'wobbler on stage' and admonished the band for their poor playing. Throughout the tour, Dee Anthony took a more active role in shaping the band's live set.*

**Steve Marriott:** He looked at our act objectively and gave us a good boot from behind. He advised us that we should cut out the softer stuff and play our heads off instead... all solid, loud and crunchy. So that's just what we did. We used to come out and sit down and play acoustic. Dee told us to kick that out for a start, cause until you're in a position to do that – until they want you to do that – they're going to boo you at the Fillmore and throw popcorn. He wasn't wrong; it just hadn't dawned on me because I was still too busy smoking hash. We dropped the acoustic numbers and played our arse off.

**Bob Garcia:** Dee Anthony is the only manager who threatened to break my arms. He thought I was hiding Steve somewhere in LA because they couldn't find him. He was staying with a bunch of friends somewhere in Beverly Hills and eventually showed up on the lot [the main A&M office in LA, there was also a large New York office] and we never discussed this again. Funny now but at the time it was, wait a minute, does Dee know where I live? That whole Mafia fantasy came bubbling up. He had a big briefcase that was handcuffed to his wrist, would collect every gig's money in hard cash. He had bodyguards. It was my introduction to this gangster culture and amazingly well-connected people. Dee had three rules for success. The first was 'always get the money', the second was 'don't forget to always get the money' and the third was 'don't forget, whatever else you've done, to make sure you get the money'. There was a character in the [Walt Disney 1940 cartoon] movie *Pinocchio* called Stromboli and that's the tender word we had for Dee [at A&M] at the time. [Stromboli is the film's puppetmaster villain who is at first portrayed as gruff but kind-hearted, but suddenly locks Pinocchio in a cage, stating that once he is too old to work, he will be used as firewood, revealing his true nature as brutal, cruel, and vicious.] Dee ran Pleasure Island [i.e. party central] and he was incredibly hands-on and a sort of respected monster. You never crossed him.

*Jerry Shirley met a friend of Dee Anthony's in New York. Carmine 'Wassel' DeNoia (1921–2015), in his late 40s, was an imposing figure: six foot two and over 200 pounds. He was described by writer Nick Tosches as starting out as a Broadway bookmaker, taking action on horses, and was 'a friend of those in the music business' dating back to the early fifties. In 2000, aged 79, DeNoia explained to Tosches how things might work when he was employed as an independent 'promotion man' in the good old days, when he would hang DJs out of windows who had welched on pay-to-play deals or how he might wrap a pipe in a rolled-up newspaper to visit a publisher trying to steal a song. Wassel (his brother J. J. was said to be a made man) was an associate of the Genovese family and the Pagano crew (he'd grown up in East Harlem with the feared brothers Patsy and Joe Pagano – exposed as ruthless killers in the book* The Valachi Papers, *in which a disgruntled soldier in New York's Genovese crime family decided to tell all). In the sixties Wassel had handled singer Freddie Scott and at one point he had inherited the contract of Van Morrison. He would be convicted of bribing radio DJs to play certain records more heavily than others and jailed in 1976.*

**Jerry Shirley:** Wassel was an enforcer guy, really well known in the business in the seventies, huge, massive guy, looked just like Luca Brasi from *The Godfather*. When we were introduced in Dee's apartment, he took my arm, his hand was so big it reached from my elbow to my wrist and he squeezed my arm and said, 'Anybody who is a friend of Mr Anthony is a friend of mine... anybody who is an enemy of Mr Anthony is an enemy of mine'... all this classic theatre. Dee wasn't associated with those kind of people as much as people believe... he knew them, he grew up with them but you didn't do business with those people too regularly other than when you had to, and in the late sixties, early seventies, you had no choice because a lot of the bigger clubs were run by mob guys.

*While the band played long stretches of dates on the American club and dance hall circuit, Anthony used his connections to secure Humble Pie support slots at a handful of bigger arena gigs with Grand Funk Railroad, including at the Chicago Coliseum (12,000) and Madison Square Garden in New York (20,000).*

**Peter Frampton:** It was good for us because we were able to reach so many people in a short space of time. They were this iconic band at the time we came over to America. We learned a lot from them, seeing a huge American band and how they did it. And Mark [Farner, guitarist and vocalist] had an incredible voice and is such a great communicator. I think Steve Marriott and I picked up a lot from him.

**Jerry Shirley:** At this time the biggest band in the States was not Led Zep, it was Grand Funk. They were the most unsung success story of the early 1970s. Their popularity was extraordinary in that it defied all logic. They got no airplay and any reviews they might have got would be bad on principle... one of the main benefits of Dee's management was his enormous number of connections, one of whom was Terry Knight, Grand Funk's manager. I can't remember why Terry was more than happy to do Dee lots of favours to help Humble Pie but he was. I'm sure Frank [Barsalona] had an awful lot do with it, as he was known as the 'most powerful man in rock'n'roll'. Frank Barsalona could get through to Steve when nobody else could. Steve respected Frank even above Dee, which was saying something.

*Barsalona (1938–2012) sat on top of a rock'n'roll empire, a kingmaker. He wore large amounts of bling, gold jewellery and one-of-a-kind gold Rolex watches. His Premier Talent was a national brand, having established a chain of 2,000- to 3,000-capacity clubs across America, where he put his bands to work on six- to eight-week tours. He controlled a long list of promoters, each running his own territory. Bill Graham, for instance, had Manhattan and San Francisco with the Fillmore East and West, Larry Magid had the Electric Factory in Philadelphia, Don Law owned Boston with the Boston Tea Party, and so on. Barsalona could dictate that these promoters could put new bands on bills with headliners whose fans would probably embrace them to build their own fan-base.*

*He'd been raised in Staten Island, New York, and started out working in the mailroom at New Yorks' GAC talent agency, forming his own agency in 1964 to handle new rock'n'roll acts such as Mitch Ryder & The Detroit Wheels, Del Shannon and The Ronettes. His wife, June Harris, a UK rock journalist, introduced him to the British Invasion acts and he took on bands such as Herman's Hermits and Freddie & The Dreamers, ultimately landing The Who. From there he established links with English record executives that brought him Procol Harum, Spencer Davis, Traffic, Joe Cocker, Spooky Tooth and Ten Years After. He was currently looking at ways to build a national circuit for some of his bigger bands in bigger arena-sized venues.*

**Mick Brigden [Humble Pie tour manager]:** Frank Barsalona was the ultimate, everyone loved Frank Barsalona as a man and as an agent... he was a king amongst kings. He built the rock'n'roll touring business in the US.

**Chris Welch:** I went to American with Humble Pie – very exciting. I was invited to go see them in New York, Philadelphia and Los Angeles, travelling around with them. I played pool with Steve in a bar in New York, we took a trip on the Circle Line cruise round Manhattan, saw the Twin Towers being built. The gig in New York was in Long Island, the support band was T. Rex... poor Marc [Bolan] playing to this really heavy rock crowd and they weren't interested at all. Humble Pie went down a storm, as they did whenever I saw them. I think they supported Alice Cooper in Philadelphia. Peter and Steve didn't really hang out together. They were like chalk and cheese as personalities. I think Peter found Steve a bit of a strain sometimes, very aggressive, in your face... losing his temper a lot, swearing and shouting. That wasn't Peter's style... there was a little bit of tension between the two even then, being cooped up together, travelling. Steve could be volatile but then again he could be very friendly. Humble Pie arrived in America without any career baggage. The audience had probably never heard of The Herd, or Peter Frampton's past associations, so they were just seeing them for what they were without being judgmental. English audiences would say, 'Oh, we know who Peter Frampton is.' It was a bit harder for them to be accepted in England.

Dee Anthony sort of cajoled them into tightening everything up and playing more solid rock material and made it the kind of band that would be a success in America. Dee would stand at the side of the stage and blow a whistle to get them into action... he was like a baseball coach. He went to all the gigs, he travelled with them, he wanted to make sure they had back-up. I liked him, he was a very jolly guy. I went to his apartment in New York, a fourteen-bedroom apartment he'd just bought... enormous, the majority of bedrooms unfurnished, virtually empty, and he explained he was going to have suits of armour decorating the hall, like the Crusades, he said. To me it seemed like Dee was genuinely fond of Humble Pie, seemed very proud of them, wanted to help them and make them into a successful band.

**Jerry Shirley:** Dee had a gold whistle that he would blow when you were flagging... he and Frank Barsalona would dissect the show, song by song. Now move this one up here, open with that one. Put this one back here. Get rid of this one. And they literally, between the two of them, with our input, completely and entirely built the set. Dee and Frank's ability to instill self-confidence in a band and steer you in the right direction on stage was second to none. They were old-school guys who went all the way back to almost vaudevillian stage sensibilities. They were particularly good at helping the frontmen. Dee was pure genius at getting the best out of some very talented people.

*Anthony was hands-on, giving pep talks, drilling stage moves into the band, demonstrating corny call-and-response routines and other tricks to win audiences over. In conversation he would repeat certain phrases, such as 'You're like a son to me' or 'I made him an offer he couldn't refuse.'*

**Dee Anthony:** I learned on the road. A performance isn't just a clump of songs, you want to lay an act out right, and have continuity, contrast and pacing. Unless you can offer a performance, people will just come to hear your last hit record and you'll always be only as strong as that record. I hope I've contributed that to rock because it was horrendous before. Sloppy. Bands would take five minutes between numbers. They were good musicians, but they weren't into show, or performance. We knew the importance of the stage show. We wanted to take the audience on a path, in a direction, so they follow you through your whole repertoire. I got into the band and worked on their act, and started to go for encores and reprises and all that, little showbiz shticks that used to work! I started that quite early with Ten Years After and kept using it, even with Cocker and Humble Pie.

**Steve Marriott:** I started coming out more. I was still introverted to a point. Dee Anthony would take me into a corner and give me a big lecture. 'You've got to come out, they want you. You're frontman, now be a frontman.' I always felt a bit inhibited about going out there and really giving my all. Now I can go out there and kick arse, man! I'm a performer first, musician second. Every night I want to leave a bit of blood on the stage, cut my fingers a bit, sweat and scream. The whole band loves that feeling you get off a crowd, the loudness of the amps, the roar.

**Jenny Dearden:** What Dee wanted for the band was for Steve to be the frontman and use that charisma he had when he was belting it out. Steve said to me, Dee always said to him, 'You're here and I want you to give blood when you go on stage.'

**Peter Frampton:** It was something to behold. Imagine being in the audience and seeing a little white guy on stage, standing four feet nothing, and every time he opens his mouth a black man's voice comes out from who knows where. He's singing instructions to them in gospel-ese. 'I want you to raise your ha-a-ands.' It was riveting.

**Jerry Shirley:** He became famous for pushing his microphone away, walking to the front of the stage and singing to the people at the back of the hall. 'Are you ready?' Winding them up until he was sure they were ready. Then, and only then, would I get the signal from him, a shake of his bum, or a twist of his hips, to start the song, he was such a master at what he did. Most of the methods Steve used to communicate with his audience have since become commonplace, the call and response, encouraging the audience to sing along or clap with the band and using the band's natural dynamics to get even more audience participation. I'm not suggesting he invented these techniques but he was one of the first to turn them into an art form.

*On this American tour the band debuted what would become their signature tune, 'I Don't Need No Doctor'. It developed from a soundcheck jam that Marriott began to ad lib over, using the lyrics of an obscure 1966 R&B single by Ray Charles, written by Valerie Simpson, Nick Ashford and Jo Armstead (garage rockers The Chocolate Watchband had cut a version of the song in 1969). They were also now opening the show with another song that would become a staple, 'Four Day Creep', a blues shuffle – mistakenly credited to Ida Cox, as she'd done a tune with that title – with lyrics borrowed from 'I Want You To Love Me' by Muddy Waters.*

**Jerry Shirley:** We were starting to get outstanding responses from every crowd we played to. Steve exuded masses of natural God-given talent and it was a joy to see how, in the hands of such brilliant coaches, he was coming to the fore again, only so much better than before. His rebirth was knocking the socks off everybody, except for one… Peter was torn in two directions. Humble Pie had started as our band but, on the other hand, Steve's resurgence of stage presence was undeniably powerful that Peter didn't want to dampen it.

**Greg Ridley:** I guess Steve's harder side sometimes didn't gel with Peter's more gentle side. But we developed into one of the heaviest rock bands in the whole world. We wanted to get louder and heavier and more cocky.

*Marriott returned to London full of confidence, spending January 1971 in Olympic Studios recording Humble Pie's fourth album,* Rock On, *again with Glyn Johns producing.*

176

**Steve Marriott:** *Rock On* was mostly harder rock with a bit of soul on there. We started going in there and creating the stage act, getting the songs down that we wanted to play in the set, instead of coming out scared thinking, oh shit, how we going to play that motherfucker [live].

**Peter Frampton:** Even though we all enjoyed the change because we were getting better, now there wasn't any room for even one acoustic number on an album, which I think we all regretted, especially live. Don't get me wrong, I enjoyed every second of every performance of Humble Pie but on the other side I was now writing stuff that wasn't fitting in with where Humble Pie was going.

*The album would feature three Marriott songs, including the wistful 'Song For Jenny' and the lyrically crude (as Marriott's lyrics were increasingly tending toward) '79th And Sunset', plus a rare Frampton/Marriott collaboration 'Sour Grain', and two songs credited to the group, alongside a cover of Muddy Waters' 'Rollin' Stone'.*

**Jerry Shirley:** Steve had a little gem called 'Red Neck Jump'. We had some group-written material we had been doing on the road for a while: 'Stone Cold Fever' was a strong favourite live. Steve was on fire on the piano during those sessions. Glyn brought in Bobby Keys on saxophone and Claudia Lennear on back-up vocals. She was absolutely gorgeous and her recent claim to fame was as back-up singer on Joe Cocker's *Mad Dogs & Englishmen* tour.

**Claudia Lennear:** I was in London singing with Leon Russell & The Shelter People and I got a call from Mick Jagger, who mentioned to me I should expect a call from Glyn Johns about a recording project. He didn't elaborate but later that day Glyn did get in touch with me to ask my availability for a project. I had never heard of Humble Pie even though that was my kind of forte to sing with English bands... but Glyn was so enthusiastic I agreed to sing background. I rounded up Doris Troy and P. P. Arnold to sing with me and we charged down to Olympic Studios and knocked out a couple of songs. P. P. knew Steve and Doris knew of him. The three of us had always wanted to get together to sing. Steve really was on top of his game. I had never been so impressed with an English singer... when I heard his vocal on 'Shine On' [a *Rock On* track written by Peter Frampton] I was totally blown away. I thought he had an incredible instrument in his voice, incomparable at the time. I had just come off the road with Joe Cocker but Steve to me had more of a higher-pitch voice than Joe, like a screaming siren, it was so in tune and so well controlled... I just thought he was amazing and then on top of it he was so small... my goodness, how can this huge voice come from this person? It was such an eye-opener. It was absolutely unique. In America if you go to many black churches you can hear a certain tonality in the preacher's voice and it's called a squall, it's that same sort of screaming sound Steve had... he had that sound in his singing.

He was also so focused in the studio, he knew what he wanted, the sound he was trying to get from us. He came out to the microphone with us, he didn't sing each person's notes but he just said what he was trying to achieve and then the three of us interpreted that. He was a lead-by-example-type person. Steve was the one who was in charge of that session along with Glyn Johns. He totally won over my confidence. I thought he was one of Britain's best exports, to tell the truth... he was just a phenomenal singer. My great friend David Bowie said the same thing. When I first met David we would talk about English singers and the first one who always came to mind was Steve... we would always have a very endearing joke about Steve, about how he was this little guy with this huge voice. It was so amazing; he would sweep you off your feet. I have never heard anything like that come from another human. I also thought he was the loveliest person.

*'Shine On' was chosen as the lead single from* Rock On. *The band played a handful of live UK gigs as promotion in late February and early March 1971, including two shows at the Marquee club, but neither the single nor the album charted in the UK. To Dee Anthony it didn't matter much. His focus was firmly on America and he had a daunting live schedule laid out, with gigs through April, May and June.*

**Jerry Shirley:** It was our longest and by far most satisfying American tour yet. From *Rock On* onwards, at that point in America, we had become the band to see. All the bands were talking about Humble Pie.

All the record companies were talking about Humble Pie. Around spring to early summer 1971, all of sudden it went from where we would normally go on stage to a polite introductory response to, as soon as we walked on stage and Humble Pie's name was announced, the place would start to go nuts. The vibe was out. The reputation was starting to precede us. We were still not headlining but everything seemed to be on the up. The four of us were getting along better than ever, Steve and Peter were individually at their very best and were playing off each other on stage better than at any time. Dee was going to find us houses in the Caribbean that we could go to between tours and make us rich enough to buy. He was also going to buy us a gold Rolex watch each once we got our first gold record. We in turn promised to buy Dee and Frank a Rolls-Royce each once we got to headline our own tour.

*The tour – with the band now routinely playing ninety-minute sets – started with a string of dates at Fillmore East and would take in familiar clubs such as the Whisky, Fillmore West and Boston Tea Party, supporting Cactus, Johnny Winter, his brother Edgar Winter, Cat Stevens and Frank Zappa. They were also booked on long stretches of arena dates with bigger, more established acts Anthony looked after, including Ten Years After and Emerson, Lake & Palmer. Anthony also had them play larger venues such as Philadelphia Spectrum and Alexandria Roller Rink with Black Sabbath. It was on this tour that young bands Aerosmith (in Boston) and Cheap Trick (in Illinois) would become major fans of Marriott and Humble Pie. Greg Ridley recalled outrageous on-the-road behaviour, bonhomie amongst guys like Taj Mahal, Ry Cooder and the Grateful Dead, drinks being spiked with acid, 'shagging' and more drugs. Marriott missed home, missed Jenny. The band stayed in Holiday Inns, the bill for the whole entourage usually coming to around $300. Now, frequently, bills were closer to $1,000 as Marriott ran up huge telephone bills calling home. Anthony's tactic of touring the band extensively was, however, beginning to pay off. Rock On became the first Humble Pie album to chart in America, reaching No 118.*

**Jerry Shirley:** It was not blowing the doors off the charts just yet, but it was a huge improvement.

**Steve Marriott:** Jerry Moss [was very supportive]… he was a guy with a bit of longevity. He wasn't talking about 'This album's got to go platinum or we'll drop you,' he was talking strictly long-term.

**Peter Frampton:** We built up the following live far more than radio. We were very much a performing band. We were playing so much. We were based in the New York area when we came over because of Dee and Frank and if Bill Graham had a cancellation or something we could be called immediately because we had such a good following. You'd get a call on a Thursday, 'Tomorrow night, so and so's dropped out at the Fillmore [East], you're in the middle spot.' 'Oh, okay.' That happened all the time. The Fillmore East had this aura about it, and it was a legendary place. I mean we played there so many times I can't remember [twenty times approximately]. It was a lot of times, and often on a moment's notice. It was a lot more easy-going and freer in that period. It was sort of our local. It's definitely why we decided to record there.

# CHAPTER 9

# I Don't Need No Doctor

**Jerry Shirley:** Dee had a very clear plan and the live album was absolutely the whole root and branch of it. Everything was planned. We were far better live [than in the studio] at that time. As the [spring/early summer 1971 American] tour rolled on we kept building momentum toward the shows at the Fillmore [East].

*Anthony's belief in the wisdom of extensive touring followed by a live album was inspired by the success of Joe Cocker's* Mad Dogs & Englishmen *album. He had the same route mapped out for Emerson, Lake & Palmer (*Pictures At An Exhibition, *released November 1971) and The J. Geils Band, who broke through with* Live: Full House *(1972). The Humble Pie live album was recorded over four sell-out shows over two nights in late May 1971 at Fillmore East in New York. The band was supporting Lee Michaels. The venue was a popular location for live album recordings: Hendrix, the Allman Brothers, Frank Zappa, Eric Clapton and Miles Davis, among others, had all cut live material here. Anthony hired producer and engineer Eddie Kramer, 29, to record the Humble Pie shows, from which they would ultimately assemble a double album. Kramer knew Marriott from his work as engineer on Small Faces sessions at Olympic. He was now based in New York working from the famous Electric Lady Studios that, at the request of the recently deceased Jimi Hendrix, he'd helped build. As well as engineering for Hendrix, Traffic and Led Zeppelin, Kramer had worked on the* Woodstock Live *album and already recorded two live albums at the Fillmore East − for The Nice in 1969 and Jimi Hendrix in 1969/1970.*

*Anthony made sure the band was in high spirits for the shows. The second instalment of their $400,000 A&M advance had recently been paid and he was* *able to inform Marriott that he had secured Humble Pie the support slot on Grand Funk's massive summer stadium tour that included mammoth gigs in the legendary Shea Stadium in New York and at Hyde Park in London. The band's set was largely made up of cover versions, with 'Stone Cold Fever' the only original included on what would become the* Performance Rockin' The Fillmore *album. A version of 'I Walk On Gilded Splinters' had been elongated to epic length, lasting for almost twenty-three minutes, while 'Four Day Creep', 'I'm Ready', 'Rollin' Stone', 'Hallelujah I Love Her So' and the closing 'I Don't Need No Doctor' were Marriott-led sound clashes of band improvisations and old blues material.*

**Jerry Shirley:** We'd interpret the covers and make them our own. An example would be 'Walk On Gilded Splinters'… that was reinvented, another was 'Hallelujah I Love Her So', we put our own stamp on the songs. Steve was extremely good at doing it. He'd say, 'We can take this old blues tune, "I'm Ready", and put it on top of this riff.' Then it developed from there, finally to the point of the live record where it was three times as long and ten times as heavy. Steve never failed to amaze me with his knowledge of the blues and old country music. He didn't know just the titles of songs, he also knew the lyrics, chord sequences… his personal mental jukebox was enormous and a tremendous resource when we were stuck for an idea.

**Steve Marriott:** There were a lot of R&B tunes and cover versions on *Performance*. By the time we did that album the audience was familiar with us and we knew what they wanted, which was hard-hitting rock – so, okay, let's give them that. It's not as if I'd stopped writing other stuff, it's just that there's a time and place for it.

**Peter Frampton:** We had no idea what would come from those shows at the Fillmore. We weren't even headlining so we only had a fifty-minute set to pull from. The first show sucked and then the second show was really good. We did two shows a night, so we didn't even start playing [the second] until about one in the morning. In between you'd end up at Ratner's, the Jewish deli next door. I think that was sort of a peak for us. It was the end of a very long tour. It was the weekend before the end of the tour. We were very well oiled as a band but we were probably a bit blasé about the material, the way you get after a six-week tour but that meant that our chops were pretty good at that point. The quality of the recording is down to Eddie Kramer. He miked the room as well as he miked the stage.

*Marriott was heavily involved in mixing the live album back in London at Olympic Studios using producer Andy Johns. Dee Anthony flew over to listen to a playback.*

**Dee Anthony:** Great, except for one thing. It's a live album and you've forgotten to include the audience in the mix.

**Jerry Shirley:** We all sat there and said, 'What do you mean?' What we'd done is we'd mixed it like you would a studio album. You had to be a brave man to tell Steve – and to some extent Peter – as Dee just had, that the mix they had slaved over sucked. We'd mixed the audience right out of it.

**Peter Frampton:** We liked the sound of the instruments when we ditched the audience; it sounded better because it wasn't so ambient. But by doing that we got rid of the vibe. Dee and the record company said, 'Where's the audience? You're doing a live album and we've got to hear the audience!' Dee came into the studio and we put up 'I Don't Need No Doctor' and Dee said, 'Okay, put the audience mikes up further, further, further…' We said, 'Really? That loud?' But then I got it. Okay, I get this now. We're missing half the conversation.

*Anthony took and remixed the album with Eddie Kramer at Electric Lady Studios in New York. With Marriott's backing Frampton was elected as band representative at the mixes.*

**Jerry Shirley:** It was a blessing in disguise because Steve had already started to develop a 'that will do' attitude in the studio, whereas Peter was much more meticulous.

*In June 1971, Marriott guested on a B. B. King album, recorded at Olympic, Live In London. He played on a cut written by his pal Alexis Korner, who also played on the album, as did Ridley and Shirley and a host of other famous fans of King such as Ringo Starr and Steve Winwood. In July, following a handful of small college dates in the UK and a series of huge exhilarating stadium shows with Grand Funk Railroad in Europe, the band played their biggest ever show – in front of 400,000 at Hyde Park in London.*

**Chris Welch:** I thought Humble Pie blew Grand Funk away… Steve was so wired up and full of enthusiasm, he just captured the audience.

**Jerry Shirley:** Hyde Park was a turning point in our career. The size of the audience meant that from then on we never again had to support anybody in the UK – we were always headliners.

*Marriott told the UK press: 'I can't kid myself. I'm an old rock'n'roller, I'll never be anything else, I've never wanted to be anything else.' Next came the band's biggest American date yet, at Shea Stadium, home to the New York Mets baseball team. It was a hugely prestigious show, newsworthy as Grand Funk had sold out the 56,000 tickets faster than The Beatles when they had played the stadium in 1965.*

**Jerry Shirley:** It was the first time I had seen Marriott nervous.

*Rain began to fall during Humble Pie's set and Marriott drew huge cheers, by announcing, 'We don't care if it rains all night long! Nothing's going to stop us from rocking our arse off for you tonight.' The headliners approached the stadium by helicopter.*

**Mark Farner:** The side door stayed open on this huge helicopter all the way, and when we got there, we looked down, and thought, holy shit, man! Humble Pie was on stage and set up on second base. The stadium was rocking, I mean visually rocking… bouncing up and down, and we could see it from the air.

*After their Shea triumph, Humble Pie remained in America for the rest of July, playing more live dates, including with Bruce Springsteen, Soft Machine and Yes. There was an 8,000-capacity arena show in Canada with Three Dog Night and Black Sabbath and a prestigious show in front of 17,500 supporting Emerson, Lake & Palmer at the Hollywood Bowl. The live album was ready for release but before Marriott could return to England (with his share of touring profit, about $5,000, approximately $50,000 in today's money) he needed to complete a* *radio edit of 'I Don't Need No Doctor' for a promo single. The process highlighted the differences in musical ambition of Marriott and Frampton.*

**Peter Frampton:** It was eight minutes long and we had to get it down to three and a half. Dee said, 'If you want it played on the radio you've got to edit it down.' Steve never wanted to do it. Dee would say, 'You want a hit?' In the end I sort of sided with Dee and said, 'Steve, we'd better do this.' I guess I was trying to say, 'Okay, if this enables us to get *Rockin' The Fillmore* on the charts, this will enable us to be the headlining band that we want to be.'

*Frampton's logic was sound but he would not survive to see Humble Pie as a headlining band.*

**Jerry Shirley:** We were planning to rehearse back in London but The Who were [supposed to be – the gig was cancelled] performing at the Albert Hall and Peter wanted to go see them. Steve insisted we rehearse. There was an argument and the gist of it was, 'If you don't come to rehearsal and you go see The Who, that'll tell us where you're at.' We went to rehearsal and Peter didn't show up. And that was the last we saw of him.

*The news quickly spread that Marriott had fired 21-year-old Frampton. The guitarist had in fact decided to quit.*

**Peter Frampton:** My mind was pretty well already made up that I was going to leave the band but the storm in the teacup over the rehearsal was the last straw for me. I called Steve [to tell him] and he went berserk. He thought I was crazy. He couldn't understand. Steve was a strong character but he was needy too. Having me, and Ronnie [Lane] before me, gave him strength, knowing that he didn't have to bear everything on his shoulders. Basically I'd grown up, got to the point where it was time for me to move on. I just didn't feel like I was part of the band anymore. It just wasn't fun. Steve had been my teacher and in a way I guess I was rebelling against the person that had taught me so much. He was no longer prepared to share the limelight with anybody. It was now his band rather than our band. Steve kind of sucked the oxygen out of the air and it was all about him. And it gets to the point where you think, 'I have to breathe – I need to do my own thing.' I was starting to feel claustrophobic. I was being stifled. Also the musical direction had changed to the point of being a lot heavier. The audience had chosen the direction we were going in, heavy R&B. Nothing wrong with it, but not all the time.

**Jerry Shirley:** I was deeply hurt by Peter. How dare you? How could you leave this after all the hard work? Steve was upset, hurt and soon lost his temper. Steve was solely responsible for getting Peter accepted as a serious musician with the media. Before Steve's public admiration for Peter he was simply thought of as just another pretty-boy pop star. But Peter just couldn't handle Steve's overwhelming side any longer. Steve was an intense person and could be exhausting to be around.

**Steve Marriott:** As soon as I started throwing my balls a bit, Peter realised that I was going to take over. It scared him and he split. I don't blame him. I would have done the same. When you see someone coming on stronger than you can, the jealousies start creeping in and there's no feeling of being a unit.

**Greg Ridley:** Steve was Captain Marvel out there [on stage]… and that sort of pushed Peter over the edge.

**Jenny Dearden:** Dee then took Peter up and Dee told me he wanted Peter to be the next David Cassidy [the world's then number one teen star as the face and voice of hit TV show *The Partridge Family*, plus spin-off merchandise including huge albums].

**Peter Frampton:** I then watched *Rockin' The Fillmore* zoom up the US charts and this gave me a feeling I had made a big mistake.

*The edited version of 'I Don't Need No Doctor' was a hit on FM radio in America and peaked at No 73 in the* Billboard *singles chart. Released in November, the live double album,* Performance Rockin' The Fillmore, *was the band's best-selling record to date, reaching No 21 in the American charts.*

**Larry Yaskiel:** The big break was the Fillmore live album. I got a gold album for that [in America a gold album represented $1 million in sales – at wholesale value, around a third of the list price. In 1975, the additional requirement of 500,000 units sold was added for albums to qualify as gold]. 'I Don't Need No Doctor' was an absolute smash, rock that doesn't take prisoners. Dee knew that's what the American public liked... Humble Pie became very much [like an] American [band]... and it was the same with a lot of groups, Deep Purple, Zeppelin, they were all 90 per cent of the time in America. In America you can tour and tour and [big-selling] albums don't need hit singles...

**Bryan Adams:** *Rockin' The Fillmore* was *the* album. It was probably the pivotal album for me as a live musician. The intro to 'I'm Ready' is a stand-out.

*The band was upbeat about their future without Frampton, initially planning to continue as a three-piece.*

**Steve Marriott:** As a three-piece we can really play what we like and we'll just call ourselves The Pie.

**Jerry Shirley:** We put on this big, heavy, tough guy exterior of 'We're better off without him,' but we were all devastated by him leaving. But I don't remember anybody saying, 'Oh, it's going to be terrible without him.' Everybody was supportive, Dee, A&M... we were on such a roll and we were so into becoming tougher and heavier and having Steve take the reins...

*Americans Rick Derringer (a former member of The McCoys now playing with Johnny and Edgar Winter) and James Gang's Joe Walsh (who would join The Eagles in 1975), as well as English player Mick Abrahams (of Jethro Tull and Blodwyn Pig), were all up for taking Frampton's role.*

**Jerry Shirley:** Mick Abrahams was intimidated by the way we sounded as a three-piece. He came to rehearsal, heard us play and said, 'I can't add anything to that, it sounds fucking amazing.' He never got his guitar out of its case. Joe Walsh and Rick Derringer both passed without ever coming to hear us rehearse. Joe had his own career, plus his manager at the time, Mike Belkin, didn't want to deal with Dee. Rick was producing Edgar Winter and didn't need it.

*Keen to capitalise on the success of* Performance *(and with another tour of America beginning in December 1971), the band tentatively began recording new material at Olympic. With Frampton went producer Glyn Johns. Marriott brought in Alan O'Duffy, who had engineered on some of the Small Faces' biggest hits. Since then he'd worked on the huge Andrew Lloyd Webber/Tim Rice rock opera album* Jesus Christ Superstar *and with bands such as Deep Purple and Slade. He was a year younger than the almost 23-year-old Marriott and, despite being drug-free, the pair had a strong, healthy working relationship.*

**Alan O'Duffy:** Andy Johns did some of the tracks on [what would become the fifth Humble Pie studio album] *Smokin'* but I did the majority of it and I mixed it. They played beautifully, I recorded it with enthusiasm and it got mixed in the same room. I had the world of respect for Steve and we were both interested in doing something great, there was a collective enthusiasm.

*Marriott was so enthusiastic he managed to sprain his ankle in the studio and had to be carried out in agony. It did not slow him for long and the band worked quickly in the studio.*

**Alan O'Duffy:** The Stones would do twenty takes of a backing track. Humble Pie would do two takes. They knew what they wanted, they played it beautiful, goodnight. Steve is a performer, a singer – he was a guy who could sing, so we'd do a vocal in one take – brilliant, next...

**Steve Marriott:** That's the album where we really got into hard rock and the soul influence started coming out. I was leaning that way, hell, I started that way with The Moments. Dave 'Clem' Clempson joined after we'd done a lot of the working-up of the songs. I don't think I would've liked being a three-piece. I'm not a good enough guitar player. I like to be able to stop playing at any point and concentrate on singing, and that was hard enough in the Small Faces, where at least we had a keyboard. We got Clem in the band, then toured Europe and the States for the first time as proper headliners. After that, we went straight into the studio to start recording *Smokin'* in January 1972.

*Dave Clempson, from Tamworth, in Staffordshire, had just turned 22. He was guitarist in progressive English jazz-rock band Colosseum, who featured Chris*

*Farlowe on vocals and had followed a late 1970 hit album,* Daughter Of Time *(UK No 23), with a live album of their own in September 1971, which peaked at No 17 in the UK. The band's drummer Jon Hiseman said Clempson was offered £26,000 (approximately £250,000 in today's money) plus the use of a Bentley to join Humble Pie. Marriott had listened to the* Colosseum Live *album and been impressed by Clempson's playing.*

**Dave Clempson:** When I heard Peter was leaving I phoned Steve's house. He was a bit wary as he didn't know much about me and Colosseum was not exactly Steve's cup of tea. He fought me off, pretending to be his non-existent brother and said he'd get Steve to call me back. He went out and bought *Colosseum Live*, listened to my blues solo and rang back to ask if I could come to Beehive immediately. We sat and jammed together on 'Natural Born Woman' for fifteen minutes and he asked me to join the band. Next day I turned up for a full rehearsal with Jerry and Greg to find most of London's music press waiting for pictures of the new line-up and I still hadn't had a chance to speak to the Colosseum guys. I got the impression Peter's problem was he couldn't compete with Steve. That was never an issue for me. The most exciting thing about the chance to join Humble Pie was that I always desperately wanted to work with a great singer that could really go up front and do his business. I was extremely happy to be in a position with somebody that was not only capable but one of the best in the world. When Pete left the band they wanted somebody who had a different style and not somebody who was going to be purely a replacement for Pete. Rick Derringer really wanted the job desperately but he played too much like Pete. They needed somebody who could fit in along with Steve's singing and rhythm guitar playing. I'd always loved Steve's voice, and his songwriting, too. He was one of a few British musicians that I considered a genius. Also, I'd never worked in the States – and doing so was every English player's dream.

**Jerry Shirley:** Clem was welcomed into the band as an equal, full-time member. We didn't say, 'Let's see how it goes,' or just put him on a wage. We had just started to headline, so the money was great. It all happened very quickly. The band was sounding fabulous. During the first year, in which Clem bought Greg's second-hand Bentley and found a derelict farmhouse near me, that he started to renovate, he also started to confide in me that the pressure was getting to him.

*The new line-up debuted in late November 1971, playing a triumphant show at London's Roundhouse in front of a sold-out crowd of 3,300. The band's live album had not charted in the UK (although over the years it would eventually go gold, selling over 100,000 copies) but coupled with the Hyde Park show the band were picking up strong word-of-mouth praise. December saw the new line-up play a two-week stretch of dates in America, focusing on major markets such as Detroit, Boston, New Orleans, Philadelphia, Chicago and New York. The live album was high in the charts, 'I Don't Need No Doctor' was a FM rock radio staple and the band were finally headlining their own shows, albeit in mostly medium-size theatres, including New York's Academy of Music (the Fillmore East had now shut). Anthony made sure the tour was a sell-out by pairing the band with strong support acts such as Edgar Winter, White Trash, Yes, King Crimson and The J. Geils Band. Humble Pie were now commanding, on average, between $12,500 and $15,000 per show as a guarantee, but they often broke into the part of the agreement that saw them take a percentage of profits over a certain amount. It meant they were often making between $20,000 and $30,000 per show. The band scored a record $25,000 guarantee at Philadelphia Spectrum, playing to 18,000 fans. With their percentage of profits added they came away with $33,000 for the gig (approximately $200,000 today). After expenses, including the promised Rolls-Royce each for Anthony and Barsalona, the band returned home for Christmas with a decent $10,000 each from two weeks' work. Marriott also brought home a cocaine habit.*

**Larry Yaskiel:** They came back from America very excited. I knew Steve had, by now, started abusing cocaine but how many of the big groups didn't have people in them taking a lot of drugs? If you take cocaine you're going to be out of it, everything exaggerated and if you take it in huge amounts it gets even more exaggerated and you can't sleep and you take something to sleep and you take something to wake up... that's a terrible spiral.

**Jerry Shirley:** Everybody was using cocaine, from presidents of record companies to roadies and all points in between. At a sold-out show in the southern part of America, the promoter came up and greeted us at soundcheck, saying, 'Congratulations, tonight's sold out,' and instead of putting a hand out to shake with, the hand that he put out held an ounce of the purest cocaine in the world. You were considered strange if you weren't doing cocaine. There was this massive misconception it was a soft drug, no more harmful than hashish but it affected a lot of people. Steve especially. From 1969 through 1971 Steve was an absolute sweetheart. He had a lovely marriage. He wasn't into hard drugs. He was a delight to know. But I never met that Steve Marriott again.

**Jenny Dearden:** He was renowned [for his cocaine use]. There are stories that you think are apocryphal but they're not. Him and Steve Stills with a bag of coke the size of a bag of flour and they just disappeared to London and Olympic for three days.

*Former Buffalo Springfield and Crosby, Stills, Nash & Young star Stephen Stills was temporarily solo and had scored two huge gold albums in 1970 and 1971. He and Marriott met at Olympic in January 1972 and Stills guested on a Marriott song, 'Hot 'N' Nasty', destined to be the lead single from the new Pie album, Smokin'. Marriott dominated the album, writing five of the nine tracks and co-writing another with Ridley. There were three covers: 'C'mon Everybody' (Eddie Cochrane), 'I Wonder' (a 1944 hit by Cecil Grant later covered by Louis Armstrong and Aretha Franklin) and '(I'm A) Road Runner' (a 1966 hit for Junior Walker & The All Stars; Fleetwood Mac would cover the song a year later and Frampton would cut it for his 1977 album, I'm In You). The sound, as engineered and mixed by Alan O'Duffy, was hard, fat and heavy. Marriott's vocals were intense and he put everything he had into the album, collapsing again with what the press were told was 'nervous exhaustion' toward the end of recording. Doctors advised rest but by February Marriott was back on the road for a four-week UK tour, the band's biggest to date, playing mainly universities, colleges, polytechnics, and finishing with a show at London's Rainbow Theatre. Smokin' was the band's best-selling album yet in the UK, peaking at No 20.*

*In March, the band began another six-week tour of America in support of Smokin'. Anthony, also now a heavy cocaine user, had renegotiated the band's contract with A&M, a deal, he said, that would make dollar millionaires out of each band member. In a haze of booze and cocaine, the band signed the new contract at the famous Los Angeles Beverly Hills Hotel, each staying in his own private bungalow. The band did not consult an independent lawyer, instead discussing the deal with Anthony's own lawyer, Elliot Hoffman, who had drawn up the contract. Hoffman was a major player, representing names such as Dizzy Gillespie, J. D. Salinger, Pavarotti, The Who, Pablo Picasso, James Baldwin, Thelonious Monk and Roy Lichtenstein. 'The need for lawyers in rock'n'roll arose when the IRS discovered that several British bands were touring the States and leaving with lots of money without paying taxes,' he said. 'They set up a special unit to deal with alien entertainers. Eventually the money started getting so big that it had to be handled in a professional way.'*

**Jerry Shirley:** In the first year and a half of Dee being our manager, his primary concern was to work us to the position where he could renegotiate our existing deal because he didn't have a piece of it. Once he'd renegotiated, he got all of it. And I, nor any of us, ever saw another penny. We saw the money being spent on things but it got channelled differently. It used to come from A&M through our lawyers and directly to us. But from the point it was renegotiated it went to Dee Anthony through his lawyers. He said, 'We're going to set up a corporation [Oven Developments] of which you are all going to be employees for tax reasons,' and he was going to be the sole proprietor, the sole officer. As soon as we signed those pieces of paper, we effectively signed, in perpetuity, our entire rights away. That was it. End of story. As soon as it was signed, we had our doubts but we chose to ignore them because we were doing so well. We foolishly trusted Dee. We did not understand the complexities of independent representation. We didn't even understand that it was illegal, in fact, to be represented by the same lawyer who represents your manager.

**Jenny Dearden:** How could Steve go from Don to Dee and not take any responsibility for his own finances? Dee provided his own lawyer, Elliot Hoffman, his own accountant, Bert Padell...

*Bert Padell (1934–2018) was born and raised in the Bronx. It was Padell who had advised Anthony to set up Oven Developments as the company through which Humble Pie's American monies were processed to reduce the tax burden on the band. Padell would become the entertainment industry's most infamous accountant; his client list would include Joe DiMaggio, Robert De Niro, Madonna, Notorious B.I.G., Mary J. Blige, Britney Spears, Blondie, Talking Heads, The Kinks, Pink Floyd, Alice Cooper and Luther Vandross. Author Freddie Gershon, a long-time friend, said of him: 'Bert did not see the world as numbers. He did not see his clientele as clients. He saw them as human beings with frailties, insecurities, anxieties, needs… He was their knight, their shepherd, their psychologist/psychiatrist/daddy/uncle and frequently their banker.'*

**Jerry Shirley:** We all thought Bert would do a great job.

**Greg Ridley:** As far as business is concerned I'm the thickest bastard on the planet. I never paid any attention to contracts and agreements. I always felt that somebody else would spot the discrepancies. Usually I'd sign them and read them later and find out, uh-oh, bad news. You usually get to sign them at the wrong time. When you've just done a good gig, you come off the stage when you're a mile high and you don't know if you're signing for a washing machine or signing your life away.

*The 'Hot 'N' Nasty' single followed 'I Don't Need No Doctor' on to the FM radio playlist and would peak at No 53 in America. Smokin' would become the band's biggest album in the country yet, peaking at No 6, and, like Performance, going gold. The spring 1972 tour of America was huge and excessive, covering every major market and several significant secondary ones. The venues the band played could chiefly hold 8,000–10,000 or more. In tighter venues, such as the New York Academy of Music (4,000) and the San Francisco Winterland (5,400), Humble Pie were booked for two nights. The gigs were often in vast sports arenas and huge auditoriums such as San Diego Sports Arena and Detroit's Cobo Hall, which both held 12,000. Playing with Humble Pie was usually The J. Geils Band, but the tour also saw them share the bill with Dr John, Sweathog, Edgar Winter, Procol Harum, Deep Purple, King Crimson and Marriott's pal Alexis Korner. Incidents piled up: Shirley added crystal methedrine to his on-tour drug intake and on one internal flight Marriott narrowly avoided being arrested when his bags were searched at airport while he was carrying an ounce of cocaine.*

**Mick Brigden:** John Hammel, Steve's guitar tech [who would go on to have a decades-long working relationship with Paul McCartney], broke his leg and they called me [Southend-born Brigden had been working for American rock band Mountain] and asked could I fill in for him on the *Smokin'* tour of the US. I worked with them until they broke up in 1975. *Rockin' The Fillmore* had given them a much bigger audience in the US and then they exploited that by doing a good album – big fat rock –

as a follow-up and then going out and just hammering it. We had a team in Texas do lighting and a team in Illinois do sound but the core of the road crew was Dave [Clarke], John [Hammel], Ted [Sellen] and me, a small unit, we got a lot of bang for our buck. John did the guitars and Ted was the drum tech who did the MCing. We put him in white tails and top hat and he would introduce the finest rock'n'roll band in the land. Dave was Steve's old Small Faces' roadie – he was the main guy for the band's gear getting on stage. Dave kept himself very simple, he liked a good meal, might have drunk a couple of beers... he would tell me stories about Steve with the Small Faces and Steve didn't change a bit. There was nothing Steve could do in moderation... nothing. If he was on stage he was on eleven the whole time and when he was off stage he was the same. In the days of the Small Faces, they were young, they could keep it going, the drugs weren't as heavy. The trouble now was evil cocaine got into Steve's grasp and that's a drug where there's never enough of it if you have that kind of mentality that Steve had... we had days upon days when me and Jerry and the other guys, we'd have gone to bed, might have been six in the morning, and Steve was still going when we got up and Steve was still going the next night when we went to bed... and we eventually got to the point when we would almost literally force him to slow down... between the brandy and the Quaaludes [a popular sedative medication often misused as a date rape drug], we'd find a way to get him to go to bed.

**Jerry Shirley:** One time in New Orleans Steve had this idea of going to the local pool hall and being a pool hustler. Now, the pool hustlers in New Orleans are nasty bastards. If you gamble with them, you better have the money or you'll end up alligator meat in the bayou. Steve was saved by two Vietnam vets who happened to walk into the bar when Steve was losing heavily. He'd been good at playing the part of pool shark but then he'd run out of cash. If those Vietnam vets hadn't managed to broker peace, Steve was dead.

**Mel Collins:** I got to know him when I was in King Crimson and we were supporting Humble Pie on the *Smokin'* tour in America. Alexis Korner & Peter Thorup were opening the show. We had some great times back at the hotels jamming and partying just to get away from the seriousness of King Crimson. Humble Pie were full-on when it came to partying... lots of the usual kind of things you have on a rock'n'roll tour, a lot of drugs, a lot of women... they were big, they were huge... at the top of their game. Steve could do no wrong.

*King Crimson broke up on the* Smokin' *tour and band members Collins (saxophone, born 1947), Boz Burrell (bass, 1946–2006) and Ian Wallace (drums, 1946–2007, a future Marriott & The All Stars band member) joined Korner to form a new band, Alexis Korner's SNAPE (Something Nasty 'Appens Practically Everyday). Marriott bonded with this tight bunch of hard-living musicians, all in their mid-20s, who were amongst the most respected freeform rock musicians in the UK.*

*Humble Pie returned to the UK in May 1972, with a gold Rolex and a bonus of $20,000 each (close to $130,000 in today's money). This was where Jerry Shirley's attaché case came in useful. It was a handheld old-fashioned school satchel bought intentionally so as to look as innocent as possible. Shirley would carry the cash, travel separately from the band and make himself look as student-like and young as possible.*

*The success of the tour and the* Smokin' *album meant that Marriott only had a few weeks' break from the road, Anthony wanting the band back in America in June for another four-week tour. Marriott could not rest. He had long harboured plans to build his own studio at Beehive Cottage and that was now a priority, with work on it progressing rapidly. He also toured Scotland with SNAPE, playing lead guitar, and contributed organ and background vocals to the band's 1972 album,* Accidentally Borne In New Orleans. *Marriott's non-stop lifestyle was fuelled by his excessive cocaine use. Unsurprisingly, his home life was suffering.*

**Jenny Dearden:** It got to the point where Steve was doing so much coke that when he was went away on tour it would be a sigh of relief. The first few tours I really missed him but now I'd sit in the garden with the animals and think, peace at last. I loved it there [at Beehive Cottage]... it was my home a lot more than his because I was there all the time. We had a stream at the bottom of the garden and these geese came, they just arrived. We had the dogs and cats. Achilles, our youngest dog, was the result of an unplanned pregnancy between Lucy, our Alsatian, and Seamus [who barked his way through a track on

Pink Floyd's hit – UK No 3 – October 1971 album *Meddle*]. We kept the last puppy and named him Achilles because he had a bald patch of skin on his heel. Steve had so many cats but he had great names for them all... Murphy and Arthur and all the names sort of suited them... it should have been idyllic but it wasn't, because of cocaine.

**Greg Ridley:** You did need something to keep you on a high, which you had to be, we all thought, to achieve what we were trying to achieve. We were trying to be the greatest band on the planet and play to all these massive crowds.

**Jerry Shirley:** It started to become apparent Steve wasn't handling the rigours of the road nearly as well as we thought he was. When he was on tour his phone bills were always big but recently they had become enormous. He'd be on the phone encouraging Jenny to go out more and then if she did go to London, he be screaming at her, paranoid about what she'd been up to.

**Jenny Dearden:** Steve was accusing me of having one dalliance that never really went anywhere and he'd be having things on the road all the time. Sometimes they'd call up, girls with American accents, 'Can I speak to Steve?' He wasn't misogynistic but he was playing the role of the macho big deal. Steve was so coked out.

*Before setting off for America again, Marriott called Shirley to tell him Jenny was threatening to leave him and had met up with Chrissie Shrimpton in London. Marriott shocked the drummer by asking if he would call Chrissie pretending to be a heavy and tell her if she saw Jenny again she would be in trouble.*

**Jerry Shirley:** Steve and Jenny arguing was nothing new but what they were arguing about had changed and the way they went about it had become much more aggressive. Unbeknownst to us he had stopped being able to turn his stage persona off once he got home. Steve would tell me how things were getting tough for him because he was on the road all the time. Jenny would confide that she sometimes wished Steve was on the road more as he had become a nightmare to live with. I couldn't argue with her because he had changed.

*Life continued to grow more out of control for Marriott as the demands on him increased. The summer tour of America saw the band playing more huge sports arenas and halls, 'sheds' – 20,000-capicity venues with the first 5,000 seated under cover and rest on a grass hill that rises on an incline away from the stage – and stadiums. In North Carolina, with the Eagles, Humble Pie played to 23,000 fans; in Tampa they played to 65,000 with Three Dog Night; in Pittsburgh, supporting Black Sabbath, to 59,000; in Akron, again with Black Sabbath, to 35,000.*

**Ozzy Osbourne:** I loved playing with Humble Pie. I'm a big Steve Marriott fan – when he died, a part of me died too. I remember when we did a show together in the Akron Rubber Bowl – it was an old amphitheatre in the open air. It was unbelievable, Humble Pie were shovelling coke up their noses like it was going out of style. They must have done twenty grammes before they went on stage. But Marriott was incredible. Somehow, he was better than ever. I remember looking for the fucking ReVox; Marriott was so good I thought he was lip-syncing.

*In Pennsylvania they played an outdoor festival that attracted a remarkable 600,000. The bill also included Black Sabbath, Three Dog Night, Emerson, Lake & Palmer and the Faces.*

**Jerry Shirley:** This was Steve's prime, he was untouchable… there was no one even close… The Faces were running around in pink scarves… they were having fun but musically they were all over the shop. We weren't 'let's think about it' rock, we were 'let's fucking do it' rock. Steve was the master of crescendo and dynamics; the way he could control a crowd and get them to do whatever he wanted was a joy to watch and be part of.

*The Faces – the Small Faces minus Marriott, plus Ronnie Wood and Rod Stewart – were at their peak of popularity. Their third album, released in late 1971, A Nod Is As Good As A Wink… To A Blind Horse, was a gold record, peaking at US No 6 and UK No 2. From it came the massive US hit single 'Stay With Me', written by Rod Stewart and Ronnie Wood, who Marriott had suggested as his replacement when he left the band. Despite this Wood had bad-mouthed Marriott in the press and Rod Stewart, who likely harboured some dislike for Marriott due to the fact he had married Jenny, his*

197

*former long-time girlfriend, had also put the boot in. 'Ronnie [Lane] writes beautiful songs,' he had told the press, 'Most of the commercial junk [with the Small Faces] was the Steve Marriott influence.'*

**Jerry Shirley:** Those two, Rod and Ronnie, were constantly having a go at Steve and the Pie in the press, even though Steve recommended Ronnie knowing that Rod would probably come along, and during that period I never heard Steve say anything about how it took two of them to replace him.

*Lane, however, was growing disgruntled with the Faces, who had essentially become Stewart's backing band, their success chiefly due to Stewart's incredible solo career. His third solo album,* Every Picture Tells A Story, *had gone to No 1 in the UK and the US, and he'd followed it, in the summer of 1972, with another UK No 1 and US No 2 album that spawned huge solo hit singles, 'Maggie May' and 'You Wear It Well'. At the gig in Pennsylvania, Marriott approached Lane.*

**Dave Clempson:** Ronnie ignored him.. Steve went up and asked him how he was doing and Ronnie looked just straight through him.

*Dee Anthony kept adding dates to the Humble Pie itinerary that, with just a few weeks break at the beginning of August, would now stretch to the end of September. It meant the band had been on the road in America for the better part of seven months.* Smokin' *was still in the American charts and a second single lifted from the album, Marriott's '30 Days In The Hole', received heavy airplay. Gigs continued to sell out and in some venues box office records were being broken. The band, at the suggestion of Mick Brigden, had hired a private Learjet to travel between shows.*

**Mick Brigden:** We'd used Learjets with Mountain and so Learjets weren't that big a deal to me. When the Pie was looking around at how can we travel in more comfort, I suggested it. In those days we didn't have tour buses. The first tour bus I ever saw was the last tour with the Pie [1975] and it was an old converted Greyhound that the crew used... nothing like the million-dollar buses we use now. The touring schedule the way Frank [Barsalona] booked it [would be, for example], you had to get up at six in the morning to get a connection between Atlanta and Chattanooga to get to Knoxville, to rent a car to drive to a Holiday Inn.

Then after the gig get four hours' sleep, get up and do it again. If you're headlining and selling out, 5- to 10- to 15,000-seaters you think, do I really have to do it that way? I'm sure I had a late night conversation, most likely with Jerry and he said, 'What does it cost?' and I gave him a number and he said, 'Well, I think we should do it,' and then he went ahead and approved it...

*Surprisingly, given his fear of flying, Marriott loved the Learjet, suggesting he could tour as long as Anthony and Barsalona liked in such style. The other upgrade the band felt they could now afford was their accommodation, no more hotel rooms. Now it was suites.*

**Jerry Shirley:** We had a suite each and then we'd hire an extra suite to use for the after-show party at which there was inevitably a snorting contest, whereby a line of coke about a foot and half long would be chopped out along the top of table to see if you could snort it – and I don't remember any band member or Dee ever failing to succeed in this endeavour. Dee had become a father figure to Steve and they'd spend hours and hours locked in the bathroom or spare bedroom of the party suite in the company of the gods of cocaine.

*Marriott's behaviour on the road was now regularly causing problems for the band.*

**Mick Brigden:** At the Philadelphia Spectrum, the basketball arena, Steve saw a black security guard pushing kids who were trying to get close to the stage pretty violently and so he went over and he kicked the guy in the arse, in front of 15,000 white rock fans and everyone cheered. Toward the end of the show the guy came round the back of stage and brought his security guys – they were waiting to do something to Steve. Dee found out and went over to confront Larry Magid, the promoter. Steve is still on stage enjoying life and the crowd was now on stage and the lighting trees were swaying. Steve had actually made the situation worse, he'd actually caused us a bigger problem because we had too many kids on stage. Larry is telling Dee, 'Steve has fucked it up,' and Dee is not taking any shit and he punches Larry in the face and now we've got a fight between the promoter and manager... we had to smuggle Steve out of the building after the show.

**Jerry Shirley:** Frank Barsalona had a driver [for his Rolls-Royce] named Willie, who carried a piece. Willie also stepped in with the security guard. Then, when you get back to the hotel, in Steve's words, 'that was a gas'.

**Mick Brigden:** We got away with a few scrapes. The Led Zeppelin security guys, plus John Bonham and Peter Grant, they physically went out after the shows looking to do some damage... we didn't do that. Steve would bust up the room he was in quite often and, in the Deep South in the early seventies, the fact you were a long-haired hippy and you were saying 'motherfucker' on stage... they were just lined up waiting to charge him with inciting a riot.

**Jerry Shirley:** We were in trouble if we weren't playing a major market because Steve hated playing anything but major markets. He was just a city kind of guy. I think the quality of blow wasn't as good in Johnstown as it was in Chicago. And Debbie and Debbie and Debbie weren't in Johnstown like they were in Chicago! Whenever we got a gig that was even slightly off the beaten track, it made Steve misbehave something wicked. We got literally chased off stage and on to the Learjet out of Florida one night. We got wind of the fact that the police were going to arrest Steve and possibly all of us because he was 'motherfucking' on stage. As we came off, they did this big diversionary tactic. They ran Steve off in one direction and took him straight to the airport while we went in the other direction in a car to the airport. It was like something out of a movie. Steve thought it was hysterical. He got the most fun out of creating a situation like that. This was the stuff that made him tick, any and all forms of authority just waiting for him to fuck with in any way he chose... he didn't care about the repercussions. Fuck consequences. While this was immensely entertaining and sometimes hysterically funny, after the hundredth time when you are one of the guys who had to cover his arse it can become extremely irritating.

**Mick Brigden:** Steve was a lovely guy; the only problem was he would never quit being on ten or eleven. His energy level coming off stage took a while to subside. That's common for musicians who put a lot out. But Steve wouldn't come back down, he'd add to it... a lot of Rémy Martin and cocaine and the mix makes you believe you can go for hours. It also makes you aggressive and Steve had that edge on him. If he saw any chance to be a little bitch, he'd be an arsehole to people who didn't deserve it sometimes and then you'd have to find a way of smoothing it out... 'Get us out of here quickly, c'mon, let's move on, Steve,' but the fire had been lit by being on stage followed by coke and alcohol. It was recipe for problems. He didn't want to be told no about anything, especially when he felt like he'd just conquered the world by doing a show.

*The year ended with five-week stretch of UK dates and a first German tour that ate up late October and all of November. The venues were between two to three thousand in capacity and, in the UK, the band was supported by Frampton's Camel, Peter Frampton's solo project – with the media reporting that Frampton and Marriott were not talking. One gig, in Glasgow, was recorded, with tracks from the show intended for use on a follow-up album to* Smokin'. *In December, the band were back in America for another four-week stretch of headlining dates with support from acts such as Aerosmith, The J. Geils Band and Roxy Music (who Dee Anthony was American service manager for). Following the American tour – their fourth that year – Humble Pie flew to the Bahamas for a well-earned Christmas break. Anthony had invested $180,000 (approximately £1 million in today's money) of Humble Pie's touring monies and record royalties in property in Nassau, a tax haven. Marriott's tour earnings often now didn't make it into Shirley's satchel. Instead he'd take his share to the Bahamas and then return to the UK broke, having blown the lot while there.*

**Jerry Shirley:** Dee and our accountant Bert Padell bought a magnificent property [in the Bahamas], which we rechristened Rock's Rest. It was a complex of six houses on five acres, with its own beach that ran the length of the property, located at the end of the road that led to the exclusive Lyford Cay Yacht Club. The houses were built three on each side of a private driveway that ran from the entrance gates down to the beach. Each had two bedrooms with en-suite bathrooms, a large living room, a kitchen and a sun-deck/patio that was built on the front of the house, looking out towards the sea... there were beautifully manicured tropical gardens, loads of palm trees, tropical fruit trees... halfway down the private drive was a large fountain and circular wishing well. It was complete and absolute paradise. Steve took the first house on the right of the drive, nearest the beach. The two houses nearest the road were for guests but actually belonged to Dee and Bert. The idea of the property was that we would use it to get some rest and relaxation between tours and rent it out to other resting rock stars while we were not there.

# CHAPTER 10
# Black Coffee

**Jenny Dearden:** Turning what had been Ronnie and Sue's place into a studio was the beginning of the end for our marriage. It was lots more coke and lots more staying up all night... and even though it was soundproofed, you'd hear the music in the garden and all through the night. This was supposed to be our sanctuary, in the country, peace and quiet. In the middle of this idyllic setting, this horror was starting to happen, one day at time.

**Jerry Shirley:** Anything Steve wanted for the studio, Steve got. It had a mixing desk, designed by Dick Swettenham [who had designed and built the desk at Olympic Studios] and built by his company Helios, and state-of-the-art tape machines.

**Alan O'Duffy:** It was upstairs above a double garage and in the garage were two white Aston Martins, one of which was a convertible. The studio had Studer 2-inch, 16-track tape machines, Lockwood speakers, an echo system...

*This was where, in early 1973, Humble Pie planned to put together the follow-up to* Smokin', *which Marriott had decided would be a double album.*

**Steve Marriott:** I thought, heck, maybe now's the time to blend in the quieter country stuff and the soulful stuff with the rock'n'roll. I had all these songs hanging about. Maybe the others had dried up as far as songwriting, they weren't forthcoming, so all I had was my own stuff. So [I planned] one side of the album as rock tunes, and one side as country-type [material], plus a side of old soul numbers and a live side [using tracks recorded in Glasgow].

*The soul covers Marriott chose to record for the album were: the Ray Charles song 'I Believe To My Soul', another Junior Walker & The All Stars song, 'Shut Up And Don't Interrupt Me' (1970), 'That's How Strong My Love Is' (popularised by Otis Redding in 1965 and covered by the Stones and many others) and Ike & Tina Turner's 'Black Coffee' from their 1972 album* Feel Good. *The three live tracks that would appear on the completed album included a new Pie original with lyrics by Marriott, 'Up Our Sleeves', plus a version of the Stones' 'Honky Tonk Women' and '(I'm A) Road Runner', the Junior Walker & The All Stars track recorded in the studio for* Smokin'. *All the original material, eight new tracks in total, was written by Marriott.*

**Jerry Shirley:** One of the big things we tried to do to keep Steve's mind off the impending doom surrounding his collapsing relationship was to tell him that we would support his musical vision 100 per cent on this album. Jenny was still there but emotionally she was gone. And everybody was thrilled with the way the sessions were developing. The music we were producing together was nothing short of sensational. It was a double album with something for everyone. There were some great songs: 'Get Down To It' was a raucous, bluesy Hammond organ gem of Steve's; there were some beautiful acoustic songs from Steve. 'Oh, Bella' [with B. J. Cole on pedal steel guitar] was a typically sweet and gentle ballad he wrote about his grandma.

*Marriott's vision of mixing genres on the album also extended to how he wanted the band to present themselves live. He talked enthusiastically about adding Sydney George, the saxophonist who played with Booker T. before becoming a staple of the Memphis Horns, to the line-up, and he asked Anthony to arrange a trio of backing singers – the very best of the very best: Venetta Fields, who he had heard singing back-up on a 1965 live album by Ike & Tina Turner; Majorie Hendricks, who sang on a 1959 Ray Charles live album; and Lorraine Ellison, who had sung on one of Marriott's favourite R&B hits, 'Stay With Me', in 1966. It's unclear if Hendricks (who would die a few months later, aged just 38, sources suggesting she had overdosed on heroin) or Ellison were approached. Anthony did contact Venetta Fields, who was already regularly working as part of a back-up singing group, known as The Blackberries, alongside Clydie King*

*(1943–2019) and Sherlie Matthews. King had worked with Ray Charles, as one of The Raelettes, and sung on the 1972 Rolling Stones album* Exile On Main St. *Dee offered Fields $3,600 a week for the group, all expenses paid, and a private jet to travel in on the road.*

**Venetta Fields:** I went to a clairvoyant on a Monday and she said I was going to get a very important call on Thursday, and sure enough Dee Anthony called me on Thursday and he told me this young man had been following my career for a long time and would like for me to come to London with two other girls and work with him. That's how it all started. Sherlie didn't travel back then, so I got somebody else in to cover her, which was Billie Barnum. Billie didn't do drugs, that's why I chose her. When I first met Steve at the apartment in London, he fell on his knees and kissed my hand.

**Steve Marriott:** They were a great influence on me, great singers all of them. I thought the backing singers would be good for the vocal side of the band. The instrumental side was virtually tied up at that point. I thought we needed something else. As soon as I find a formula I want to break it. What I was originally going for, which the rest of the band objected to, was a 'revue' format, like the old Ike & Tina Turner show, which the rock audiences hadn't really seen. I wanted to get Junior Walker to tour with us. He'd set out, we'd back it up, and do (say) 'Shotgun', and we could do a couple of our numbers, and The Blackberries could step out and do a couple of the old Ikettes things, 'Peaches 'N' Cream' and stuff.

**Dave Clempson:** I was a bit dubious. I liked the music with a hard edge to it. I was thinking, what are the girls going to do? Are they going to add or subtract to the band? But when they did come in they were great. To be honest, the record company wasn't crazy about a lot of what was going on back then. I would think that they'd want us to consolidate the success we'd had with *Rockin' The Fillmore* and *Smokin'*, which was [being a] good hard-rocking English band. If I'd been involved with the record company I would have been worried about not so much the direction the band was going in but the rapidity in which we were travelling in that direction.

**Venetta Fields:** We were staying very close to Steve in a motel in Moreton and we would spend most of our time [recording] at Beehive Cottage. It was a very funny, exciting time, and we started bonding with each other and that grew, allowing us to make the music we did. In the studio when he started to sing... at that time I had never heard such spirit come from a voice. Lot of spirit, lot of honesty – that's why we bonded because I liked his voice so much and we had the same sort of spirit. That's what made him unique – he had a gospel tone to his rock'n'roll, not like The Who or David Gilmour. Not only could he sing it but he knew how that felt... so that's why he could do it so well. He didn't copy it. It was in him. The sessions we did were electric. We'd be in a daze after we rehearsed or recorded a song. We felt the vibe. Like being in church. Our voices blended musically and spiritually. He was teaching us something and I was teaching him my spirit. We were fusing our music together. It was the same with Pink Floyd [who followed Marriott's lead and used The Blackberries for their *Dark Side Of The Moon* follow-up album, *Wish You Were Here*, a US and UK No 1, selling 13 million copies]. What did they want from us? They wanted our spirit, our blackness, the sound, the phrasing... and Steve almost had it already, so when we got together he got it more and more because he was around us a lot. They had heard black singers but they had never been exposed to it one-on-one. That's what they wanted.

**Jerry Shirley:** The record company and management thought it was the wrong thing to do. The girls were a distraction, financially. They were a subversive force. Clydie told Steve Dee's pay scale was a bit on the cheap side... and she wasn't sure if she would want to continue much past making the album. He promised them $3,600 each per week and on top of that he offered to buy them each a mink or sable coat. Steve, as only Steve could, had told the girls that their pay scale would be so huge that, if we were to abide by it, the entire band and crew would be working for The Blackberries... coke was making everybody's decision for them at the time. Steve had changed by then. He'd become very out of control on the coke... the lunatic was definitely running the asylum at that point.

**Venetta Fields:** We went to New York to spend a few days and we went to this furrier and they had lots of mink coats, $5,000 and $6,000 and $7,000 but they were nice coats. I bought one for my mother for Christmas, one for myself. We, as The Blackberries, had not had that much money before at one time. We were doing session work, a few tours but nothing as grand as Steve Marriott and from Steve it started happening for us… we started making more money.

*The Blackberries' wages were renegotiated to everybody's satisfaction. Alongside the new Pie album, Marriott started to produce an album with The Blackberries at Beehive, cutting a version of 'Twist And Shout'. Marriott was pleased when A&M agreed to release it as a single.*

**Jenny Dearden:** Steve had a thing [relationship] with Clydie when they went on tour in the States but that didn't last. They all had a relationship with people in the band, except Billie. I loved Venetta and I liked Clydie. She [Clydie] had this thing with Bob Dylan for quite a long time when he was going through his religious phase [during his born-again years in the eighties. 'She was my ultimate singing partner,' Dylan told *Rolling Stone*. 'No one ever came close. We were two soul mates.'].

**Venetta Fields:** Steve didn't seem to get that far away [on drugs] with us. He held himself back, especially in the early days. He could be outlandish sometimes but we loved him. I thought he was my brother and he was naughty. The band was fine, polite, giving, funny, worked hard, wonderful… nobody had an attitude but Steve. There's always a prima donna in your band and that was Steve but it was more the worry than anything else with him, thinking he was not all that good. It seemed his talent was more of a hindrance to him than a blessing… Humble Pie had gotten big and he had to work hard and he had to steer the rest of the guys too… there was a lot of pressure on him at that time.

**Dave Clempson:** I think overall we were quite happy with the album but there were problems… we weren't going to the studio as a band and working as a band and leaving as a band. Basically when the rest of us left, Steve was still there and would often want to carry on. Some of the stuff that Steve had done in those circumstance was okay and sometimes we didn't like what he'd done. It became difficult… he was playing other people's parts sometimes. I mean, there's no reason why he couldn't have done that occasionally but because it was done after everyone had left it kind of created some bad feeling. His intentions were never malevolent but he was just full of energy and wanted to keep working. The quality of the recording was something I was concerned about. The studio wasn't really up to the standard that was required...

**Jenny Dearden:** The sound in the studio was not good at all and that was not helpful for his career.

**Alan O'Duffy:** I made the album with Steve and with Clydie, Billie and Venetta, and what a lovely moment that was in our lives. Steve was surrounded by three Californian, Baptist soul singers. They loved Steve and Steve loved them. He was up to speed with them. There aren't a lot of singers in England who you can put up against those guys. I got a great sound out of Beehive but when it came to the mix, Steve was very headstrong, he insisted on doing it and he had an idea he wanted it to have lots of bass. I told him that's not correct but it was not possible to argue with the guy. I'm getting paid by Dee Anthony so I can't walk away from Steve doing all this but I washed my hands of the sound of the mix. I said, 'You can't do a mix with that amount of bass...' but Steve was impossible to tell otherwise. If I'd have been a little more arrogant, I'd have told him where to put his bass... there were fashions in mixing and his fashion was we need to have a very strong bass but it was OTT on the bass.

*In the UK the band debuted their new line-up and soul sound on BBC 2 TV music show* The Old Grey Whistle Test. *They performed 'Black Coffee' as an ensemble and then The Blackberries took the lead to sing 'Twist And Shout'.*

**Jenny Dearden:** That famous clip they show of him on *Old Grey Whistle Test* doing 'Black Coffee', he is just out of it on cocaine... his eyes have gone. Steve could be very hyper and he could be very low. They used to call it manic depression and coke hugely acerbates that because, when you run out and haven't got it, you plummet anyway. It could have been ADHD, could have been bipolar. You didn't deal with those things... back then it wasn't discussed, in fact it was shameful. Today, you could see he was manifesting symptoms that meant he could probably have been helped... but he was using substances to self-medicate.

*Marriott titled the double album* Eat It. *It was launched in London with a prestigious show at the Palladium in front of 2,200 and would peak at UK No 34. As usual, Dee Anthony was unconcerned with the UK market and had chosen Marriott's 'Get Down To It' as a lead single for American radio while overseeing the planning of a huge A&M marketing campaign for the album, including billboard ads in Times Square in New York. He had also arranged for A&M to repackage the band's first two Immediate albums as a double,* Lost And Found *– meaning the band would be releasing two double albums in America almost simultaneously. He and Frank Barsalona had also lined up a huge American tour stretching from March 1973 through May and June, set to climax with a headlining show at the 20,000-capacity Madison Square Garden. He had reserved ten days in May for a handful of dates in Japan, which he intended to film for a theatrical release and harvest another live album from, in imitation of Joe Cocker's* Mad Dogs & Englishmen *documentary and soundtrack album.*

**Alan O'Duffy:** When Jerry Shirley first heard the single ['Get Down To It'] in New York... he said it sounded awful and the reason was it was booming because of the excessive amount of bass Steve had insisted on using.

**Jerry Shirley:** Alan had told him you could not put that much low end on it, it won't transfer to vinyl and Steve's reply was, 'Nah, it'll be all right... it'll be fine'... but it sounded like someone trying to talk with a sock in his mouth.

**Dave Clempson:** We didn't understand straight away what a disaster it was, because we barely had time to complete *Eat It* before rushing off on another tour. Then we heard a track on the radio in our limo. Greg's bass was shaking the whole vehicle, and you couldn't really hear much else.

*'Get Down To It' proved to be a disaster for the band and failed to chart. A second single was quickly pulled from the album, 'Shut Up And Don't Interrupt Me'. It also failed to gain the radio play expected and failed to chart.*

**Jerry Shirley:** As soon as the album was released and it went into the charts with a bullet at No 10, everybody was happy. The following week it stayed at No 10 but lost its bullet and the week after that, when it dropped to No 140 or something, then all the noises started, oh dear, things are going drastically wrong.

Eat It *peaked at No 13 on the American charts. A third single from the album, 'Black Coffee', did get some airplay, peaking at No 113 in the US. The repackaged Immediate album,* Lost And Found, *peaked at US No 41.*

**Bob Garcia:** *Eat It* didn't sound very good when it was released. There was so many discussions about the title too... it was a sexual thing, [meaning] muff diving or sucking cock and nobody thought of it any different. And Steve wasn't good at hiding his problems. I didn't have to discuss [his cocaine use] with the company because a lot of our folks seeing him live absolutely knew [he was using cocaine]... nobody was that stupid. And all too many times on the road he'd simply disappear with some guy who was probably a dealer and then would come back in such a different state... you just knew. It was like Cocker, everybody knew he was drunk and throwing up behind the speakers but he was 'good old Joe' and this was 'good old Steve'... his livewire personality was so implanted in people's minds it was kind of expected of him to be a bit off... you never expected to have an absolutely predictable time.

*The band travelled between dates on a Falcon Jet – big enough for the band, Blackberries and luggage – but in Chicago the Falcon was replaced by two smaller stretch Learjets. Marriott refused to have The Blackberries separated from the band and so one Learjet was used to simply transport luggage. It seemed excessive even at the time. The touring personnel had expanded to include Anthony's chauffeur and Shirley's brother. Pie's biggest markets remained major cities such as Los Angeles, where they played two nights at the 17,500-capacity Forum, generating the band's then biggest gross of $48,000 (over $275,000 in today's money). In Chicago there were two nights at the 12,000-capacity Cobo Hall. Marriott continued to protest at having to play dates in secondary markets. On this tour Anthony had booked a series of smaller gigs in virgin territory, 5,000 capacity and under. Led Zeppelin had recently done a three-week tour of just those markets. Anthony and ambitious band members such as Shirley found Marriott's attitude grating. It was not the only annoyance that surfaced on the tour. Marriott was now calling Clempson 'bitch'.*

**Steve Marriott:** The chicks called me 'nigger'.

**Venetta Fields:** Steve picked up some of the language we used. Oh yeah, he'd be outrageous on the road but he was funny most of the time. He wasn't rude and he wasn't nasty. There was not a mean bone in his body... he was a good guy that was high. There were some huge gigs... the bigger the gigs were, the more he would perform.

**Jerry Shirley:** He had started mimicking the girls, how they would speak backstage. They told him off a number of times for talking like that on stage. He had gotten very into almost being a caricature of himself as a James Brown on stage... frankly a lot of people got down on him in reviews and stuff because of that.

*The* NME *criticised an American Humble Pie live show, picking on Marriott's between-song raps (about politics and race relations) and how he reminded the reviewer of 'Sammy Davis Jr doing an imitation of a black man singing the blues', how 'they'd laugh him off stage at a place like the Apollo... somebody send that boy a scholarship to church school so he can get it all out of his system and get back to what he does best'. He was also picked up for changing the lines in 'Black Coffee', singing: 'My skin is white but my soul is black.'*

**Steve Marriott:** Who does he think he is? But you know Tina Turner sang, 'my skin is brown and my soul [sic: mind] is black.' Even funnier if you think about it. I just sang it because I loved the song and it was my interpretation of somebody else's lyrics. People should have known that I've been into black music for years anyway.

**Mick Brigden:** They played two nights at Winterland [in San Francisco, 5,000 capacity] and had a great weekend, and then we were going to get up early and get on the plane to fly to Japan from San Francisco airport. We got down there in the morning and we go on the plane and it wouldn't start. We'd been up late and we had a couple of Bloody Marys like you did on a plane, we all crashed out and then we woke up eight hours later and we were still sitting on a plane in San Francisco airport. We drank the plane dry... that might have been a forewarning that this wasn't going to be the pay-off we hoped for.

*The band was set to gross $50,000 for five Japanese gigs in ten days. This was the trip Anthony had proposed to film. The band was encouraged to invite their* *partners, Marriott had persuaded Jenny to come with him. Anthony had hired a Boeing 707 jet that could hold 130 people.*

**Jerry Shirley:** But when we got on the 707 there were no cameras, and only three reporters, and only thirty-five people on board. The weird thing was that nobody said anything about it. The only thing we said was, 'Where's the blow?' The expense of all this was astronomical. We were spending money like it was going out of style. It was more than clear that the film was not going to happen but nobody questioned it and no one gave an explanation. It simply didn't happen. So there we were with all the trappings of a big-shot movie documentary without one major ingredient, the movie crew.

*They returned to America, loaded with cutting-edge Japanese electronics, to play their headlining show at a sold-out Madison Square Garden. Marriott had invited many of his family to the show, 'quite a few aunties and uncles', said Shirley, paying for them all to stay in New York at the Regency for three days. His mum Kath, now 47, was working part-time in a pub, a job she said that made her 'feel like a woman again'. Marriott would routinely plead for her to quit, saying he would give her money if she needed it.*

**Kath Marriott:** At Madison Square Garden he said, 'Mum, if I died now I'd die happy. I've done it all. I've loved it, I've enjoyed every moment. I've done things that kids my age would never do... I've had a wonderful life.' I said, 'Don't talk like that.' I always had the fear that he would [kill himself]. Because it's such a fast life, isn't it? He was a big softie underneath. You have to build a wall around you when you're meeting all these people, make out that you're tougher than what you are.

**Kay Marriott:** I'll never forget it. We were escorted in there by policemen with their guns out. And we all had little English flags in our hands. And at the end the whole audience lit a lighter or a match! That sticks in my mind. I couldn't believe that. And we didn't understand what the lighters were for! My mother was saying, 'Sit down or duck!' She thought something was going to happen because we had gone in with English flags!

**Jenny Dearden:** Suddenly, after having had this difficult relationship with Steve, his mum became somewhat overprotective... I did try to talk to her. I said, 'I've just been totally lonely at Beehive, left on my own for months, and when he's back he doesn't want to do anything.' She said, 'Don't talk to me about my son'... so I sort of gave up. When I saw him on stage at places like Madison Square Garden it was that bipolar thing, reaching the heights so to speak, probably a lot of anger and trauma coming out... and it gave him power, he was small, and it gave him this enormous power... but it does burn you out in the end. You can't do that forever.

*Marriott threw a tantrum to ensure his parents and family were upgraded, at some cost, to first class to sit with him on the flight back to the UK. While in New York, Bert Padell had pulled Shirley aside to tell him that following the Japanese trip, which had actually lost rather than made $50,000, the band was a remarkable $100,000 (over $500,000 today) in debt. Padell also highlighted the costs associated with The Blackberries and the studio at Beehive.*

**Jerry Shirley:** Padell asked me, 'How did Steve manage to spend over 100,000 bucks on a little studio in his barn?' I nearly fainted. Steve had led us to believe that the studio only cost $10,000. The trouble was Steve was spending it faster than we could earn it. So long as we were getting our fair share out of all the work we were doing, it was fine, but when Steve started to get into the habit of spending all his share and then going on effectively to spend ours as well, that began to grate on our nerves. He used the studio as a red herring to draw us away from the real issue of his overspending. This was all a product of his reasoning while he was on coke, which was pretty much all the time. He insisted that the money being spent on the studio was a fraction of what we were told it was and this was a sign of our money being systematically ripped off... this led to an atmosphere of backbiting and Chinese whispers. Steve was certain that all who represented the business side of the group's life were Al Capone's right-hand men. And he also claimed ownership of the studio. The group's money financed the studio but no sooner had it been built then all of a sudden it became Steve's studio. His rationale was, 'Well, after all, I'm doing all the writing. So by the time all the publishing money comes in, I'll have that much more owed to me anyway, so I'll just have the studio.'

**Venetta Fields:** One time we weren't getting paid and Steve confronted Dee Anthony and within two hours the money was there [Marriott told Shirley, who went to Bill Anthony, and the issue was sorted]. He really protected us and I sort of wanted to protect him... because they had no idea what was going on as far as Dee Anthony was concerned. I hinted that he was doing what he should not have been doing. He was a manager who I thought of like Elvis's manager... controlling but not giving. Humble Pie got taken for a ride. I was watching it going down. I wasn't so much into business in those days but I had watched it through my Ike & Tina Turner days...

*There was a tour of Germany in June 1973, followed by another four-week tour of America throughout July, mostly in the secondary markets Marriott dreaded, with the occasional cultural highlight including dates in New Orleans and Memphis. Carlena Williams had now replaced Clydie King in The Blackberries. Support chiefly came from The J. Geils Band, Frampton's Camel and Leslie West, former Mountain frontman. The band played to 20,000 at a stadium gig in Toronto and to an incredible 125,000 in Milwaukee, topping an outdoor festival. Benedetta 'Benny' Balistrieri, daughter of Frank Balistrieri, the mob boss of Milwaukee, had met the band's Learjet at the city's airport, driving her Mercedes right next to the plane on the tarmac. Following the tour, completing what had essentially been a five-month stretch on the road, an exhausted Marriott began laying some ground rules for future touring.*

**Jerry Shirley:** He kept putting conditions on how we toured – we can only tour three weeks at a time and then we have to have two weeks off. That's a nightmare because by the time you've wound this big machine up it does not make sense to wind it down after three weeks and then wind it back up again two weeks later... any profit you were going to make would be cut in half right there. We should have gone out and made hay while the sun was shining after doing all that legwork to get into a position where we were making fantastic money... but he suddenly put the brakes on. His attitude was, 'Oh well, we've done it now, let's just stop.' No, Steve, that's not how it works, this is when you're supposed to go and rake it in for a rainy day... that's a sensible, normal person's way of looking at it, right? That's not being a breadhead or a mercenary... he loved those two words. There was one perfect example [after the tour]: we were on an extended break we'd promised him so he could try and fix his marriage and we got a remarkable offer for a long weekend, four festivals over a five-day period, $75,000 per show, all expenses paid, go in, do it, turn around, come home. Even after commissions you were talking $50,000 each [$250,000 today] and he said no. His quote was, 'Ah, there'll be others...' Well, there never was... not like that. We were all pretty pissed off at the time but that's just the way he was. Something happened to Steve in America. It had to do with the coke. He turned into a scary character. I'd always be looking forward to the next American tour but Steve got the point where he dreaded it.

**Jenny Dearden:** In the end he didn't want to tour anymore, he was burned out. He'd say, 'If I have to go on and be that other person again, I'll go mad.' He had all these other people who had expectations that he'd tour and who relied on him to tour.

*Frustrations within the band grew as they began to record the follow-up to* Eat It *at Beehive in September 1973. Marriott did not seem committed to the project. In direct contrast to* Eat It, *he did not contribute any solo written material to the album that would be titled* Thunderbox.

**Steve Marriott:** I remember Clem saying, 'Look, we've got make a rock'n'roll album.' I didn't understand that kind of logic. What the hell is rock'n'roll? Is it Black Sabbath? Chuck Berry? I thought when we were working with The Blackberries that was the best period of the band. But they were asked to leave.

**Venetta Fields:** By that time things were falling apart. We went to America [to finish The Blackberries album Marriott had started] and recorded at the A&M studios. Billy Preston became our producer. There were lots of things going through Steve's mind at the time: it was the wife, the management, the money, the good times, the people, the crowds, the limousines, the whole lifestyle. I tried to talk to him many times; we had many heart-to-heart talks. He was afraid at that time – he knew he was messing up and just didn't know how to get it together. It was, 'What are you going to do for your next [Humble Pie] album?' and he wasn't feeling as good as he did during *Eat It*. He was a little down after that and he got lost, really and truly, but he still wasn't a violent man at all, he was just going through his own thing... falling apart, little by little. The band, the wife, the business, and then the drug taking, the whole thing was on his shoulders and I bet he could see it coming apart sooner than the other guys did. He was going through that phase when everything that could go wrong did go wrong. I never told him, 'You've got to look after your voice.' I said, 'You've got to look after yourself, the voice will take care of itself if you take care of you.' I said it many times, many times. Everything that I had heard about the rock industry, they were the epitome of it... they all want to come to America and the managers say they'll make you a star... and they introduce you to the drug thing. I think Dee Anthony had something to do with that: the abundance of it all. Jenny and I were good friends... and she didn't know what to do about Steve. Steve was in such a bad way she couldn't control him anymore... and she was a very nice girl, very strong.

**Jerry Shirley:** Clem turned from being an easy-going, normal, well-balanced young lad from the Midlands into a scheming, backbiting menace to society. Greg just wanted to pick a fight with the world. Steve became verbally violent and he'd get physically violent as well if he thought he could get away with it. I was just as bad as everybody else in that all I seemed to do was piss and moan behind Steve's back. Dee was developing this routine of calling anybody but Steve and going on and on about how much Steve was going to screw up everything if he didn't shape up and sort himself and his marriage out. We in turn did our own bitching about the way Steve was behaving. Particularly when it came to money. Steve's downfall was cocaine. It was when he started doing it in a big way that his world started collapsing around him.

Thunderbox *developed into a strange rock/funk/soul mongrel. Former King Crimson/SNAPE man Mel Collins guested on saxophone and The Blackberries also contributed. Marriott collaborated with Clempson on the hard-rocking title track, 'Thunderbox' (a precursor to AC/DC's screeching vocal and riff shtick), with Ridley on another and with the band on two others, including the Muhammad Ali-inspired 'Rally With Ali'. The album's direction was, however, steered by a remarkable seven, largely soul, cover versions: 'Oh La-De-Da' by The Staple Singers, 'Ninety-Nine Pounds' written by Don Bryant for Ann Peebles and another Bryant/Peebles collaboration, the minor US hit 'I Can't Stand The Rain' (yet to be released in the UK). There was also a cover of*

Celebrity couple – Marriott and Chrissie Shrimpton, Mick Jagger's ex, 1967. The pair made the front pages when they were busted by police on suspicion of drug possession. The relationship was short-lived and, says a pal,'disastrous'. MIRRORPIX

Small Faces posing with Loog Oldham, 1968. 'Andrew had a lot of influence over us,' said Ronnie Lane. FAIRFAX MEDIA/GETTY IMAGES

Small Faces and The Who on tour in Australia and New Zealand. Marriott chatting with Pete Townshend, the pair wound up having a fight in a hotel corridor, 1968.
DOMINION POST/ALEXANDER TURNBULL LIBRARY, WELLINGTON

With wife Jenny Rylance, model and hip face about town, at their beatific, remote Beehive Cottage, 1968. 'She was the love of Steve's life,' says P. P. Arnold. PICTORIAL PRESS LTD/ALAMY

New 'supergroup' with Peter Frampton (right), Humble Pie, 1969. 'Steve wanted us to be like The Band, where they're sharing vocals and playing musical chairs, instrument-wise,' says drummer Jerry Shirley (left). CROLLALANZA/SHUTTERSTOCK

Humble Pie on their debut UK tour supported by David Bowie, who Marriott had, pre-Small Faces, discussed forming a duo with, David & Goliath. Peter Frampton (right), 1969. NME

Post-Immediate, Humble Pie signed to A&M and developed 'into one of the heaviest rock bands in the world,' said bassist Greg Ridley. The move alienated Peter Frampton (left) who quit, 1971. GAB ARCHIVE/REDFERNS

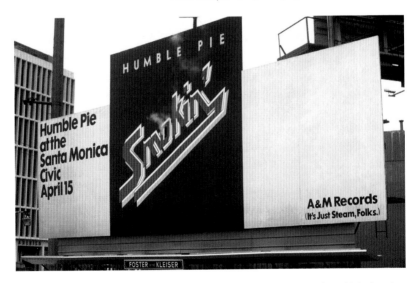

The band's hard-rock fourth album *Smokin'*, released in 1972,was a huge hit in America. This advert on Sunset Strip in LA typified the scale of their success as the band toured huge American venues. ROBERT LANDAU/ROCKANDROLLBILLBOARDS.COM

Humble Pie, with new guitarist Dave 'Clem' Clempson (far right) and new backing singers The Blackberries, (from left) Billie Barnum, Venetta Fields and Clydie King, Tokyo, 1973.

KOH HASEBE/SHINKO MUSIC/GETTY IMAGES

Humble Pie manager Dee Anthony, 'the hottest manager in America for our type of rock'n'roll,' said Jerry Shirley. He is credited with turning the Pie into a stadium act, 1974.

RICHARD E. AARON/REDFERNS

One in a series of personal letters sent to wife Jenny, 1974. Long stretches of American touring and Marriott's heavy cocaine use led to the collapse of their relationship. 'Steve was falling apart,' says Rylance.

COURTESY JENNY DEARDEN

Marriott on stage with Greg Ridley, Miami Baseball Stadium, 1974. 'Steve respected Greg,' says Jenny. 'He was macho, quite stable and kept an eye on Steve.' RICK DIAMOND/GETTY IMAGES

With Pam Marriott Land, 1975. They met in her native Atlanta in 1975. Marriott, on tour with Humble Pie, persuaded her to drop everything and move with him to England. 'I was infatuated,' Pam says. COURTESY PAM MARRIOTT LAND

With maternal Grandma Kathleen, 1976. 'He worshipped her,' says Pam. 'She was the one who turned him on to the blues. She was a huge influence on him.' COURTESY KAY MARRIOTT

*Arthur Alexander's 'Anna', an old Marriott staple dating back to his pre-Small Faces days, plus a strutting take on 'No Money Down' by Chuck Berry and a brave stab at 'Grooving With Jesus', a 1971 song by gospel group The Violinaires.*

**Dave Clempson:** *Thunderbox* was us trying to push the band back in the *Smokin'* direction. I thought it was a noble attempt but the band was past its creative peak. Greg was beginning to sing more [on the cover version of 'Drift Away', which Dobie Gray had taken into the US Top 5 earlier in the year], which was something he personally wanted. I was writing a bit more [as well as contributing to the group songs and collaborating with Marriott on the title track, he had written a solo song for the album], which is something I wanted.

*The band did a short tour of the UK in October, playing in 2,000-capacity venues, supported by the Heavy Metal Kids, a glam-rock band, featuring future Marriott All Stars guitarist Mickey Waller. The band was managed by future Marriott manager Laurie O'Leary. Humble Pie were back in America for another four-week tour in November/December. The band's precarious finances had little impact on Marriott. He argued for a brass section to complement The Blackberries, who he again insisted accompany the band on this tour. With support from Foghat, Electric Light Orchestra and Frampton's Camel, the tour hit many familiar 10,000–20,000-capacity venues such as the LA Forum (there were four further big Californian dates, including San Diego Sports Arena), Denver Coliseum and Chicago International Amphitheatre, with the band able to command crowds of 5,000–8,000 in secondary cities such as Tulsa, Oklahoma, and Dayton, Ohio. Marriott was in poor physical and mental shape throughout.*

**Mick Brigden:** He was self-abusing to such an extent it took down his creative forces and his singing suffered because his voice was getting torn up. After a show he would sing all night in his room, singing to Motown and James Brown. If he had anybody to listen to him, he'd talk and talk, have fun and tell jokes. He was always a joker... he was great to hang out with if you had the energy. But I felt that there was a definite dip in quality, we all felt it in the band. I don't know if it showed out front... Steve was such a showman... he would put on the greatest show, no matter what.

**Jenny Dearden:** Dee said, 'Please Jenny, can't you come, because the tour's at stake?' Steve was falling apart. It was the coke. I remember weeping on the phone to Dee saying this is ruining his life. I didn't like it at all. His personality changed when he was on coke. I had all this pressure from Dee. Steve thought I was having an affair with somebody, which I wasn't. Steve had me followed in London. The guy was a photographer and he was very keen on me but I couldn't have been less able to have an affair, I was completely done in by Steve because he'd been so difficult. But it was nice to have somebody be nice to me. I think Steve must have been threatening to walk out on the tour and finally I got persuaded by Dee to go and stay with his wife in their house in Nassau and then I was flown to New York for a meeting with Steve.

**Jerry Shirley:** It had got so bad that Jenny would only agree to be in the same room with him alone if she got a guarantee that he would not touch her. The band thought it was a possibility. Steve was so crazed. They walked into the room and within thirty seconds... he's lost it.

**Jenny Dearden:** Steve never hit me and he wasn't that sort of a person normally but what happened was they'd all apparently laid into him, said, 'Do not lay a finger on her.' I then had to sit there and read this completely mad letter from Steve. It said, 'If you say you love me then save me and you'll be back on the pedestal,' sort of thing... 'if you don't you'll be in the gutter and you won't have anything, you won't have a penny, you'll lose all your animals.' That's hardly likely to induce one to say yes, of course, I want to stay with you. It was horrific. I said, 'Steve, I don't want to stay,' at which point he lunged at me and we ended up on the floor... he didn't slap me around or anything, it was a violent act but I wasn't black and blue. I didn't mention it to anyone until a few days later, when Dee said, 'Did he hurt you physically?' and I said, 'Y'know, he pushed me over'... and it was the one time it happened, the only time he ever had a go at me physically like that, and he was so coked out. I think he must have snorted several grammes just in order to see me... he had this irrational thought that I was the key to happiness in his life... I became a sort of fantasy.

*At the end of the tour Anthony gave Marriott a sum of money to give to Jenny to help her start an antiques shop. Marriott gambled it away while supposedly resting up at his house in Nassau.*

**Jerry Shirley:** On the first night at the casino they allowed him to win $15,000 and he returned home full of beans. Sure enough he went back the following night to clean up again, only this time he didn't do quite so well. The casino got all their money back and more, they cleaned him out.

**Jenny Dearden:** Steve told me that the money was stolen by somebody in baggage [at the airport] and I believed it. I do remember saying, 'Why on earth did you put it in the suitcase?' He was a terrible liar as well, I'm afraid. We ended quite disastrously and he never forgave me for going despite the fact it was dire while I was there. When Achilles' Heel, who nearly died when he was born and who I loved desperately, got run over in the middle of the night – in the middle of nowhere this woman had run into him on this tiny lane – and had to be put down, I just thought, this is not working for me anymore, I just have to get out. I loved our animals and I had to let them down. I couldn't find homes for them all when I left. Steve was desperate. He didn't want me to go. He suddenly got completely panic-stricken. Steve was spoilt because everything had been done for him from an early age and he hadn't learned how to deal with things or find his own road map. I was punished or put on a pedestal… it sort of varied constantly. What he did in the end, when we split up, he always had to blame somebody else, so he'd blame the music business… and the pressures… he'd say to me, 'I put music first and you should have been first.'

**Jerry Shirley:** She just couldn't stick around and watch him destroy himself anymore. Steve was a very fragile guy. He had the most down-to-earth nature and the most complicated ego all wrapped up in the same package. He was never the same person as soon as his marriage to Jenny ended. His drug intake increased. Steve's marriage to Jenny was his only piece of normality and when that went down the pan so did he. Bigger and stronger men than him would have overcome it but he wasn't equipped to deal with it. The marriage was probably the first failure of his life and that led to lots of other failures.

*Marriott holed up in the studio to complete* Thunderbox *at Beehive, shovelling cocaine up his nose and drinking heavily. He was also snorting heroin. He began talking about recording a solo album. Anthony and Padell visited Beehive to hear the new Humble Pie album and for a clear-the-air business meeting.*

**Dave Clempson:** Steve was becoming concerned about the management situation and management was becoming concerned about Steve's behaviour. And the rest of the guys, we were a bit confused! We started to see a way of easing the situation at first. We tried to kind of make ourselves a bit more independent of management by trying to establish some kind of set-up in England and Europe. But of course that caused all kinds of problems and conflicts as well because management didn't want that. They didn't want us to be involved in any situation from which they weren't profiting.

**Jerry Shirley:** It was a shame to see a great relationship between an artist and a manager break down because of cocaine. In the meeting Steve was being awkward. I was obviously hot and bothered by the whole situation. Greg and Clem were getting fed up. Steve believed that there were literally millions of dollars stashed away, not only with Dee but with A&M, that was owed to us. There was lots of finger-pointing from Steve. I wasn't defending the management but I was saying if there's something wrong let's try and figure it out and fix it and he didn't want to do that. He just wanted to go hide in his studio and get high... he was not in a good place. I lunged at Steve, he lunged back and Bert and Dee grabbed me and prevented me from slapping the shit out of him... Dee had already booked a tour of America [to support the release of *Thunderbox*]. Our initial reaction was, 'Cancel it.' In fact the band broke up. We were looking for a new singer. I would tell Steve things he didn't want to hear. But that had its comebacks...

*Marriott quit after the fight with Shirley but Humble Pie felt they could continue without him and eyed Bobby Tench, former singer, guitarist and bassist with The Gass, a hip sixties band who had counted Jimi Hendrix and Led Zeppelin as fans. Tench had been a member of the Jeff Beck Group from 1971 until they disbanded in mid-1972. Shirley went to see Derek Green, who had replaced Larry Yaskiel as head of A&M UK, with the idea. Green told him Tench was unavailable, A&M having just signed his new rock/soul band called Hummingbird.*

**Jerry Shirley:** Dee suggested that we go check out Billy Joel of all people. Obviously that went nowhere and immediately thereafter Steve was back in the fold anyway [Shirley called Marriott to apologise and they agreed to get back together for an American tour]. We were falling apart at the seams and it was no longer hidable. There was a lot of dissension going on behind the scenes regarding the management. Everybody knew it, from Jerry Moss on down… everybody knew what kind of trouble we were in. Jerry Moss tried to help, counselling Steve, who took great pride in his negative attitude regarding the business and took the piss relentlessly out of anybody who even tried to keep an eye on it. He was so angry with the whole situation and deep down so angry with himself.

**Dave Clempson:** There were several occasions of flare-ups between different members of the band. I had a row with Steve about something to do with money. He said he couldn't work with 'breadheads' anymore. Up until the *Thunderbox* time we had been kept very happy with wads of cash, even though we didn't have a clue how much we were making or what was happening to it, and the assumption was that everything was taken care of. But then that suddenly started to dry up and we actually started to find ourselves in a debts match in England. That again caused a lot of internal problems. We had different ideas on what we had to do to deal with it. Though I don't remember Dee ever standing up to Steve, he would always sort of blame Steve when he was speaking to the rest of us for any kind of problems we were having. 'You know how long this guy spends on the telephone?' And as soon as anyone breathed a word of that to Steve all hell would break loose. At that stage we didn't have any idea what the truth was at all.

*It was decided that* Thunderbox *would not be released in the UK. It limped out in America in February 1974 to coincide with a six-week tour – a recalcitrant Marriott insisting it would be the only American tour that year. The gospel-tinged 'Oh La-De-Da' was lifted as lead single.*

**Bob Garcia:** *Thunderbox*, there's another one: nobody took it any differently [a reference to a vagina]… some of us thought it was funny but trying to explain it to people who were listening to it or seeing a live performance and asking that eventual question…

**Jerry Shirley:** A&M did not promote it. It didn't get any airplay. It didn't sell. At the same time, for the first time, we started to notice that we weren't selling tickets with the same strength as we were before. They talked us into getting rid of the girls and going back to basics. We didn't know from day to day which Steve we would be dealing with on that tour, so even the smallest band get-together was fraught with danger. Nothing seemed to work unless there was some coke around, and even then all it did was make him be the old mate who would be ready to do this and do that – but when the following day came, he would run for cover and wouldn't do any of it.

*Humble Pie were still playing large venues: in Uniondale, New York, they played a 14,500-capcity venue, 10,000 in Memphis, 16,000 in Atlanta, but there were no Californian shows on this run of dates and a noticeable increase in smaller, 4,000-seat gigs. The Learjet was gone, the band now travelling between dates on regular aeroplanes. A second single was pulled from* Thunderbox*, the deeply soulful and impressive uptempo 'Ninety-Nine Pounds', but it sank quickly, as had 'Oh La-De-Da'. The album peaked at No 53 on the American charts, a disappointment for everyone. Marriott's behaviour was growing increasingly erratic.*

**Jerry Shirley:** In Dallas, with Greg's assistance, he completely trashed an entire suite. There was very little left that you could identify as a hotel suite. It would cost a fortune. If Steve were responsible, he would have to personally pay the bill. He had to do some quick thinking… he noticed an American Wrestling Federation sign in the lobby, 'Welcome Wrestlers'. So when he was asked by an exasperated Bill Anthony the following morning what had happened, he said, in a typically convincing way, that the party had been gatecrashed by a bald wrestler called Melvin who had run riot through the suite and trashed the whole place. So convincing was he that the hotel bought it. Thus Steve's drunk, coked-up, pain-in-the-arse alter ego was born and christened Melvin.

Cocaine, sadly, in Steve's case, was definitely bringing out the worst. He became someone else...

**Steve Marriott:** We'd been on tour for about four years and we were just very tired. I was tired with the responsibility, of having the responsibility of producing our albums.

*Marriott was supposed to recuperate in Nassau once the tour was completed, in preparation for UK dates. Instead, in early May 1974, he was arrested there for being a public nuisance. A week later the band played their biggest UK show since Hyde Park, supporting The Who at Charlton football ground in south-east London. They were one of a number of supporting acts, including Lou Reed, Bad Company, Maggie Bell and Lindisfarne. Incredibly Marriott was back to his best, as were Humble Pie, suggesting they would rise from their career nadir.*

**Jerry Shirley:** He'd no cocaine for the week he was in Bahamas... the experience [of being locked up in jail there] had given him a slight pause for thought, jail down there can be a scary place... and he'd had his hair cut off into a classic Mod crew cut and he was wearing blue jeans with turn-ups and bright silver braces. I suggested to Steve we open with 'Whatcha Gonna Do About It'... we nailed it, completely tore the place up.

**Mick Brigden:** The Charlton gig was such a great homecoming, for Steve especially. We'd never done a Small Faces song before... there was never ever any bringing out old chestnuts with Humble Pie. Steve in his bovver boots and a denim shirt open and a black Les Paul... wow... the Pie really tore it up. They got forty-five minutes to do their thing... it was great... it was perfect for him, and he was having a great time and he just let everybody in on it... when a rock singer isn't acting like he's better than you, when he's one of you, it's a nice feeling... he always could do that... I loved the way Steve talked to the audience with his gospel voice singing. I think the headline was 'The Pie 3, The Who 0'.

*Sounds put the new-look Marriott on the cover the following week, amid a glut of overwhelming positive reviews: 'the day's working-class hero with fun and funk band'... 'one hour of spectacular attacking play by rank outsiders and underdogs Humble Pie left the rest of this festival reeling and unable to draw level'...*

*'bovver boy Marriott took the crowd by the scruff of neck'... 'what Marriott had and the rest seemed to lack was the ability to communicate with the crowd'... 'lengthy encore, "C'mon Everybody" put the crowd in a frenzy'... 'a complete triumph for him'.*

*'Whatcha Gonna Do About It' stayed in the set for two more UK dates in early June: a headline show at the Rainbow; and another blinding outdoor set, with Marriott on fine rabble-rousing form, in front of a boozy, laddish crowd of 10,000, at the Buxton Festival in Derbyshire, where they were billed as special guest stars to headliners the Faces and Rod Stewart backed by the Memphis Horns. That night Humble Pie added a new cover to the set, Betty Wright's 1973 R&B hit 'Let Me Be Your Lovemaker'. Afterwards Marriott was asked why there were so many cover versions in Pie's set and on the latest album.*

**Steve Marriott:** I hate to force my music and it's relaxing to feel that you do not have to write. There are other people writing songs that you feel say something for you. I don't think you should be too intense about making music. If you lose the joy, you should stop. A lot of my songs are so personal that it really hurts me to write them or even sing them out loud. Sometimes I think it's very important to reveal a truth and then at other times I think it's silly to expect anyone to identify or feel strongly with something deeply personal.

# CHAPTER 11

# Captain Goatcabin's
# Balancing Stallions

*Summer 1974.*

**Dave Clempson:** Jerry and I were convinced that recording another Humble Pie album at Steve's house was a mistake, for all kinds of reasons. It seemed the obvious thing to do was go back to Olympic, where we'd done *Smokin'*, but Steve was dead against it. So he started to get other musicians up to his studio. His attitude was that if we weren't prepared to go and indulge him at his place he'd bring people along that would. And there was no shortage of them and no shortage of stimulants to keep them all going.

**Jerry Shirley:** He did everything he could to avoid going back to Olympic. It was a nightmare of a time and, no matter what got done, it seemed counterproductive. The more I pressed for a businesslike approach, the more Steve would derail the whole idea. Steve's way of dealing with things was buying an ounce of cocaine and burying himself in the studio. Therefore, when you've got nothing but carte blanche studio time and all the coke in the world, all you do is record. So suddenly he had a solo album, he had an album with Greg and all kinds of stuff going on. And none of it got done very well. There were great bits here and there but there was no one focus on one record. The studio at Beehive was the biggest mistake he ever made. It meant he didn't have to go anywhere and all kinds of hangers-on would show up and bring their big bag of cocaine... and it meant all Steve had to do was

225

get up, walk twenty yards and start making music – which he loved – but the attention to detail was getting lost and he'd be staying up night after night and his health would suffer. His entire life was completely crumbling around him.

*Among the visitors to Beehive was Tim Hinkley, 29. He'd been around the London scene since the early sixties and by the seventies established himself as a session keyboard player, recording with acts such as Al Stewart, Alexis Korner's SNAPE, Graham Bell, Vinegar Joe, Alvin Lee and Esther Phillips. There were many people, whom Humble Pie dubbed 'coke whores', seeking to inveigle their way into Marriott's musical life via drugs and their access to a supply, and Jerry Shirley, particularly, was circumspect of Hinkley's intentions. Shirley's dislike of Hinkley intensified as Marriott's drug intake seemed to increase. He was further aggravated when Marriott suggested Hinkley might join Humble Pie as keyboardist. Dee Anthony, keen to appease Marriott, even talked with Hinkley's representative, Nigel Thomas, who was best known as Joe Cocker's manager.*

**Tim Hinkley:** Dee asked Nigel, 'Is there anything in your contract that says if he dies your contract is null and void?' He also said, 'You know what it's going to have on Nigel Thomas's tombstone... here's the guy who's got so many contracts he finally got one on himself.' Nigel said he was full of shit but it did worry him. Dee was a trip. He came to listen to the Alvin Lee album I was playing on at the time [Lee, the former singer and guitarist with Ten Years After, was now managed by Anthony]. He sat down at the recording desk in the engineer's seat with his face in his hands, whole album, and it finished and he said, 'I smell gold!' He was an act himself.

*Hinkley began steering Marriott away from Shirley, Clempson and Ridley and toward putting together a new line-up. Saxophonist Mel Collins was one musician contributing to the sessions at Beehive. He had played on* Thunderbox *and knew Hinkley from playing with him with Alexis Korner's SNAPE. Then there was Collins' King Crimson/SNAPE pals, drummer Ian Wallace and bassist Boz Burrell. Wallace had been drumming since the early sixties, backing acts such as Sandie Shaw and Lou Christie. He'd played with Viv Stanshall of the Bonzo Dog Doo-Dah Band before joining King Crimson. As well as playing with Alexis Korner, he was an in-demand session drummer, playing with*

*Billy Burnette, Lee Jackson, Alvin Lee and Esther Phillips, the latter two sessions had also included Hinkley and Burrell. Relations between Marriott and Shirley remained strained. Wallace was keen to step in on drums and struck up a relationship with Marriott.*

**Mel Collins:** Ian was one of my best friends, bigger than everybody, could drink more than anybody, could consume all sorts of things more than anybody. As much as Ian was serious about his music he loved to party, so Steve and Ian was a dangerous liaison. Steve was a real party animal but so were we. There was a circle of musicians who used to play together: Tim, Ian and Boz. Steve was putting various albums together at the time. Alvin Lee was involved. Angie Bowie was around, Bowie's wife, on a couple of occasions when I went to the studio. She was very out of it, draped over the sofa. Steve was so manic, always recording something. We'd be playing through the night and it'd be ten o'clock in the morning and he'd get another idea – let's put some horns on this one – and he'd have all these reels of tape. We just recorded all these songs and he built up a big library. There were so many tapes of this and tapes of that and I never really got to hear what the end results were. I never got paid. I never got given anything apart from the white powder. I didn't mind. We did it for fun. Steve was losing his way and a lot of it was due to the white powder. He was excessive in every way. He had all this talent but it was on the edge of being destructive... the drug thing was really heavy. When he ran out he'd send somebody off to get some more. It never ended. Steve would stay up for five or six days and then would just collapse and be comatose for two or three days after that.

**Tim Hinkley:** I mistakenly thought that what we were working on would be another Humble Pie album. Steve and I wrote all these songs. Steve wanted Ian to be the drummer. Dee said Humble Pie is not going to have Ian Wallace as the drummer, Jerry Shirley is the drummer. All those emotions were flying around. The vibe was so bad... and Steve created most of that himself. But we believed in the album we were making. Clem played the Dobro on 'Hambone'. We were doing [Steve's song] 'Captain Goatcabin's Balancing Stallions'... all this crazy shit. Joe Brown and [his wife] Vicki used to come over quite a bit [Brown contributing fiddle and Vicki sang on the sessions]. Steve's dad came over to record with us, he was a real ham-fisted pub piano player. [Small

Faces founder] Jimmy Winston came over. He was a real dear friend of Steve's and he sort of gave Steve a bit of a talking-to. Ronnie Lane came over but just once... they had fallen out big time, so it was an odd visit. He came in and stayed two or three minutes and sensed the vibe, there was so much shit going on in the air... thick with it. Steve thought he might come play on a track.

**Jerry Shirley:** The truth is that Steve didn't want to do anything but stay in that studio with a bunch of coke and musicians that wanted our jobs. Hinkley had got his little gang in to replace us all. Steve had probably promised them our jobs but we weren't about to let them have our jobs. Ian Wallace had been trying to get my gig ever since he toured with us [in 1972]. In this period Steve went to a place that he never really returned from – really, excessive cocaine use, heroin, lots of booze and staying up for days. At the time Steve was blaming Humble Pie for breaking up his marriage and for his lack of money. I felt Hinkley was trying to take advantage of the situation, replacing us with his cronies. Greg was the only one that he couldn't get out because his preferred bass player Boz Burrell had just got a great new gig [Burrell had joined rock supergroup Bad Company].

*Elkie Brooks was another visitor to the studio during the recording sessions. She was pals with Boz Burrell, and knew Hinkley as he'd played with her in Vinegar Joe, the band that launched both her and Robert Palmer's solo careers. She recalled recording a duet with Marriott on a Ray Charles song. Pedal steel player B. J. Cole also played on the sessions.*

**B. J. Cole:** We were supposed to be doing this country-rock album, but as the recording went on Steve lost it more and more and the drugs took over... he was a mess and the house was a mess, there were ducks wandering about in the kitchen! When you were there together working, just the two of you, he was the most delightful, sorted person with a great personality and a lot of interest in music... it went wrong when everybody else turned up.

*One visitor during this period would become a long-standing feature in Marriott's life, one of his closest friends. John Skinner lived locally and had first visited Beehive as a nervous fan in 1972, aged 21. He wanted advice for his band.*

*Marriott told him to practise and invited him in for a cup of tea, watched over by the 'huge' Alsatian Lucy. Skinner had been dropping by infrequently over the intervening years. He recalled finding Marriott one time acting as car mechanic.*

**John Skinner:** I could hear this banging. It was when he had an Aston Martin DB5 white saloon and a green convertible DB5 Volante [both cars now worth hundreds of thousands, if not millions]. He was in the boot of the white Aston with a mallet. He said he'd been driving along and this wheel had gone by and 'I laughed like a fucking drain until the back end of the car dropped down and all sparks flew.' A bloke helped him put the wheel back on but it had dented the bottom. He said, 'I'm just banging it out.' I said, 'Take it to a garage.' 'Nah mate, I can do that, just bang it out.' Another time, me and my wife were sitting in the front room at Beehive and Steve was playing us some records and I said to him out the blue, 'That's some good old music you got there, lovely old Ray Charles, he's lasted well – what do you reckon you'll be doing, Steve, at 70?' He turned to me and Jill and said, 'Oh, I won't make old bones, mate, I know that. I won't make that age.' Then he just turned back to the records. He knew he'd only got a certain amount of time and he had to make the best of it for himself.

*Skinner witnessed the steady decline in Marriott's health.*

**John Skinner:** I was there for some of the 'Scrubbers' sessions [as these recordings became known, with Marriott likely referring to the line-up by the name, a derogatory slang term for a prostitute, similar to 'slag' or 'whore']. Steve was thin and emaciated; he wasn't eating properly. It was sad to see him like that but between them they made some good songs... what's come out [since] are just rough mixes. It was madness with Hinkley, and the cocaine, and Ian Wallace... there was a drunken, drunken coke session when they wrote 'Captain Goatcabin's Balancing Stallions' and there was a woman who was so drunk she got up and danced on the table and Steve recorded her tap-dancing and put it on the record. I went round once, the back door was open, ducks were in the kitchen, they'd shit all over the place, the dogs were in the house, the cats were there... plates and cups on the table but he was nowhere to be seen. Another time I knocked on the door, no answer, but he was hiding inside. I could hear him so I shouted and he poked his head out.

'Oh, thank God it's you. I thought it was Jimmy Winston. I was hiding – I want to keep out of his way... Don't want to see him no more.'

**Tim Hinkley:** Nobody would stay for very long because Steve was so wearing. He was very lonely, very insecure. One time I put the track 'Stay With Me' by Lorraine Ellison on the record player and he freaked out and crunched down into a ball, crying. He said, 'Take it off, take it off'... he was just a mess... I felt sorry for him. He went crazy during that time, he should have been locked up... he was smashing the place up, he was in a terrible state.

**Jerry Shirley:** You'd call up the studio to find out whether or not it was worth going there. You'd ask, 'Is Melvin out tonight?' Or you'd be told, 'Careful, Melvin's out.' Melvin was not a pretty sight. The back door would be left open and cats, dogs, ducks and chickens would come in and shit all over the place. He never cleaned and the place was disgusting. It had become a crash pad for every drug-addicted bastard in the business. When I walked in some dealer would say, 'Who the fuck are you?' I'd say, 'I'm the cunt who helped pay for this place.' Steve was doing mountains of blow and he was staying up for five days straight. And there's nothing more ugly in this world than what we used to call a 'five-day Marriott'... It was just uncomfortable.

**Kath Marriott:** ...that was Steve at his unhappiest. Bill and I had gone round to try and keep him together and he was walking around the grounds screaming, 'I want my wife!' It was terrible. Jenny was the love of his life. Jenny was smashing. That was very sad.

**Kay Marriott:** From then on he wasn't as good to women and he had a lot of hangers-on.

*Marriott played the results of the recent sessions to A&M. They were unimpressed.*

**Jerry Shirley:** Some of the music Steve made in that period was magical but a lot of it wasn't.

**Tim Hinkley:** We'd be playing soul music, New York funk music. We were into [funk drummer] Bernard Purdie [who led the 1973 *Shaft* album]. Boz and I had been over with those guys doing [the] Esther Phillips [album, *Black-Eyed Blues*, 1973] and Steve loved all that. The 'Scrubbers' sessions was him completely unfettered. It was crazy for the time.

*Twenty tracks from these sessions came out as a bootleg album,* Scrubbers Sessions, *in 1991. There were five cover versions included: 'Shake' by Sam Cooke, 'Mona' by Bo Diddley, 'Send Me Some Lovin'' by The Crickets, 'Be My Baby' by The Ronettes and 'You're A Heartbreaker' by Elvis. Marriott, Ridley and Hinkley were credited with co-writing twelve of the other songs, while 'Star In My Life', 'Street Rats' and 'High And Happy' – songs that would resurface beyond these sessions – were credited to Marriott alone. 'Star In My Life' was said to have been written for his sister Kay, whose fiancé had recently been killed.*

**Jerry Shirley:** A&M finally gave Steve an ultimatum, 'You must record in a professional studio, preferably Olympic, and you must get an outside producer for the next [Humble Pie] record.' *Smokin'* and *Rock On* were Steve's favourite records with Humble Pie by far and they were both recorded at Olympic. He loved the place. That's what was so weird about it all. It was where we had recorded our best albums to date, as had Steve when he was with the Small Faces. *Ogdens'* was recorded there. The environment that surrounded the studio at Steve's house was the problem. It was designed and modelled on Olympic, for heaven's sake, except the room was tiny whereas the room at Olympic was huge.

**Steve Marriott:** If we must, let's bring in Andrew Oldham… the whole thing was disgusting. The album was disastrous. I had nothing to do with the fucking thing. Andrew used the wrong vocal track on the title track ['Street Rats'] and that wasn't intended to be on the album anyway. 'Street Rats' was a track with me, Ian Wallace and Tim Hinkley playing piano. It was nothing to do with Humble Pie. Somebody stole the 16-track mix and put it on the Humble Pie album. I'd backed out by then and would just show my face every now and then to do a vocal and split, because I was fed up with the whole situation.

*Oldham, who was based in New York, had asked for and got a high fee to take on the project. He had kept busy since the demise of Immediate, having been involved with producing acts for Rare Earth, a Motown offshoot label, repackaging the 1963–1971 Stones material he had a financial interest in, and working with Donovan and a new glam solo act, Brett Smiley. For the Humble Pie recordings at Olympic he hired his old pal Alan O'Duffy, who had engineered on* Smokin' *and* Eat It.

**Andrew Loog Oldham:** On arrival things were not as they had appeared. It would become apparent there was a reason that my high price had been agreed to without a moment's pause – with all expenses, travel... everybody had forgotten to tell me that the group was no longer. Humble Pie had broken up. Basically, I had been hired as a friend, perhaps the only one who could get out of them one last album while they were breaking up, breaking down and going around the bend.

**Jerry Shirley:** Dee and A&M had all but given up on the whole shooting match. They hoped and prayed Andrew might pull off some bit of magic in the place where it all started, Olympic. We also had a certain amount of hope for what was looking like a last-ditch effort... five years earlier Steve would have bitten your arm off for a 24/7 booking at Olympic; now you could barely get him to show up. Cocaine had turned him into a monster. Andrew did his very best to make the best record that could be made but Steve's cocaine sessions started back up apace and, even though we were committed to making this album as part of our record deal with A&M, Steve treated it as an inconvenience that he would grudgingly tolerate.

**Andrew Loog Oldham:** 'Steve's having problems,' explained Greg [Ridley]. 'I think he'll come to the session if first you'd go out to his house in Essex for a talk'... Steve was ranting and raving. He'd had it up to here with A&M, up to there with Dee Anthony. He'd worked four years and was tired and broke. The taxman was after him, there were problems at home and Steve had just learned that the real estate, a compound named Rock's Rest that he thought he owned with the rest of the group somewhere in the Bahamas, wasn't his at all. He said he'd come to town to grind out the album if I'd come to his home studio and make a solo Steve and Greg effort on the side, then take it to New York, mix it and guard it until it was deemed releasable.

*Oldham agreed. A pattern emerged. Oldham and O'Duffy would show at Olympic for an 8 p.m. start, the band would drift in over the next few hours and 'order and receive some terrible coke'.*

**Andrew Loog Oldham:** Steve would get bored on the run-throughs, so Greg would take over the singing chores. Steve was at an all-time self-destructive paranoid high. We cut basic tracks that were note-for-note rave-ups of well-known Beatles songs, 'Paperback Writer', 'Rain', 'We Can Work It Out', a couple of others. Steve wanted to rip off John and Paul and come up with sufficient variance on the melody, welded with some James Brown cockney patois verbiage to be able to call the song his own. I let him change 'Paperback Writer' into his own 'Street Rats' but drew the line at letting him plagiarise 'Drive My Car', 'We Can Work It Out' and 'Rain'... it was just too obvious and grim. Steve didn't care. The insidious madness grew... his mind was badly coked and frazzled, his human resources undernourished and scarily thin. He wrote average lacklustre songs and took it all as a sick payback joke, which it would be – on himself. Then he did a couple of breathtaking vocals, incredible 'I'll show you, don't count me out' performances, each of them delivered in one tasty take... [it] only made it more frustrating.

*Tim Hinkley was still palling around with Marriott, and was often at Olympic, although the band did not invite him to record with them. It was with Hinkley, after one session, having scored drugs, that Marriott almost died after snorting Thai heroin – heroin now creeping into the fringes of the group's social circles. Marriott occasionally dabbled in heroin but it never became a habit and he would soon eschew the drug entirely.*

**Tim Hinkley:** The next thing I know we woke up in the morning in my apartment with my wife making sure we were still alive. She'd stayed up all night.

233

*Marriott also abused Premier Talent's Hertz Gold Card, hiring flash cars for the sole purpose of drug deliveries. While Hinkley still had Marriott's attention, there was more recording at Beehive; the hard-living 'Scrubbers' crew – minus Boz Burrell – out in force.*

**Andrew Loog Oldham:** I went out to Essex and stayed there [at Beehive] a good week. The sounds Steve had come up with for Steve and Greg's now titled *Joint Effort* were fresher, had a great vital groove and were much better than anything we'd produced at Olympic for Humble Pie. Steve and Greg had opted for Ian Wallace on drums, Tim Hinkley on piano and Mel Collins on horns. There was a darkness about Hinkley. Alan O'Duffy ran the board with zest and vigour. It was an instant groove, clever… in that week Steve spiked Alan's tea with acid, took over the board, added all the right stuff and was very much grooving and in control. Steve was bopping and happy, at one with himself and all at once young again. We finished on Tuesday and on Friday Steve agreed he would come down to London and Olympic and dub his voice over the remaining three Humble Pie songs he'd promised he'd sing.

**Tim Hinkley:** Greg Ridley was a shining beacon through all this. Steve would change his character when Greg was around and Greg knew how to handle him. Steve bad-mouthed everybody behind their back but never Greg. He needed one person in the world who would stick with him. Greg was a great guy, lovely man, a sweetheart.

*A contentious ten-track album called* Joint Effort, *credited to Humble Pie, surfaced in 2018, advertised as a 'lost Humble Pie album'. It featured two Ridley/Marriott songs, three Marriott originals and a Ridley original (none of which appeared on* Street Rats*), plus cover versions of 'Think' by James Brown, 'Rain' by The Beatles and Betty Wright's 'Let Me Be Your Lovemaker' (the latter two covers would also be featured on* Street Rats*). The Humble Pie recording session at Olympic ended with Marriott walking out of the studio after an argument that left Oldham in tears. The band had hit a groove and Marriott had jammed lyrics and the melody of an old song on top, this time Chris Montez's 'Let's Dance'.*

**Andrew Loog Oldham:** I couldn't believe it. This was the moment I'd been waiting for... Steve turned to me in the control room, saw me getting off... suddenly he shouted, 'Hold it,' like a sergeant major, and Greg, Jerry and Clem did, and with that went this magic sound... 'Got you this time, didn't I, Oldham? You think I'd do that fucking song?' Steve and I had said we'd never lie to each other. He'd got me going, then, in my view, pulled the plug on both of us. He needed a hit. I needed a hit. He had to show me the commercial cunt in him and pull it all away... Steve then let me know that the scene wasn't over and read the lines he knew by heart. 'Hey Andrew, what would you like us to do next for you, "Sha-La-La-La-Lee"?' 'It depends on how you do it, dear. We do know the song's a fucking hit.'

*'Oh, fucking leave me bleeding alone,' said Marriott, threw down his guitar and exited. Oldham went to work putting together the album as best he could. There was confusion and acrimony. Shirley, who was still just 22 while all this was happening, said his drums were overdubbed by a session player in New York. Hinkley claimed tapes he played on, recorded at Beehive, went missing and were used on the album. Ian Wallace said he played on four tracks uncredited, as well as co-writing the title track. Marriott went back to Beehive. He had seduced the wife of Loog Oldham's long-time driver, Eddie Reed, and she was now living with him at Beehive. It didn't last long. There were also rumours of affairs with the wives of both Greg Ridley and Tim Hinkley.*

**Tim Hinkley:** There was a succession of women... he'd fuck anything wearing a skirt. He wanted to take my wife to LA! I said, 'Fuck off, what are you talking about?' He got weird. When you walked in to meet him, he'd go, 'Whaaaooo,' and he do this thing where he'd pretend to give you a head butt and stop. He did it to everybody. He just did it a little bit close to me one day and caught my lip. So I punched him and he fell down. He was going to get up and I said, 'Why don't we leave it there?' because I didn't want to get into a full-scale fight with him... not because I couldn't handle it but because he was almost suicidal... and people in that state could do things they would normally not. I said, 'I've had enough,' and left and he came chasing after me in his Aston Martin [V8]. I went to Greg's house, we were having a joint and Greg said, 'Steve's crashed his car.' He'd driven the Aston Martin through a railway bridge and into a river. He had taken two downers and got in his car... he had a death wish. It just followed him everywhere, disaster upon disaster.

**John Skinner:** It was 200 yards from his house and his version was the bridge is on a bit of a bend and as he got to the bend he reached down to put a tape in his tape player and he never turned the corner and the Aston demolished one side of the bridge and ended up in the river... it went to Newport Pagnell, the Aston Martin factory, to be repaired but he didn't have the funds to pay for it and release it.

*Since creating Oven Developments to oversee their finances, the Humble Pie members had been placed on a monthly wage. Anthony now cancelled the payments. Marriott's electricity was cut off. He was belligerent and enjoyed playing the role of martyr. He asked Anthony to sell off his property in Nassau. 'I don't need it,' he said. 'I certainly couldn't afford to go there.'*

**Jerry Shirley:** The argument was that Steve had spent far too much for management to sustain our outgoings. Steve could spend money like water; part of why he always claimed to have been ripped off so much was to cover his own crazy spending. I started making what I thought was a manly attempt to get the group to look at what was going on, financially, and to get other management involved. I was trying to get us away from Dee and go with Bill Curbishley, who was prepared to help, but Steve wasn't having it.

**Greg Ridley:** Well, we were all having problems. Whether it be women or drugs or your mortgage ain't paid or you're getting stale or you want something to excite you. We all had to start selling off things and moving out and whatever.

**Dave Clempson:** The screws were being tightened on us financially. We scheduled a meeting with Bill Curbishley, who handled The Who's money. They were the only people we knew of that we thought would be big enough to take on Dee. And they agreed to see if they could help us out.

*Curbishley was 33, born close to Marriott in West Ham, pals with the Kray brothers and had served a prison sentence for armed robbery in the sixties. He was*

CAPTAIN GOATCABIN'S BALANCING STALLIONS

*de facto manager of The Who, in charge of their lucrative tours and currently producing the* Tommy *movie. In 1976 he would officially become the band's manager, and would go on to manage Roger Daltrey, Judas Priest, Robert Plant (for twenty-six years) and Jimmy Page (for over a decade).*

**Jerry Shirley:** Bill Curbishley was one potentially shining light... he took over day-to-day managerial chores, starting with the road. He was able to find us ways of getting money from some European promoters so that we could function. Plus, he was financially able to advance us money from upcoming gigs. On one occasion he agreed to advance us £8,000 [£80,000 in today's money] on a week or so worth of dates... Bill stuck his neck out a long way to jump in and act on our behalf. Dee could have sued Bill for poaching us. And then there was the fear side of Dee which Bill didn't care about. You couldn't scare Bill like that.

*In late September, Humble Pie played their first live dates in over three months, joining a package of acts that included ELO and Peter Frampton for two shows at 8,000-capacity venues in Germany. Tim Hinkley accompanied the band.*

**Jerry Shirley:** Tim Hinkley tried everything in his power to join the band, even told some people he had. He came on the road with us, paid his own fare, but the three of us wouldn't let him on stage by this point. Steve had tired of him too, as he had by then probably succeeded in screwing Mrs Hinkley, so he loved the fact that we all said no as it meant that Steve could say, 'Sorry, can't help you, the guys won't have it.' It was me, with Greg and Clem's support, who finally told him to hit the road.

*In November, using some of The Who's road crew, Humble Pie took on a four-week tour of the UK – playing venues that held between 2,000 and 4,000, such as the Hammersmith Odeon (3,500 capacity). There were also a handful of similar-sized European dates, including at the Olympia in Paris (2,000 capacity). After the dates, a meeting was scheduled with Curbishley and the band at Marriott's Beehive Cottage about how best to proceed.*

**Jerry Shirley:** This was the most important meeting we had ever got together over. The whole thing was either going to make it or break it. As I walked into the studio my heart sank. There was Steve messing

237

around with something he had recently recorded and trying to avoid eye contact. I'd seen it a thousand times before, the little dance, the look of absent-mindedness, the half-smile that he would do, this sinister little chuckle... he still had a white ring around his nostrils. When Bill arrived with Greg he looked at Steve and then me and winced as if in physical pain.

*Curbishley said he had spoken to Anthony, who had stated that as far as he was concerned the band were under contract to him for another five years.*

**Jerry Shirley:** Marriott said, 'Oh, well, sorry you couldn't help,' flippantly... and went back to his recording.

**Dave Clempson:** Steve had been on a bender and was completely out of it. Jerry and myself just went down to the pub and had a drink. And that's where we first said, 'That's it, it's over.'

**Jerry Shirley:** I couldn't watch him destroy himself any longer. But we neglected to realise Dee had booked us for one more [American] tour. So we agreed to do that as a farewell tour and that would be the end of it...

**Steve Marriott:** Nobody really left, exactly; a roadie came round to tell me my band was breaking up. Why are you telling me this? It made me a bit sick. I'd said I hadn't wanted to tour but we were contracted to do one more... it was a nasty period.

*Marriott appeared less concerned with Humble Pie than the new band he was joining.*

**Tim Hinkley:** After I split I was living on the King's Road and Steve came round to see me and said, 'Great news, I'm going to join the Stones.' I said, 'Wow, you're going to take Mick [Taylor]'s place?' [Taylor officially quit the Stones in December 1974.] He went, 'Yeah.' And after he'd gone I thought, there's no way Mick [Jagger] is going to let Steve join the Stones. But he was hanging out with Keith Richards... Marriott was full tilt at the time, half ounces of coke and smack and God knows what. So Steve and Keith and Anita [Pallenberg] were getting completely wiped and they had been playing together.

**Jerry Shirley:** Steve was hanging out with Keith Richards from time to time, jamming and going over to his house... up all night. The only person that could out-Steve Steve was Keith. Steve could stay up for five days straight without so much as thinking about going to bed. Keith could go ten. He was definitely Keith's number one choice after Mick Taylor left. It was Steve losing the gig with the Stones that led him back to us. When I called him to apologise and see if we could tour again, he said in a very coy but nice way, 'Well, mate, I have already joined another band but I will speak to them and see if I can do a tour with Humble Pie.' Which means he probably still thought he had a chance with them, i.e. waiting for the confirmation call, or he had just found out and this was his way back into work and saving face. Who knows?

**Ian McLagan:** Steve was Keith's number one choice for the Stones when Mick Taylor left. There was auditions in either Munich or Rotterdam, with Richards offering counsel to Steve: 'Stay cool, Let Mick do all the singing, don't get in Her Majesty's way and the gig's yours.' Marriott lasted two minutes, leaped to the mic, upstaged Jagger for the next twenty minutes and blew the audition.

**Steve Marriott:** Keith always wanted to have me. It was, 'My mate Steve's got a great voice, plays a bit of guitar.' And I spoke to Mick about it, and I played with Keith for a while and I thought it was great. Keith would have liked me with them, playing second guitar and singing backing vocals but Mick didn't want to play ball and I don't blame him, he was absolutely right.

*The farewell Humble Pie American tour was scheduled to run for six weeks, starting mid-February 1975, set to coincide with the release of* Street Rats, *Humble Pie's ninth album in six years. A cover of Chuck Berry's 'Rock And Roll Music' sung by Ridley was chosen as the lead single from the album. There was a remarkable three Beatles covers included on the finished Oldham-produced album: 'Rain' (Ridley sharing lead vocals with Marriott), 'We Can Work It Out' (sung by Marriott) and 'Drive My Car' (sung by Ridley). The band's cover of 'Let Me Be Your Lovemaker' was also sung by Ridley. Marriott was credited with writing two songs, including the title track, collaborated with Clempson on two others, and there was one band song, 'Queens And Nuns', sung by Marriott. When it came to organising a group photo for the album sleeve the members refused to pose together so A&M were forced to take four solo shots that were then spliced together. On the eve of the tour, Marriott refused to take part.*

**Jenny Dearden:** Steve was bombarding me, so was Dee. Steve was saying, 'I'm not going on the tour unless you come.' I'd rented my friend Alice Pollock's flat over Manolo Blahnik's in Old Church Street [Chelsea] and an old friend, Sally Miles, introduced me to this guy she was going out with, James [Dearden, screenwriter/film director]. I suggested to Steve he ask Sally to go with him because I knew she was quite keen. Sally did go but while she was in the States she found out James and I had started seeing each other and she said to Steve, 'It's so funny because me and you, and now James and Jenny are—' at which point he smashed the whole hotel room up and she was sent home. He used to call me all the time... the phone would go in the middle of the night, James would pick it up and he'd say, 'Can I talk to my old lady?' It went on and on and it was awful. The time it stopped was when I'd just got home from hospital with my youngest. He called up and I said, 'Steve, I've just come back from hospital with a baby.' 'Okay,' he said and just put the phone down and that was it. The last I heard from him.

*Marriott's behaviour on the farewell tour was unpredictable at best. Money was at the forefront of the band's mind: the members had each been presented with tax bills in the UK said to amount to approximately £10,000 (or £100,000 in today's money). It was the sort of cash they did not have.*

**Jerry Shirley:** Dee agreed to make the payment... there was a serious misunderstanding about this that resulted in some considerable anger and unfortunate accusations.

**Greg Ridley:** The tour was sad. It was bloody sad. It was terrible.

*The mood was worsened by the poor performance of* Street Rats. *The album peaked at No 100 in America. The single 'Rock And Roll Music' barely caused a ripple. To ensure solid ticket sales for the tour Anthony had heavily publicised the farewell/final tour aspect and booked support from a varied selection of strong opening acts, such as REO Speedwagon, Robin Trower, Iron Butterfly, John Entwistle's Ox and Peter Frampton. The band were back on the Learjet and the schedule packed with huge gigs such as the 17,000-capacity Pittsburgh Civic Arena, the 12,000-capacity Cobo Hall in Detroit, the 12,000-capacity San Diego Sports Arena, two nights at the 4,000-capacity New York Academy of Music, a night at the 13,000-capacity Long Beach Arena in California and two nights at the 5,500-capacity Winterland in San Francisco. In New Orleans, at the Warehouse, in front of a capacity 3,500 crowd, Led Zeppelin's Jimmy Page, Robert Plant and John Bonham came to check out the band. Dee Anthony took the opportunity on this tour to expose a new act he'd signed, Montrose, and they provided support at the 9,000-capacity International Amphitheatre in Chicago, at the 9,000-capacity St Louis Kiel Auditorium, the 5,000-capacity Memphis Auditorium North Hall, and the 5,000-capacity Municipal Auditorium in Atlanta. The band's singer was Sammy Hagar.*

**Sammy Hagar:** I watched Steve every night when I opened for them. The first time I ever hung with him, I went to his suite. He's got a framed picture sitting on the table covered with a road map of cocaine. At least half an ounce. Half of it gone, big chunks missing. He's got a couple of chicks and couple of other guys hanging out. I'd done coke twice in my life. 'Hey man, you got like a $100 bill or something?' he asked. I pulled out a $5 bill… he rolled it up, did his blow. I did mine. He was cool. He didn't give a fuck. He was completely on the moon all the time. He'd stay up until he passed out. He'd do blow until he ran out. He'd just live like that, really a reckless guy.

*After the show in Atlanta, Marriott invited Hagar to a late night club in the city called Poor Richard's where blues legends Junior Wells and Buddy Guy were playing. In the limo on the way to the club, swigging on Courvoisier, excitedly talking about jamming on stage with Wells and Guy, Marriott gave Hagar a Quaalude and he promptly collapsed. Marriott got on stage, jammed, and then continued to party, meeting the woman who would become his second wife in the early hours.*

**Pam Marriott Land:** A friend of mine, Andie, met him. She had gone to a Humble Pie concert and brought him over to my apartment [in Atlanta]. I was having a little party that night. He was the smallest little

241

thing I'd ever seen. I'm from the South, all the men are big, and my room-mate, as soon as we opened the door and saw him, said, 'Boy, he's a little shit, isn't he?' So he was always called that, 'the little shit'. At the party he called a friend of mine a cunt, which I know in England is really not that big of a deal but in the South we just don't say that word, so I called him an arsehole and I wanted him to leave my apartment but the girl who brought him had already left, so I just kept making fun of him. I had just read Lenny Bruce, I was obsessed with Lenny Bruce, and every time Steve would say something – Lenny Bruce's saying used to be 'Yadda yadda warden' [from the controversial American comedian's 'Father Flotsky's Triumph', the closing track on his 1961 album *Lenny Bruce – American*] – I'd say, 'Oh, yadda,' and finally Steve looked at me and said, 'If you're going to quote Lenny Bruce, do it properly, it's "yadda yadda warden,"' and I said, 'You know Lenny Bruce?' He said, 'Yeah, I just finished his book'… and that's actually how we started talking.

He was about a week into the tour and had probably been up for three days. One minute he's talking and the next minute he was out cold. We couldn't wake him. I didn't know what hotel he was supposed to be at. I didn't know anything about him… so me and my room-mate put him in my bedroom and he slept for almost a whole day and when he woke up, he said, 'Oh, I'm so sorry for the inconvenience – would you like to go to Pittsburgh?' I said, 'For what?' He said, 'I've a show in Pittsburgh [there was a day off between the Atlanta and Pittsburgh Civic Arena show] so if you could get me to my hotel I'd love to invite you to Pittsburgh.' My room-mate said, 'Go'… I'd never been backstage or anything like that before. I'd just turned 22. I had one of the Humble Pie albums and I loved rock but I wasn't a big music buff. I went to Pittsburgh, saw him perform, rode in my first limousine… I had never met anyone who could transform themselves into what he did, to be that little shit and then on stage perform like that, I was blown away by the talent. I could not believe it was the same person. Anybody who witnessed Steve on stage, God almighty, he put his whole heart into it… and he had a little sick sense of humour that I have too. I was madly in love after about five days. Probably, I was seduced by the lifestyle because I had never seen anything like that, huge arenas, limousines… it was all totally new to me. I was infatuated.

**Jerry Shirley:** She was fun and easy to get to know, a typical laidback Southern lady. I felt extremely grateful to her and at the same time very sorry for her as she had no idea what she was getting herself into.

*Marriott continued to cause chaos on the tour.*

**Sammy Hagar:** I remember one time in Chattanooga, Tennessee. We were sitting in the hotel room of [the Humble Pie] tour accountant Jerry Berg, picking up our $10 per diems on Monday morning, first in line for the weekly payout. Jerry was filling out the paper, sign here, when Steve came busting into his room, fucked up in the middle of the day. He'd been up all night doing blow and drinking. 'How much fucking money we got, mate?' he asked. Jerry started to close his briefcase and Steve punched him in the mouth, grabbed the briefcase, and dashed out the door. Jerry was bleeding. Steve was gone. He had a limo parked out front. Berg got on the phone with Dee Anthony, who wanted to know how much money was taken. When Berg told him $40,000 [about $200,000 in today's money] and change, Anthony went nuts, chewing him out. As far as he was concerned, it was all Berg's fault. Marriott didn't show up for the concert that night. The next day pulling into the Holiday Inn parking lot, here comes fucking Dee Anthony, rolling in like the president... he gets out, grabs Jerry by the neck, throws him against the wall and gives him another pounding. They found Steve in jail. He was arrested with a bunch of drugs, hanging out with some black dudes. They got him out of jail and the tour continued.

**Jerry Shirley:** He [was] very destructive. Smashing up rooms, causing trouble. Steve was in an advanced state of Melvinosity... had not seen a bed in over a week. Here we were, watching every penny, having no idea what would happen after this tour, while Dee had very quickly put into place Steve's right to make a solo record under the terms of the record deal as it stood. Steve's spending, therefore, went on unabated as he knew he was going to be walking straight into a solo record deal that gave him $25,000 when he started recording and a further $25,000 when he delivered the final mixes [and it was suggested another $25,000 when the album was released].

**Pam Marriott Land:** About four weeks after I met him [when the Humble Pie farewell tour was ending] he said, 'I want you come to England.' I went home and told my parents and my father had a massive heart attack three days later. I was raised working class, little Christian girl, extremely naive, not seen much of the world. I was pretty much a goody two shoes. I played professional softball, to give you an idea of what a nerd I was! My father had severe PTSD from the Second World War and he was sick too... and back then to get a job as an air stewardess [Pam flew for Eastern Air Lines], especially for a working-class person, that was a huge thing, that was *the* job. So for me to come home after knowing a man for four weeks and say to my father, 'I've fallen in love, I've quit my job and I'm going to England.' My father said, 'You're not going to do that, you're not going to ruin your life.' 'Too late, I'm leaving tomorrow.' So I flew to Houston [the tour's final show] and the next day I got a telegram that he'd had a massive heart attack... he had a blockage but let's just say the shock of seeing his kid daughter all of a sudden dressed like a hippy, saying, 'Oh, I've given it all up for musician'... that was way too much for him and Mum. Steve got a Learjet and we flew to the hospital and Dad was in intensive care... my whole family looked at me like I caused it. I certainly didn't cause the blockage but let's just say I sped things along. They didn't speak to me for two years because of that. By the time I got to England I knew I'd probably made a mistake because I'd given up everything on this spur-of-the-moment thing. His mum and dad were there to meet me. Beehive was so remote; driving on this little two-lane road, all I could think of was, where in the heck am I? I'd never seen a house that old, it had a thatched roof and the ceilings were really low inside... it was just strange, completely different to Atlanta. I was homesick twenty minutes after I got there. I didn't know anyone – I could barely understand anyone. I had a broad Southern accent back then. I had no idea Steve was still married to Jenny. If I had, I wouldn't have given up my whole life to run off with him. It was the first night we got there that he informed me he was only separated, not divorced. He also said I didn't need to take birth control because he was sterile. I guess he thought that because Jenny never got pregnant with him.

*In April 1975, Humble Pie officially split up. Clempson joined new band Rough Diamond, was then considered for Deep Purple, and ended up forming a band with Greg Ridley and Cozy Powell called Strange Brew. Ridley, however, gravitated back toward Marriott. Jerry Shirley left England for America and joined a band called Natural Gas.*

**Jerry Shirley:** I offered my share of the Bahamas property in exchange for my freedom, writing in a one-paragraph letter that it was in lieu of any debts I may have had then or in the future to Dee or Bandana [Anthony's company]. Everything I had got quickly sold or liquidated because I had no money. At the beginning of 1975 I had the spoils of war. The house in the country, a Mercedes, a Rolls-Royce, a Range Rover, a BMW, a marriage, a kid, money in the bank and all points in between. At the beginning of 1976 I was sitting in the living room of a rented home in upstate New York alone, surrounded by a few boxes.

# CHAPTER 12
# **Soldier**

*It is unclear what further discussions occurred between April and August 1975 regarding Marriott's planned solo album with A&M. It is also unclear what happened to the reputed $75,000 Dee Anthony-brokered advance Marriott was to receive for the album. We do know Marriott was still contractually tied to Anthony, as was Greg Ridley, and that he had bought a horse, Bim, which he rode down to the local pub, where he enjoyed afternoons playing darts. And that he also attempted to turn Beehive studios into a commercial enterprise and himself into a producer for hire. One client was the Noel Redding Band, featuring the former Hendrix bassist, singer Dave Clarke and Eric Bell from Thin Lizzy. Their label, RCA, paid Marriott a significant advance for him to produce an album with the band at Beehive but the enterprise ended swiftly and abruptly. After the first day's recording – two tracks cut, one of which would become the title track of the eventual album* Clonakilty Cowboys *(1975) – Marriott stayed up all night mixing the material.*

**Dave Clarke:** The next day Steve was in a terrible condition. He said he'd stayed up all night because he just found out from Pam that she'd had the baby in America and he'd been celebrating [Toby was born February 1976, so conceivably Pam had just found out she was pregnant]. The management and Noel got a bit pissed off. Noel had come over from Ireland, we were all staying at a nearby hotel, and we'd given Steve a big advance. The management stopped it and we ended up doing the album with Muff Winwood at Island. I carried on hanging out with Steve. He shouldn't have done what he did but we'd all been in that shape at some time. Tony Henderson was driving for Steve when we went to record there, he was an ex-wrestler. There was

246

no management, nothing. Steve talked to me about a trip he'd made to the States. He'd been getting all the money in cash and had a gun in his briefcase. He claimed there was an attempted robbery and so he got a gun.

**Pam Marriott Land:** Steve wouldn't even go into the studio unless he had cocaine. As soon as the man came with a quarter ounce of cocaine Steve would go in the studio and he'd lay down something that was just great but then he would just keep doing it, keep editing it, put more stuff on it, overdoing it, for days and days, until it sounded like crap and then he would pass out. I'd go in and pick him up and carry him to bed and he'd sleep for three days, and then I'd nurse him back to health and we'd be okay for a few weeks while he got well and then when the next cocaine dealer came round the cycle would repeat itself. He was just totally addicted at that time. He had a terrible drug problem. And we were broke. We literally had no money to eat. We were actually stealing food… we had to sneak out in the middle of the night to the farmers' to steal corn and potatoes to eat. Steve was very childlike – he'd been performing his whole life, so all Steve knew was to say, 'I need money,' and Dee took care of it. He tried to call Dee and couldn't reach him. It was highly stressful. He was just calling and calling and the man wouldn't even take his phone calls. It broke his heart. We got calls from the Mafia threatening death to us and Steve's family if we spoke out against Dee. Steve was going through anguish, you have no idea. He wouldn't even answer the phone in the end. The first year with Steve was the worst of my life, but I thought I deserved it because of all the heartache I had caused everyone I loved in Atlanta. I had been dating the same guy for five years. A wonderful man who loved me very much, and when I ran off with Steve he was in the hospital with a ruptured appendix. Didn't even tell him. He came out of the hospital to find me gone. What a self-centred cow I was!

**John Skinner:** In that difficult period between Humble Pie finishing and the Marriott solo album coming out, me and my wife did our best to feed them, keep them warm. We'd go round there on a Sunday with a leg of lamb, some veg and wine… and a bag of coal. He'd cook. Very often we'd go round to find the electricity cut off, it'd be dark. Steve and Pam were our friends and we were looking out for them. He did repay us in his own way because he bought us a car, but we didn't want anything. Pam was pregnant with Toby. My wife was pregnant with our second. They drove a battered old Mini and only one door opened on that. One Sunday his dad turned up and he looked at us and went, 'I see the liggers are here again, poncing off you, Steve,' and Steve was embarrassed. He said, 'No, we're all right, Dad,' and then Bill turned to him and said, 'Don't forget you ain't paid the television rental for us this week. You will get that done, won't you?' I always thought Kath wanted to be the next Marilyn Monroe, she wanted to be a star herself. She was a very elegant lady. They were living their life through Steve, always wanted to get in on the limelight. Bill was much older and the penny-pincher. I always got the impression with his mum it was, 'I wish that was me being famous. I'll live my life through my son. Steve, go and do this, go and do that.'

*Laurie O'Leary, the manager of the Heavy Metal Kids, who Humble Pie had toured with in late 1973, visited Beehive.*

**Laurie O'Leary [1932–2005]:** He had no electricity. He said, 'Dee's stopped my money; Pam's up the duff and all I've got is candles.' I couldn't believe the state of the place. In the kitchen there were ducks and chickens running about tipping over the waste-paper basket looking for scraps of food. Steve would just shout at them, 'Get out of the fucking way!' I'm thinking, he's had all these hit records, he must have an income somewhere. Steve was a tough cookie and you had to be a tough cookie yourself to handle Steve.

*Marriott told O'Leary that Dee Anthony was 'fucking Mafia', 'always threatening', had left him 'potless', that he 'didn't have a pot to piss in'. Despite the obvious signs Marriott was a raging cocaine addict, O'Leary was sympathetic and agreed to become Marriott's new English manager 'on a handshake' and began to help him assemble a band. O'Leary said he had 'always respected' Anthony.*

*O'Leary was an East Ender and a childhood friend of the Krays. He had run their Knightsbridge nightspot, Esmeralda's Barn, from 1960 to 1963 (used as rehearsal space by Eric Clapton and, it is claimed, a young Steve Marriott). His stock rose throughout the sixties as manager of two famous nightclubs, the first being Sibylla's in Mayfair, where The Beatles, the Stones, Frank Sinatra, Richard Harris and a host of famous faces partied. Sibylla's was on the same street as the infamous Stork Club, where the Krays were regulars, and O'Leary booked live entertainment such as Tim Hardin and Joe Cocker for the club through a company, he said, 'we had already established, namely The Charles Kray Agency'. The infamous criminal Freddie Foreman, a Kray associate, said, despite the exclusive door policy at Sibylla's, he was always welcome. In 1968 O'Leary took on the famous Speakeasy Club as promoter and publicity manager. Pauline Cutler, a young dancer who worked the club and became attached to O'Leary, said: 'He was hired because he was connected, and good at what he did.' The club quickly became the leading music business hang-out with executives and hopefuls mixing with members of The Beatles, Stones and Led Zeppelin, plus celebrities such as Oliver Reed, Jimi Hendrix, Eric Clapton and David Bowie. The Who had mentioned the club on* The Who Sell Out *album: 'Speakeasy, drink easy, pull easy'. O'Leary would also brag of 'tour managing' superstars such as Edwin Starr, Otis Redding, Chuck Berry, The Drifters and Glen Campbell and claimed to have managed Marvin Gaye, Martha & The Vandellas and Barry White.*

*By mid-1975, however, the Speakeasy was past its peak. Charlie Kray had just been released from prison, after serving seven years of a ten-year stretch, for his involvement in a double murder that saw his brothers, the infamous Ronnie and Reggie, receive life sentences. It was heavily rumoured that, not only had O'Leary been the face of the Krays' showbusiness and West End club operations, but while the three Kray brothers were inside he had been acting as business manager of their various other operations. In 2001 O'Leary wrote a best-selling book about Ronnie Kray,* A Man Among Men, *describing himself as Ronnie Kray's closest friend throughout his life. Ronnie had asked O'Leary to write the book just before his death in 1995. He said he had many calls from 'various friends of the Kray family giving their condolences' over Ronnie's death. He stated that Carmine 'Wassel' DeNoia – who Jerry Shirley had met at Dee Anthony's apartment – phoned with respects from himself and the Pagano family (DeNoia and Dee Anthony were said to be familiar with Joe Pagano of the Genovese crime family).*

**Laurie O'Leary:** I was going to manage Steve in England to the best of my ability.

*His first visit was to Tim Hinkley, who he said had served a court order on Marriott claiming co-authorship of some of the songs they had recorded together in 1974. O'Leary said he found the paperwork in the grass outside the kitchen at Beehive and that he 'instantly killed the claim'. He also sought out paperwork to establish who owned the studio at Beehive and called 'his friend' Derek Green, head of A&M in UK. Green said he had already received orders from Anthony not to deal with O'Leary. Jerry Moss, Green told O'Leary, had already given Anthony an advance for a Marriott solo album. O'Leary said he persuaded Green he was the one who could get Marriott to the studio and extracted an $12,000 advance 'to help with the band'.*

**Steve Ellis:** Laurie managed Steve and me [former Love Affair and Widowmaker frontman Ellis was now pursuing a solo career] at the same time. Laurie was very intelligent, a sharp businessman. He went to America, to have a meeting with Dee Anthony, about Steve's contract. Laurie was a magician and his brother, Alphi, was lovely too. For many years Alphi was Eric Clapton's road tour manager. I've been at meets with Laurie… he never took any prisoners; he'd just get right to it. Laurie was a stand-up guy. He wasn't a gangster.

*The new Marriott band – christened Steve Marriott's All Stars – featured Ian Wallace on drums, Greg Ridley on bass and East Ender Mickey Waller (1947–2013) on guitar. Waller had left the O'Leary-managed Heavy Metal Kids in early 1975. His association with O'Leary, however, went back to the early sixties and his first band, Mickey Finn & The Blue Men (Waller had changed his name to Finn, a Mickey Finn being a drugged drink intended to make the drinker unconscious).*

*In August 1975 the band was unveiled via the front cover of the NME. The headline read, 'The Horse That Steve Marriott Ate', after a quip Marriott made, suggesting that he was so poor he had been forced to eat his horse. Marriott's financial plight, in light of the huge success Humble Pie had enjoyed in America over the past three years, was a focus of the interview. 'We earned a hell of a lot but we spent a hell of a lot,' he said. Of the band's property investment in the Bahamas, he added: 'The land is a bad thing. There's about ten acres with six houses and a lot of beach.' He was quick to add: 'The situation between me and Dee is fine. Dee hasn't ripped me off. He made us so we have got a lot to thank him for. He's still the heaviest manager to get for America.' Ridley was quoted as suggesting Marriott would not dare say anything different about Anthony, at least in print. Wallace added that legs could 'get sawn off' otherwise.*

*The same month Marriott joined his pal Alexis Korner to play live on German TV to help promote Korner's latest album, 1975's* Get Off My Cloud, *on which he had also guested, as had Keith Richards and Peter Frampton, who had just released his most successful solo album yet,* Frampton, *peaking at US 32 (on the cover he was pictured wearing a T-shirt featuring the face of Marriott). On the show, Marriott shared lead vocal and guitar with Korner in a four-piece band that included Ian Wallace on drums. They ran through live versions of the Stones' title track, a Korner original from the album and a cover of 'One Scotch, One Bourbon, One Beer', a fifties drinking song popularised by John Lee Hooker.*

**Alexis Korner [1928–1984]:** We had a ball. He loved it. But I couldn't work with him on a regular basis any more than he could work with me on a regular basis. I think Steve is one of the most exciting stage performers I've ever seen in my life. He's an incredibly intense blues player and his whole life is really what happens to him on stage and when he's recording. Music is his whole life.

*Despite the platitudes, the two close friends fell out badly during this period. Korner, who was 47, felt Marriott had treated Jenny appallingly and told him so, advising him to grow up. They would never be reconciled.*

*O'Leary moved quickly to score a publishing deal, reputed to come with a £100,000 advance, for Marriott with former Belinda Music boss Freddy Bienstock. Bienstock now owned Carlin Music, which was on its way to being one of the most successful modern music publishing companies in the world, controlling over 100,000 song titles. He would buy the venerable Chappell Music in 1984, then the world's largest music publisher, with a 500,000-song catalogue, for $100 million. It is unclear what songs the advance Bienstock paid Marriott brought him, or for what length of time the deal was set to last, or what cut O'Leary took of the deal. It is unlikely Marriott received the £100,000 in full on signature and more than likely the deal was staggered.*

**Steve Ellis:** Laurie would tell me all these mad stories about Steve... 'You know what he's gone and done now? I've had to go sort out this mess he's got himself in,' and blah blah blah. Steve could be a nightmare and Laurie got him out of a lot of bother. One time Laurie said, 'I've just got him a big publishing deal and he's gone and spent it all...'

*This large advance for publishing was also mentioned by Jerry Shirley in his book* Best Seat In The House *in a section detailing Marriott's ownership grab of the studio at Beehive. 'His and our publishing money was tied up in a dispute between our old publisher Immediate (who had sold our rights to United Artists) and Almo Music (A&M's publishing branch)... he was paid a small fortune by Freddy Bienstock and Carlin Music, and we didn't receive a penny.'*

**Pam Marriott Land:** I don't think Steve turned to Laurie in the hope he might outmuscle Dee, it was to negotiate with him. Laurie had contacts in America, the Pagano family. There was a Godfather wedding at a place called Motel on the Mountain and Laurie had set up a meeting for Steve to talk to Joe Pagano, who was the music don and supposedly in charge of Dee Anthony. So we went and it was nothing but gangsters, and at the bottom of the hill it was just the FBI. I said to Steve, 'What are we doing here?' He said, 'I don't know but this is weird'... it was straight out of *The Godfather* movie. Laurie was going, 'Oh, that's so-and-so by the way and that's so-and-so'... and of course by the time it was time for Steve to talk to Mr Pagano we were scared to death and he told Steve that Dee Anthony had testified during a murder trial and saved someone and that's why they loved him so much... and then Mr Pagano explained to Steve, 'Too bad, too sad, if you make any waves you're a dead man, because we're standing by Dee'... so we knew... Steve said, 'Well, we've lost it, they will literally kill me if I say anything, so let's just cut our losses.'

*The wedding was likely that of Englishman Wilf Pine (1944–2018), organised by Joe Pagano at the Motel on the Mountain in October 1975. The Motel on the Mountain was past a village called Suffern, in Rockland Country, New York. 'When the car could go no further they had reached their destination. Perched on the mountaintop, set in the autumnal woodland, it could have been Shangri-La,' wrote John Pearson in the 2003 book about Pine,* One Of The Family: The Englishman And The Mafia. *Pine had fourteen guests at the wedding. Pagano had around 200. Charlie Kray was invited but refused entry into America. Carmine 'Wassel' DeNoia was in attendance. The wedding, it seemed, was a cover for a mini Mafia meeting. Pine was another good pal of the*

Krays, a pallbearer at Reggie's funeral, and a regular visitor to the Krays during their latter years in prison. He was also connected to Charlie Richardson and Freddie Foreman, two of England's most feared criminals.

It was said Pine was one of only two English men allowed entry into the Mafia. For now, he was in the music business. He had started out as 'muscle' for Don Arden in the late sixties, a petty criminal, lethal fighter and nightclub bouncer who ran a tidy tooled-up firm, happy to undertake 'heavy work' – intimidation, including shootings intended to wound rather than kill, and armed robbery of gambling clubs. Pine, who bore distinctive tattoos on the backs of his hand and fingers (LOVE and HATE across his knuckles), was prepared to go 'all the way' for Arden, who rewarded him with a promotion from bodyguard to personal assistant. 'He taught me almost everything I know about the business,' said Pine.

In the early seventies Pine had struck up a relationship with Patrick Meehan Jr, the son of Don's old associate Pat Meehan, and the pair struck gold when they took over – or in Pine's words 'nicked' – the management of Black Sabbath for Meehan Jr's company, Worldwide Artiste Management. Pine began to run his own operation within Worldwide, scoring a Top 10 hit in 1973 with an Andrew Loog Oldham-produced single by American soul singer Jimmy Helms, called 'Gonna Make You An Offer You Can't Refuse'. Ken Mewis, the former Immediate promotions manager, worked for Pine, signing proto-punk band The Hollywood Brats to Worldwide. Mewis was told that even though the Krays were in prison 'business goes on as usual', and that both the Speakeasy and Worldwide Artiste Management were part of the Krays' empire. In his book Sick On You, The Hollywood Brats' singer Andrew Matheson recounts how senior Mafia figures would show up at the office and Mewis told him the band had 'signed to the Krays'.

Through Jimmy Helms, Pine had met American Irwin Schiff – six foot five, weighing 350 pounds, looking like Al Capone – who was touting a singer called Jimmy Price, the son of Joe Pagano, and also interested in buying out Worldwide for $6 million. Pine took an active interest and, via Schiff, he said, he became pals with Joe Pagano, and over the years increasingly involved with many of the most powerful figures in organised crime in America. Mewis said he felt it was actually O'Leary who had introduced Pine to Pagano. Either way, Pine said he was now prepared to go all the way for Pagano, one of the most senior figures in the Genovese crime family who were considered, by the FBI, as 'The Ivy league *family among the five crime families of New York', with Joe Pagano and his brother Patsy considered 'Mafia royalty'.*

*Pine had put up Charlie Kray on his release from prison and one of his staunchest friends was Laurie O'Leary, described by Pine as 'a friend of almost everyone'. Pine used the Speakeasy as a sort of office. In* One Of The Family, *Pine told a startling and revealing story about how he saved Don Arden's life after Arden had upset a powerful figure in the American music business. First Arden was visited by Carmine 'Wassel' DeNoia and told that Joe Pagano had a connection with the powerful figure. It was a warning. Arden responded by calling Pagano 'a faggot'. Pagano received the message and called Pine to instruct him to set up a meeting with Arden. At the meet Pagano was accompanied by a man Pine knew dispensed with people. Pine persuaded Pagano that Arden would be worth more alive and the two men became friends.*

*It was a complex, covert web of connections that transcended the music business and relied on codes of silence and respect, but Marriott was well aware of what it meant for him: Anthony was protected by the Mafia and even O'Leary and Pine – two of the British music business's most connected players – could not force his hand to release him from his contract. And, despite all the vitriol and accusations, Anthony had plans for Marriott in America.*

**Pam Marriott Land:** Dee wanted to make Steve the white Sammy Davis Jr; he was trying to get him a gig in Vegas. Steve was like, 'Are you kidding me? Me, on the stage in Vegas?' It was insane... but that was the idea: the little white guy who can sing like a black man. He had to do what he was told because Dee was kind of with him and had gotten him a little bit of record deal so we could eat. He was under the thumb. He had to do it.

**John Skinner:** When they did the *Marriott* album he got a bit of an advance; he went out and bought an E-Type Jag and he bought us a car, totally unexpected – an Austin 1300 Estate.

*Marriott recorded a solo single, 'Soldier', in Los Angeles. It was a song written by his pal Joe Brown and arranged by David Foster, with backing from the Los Angeles Philharmonic Orchestra. Canadian Foster, 26, was someone Marriott had clicked with. He was something of a prodigy: 13 when he started a music*

254

*programme at university, 16 when he led a nightclub jazz band and 17 when he started backing Chuck Berry. He'd moved to LA around 1974 with his band Skylark, who were known for their 1972 hit 'Wildflower'. In 1975, as well as taking on the Marriott project, Foster played on a George Harrison solo album,* Extra Texture. *He would go on to score big in the late seventies as arranger and songwriter with Earth, Wind & Fire, before composing, arranging, writing for, producing and playing with a galaxy of stars including Chicago, Kenny Rogers, The Corrs, Mary J Blige and Bryan Adams. He would also write successful film scores and Olympic theme songs, winning sixteen Grammy Awards from forty-seven nominations.* Rolling Stone *would call him the master of 'bombastic kitsch rock' and he would become a well-known celebrity in America, with his own reality show and guest appearances on shows such as* American Idol.

**David Foster:** I don't remember anything about those sessions except that I was a huge Steve fan and thrilled to be working with him and we recorded at the old Record Plant on 3rd Street [hourly rate $120] – I ended up buying that recording desk, strangely. I remember Steve being super musical, very respectful of what I could bring to his musical world (even though I was not a 'rocker') and it just being an incredible experience overall. I remember being really impressed with his vocal abilities but I already knew I would love his singing because I was such a Small Faces fan and one of my fave records of all time was 'Itchycoo Park'. Steve took the time to recount how they came up with the 'phasing' idea that I thought was so unique and outside the box. A real gentleman and a hard and dedicated worker he was in the short time I spent with him.

**Bob Garcia:** The first time I heard a rough mix of 'Soldier' it just blew me away. Wow! All I could think about was why wasn't this earlier in the game? It could have really done the business for Humble Pie. Where was this coming from? I guess it was there all along but not part of the particular self-view at the time... my biggest hope was this was going to develop into something but it didn't. Steve's career didn't have enough breathing room to change... Humble Pie was stamped [as a heavy rock band]. As great as Marriott was toward the middle and end, he was becoming a one-trick pony and that to me was very sad because he was a stellar performer and powerhouse of a vocalist. Management had also become difficult to deal with... those stories are legion. No one really wants to get into them but everyone has a fun story about Dee and a horror story about Dee… there was always the story about him causing Peter Frampton's car crash [in 1978] so he would break his arm and never play again. Everybody had trouble breaking free from Dee Anthony, there was never a happy leaving during that era.

*Marriott was back in the UK for a handful of British dates with his All Stars band at the end of 1975, including two nights at the 1,700-capacity Roundhouse, when the four-piece was joined by Dave Clempson, picking up promising reviews. Marriott was optimistic.*

**Steve Marriott:** The All Stars are going to the States. I'm going to take out The Blackberries again and hopefully also David Foster on keyboards. It'll be augmented in the States and if it's successful I'll bring it back here. I'll do a six-week tour and then cool it.

*Marriott returned to the Record Plant studio in Los Angeles to record more solo material. 'Soldier' had been shelved as Marriott now hoped to use the All Stars on the recordings. A&M tried to dissuade him. They had hired producers Kenny Kerner and Richie Wise, fresh from success with KISS, Elkie Brooks (her debut solo album, Rich Man's Woman) and Gladys Knight & The Pips, and Kerner and Wise had the cream of LA session musicians on tap. Foster was retained to arrange the material and play keyboards. The conflicts over what the album should be and who should play on it were never satisfactorily reconciled and the material ended up confused and unfocused. The final concept, one side for the English band and another for the American, was ill-defined and the album incoherent.*

**Richie Wise:** Steve Marriott, to me, was one of the greatest rock'n'roll singers, one of the greatest talents and energies that ever walked this planet. I disappoint myself when I put that into words and think, wow, I did an album with him and then I think of that album… there's a couple of moments that are good and that's about it. Steve wanted to work with some of his English friends, the left-handed drummer Ian Wallace and a couple of other players. We used David Foster, a brand-new keyboard player that I was giving more work to than just about anybody back then, and a lot of the LA session guys, quite a few session guitar players – Ben Benay [who had played on albums by Neil

Sedaka, Barbra Streisand, Steely Dan, The Four Tops, Glen Campbell and the Wise-produced Elkie Brooks album] would have been one. It was an expensive record to make. Record Plant studio was one of the hot places to record. All the LA guys were getting union rates, double scale.

*Venetta Fields, Carlena Williams and new Blackberry Maxayn Lewis also added vocals to several tracks. Foster was credited with keyboards and writing, arranging and conducting strings and horns. During recording Marriott was in typical livewire mode, asked to leave two hotels for incidents such as obscene behaviour and for keeping a dog he'd adopted at the Hollywood dog rescue centre in his room.*

**Richie Wise:** I don't remember anybody from A&M coming down; they let us do our thing. Dee Anthony was not around, never met the man. Bad Company was working in the studio next door. One night, Steve, extremely high, and [Bad Company singer] Paul [Rodgers], extremely high, were in my studio in front of a couple of microphones jamming… the bass player from Bad Company [Boz Burrell] was in our studio all the time just sitting around. There were some songs [on the album] I chose: 'Are You Lonely For Me Baby' I think is one of the great Bert Berns gems and I'm glad we did that one. 'Wham Bam Thank You Mam' [Lane/Marriott] was Steve's idea… most of the songs on what they called 'the American side' came from me. The British side, he did what he wanted to do.

*Alongside the old Small Faces song (included on the band's 1969 posthumous Immediate album, The Autumn Stone), Marriott contributed two further songs to the 'British side' of the album, one a co-write with Mickey Waller, and the other co-written with Pam. There were also two covers, 'Lookin' For A Love', originally cut by The Valentinos in 1962 (the song had been part of the early seventies live set of The J. Geils Band and The Valentinos lead singer Bobby Womack had cut it as a solo track in 1974), and 'Help Me Through The Day' (written by Leon Russell), first cut by Freddie King in 1973 on A&M album Woman Across The River. On the 'American side', alongside the Bert Berns track, there was (puzzlingly) a new Marriott original, and two other Marriott songs dating back to the aborted 1974 Beehive sessions, 'Star In My Life', credited to Marriott and Ian Wallace, and 'Late Night Lady', credited to*

*Marriott, Ridley and Hinkley. There was also a more thematically fitting song written by American country music superstars Eddy Arnold and Cindy Walker.*

**Richie Wise:** Steve gave it his all; he was never under the weather, never not into it. He had to be depressed about the fact his career was in the dumps but he didn't show it. He rolled these big-ass joints but he was never incoherent, never in an argumentative state. He was never down on it. It was like he was leaving it all to me. I'd worked with a lot of singers, I had a lot of good records, the first KISS album was a good album, I had many hits with Gladys Knight & The Pips, one of the greatest female singers who ever lived, but Steve Marriott when he would get in front of the mic was something else... he did not stand there and sing... he was performing, in between phrases he would move away from the mic and groove and then he'd be back on the mic and then he'd move back and do his thing... it was astounding. I never worked with anybody who performed like that at the mic. Whether the material was mediocre, whether it was great, no matter what the track was, he performed that son of a bitch, he was on fire... when I think of him now, and this sounds stupid, I think of him like a rock god... that's how great I think he was.

**Steve Marriott:** My solo album wasn't my concept. It was a pressure situation A&M had put me in. I'd given them songs done by me at my studio but they said, 'No, it's not good enough quality.' It cost me $300,000 to have the same songs sound like an LA clinic but I didn't really have a choice. They brought in Kenny Kerner and Richie Wise to produce it, they're nice people but, let's face it, the album's no great shakes. They didn't know how to produce English rock musicians, guys used to thrashing it out. It sounds like they put a limiter on everything and squashed it into a can. The other side is too clinical, they said my version sounded too black but the LA side came out sounding blacker, or rather more contrived 'black'. They're mostly my songs but they didn't come out as I'd visualised them or as I'd already done them.

**Pam Marriott Land:** Those songs were wonderful until they were produced... we knew it was going to be a flop and Steve just hated it.

*The album, to simply be titled* Marriott, *was scheduled for release in April and Marriott agreed to a six-week tour of America to support it. In the meantime he returned to the UK to find 'Itchycoo Park' had been re-released and was proving popular. There were requests for him to reunite the Small Faces to shoot a promotional video. Strangely, the hand of Wilf Pine was not too far removed from this development. With Black Sabbath scoring huge success in America, chalking up six platinum or gold albums, Patrick Meehan Jr at Worldwide Artiste Management had been empire building and had acquired NEMS, Brian Epstein's old company, which had acquired rights to the Immediate back catalogue from the liquidator. And Tony Calder was involved.*

**Tony Calder:** Patrick Meehan's father [Don Arden's old associate and a partner in Worldwide] came to stay with me in Antigua and said come back and change Worldwide Artiste Management into NEMS Records for me. We bought what rights the receiver had for Immediate – for the UK only.

**Kenney Jones:** In the Small Faces we used to take Patrick Meehan Jr, when he was a young kid, on some of the gigs we did if we ever played south of the river. We used to pick him and his dad up. Not knowing this little kid would come back to haunt us.

*As well as concocting plans for the Small Faces – there was talk of the band cutting a new album – NEMS had signed Marianne Faithfull, who would release a single, 'All I Wanna Do In Life', and an album,* Dreamin' My Dreams, *with NEMS in 1976.*

**Ian McLagan:** Fucking Tony Calder… a long-tangled tale over the rights… it was sort of a shuffle from one hand to another. They re-released 'Itchycoo Park' and it was going up the charts and they asked us if we'd get back together for a video and promised us £1,000 each if we'd do it and do one live show, and they could film, it, record it and release it. The thought of even being in a band with Steve again made me tense up.

*The All Stars played a few Christmas dates, in Germany in 4,000-capacity halls and as part of the bill at the Great British Music Festival at the 10,000-capacity Olympia in London alongside Status Quo and Thin Lizzy. Marriott had money again. Then, in mid-January 1976, Marriott jammed with Ronnie Lane at a Slim Chance gig at Essex University. O'Leary claimed there had been phone calls over Christmas with Mark Fenwick, Lane's manager, who had suggested the get-together. Fenwick (of the Fenwick department store dynasty) ran EG management, who looked after King Crimson, T. Rex, ELP and Roxy Music (and later Roger Waters) and had a close relationship with Dee Anthony, who 'service managed' the EG acts in America. Fenwick had even been asked to manage Humble Pie in the UK circa 1973 in a similar way that Anthony looked after EG acts in America.*

**Mark Fenwick:** I think Dee really wanted to be able to tell his acts that he had an office in the UK; he probably never formally told Steve of our management arrangement. I knew Dee very well; he was a good friend to us all. I knew Steve very well. I knew the other guys very well.

*O'Leary said he detected 'a little animosity' between Marriott and Lane and that after sitting through several songs it was only when Marriott was on the verge of leaving the Slim Chance gig that Lane called him up on stage. They played five songs together, including 'All Or Nothing', 'Whatcha Gonna Do About It', 'Honky Tonk Women' and the old standard, 'Side By Side'. By the end, O'Leary said, Marriott had completely taken over the gig, with Lane adopting a background role.*

*Lane had formed Slim Chance in 1973 after quitting the Faces. They had started out with a hit single but three subsequent albums had all failed to make the Top 40, and Lane was living in some poverty on a sprawling ramshackle farm in Wales. McLagan and Kenney Jones were also down on their uppers now the Faces had split, with Rod Stewart going solo and Ronnie Wood joining the Stones. All four former Small Faces met up at Beehive.*

**Steve Marriott:** We shouted at each other for a few hours and then made friends again.

*The videos for 'Itchycoo Park' and 'Lazy Sunday' (which NEMS planned to release as a follow-up single) were filmed in late January at Island Records' Hammersmith studios. McLagan recalled a 'scruffy Steve' looking as if 'he'd seen better days'.*

**Pam Marriott Land:** I had never heard of the Small Faces. His mum had old clippings and when I saw pictures I couldn't believe that was Steve because I had to go make him take a bath. He'd bathe maybe once a week if I was lucky and that's if I ran the bath for him and forced him to go in there... he never wanted to get fancy clothes. I looked at the pictures and said, 'This was you? I cannot believe it, look how cute you were... you even bathed back then...' but he was just rebelling against all of it... he went a little insane.

*'Itchycoo Park' peaked at UK No 9. 'Lazy Sunday' was scheduled for release in March (it would peak at UK No 39) and Calder was readying a reissue of Ogdens' and a Small Faces greatest hits album package. In the pipeline were also greatest hits packages for Humble Pie (the Immediate-era material), Amen Corner, Chris Farlowe and The Nice. Marriott was non-committal when asked by the press about future plans for the Small Faces.*

**Steve Marriott:** We have talked about playing together but as yet there's nothing definite... we did the films [videos] and we said, 'Wouldn't it be nice to play somewhere?' I think there's a definite possibility of something... it wasn't my idea [to get back together].

*Foremost on his mind was the upcoming All Stars tour of America. Dave Clempson had agreed to join the band, as had a friend of his, the young classically trained keyboard player Damon Butcher, who would later find success in the eighties and nineties with Everything But The Girl, Tricky and The Beautiful South. Tim Hinkley, who had, post Street Rats, arranged and conducted Rock A Memphis, Johnny Hallyday's 1975 album, was looked over for the role. Before leaving for America, Marriott became a father for the second time, Pam giving birth to Marriott's son, Toby, on 20 February.*

**John Skinner:** Me and the missus got a phone call from Pam: the baby's coming. We jump in the car, get over to Beehive, get them in the car and we are on the way to hospital. Steve says, 'Hang on a minute, John. I've got to get some tobacco.' Steve gets out, Pam's in the car, Steve's taking his time, what's he doing? I think he's having a conversation with the bloke in the shop... beep, beep. He comes out, 'Oh, I'm just talking to this bloke a minute, won't be long.' 'Steve, Pam's having a baby.' 'She'll be all right, I'm just telling him something.'

*Marriott and his sister Kay celebrated at the local pub.*

**Kay Marriott:** He was so chuffed and everyone was making a fuss. I left him for just two minutes to go to the loo, and all of a sudden I could hear all this shouting and yelling. I come out and Steve is staggering and he's got a black eye. Someone had punched him in the face.

*Joe and Vicki Brown were asked to be godparents, with Toby given the middle name of Joe.*

**Joe Brown:** His name Toby was taken from a Toby jug, so he was named after a beer glass. We were chuffed to be asked to be godparents, especially when Steve gave him my name. Steve only referred to him as 'Toe Rag' though, and it's a wonder that he didn't grow up deaf. I remember Steve just propping him up against an amplifier and just plugging in. Steve didn't stop and think... he was never cut out to be a father. I liked Steve and most of the time he was good company but when he was on certain substances he became quite unbearable. When he was sober or even when he was pissed he was a very funny man. We'd sit up all night at either his place or mine just exchanging jokes. We had the same sense of humour. We'd pull out acoustic guitars and spend hours playing old country tunes. Steve loved country music, particularly Hank Williams and Willie Nelson. He also loved to play old Everly Brothers songs.

**Pam Marriott Land:** At the time, Joe and Vicki were a great help. We depended on them. Vicki was an absolute angel, I wouldn't have survived without her. Of course, Steve's family was great too. He loved his parents and his nan was a beautiful woman and they all adored Steve. He always took care of them. Steve's sister and I became very close.

**Kay Marriott:** Pam was my favourite [of Steve's wives]. I loved her. She was so funny. We really, really got on. We were mates. We used to go out clubbing and all that when he was away.

*In America, a lead single from the Marriott album, 'Star In My Life', had failed to ignite much interest, and the album was destined to sell poorly.*

**Richie Wise:** With record promotion, sometimes they would just shove the album in an envelope, send them to the music or programme director at a radio station, do a 300 mail-out... follow up with some phone calls and if it doesn't get an immediate burst of excitement, that's it, they don't push anymore. The old adage of throwing shit up against the wall and seeing what sticks.

*Despite the lack of interest in his current material, the Marriott name still held sufficient cache for the All Stars to be booked into large 5,000–10,000-capacity venues such as the Spectrum in Philadelphia, West Palm Beach Auditorium in Florida and Winterland in San Francisco, although often supporting acts such as ex-Procol Harum guitarist and singer Robin Trower, who had scored a recent Top 10 American solo album. The band – Marriott, Ridley, Wallace, Waller, Clempson and Damon Butcher – headlined smaller halls, clubs and theatres, sometimes joined on stage by Venetta Fields and Carlena Williams.*

**Laurie O'Leary:** He wanted me to go with him. I just said, 'Go on your own, Dee isn't a problem.' See, I had spoken to Anthony already and he was totally unperturbed. He was getting into much bigger things.

*Peter Frampton, Marriott could not have failed to notice, had suddenly, from out of nowhere, become the biggest rock star in the world.*

**Tim Hinkley:** Frampton's success would have affected him a lot. He never stopped bad-mouthing people but especially Peter...

*Released in January 1976, Frampton's fifth solo album, the live album* Frampton Comes Alive!, *was now at No 1 in America and would stay there for ten weeks – covering the entire period Marriott was touring there with the All Stars – eventually selling 12 million copies. Frampton was all over American radio and TV, with three massive hit pop singles taken from the album, 'Show Me The Way' (on which his talk box gimmick gained notoriety), 'Baby, I Love You' and 'Do You Feel Like We Do'. There were mega-concerts being planned – two 50,000-capacity gigs at Oakland Coliseum and a 118,000-ticket show at JFK Stadium in Philadelphia. It was estimated the album and gigs would generate $50 million.*

**Peter Frampton:** Dee Anthony and Frank Barsalona had great success with live albums. We just went, 'Look what we did with Humble Pie, should we go there again? Should we try it?' And we followed the template, basically.

**Bob Garcia:** A&M at that time was small enough and snappy enough to be able to just jump into the breach and kill for that album and that artist. So much groundwork had been laid, Peter had been going all over the place glad-handing our reps, meeting retail, just doing everything he could for the release of this record. Peter was so well liked. This was not an abrasive rock star. He was always a very friendly guy in whatever he did and whomever he had to engage with. I think everybody wanted to return his graciousness and it came back in spades.

**Jerry Moss:** He became Mr 1976.

*Anthony's handling of Frampton would see him named manager of the year in* Billboard. *For a reputed $1 million Anthony had signed him up to star in a big-budget film musical, alongside the Bee Gees, based on The Beatles'* Sgt. Pepper's *album. His intense focus on Frampton, however, saw complaints from his other acts. The J. Geils Band dropped him as their manager. Marriott was convinced Anthony had used Humble Pie money to keep Frampton afloat over the past five years – he was said to be $250,000 in the red prior to the release of the live album, with A&M, at that stage, having invested about $1 million into his career. At the start of June 1976, with the tour over and his solo album a flop, Marriott split his All Stars band. Ian Wallace joined Bob Dylan's road band and Waller and Ridley formed a new band, Fallen Angels, crashing their van on the way to their first gig.*

**Steve Marriott:** I was disillusioned by the whole thing. After that tour I started talking to the rest of the Small Faces about a reunion.

# CHAPTER 13
# Filthy Rich

**Kenney Jones:** This episode of my life still pains me. We got together and, instead of playing the old stuff, everybody was writing new songs and some of them were good. And then things got out of hand when people began to say we should stay together permanently. That frightened me but I thought, well, I'm not doing anything else. And it frightened Ronnie. He didn't want to do it, though he loved the idea of a [one-off] reunion gig [as had originally been the plan].

*Initially it was Marriott and Ian McLagan who were writing songs together, in all-night sessions at Beehive, and who, buoyed by their shared heavy cocaine habits, were the chief agitators behind the proposed Small Faces reunion.*

**Steve Marriott:** Me and Mac really loved each other at the time. I built him up to feel really good, because he was always the underdog with the Faces, right? All the time I'm going, 'That's great, Mac, that's *great*! Let me rewrite this, rewrite that, don't play A, play G, now play a B.' And I'm trying to help the little motherfucker. Then, all of a sudden, when I turn around *one time* and say, 'Mac, that sucks,' he went crazy! Slamming doors – I thought, oh my God!

*The money he had earned from the* Marriott *album and American tour was, typically, splurged on fast living. He sold the E-Type Jaguar and got the repaired Aston Martin V8 back from the factory and took Pam and pals out for expensive meals in London. Lane remained non-committal to the proposed reunion but he needed the money, being a reputed £35,000 in debt to EG management. Laurie O'Leary met Mark Fenwick at the EG offices on the King's Road. Lane would*

*join the reformation if Fenwick managed the band. 'Fuck that, what about you?'*
*Marriott shot back when told the news by O'Leary. 'I'll continue to manage you*
*but I don't want to manage the Small Faces,' O'Leary said.*

**Kenney Jones:** I looked upon Laurie managing Steve as 'that's desperate'. Laurie was a smart guy but not really looked at as being a manager – he's known for looking after people, more as a bodyguard. Laurie looked after Steve because he felt sorry for him. Steve had problems in his business life but the old story is, if you're in a hole stop digging. You can't run away from problems, you've got to face up to them, and Steve ran away from them. And he didn't want to know about business because he felt it got in the way of him being a musician. And then he'd play at being a businessman...

**Ian McLagan:** Mark Fenwick flew to New York and was negotiating a $1-million, five-album deal of which the band would get 25 per cent.

*Lane got cold feet but Marriott talked him into attending a recording session he'd*
*arranged at Joe Brown's Grange Sound studios in Chigwell in the early summer*
*of 1976. Marriott had promised Brown he would pay for the studio time when*
*the band got a deal. It did not go well.*

**Steve Marriott:** Ronnie had just found out he had MS [multiple sclerosis] and was still trying to come to terms with it. In the studio he kept falling over and I couldn't work it out and I got angry with him. I thought he was drunk. He had a bottle of brandy. He was trying to sing and he'd sway and fall. If he'd told me about the MS, then I would have been a lot more sympathetic towards him instead of being annoyed.

**John Skinner:** Ronnie kept falling over, losing his balance, and Steve thought he was drunk... he fell over near Steve's guitar one day and nearly broke it and Steve had a row with him, accused him of being drunk and Ronnie got the hump.

**Ian McLagan:** Ronnie was a fly in the ointment. As Steve and I had written a couple of songs together it put Ronnie's nose out of joint... the Marriott/Lane glory days were over, nothing creative was happening between them. Steve and I had been doing vast amounts of charlie and, after working through the night, we took a break at lunchtime to go for a drink at the local pub... Steve and Joe [Brown] were telling jokes and, all of a sudden, Ronnie got pissed off and started talking about going home. He got nastily drunk... he said it was all a load of bollocks in the studio, then he became abusive and Steve and I chased him out of the room and up the driveway, screaming at him.

*Marriott took particular offence when Lane said he hadn't written a decent song since leaving the Small Faces.*

**Steve Marriott:** There was an insult given out and I still take it as one today. At which point I whacked him [punched him in the face] and Ronnie said goodbye. It was a minor fracas but it was heavy. It'll obviously all turn out to be my fault.

**Kenney Jones:** Ronnie was drunk... he had changed, become more angry, belligerent, frustrated and upset... Marriott was acting like an arse, constantly taking the piss, overly confident and arrogant. Strutting. He was bossing Ronnie around. The two of them clashed. Verbally and physically. Ronnie stormed off and did not come back. We should have got to know each other again first. Ronnie still had his head in the [Slim Chance] Passing Show [a circus-style tour that had been a passion but cost him huge amounts of money] and didn't want to go backwards in life. He thought, if Steve was going to be acting like this, nothing's changed, so I'm off. I wished I would have walked out at the same time.

**Mark Fenwick:** It was a twenty-four-hour reformation, which ended as quickly as it started. The rest didn't involve myself or EG.

*Marriott stayed up all night to rescue the one song the band cut with Lane, 'Lonely No More', and quickly arranged a replacement bass player.*

**Rick Wills:** Steve rang me about four or five in the morning. He was bright as a bee, as if it was the middle of the day.

*Wills was 28, a few months younger than Marriott. He'd started out in the late sixties playing with David Gilmour and had been friendly with Jerry Shirley, through whom he had initially met Marriott. Wills had been the one who arranged for Marriott to guest with his early seventies band Cochise (that featured B. J. Cole) and they had become close pals. Marriott gave Wills his Alvis car and he and Jenny had attended when Wills got married (Jenny had organised an Ossie Clark dress for the bride). After Cochise broke up, Wills had toured and recorded with Peter Frampton for a few years up until 1975 and enjoyed a short tenure as Roxy Music's bassist, but was currently out of the music business.*

**Kenney Jones:** It was Steve's idea to get Rick in. He was a plumber… we didn't have a say who was there.

*With Wills on bass, the reformed Small Faces continued to record material through to the end of July at Joe Brown's home studio, encouraged by the thought of a lucrative deal for the project.*

**Rick Wills:** Steve was a heavy drug user and was drinking a lot as well. He was bloated and he was losing his hair. He'd also got into country music, so all the songs had a country tinge. I couldn't understand why he wanted to go in that direction. I never felt comfortable taking Ronnie's place.

**Kenney Jones:** I'd do the tracks and go home, because I refused to work through the night. They wanted to stay up all night and blow their brains out. So I'd go home and when I came back they'd finished it and it wasn't very good.

**Steve Marriott:** Don't say, 'Well, I think I'll go to bed, have a listen tomorrow.' I hate that attitude… We did stay up for a couple of days but that's nothing. Have I got to go to bed at ten? Mow the lawn in the morning? If you're into something, you're with a sound and you want to finish it, then go for it.

**Pam Marriott Land:** When the Small Faces reunited, the main thing was how much he missed Ronnie… it completely ruined it in the beginning when Ronnie didn't want to be there.

*Kenney Jones asked Mel Bush, one of the most successful promoters in the UK, to manage the reformation. Bush had handled acts such as Joni Mitchell, The Band, Crosby, Stills, Nash & Young, as well as teenyboppers such as David*

*Cassidy and David Essex. His brother Bev (RIP) was a bodyguard to the stars, looking after Elton John, Jimmy Page and Brian Ferry.*

**Kenney Jones:** Mel was handling David Essex. We needed a manager... and Mel Bush offered to do it. David Essex and I were mates. Steve had changed. He had a success death wish. Every time he'd get near success he'd find a way to destroy it.

**Mel Bush:** I negotiated with Dee Anthony to release Steve from his contract and negotiated a record deal for them with Ahmet Ertegun at Atlantic Records. I did two tours, one in the UK and one in Europe, and then the band broke up.

*It was not easy for Bush to deal with Anthony. Chiefly due to the success of Frampton, Humble Pie were still considered a commercial entity in America – A&M were preparing the release of* Humble Pie: Greatest Hits *for 1977. Anthony's ego had also exploded as the success of Frampton continued apace. A follow-up to* Frampton Comes Alive! *had produced another huge hit single, 'I'm In You' (the album's title track), and there were weeks, he said, when his cut of Frampton's concert earnings was above $100,000. The* Sgt. Pepper's *film was also close to going into production and Anthony had eight corporations to run. Frampton, for his part, was struggling to cope with his huge fame, drinking heavily and hooked on coke. It would not be long until he drove Anthony's Rolls-Royce into a tree in Nassau, resulting in serious, career-threatening injuries and thereafter severing ties with his long-time manager, discovering he did not have as much money as he presumed (a settlement prevents him from discussing the matter). In a final twist, in June 1977, Anthony's mansion in Nassau, burned down due to an electrical fire. The Humble Pie complex, Rock's Nest, was eventually sold for circa $5 million.*

**Steve Marriott:** There were lots of managers interested but they were not able to get to grips with Dee Anthony, the record company and the publishers. Mel was the one who had the guts to go out and get me out of my commitments.

**Ian McLagan:** That's when the penny dropped that Steve needed us, and this deal, to bail him out of the mess he was in.

*Negotiating Marriott's freedom and securing the deal with Atlantic on the back of the demos recorded at Brown's studio would take Bush several months. In the meantime Marriott and the band were left in limbo. With punk rock and the Sex Pistols breaking (the Pistols were the last band to ever play O'Leary's about-to-close Speakeasy and also included 'Whatcha Gonna Do About It' in the early live shows), Marriott was in a provocative mood. He went along to see McLagan guest with The Rich Kids, featuring former Sex Pistol Glen Matlock on bass, at the Lyceum Ballroom in London (the band featured 'Here Come The Nice' in their set). Iggy Pop was also at the concert.*

**Glen Matlock:** Marriott thought we were trying to nick his keyboard player. He came backstage and had a run-in with Iggy Pop... he was in a real stroppy mood.

*In August he was seen in Paris accompanied by Pam, jamming at the city's hip Nashville club with The Spamm Band (featuring future Status Quo bassist John 'Rhino' Edwards), Led Zeppelin's Jon Bonham and Bad Company's Simon Kirke and Boz Burrell.*

**John 'Rhino' Edwards:** Steve wanted drugs. We introduced him to the club owner and he came out happy... and then sat in with us for four nights at the Nashville. It was quite a big deal he was in town. He was charming but he did spit at the photographers and was horrible to his wife one night.

*By Autumn, Bush was finally in a position to sign a $600,000 (over $2.5 million today), two-album deal with the illustrious Atlantic Records. The cost, however, to untangle Marriott from his various contracts was said to be £250,000 (close to £700,000 today). The advance from Atlantic was staggered – an amount being paid on completion of each album. Marriott may have now been free from Anthony but he was not rich – in fact there was very little money for the band members in the reunion.*

**Ian McLagan:** We signed for a huge advance but before any of us could dip in the pile, Steve's old partners got their hands dirty first and after bailing Steve out of his contracts there wasn't that much left to get excited about.

*The band's unveiling was delayed by another several months when Jones and Wills had a bad car accident, careering off the road and smashing into a tree, after a late night recording session at Beehive. Wills suffered lacerations, fractured ribs and a broken collarbone. Jones was thrown from the vehicle, escaping serious injury.*

**Steve Marriott:** Two months wasted.

*It seems to be in this period that Marriott began to make plans for a future beyond the reunion or beyond Britain. On 23 March 1977, he married Pam at Kensington and Chelsea Register Office.*

**Jenny Dearden:** The day before Pam and Steve were going to get married, he called me up and said, 'I just want to say, any chance of you coming back because I've got to marry her tomorrow because her visa is going to run out...?'

**Pam Marriott Land:** Yes, Steve called Jenny before we got married. I would know that, because I was standing right there listening with my fingers crossed hoping she'd take him back! I'm the one that needed that marriage certificate so I could legitimise Toby. Steve asked me to marry him on Greg Ridley's front steps. I left Steve for Greg... but that's another story all-together.

**Jerry Shirley:** Now, what they may have done was that they may have not bothered to get married until such time that they decide to get out of England and move to America and therefore to make his green card accessibility easier. But they were long and deep into that relationship. It wasn't, 'Oh, let's get together and get married so I can have a green card.'

*Marriott was also now in the process of dismantling the studio at Beehive, selling off equipment (at a fraction of its worth), and Beehive Cottage was also put on the market. He was also selling off his guitars. John Skinner, who was now employed as Steve's guitar tech, witnessed the desperation.*

**John Skinner:** Steve, unbelievably, was pretty much out of money. He was selling things left, right and centre just to get a bit of cash. One day in 1976 Steve and I went to Mick Jagger's mansion near Newbury to look for the Cherry Les Paul [guitar] that Steve swore blind he had given to Keith Richards and now wanted back. After searching through what seemed like 200 guitars at Mick's we gave up and came home. Maybe Steve had forgotten that he had sold it to Top Gear Music, bless him. The studio was dismantled and gone. It had been the most expensive stuff you could get at the time: customised Helios desk, 16-track Studer machine, 2-inch Studer for mixdowns, four Tannoy speakers. I believe it went to a studio in Kent. Steve was doing some recording down there. It was where we met Angie Bowie.

*Rehearsals for the upcoming Small Faces gigs in April were joyless. 'That's when the rot set in,' said McLagan.*

**John Skinner:** Steve Marriott was his own man. There was no stopping him. He was like a force of nature. Mac would moan, 'Can't you keep control of him? We want to start rehearsing at eight, it's no use him coming at twelve.' I said, 'I can't tell him, he'll tell me to fuck off,' which he did. 'C'mon Steve, we've got to go to rehearsals.' 'Oh, fuck off, there's a good film on the telly, we'll go about ten...'

*A small show for 400 family and friends, including David Gilmour, at the Mean Fiddler, in Harlesden in north-west London, briefly raised spirits but they were quickly dampened.*

**Kenney Jones:** The early gigs [two in Germany] were particularly bad. Marriott was all over the place, drunk. We told Steve we weren't going to put up with it and he did eventually listen.

*For a short UK tour, which included two nights at the 3,000-capacity London Rainbow Theatre, Marriott persuaded former Immediate act P. P. Arnold to sing backing vocals.*

**P. P. Arnold:** I was at Island Studios, where Bob Marley was recording *Exodus*, my friend Junior Marvin was playing guitar with them. I came out the studio one day and I saw Steve walking down the street and he goes, 'Pam, where you been? We're going on tour, you've got to come on tour with us.'

**Dave Clarke:** I went to the Small Faces show at the Rainbow and the party afterwards; I recall that Michael Jackson was there, David Essex and a whole lot of people. [Elton John came to watch the band in Bristol.]

*The Small Faces were invited on to David Essex's 1977 BBC TV show,* David Essex *– a prime-time light entertainment song and dance affair that featured special guests. Marriott was contemptuous of Essex, who was at the peak of his popularity. He had emerged as a major teen idol, with starring roles in* That'll Be The Day *and* Stardust *spawning huge hit singles including 'Gonna Make You A Star'. In 1976 he'd scored a No 1 with 'Hold Me Close' and crossed over to the stage playing the role of Che Guevara in the smash hit Andrew Lloyd Webber/Time Rice musical* Evita *– a role initially offered to Marriott. O'Leary said a dishevelled and drunk Marriott had accepted an offer to meet Lloyd Webber to listen to the musical score but afterwards exclaimed, 'What the fuck was all that about? Don't think so, mate. I'm not a puppet.' The Small Faces played 'Whatcha Gonna Do About It' on the David Essex show but Marriott refused the offer of a duet with David Essex (standard practice for guests), snarling, 'He's taking the piss, isn't he?'*

*In Edinburgh, after a gig at the 3,000-capacity Playhouse, the 30-year-old Marriott collapsed from a suspected heart attack. He and McLagan had partied with Billy Connolly and then stayed up late drinking and snorting cocaine. At some point Marriott had smashed a fire alarm, causing the hotel to be evacuated. When the police finally arrived, McLagan panicked and hid the stash of cocaine. It was then that Marriott collapsed. McLagan could not detect a heartbeat. He tried to recall basic lifesaving techniques, banging on Marriott's chest and blowing into his mouth. Marriott briefly roused before slumping back. An ambulance was called and Marriott was taken to hospital.*

**Rick Wills:** All this mayhem was going on, police cars everywhere, fire engines... just another night with Steve, basically. With Steve you were living on the edge all the time. It was pretty scary at times... you never knew if you were going to get thrown in jail or get the crap beaten out of you. It terrified me. There was this craziness that surrounded the band and you just had to go along with Steve. He was the glue that held it all together.

*Marriott was soon back at the coalface. He had collapsed from heart palpitations (possibly a seizure), caused by stress, anxiety, alcohol and cocaine.*

**Ian McLagan:** Steve had experienced several of these heart tremors or palpitations before. He was the most highly strung person I've ever met… a heart attack waiting to happen.

**John Skinner:** Mel Bush would give me £125 a week for petrol and expenses and he was a stickler for getting a receipt. On Monday, Steve would be, 'John, get us £20 out of the float?' 'Er, well I can't really.' 'Oh, go on, fuck off. Mel Bush, he's a cunt, he won't worry.' That afternoon, 'John, I want to get some tobacco, have you got any money?' 'Hang on, I just gave you £20, but here's another £5, but I really need to get receipts.' 'Oh, don't worry about it, it'll be all right, tell him I've had it.' Next day, 'Have you got £20?' I've never seen anyone get through so much money in my life and really not have anything to show for it.

*The band began now to record new material with (then) 40-year-old producer Shel Talmy, the American celebrated for his string of innovative and hard-hitting, massive, mid-sixties breakthrough hits with The Who (in 1965, including 'I Can't Explain' and 'My Generation') and The Kinks (between 1964 and 1967, including 'You Really Got Me', 'All Day And All Of The Night' and many more). Marriott had bumped into him at Morgan Studios (where Humble Pie had originally recorded) while guesting on a Vicki Brown album that Talmy was producing. Marriott initially chose two songs to record with Talmy at Morgan, 'Lookin' For A Love' (the Valentinos cover featured on the* Marriott *album) and Albert King's 'Don't You Lie To Me'. The results were encouraging.*

**Shel Talmy:** The first few takes had been god-awful and then he had a flash maybe of how good he was and it all happened. It was not the easiest thing I've ever done but we finished the songs and I was pleased with them and so was everybody else. Then we went on to Steve's home studio in Essex with a remote [recording] truck [Ronnie Lane's Mobile Studio, LMS] and that's where the problems really began. We were scheduled to start at eight o'clock at night and we never got started before midnight because, with all due respect to Steve, who I loved, he was stoned. He did this several nights in a row. He kept everybody waiting and he was acting strangely with the other guys. Mac in particular was really pissed off... I got five or six tracks down at his home but we never finished because, basically, he wasn't capable. There was no point hanging around, there was nothing going on, it wasn't happening. I walked out along with pretty much everybody else. I talked about it for years afterwards with Mac, how disappointing the whole thing was... both of us wished we hadn't been there.

*The band had set up and played in the old Beehive studio but all the recording equipment had been stripped out and sold, hence the need for Talmy to hire the mobile recording studio. Talmy and his secretary were surprised that Marriott had no manager or handler to look after him.*

**Shel Talmy:** Steve was aware enough to know he wasn't up to where he used to be [vocally] and his playing was not as good either. I would in no way ever demean Steve, because he was a great artist, but unfortunately he fell into a period where he started losing parts of what he could do so well. He would have a moment where he was brilliant but they didn't sustain... and that was the major problem. I've run across other artists like that and they wind up hating themselves.

*Atlantic managed to patch together (using some material cut at Joe Brown's studio) a Small Faces reunion album,* Playmates, *released in August 1977. It sank without a trace; the lead single, the Talmy-produced 'Lookin' For A Love', made little impression. Marriott blamed Atlantic for the failure, claiming they had chosen the single and then failed to promote it. Among the other nine songs on the album were 'High And Happy', a song Marriott had written in 1974, and two new solo compositions, 'Saylarvee' and 'Playmates'. There was a track credited to Lane, Marriott, Jones and McLagan called 'Find It' and three Marriott/McLagan compositions, plus a Marriott/John Pidgeon (RIP) song. Pidgeon was a music journalist and author, a close associate of the Faces, and a songwriting partner for McLagan.*

**Kenney Jones:** The material wasn't particularly strong and Steve was over-exaggerating his rock'n'roll persona.

*Beehive was sold. Laurie O'Leary, who handled the sale, said a local baker bought the property. It fetched a figure of around £80,000 (about £500,000 in today's money). John Skinner and his wife moved the furniture out while Marriott, Pam and Toby moved into the Royal Garden Hotel, Kensington, and lived the high life. 'Extravagant meals for family and wild coke nights for cronies,' recalled O'Leary. This was an extension of the party atmosphere that surrounded Marriott's marriage to Pam and indicative of how Marriott spent large sums of money quickly.*

**Pam Marriott Land:** I think Laurie did the best he could. He was always immaculately dressed and was just lovely but how can you help somebody who you can't get off drugs? There's one article where Steve is holding Toby when he was an infant and it was 'Sleepy Superstar' or something... Laurie had set up all these interviews and people were coming but Steve had been up three nights on coke and wouldn't even get out of bed. Steve's thing was, 'Fuck them, I shouldn't have to be explaining myself'... I said, 'You've been doing this for years, you know this is what you've got to do.'

*The Small Faces played a handful of huge festival shows in Germany in September 1977, playing to upward of 10,000 people, before embarking on a second, lengthier, UK tour, including two nights at the Hammersmith Odeon.*

**Rick Wills:** He'd go on stage and say outrageous things, especially in Germany. Very much in Hitler mode, doing Nazi salutes, which didn't go down well. He had a lot of bad, evil thoughts festering inside him. He became a really nasty person. He looked around at Rod Stewart and all these guys having success and he knew he was going the other way.

*Marriott had persuaded the baby-faced 24-year-old Jimmy McCulloch (1953–1979) to join the tour on second guitar. McCulloch had been a member of Thunderclap Newman, who scored a huge No 1 in 1969 with 'Something In The Air', and subsequently played with John Entwistle, Roger Daltrey and John Mayall before joining Paul McCartney's band Wings in 1974.*

**Rick Wills:** Without consulting the rest of us, Steve asked Jimmy to join the band. Jimmy and Steve had been pals for years and Jimmy had often visited Steve at Beehive and they'd get completely out of their minds together. Jimmy was unhappy with the situation in Wings. I think Paul McCartney had enough of him. Jimmy was a bad influence on

276

Steve. Kenney and I used to drink but Mac and Steve were social in another way. Mac could sort of control it but Steve and Jimmy couldn't and they sort of let themselves go, Steve more so [McCulloch died from a drugs overdose, aged 26]. On stage Steve would just gob up into the air and think it was funny if it landed on Kenney's drum kit. Kenney used to get furious. Steve also became so scruffy… he had very few clothes and those that he did have didn't fit him.

**Kenney Jones:** On the second tour, Steve turned punk, swearing and spitting at the audience. We had a much bigger sound [with McCulloch] but Marriott blew it. It was such a shame. I don't like to think of him in those days. I was cringing every time we stepped out on stage. He was fucked up… he became really uncontrollable. He thought it was cool to act like a prick… normally he was a nice polite guy with a piss-taking attitude but when he became like that I thought he doesn't a give shit. There were a few gigs with Jimmy that were great but Steve was spitting and pissing on people and God knows what… rude to everyone. I just wanted the stage to open up and swallow me. As soon as the tour finished I was off, gone.

**John Skinner:** Unfortunately this was the new persona of Steve Marriott. I think he was trying to emulate the punk scene. Nobody in the band liked it, or liked to be spat at but Steve thought it was funny. Mac said, 'If he spits at me, I'll chin the cunt.' Steve was like, 'Punk boys do it, so why can't I?' The other habit he had – I'd have to buy ten or more blues harps because he used to throw it out into the audience. He'd play a harp solo and then throw it out… and of course he threw it out one day and it hit a bloke on the head who wasn't watching. I got the impression the band were all a bit unsure of each other. They were mates once and now we're back together but we're not really mates again.

One of the gigs in Germany was the best we did, blinding, the band was tight and the encores were brilliant. Steve walked off, gave me his guitar and he said to me, 'How was it John – was it all right?' I said, 'Yes mate, it was blinding.' He said, 'Oh brilliant, only I can't remember what it was like.' Ah, the performer Steve Marriott has been out there but Steve Marriott the person hasn't been party to it.

**Ian McLagan:** Steve would never just be cool... he would try and do 'Itchycoo Park' in a spitting frenzy on stage. It was fucked! He was a mess. He had a big old moustache and he was dirty. He didn't have any decent clothes. He was a coked-out, over-singing arsehole and he was getting worse and worse. When he came to your house he'd pretty much stay until there was nothing left to drink, he drank us out of everything. Three, four days, we had a lot of booze, beer, vodka, gin, rum... and he had every drop... and we were still doing coke and after a couple of days my missus, Kim, would just have had enough. So I avoided him. My heart wasn't in it anymore. It was an excuse to pay off Steve's debts. We'd become a tired revival band. Eventually I stopped answering the phone to Steve. Even if Ronnie had stayed, you couldn't have saved that project. It was a train wreck. It was awful. It was a rotten idea.

**Pam Marriott Land:** They'd call me when they were on the road and say, 'You got to get here, Melvin's here,' because I could handle Melvin sort of. It was not much fun, he literally had a different personality. He'd drink and his eyes would get real glassy and he'd look up and I'd say, 'Steve?' And he'd go, 'No, Melvin'... and that's when he got crazy. He never remembered it the next day. You could not tell him he wasn't Melvin, a bald-headed wrestler named Melvin; that's who he was until he came to. When he was sober I'd start tell him things he did or said and he'd start crying.

**Steve Marriott:** The Faces would only work one German tour and one English tour a year. I booked a week in the Marquee in London. Okay, so it only holds a thousand people, so it's a pisshole, so what? They wouldn't do it. I said, 'Oh, come on!' We got a week in there – the place where we started, where The Who started, where The Yardbirds started, where The Action started. They said, 'No, no, no, it's not enough money, Steve.' I said, 'Well, fuck the lot of you, then.' That's when I left.

*Plans for an American tour were abandoned. After one final round of gigs in Germany in early 1978, without McCulloch but with more Marriott mayhem, including hotel-room-wrecking, the Small Faces reunion was over. Plans for a live album were scrapped. A second Small Faces reunion album, 78 In The Shade, was released posthumously in August 1978. Again, it was patched together, with some cuts taken from the aborted Talmy sessions, others from sessions at Joe Brown's studio, while other tracks featured Jimmy McCulloch on guitar. Marriott revisited the 1975 Joe Brown song 'Soldier', there were a couple of McLagan songs, two McLagan/Pidgeon efforts, a song by Wills, a group composition, and three new Marriott tunes: 'Filthy Rich', 'Brown Man Do' and 'Stand By Me (Stand By You)'. The last was chosen for the lead single, not that it mattered much. Marriott again blamed Atlantic's lack of promotional support for its failure.*

**Kenney Jones:** The accountants distributed the money that was left. We were each owed £15,000 [about £90,000 in today's money] from our deal but we didn't receive that. Steve's share was eaten up by more contractual problems. Mac and I had agreed to pay production on the albums. With that settled, we were left with pennies. Only Rick walked away with any cash...

*Kenney Jones joined The Who in 1978, after briefly playing in a band with Joe Brown and Tim Hinkley. McLagan worked as a sideman to the Stones before taking up session work. He married Keith Moon's ex-wife Kim in 1978. Rick Wills guested with David Gilmour before joining rock band Foreigner.*

**Kenney Jones:** When I joined The Who, I had a party at Stringfellows and Steve and Ronnie turned up. They were getting along really well and I found that strange after the bust-up. Steve looked at me with his cheeky Artful Dodger look and said, 'Lend us a few bob, Ken.'

*Marriott guested on the debut solo album by Johnny Thunders, the famously dissolute former singer/guitarist with the New York Dolls and Heartbreakers – who had broken up after touring the UK with the Sex Pistols. Thunders had found a level of notoriety in London and was using both Paul Cook and Steve Jones from the Pistols and Thin Lizzy's Phil Lynott as a core band, while other guests on the album included the equally dissolute Peter Perrett of The Only Ones and Chrissie Hynde of the Pretenders. Marriott sang on a version of Otis Blackwell's 1953 'Daddy Rollin' Stone'. Many involved in the album were noted for their heavy drug use.*

*The hook-up is likely to have come via Christine Lore, a young American who had met the Marriotts at a party and was now living with them in the two-storey*

*detached townhouse Marriott had recently bought in the residential area of Golders
Green, north London, close to Hampstead. Lore had been sharing a London flat
in the same building as punk/new wave label Stiff Records with fellow American
Liam Sternberg, who was associated with Stiff's American act Devo (and was the
future writer of Bangles hit 'Walk Like An Egyptian'). Sternberg was producing
material for Lore's best friend Kirsty MacColl, who had signed a solo deal with
Stiff. The Thunders album – cut in intermittent sessions between January and
June 1978 – was produced by Lore's friend (and MacColl's future husband)
Steve Lillywhite, then a 23-year-old staff producer at Island Records.*

**Christine Lore:** The house in Golders Green was beautiful. It was
detached but with very close neighbours on one side, who didn't really
appreciate them there. The three of us got on so well. It was great fun.
Their home was beautifully decorated, beautiful antiques... gorgeous.
They had their collie and Steve's macaw parrot and their child Toby Joe.
Pam had a good head on her shoulders. He was lucky to find her. She
was a nurturer, loving, caring and responsible... quite a lady. People
write that he was five foot four inches but that is stretching it, I'd say
more like two inches or three inches because I'm five foot six and I
towered over him. Pam always had her arm around Steve... she was a
head about him in their marriage photos. If Steve got drunk he was the
most evil person, he called himself Melvin, his alter ego. It was too much
Bushmills [Irish whiskey], very ugly, so much so that Steve wouldn't
take responsibility for knowing a person like that. It was weird. If Melvin
came out and afterwards he was hearing stories of how shitty he had
been, he'd say, 'That was Melvin,' and 'I didn't have anything to do
with it, you'll have to take that up with Melvin next time you see him.'
I'd say, 'I don't ever want to see Melvin around me again,' and he'd say,
'Nobody does, but he tends to come out when I drink too much.' It was
night and day.

**John Skinner:** Golders Green was a nondescript townhouse, a pig to
get to, garden backed on to the North Circular, noisy. The one thing
Steve didn't want in life was neighbours and he had people right next
door. It was an odd choice... he was a little country boy, all his other
places were solitary, out of the way, so he could be private. Christine
had done some murals for them in the bedroom, lovely artwork, on the
walls and cupboards, so Steve, in his wisdom, wanted to make a

statement and he painted the bathtub with green gloss paint! He'd got no idea how to do things: he'd say, 'John, my telly don't work, there was smell of smoke and the telly went off.' I'd say, 'Have you got any fuses?' No? Okay, I'll get some and be round.'

**Pam Marriott Land:** Steve was really morose. He was going to go on the medication Keith Moon was on [clomethiazole, to treat symptoms of acute alcohol withdrawal. Moon overdosed on the drug and died in September 1978] but he didn't. One day, after a two-day binge in Golders Green, we found him asleep on a neighbour's couch. He didn't even know these people. I got him out of quite a few fixes. So did Laurie [O'Leary]. He went to one doctor and I guess he was diagnosed... when you've got a split personality, I don't even know what you would call it but he most definitely had something because he was not Steve when he got that drunk... and he would tear up everything and anybody around him... and the next day he'd be crying half the day... there was definitely something in his psyche. Steve just had so many demons that unfortunately didn't get straightened out and the drink and drugs, unfortunately, changed him. I would say Steve was bipolar. He could be so much fun when he'd just done a little bit of coke, a little bit of alcohol; the problem was he couldn't stop. He was the funniest, sweetest person in the world and he could charm the socks off anyone. You couldn't help but love him. He was so funny but he had demons. The drugs were just for him to cope because he was so bitter – to have worked as hard as he did and to have nothing to show for it just slowly drove Steve insane. We'd go to see a friend and there they are with their nice house and they'd made money and here we are without £5 in our pocket. 'Filthy Rich' [the standout track on *78 In The Shade*] was written after he'd talked to Keith [Richards] or someone. He said, 'Look at all them, they've done half of what I've done and they can afford to feed their family and I can't' – that drove him to drugs more than anything. People wouldn't even take his calls at that time. It was sickening. He just felt people hated him and his music was shit – the solo album was a flop, the Small Faces reunion was panned – it was so incredibly hard for him. I said, 'Why don't you just do the nightclub circuit? People do love you.'

**Steve Marriott:** So I formed a band called Blind Drunk.

*Marriott recruited Joe Brown, guitarist Mickey Waller and two members of Joe Brown's band, drummer Dave Hynes (RIP) and 32-year-old bassist Jim Leverton, and booked a gig in August 1978 at the 500-capacity Bridge House pub in Canning Town, east London. The Bridge House would become celebrated for its live music, putting on shows by Iron Maiden, Depeche Mode and Charlie Watts, amongst a list of hundreds.*

**Joe Brown:** Steve's idea was that we'd all start the gig with a bottle of brandy each and slowly get pissed as the evening wore on. We filled the place, over 400 people, and played good old rock'n'roll.

*The gig would be the start of a professional relationship, and friendship, with Jim Leverton that would continue until Marriott's death. Leverton was a pal of Noel Redding, and had jobbed around with acts such as Henry McCullough, Savoy Brown and Leo Sayer. He had first met Marriott when the reformed Small Faces were recording at Joe Brown's studio and they had bonded over a shared love of American soul and R&B. After the Canning Town gig, Marriott wanted to continue as a three-piece outfit with Leverton and Hynes.*

**Jim Leverton:** He came to Joe's show at Baileys nightclub in Watford one night with his grandma, because his grandma loved Joe Brown. He came in the dressing room and I heard him say to Joe, 'I'm going to steal your bass player.' He came up to me and said, 'I want you to join my group because I like the way you play the bass but you can also sing pretty good, I need that, I need to take a bit of a breather [on stage] these days.' Steve nicked Dave Hynes [from Joe Brown's group] as well. It was a difficult period to be in a band with Steve…

**Christine Lore:** Steve took me and Liam [Sternberg] into the studio and played us this incredible music, treasures he'd made with Dave [Hynes] and Jim [Leverton]. Then, in August 1978, when I'm living with them in Golders Green, Steve gets a letter saying he owes the Government so many thousands of dollars [in tax], it may as well have been a billion, because he didn't have any money. Things were bad. The letter said Steve had thirty days to pay or he was going to have to go to debtors' prison… so he was screwed.

**Pam Marriott Land:** He couldn't catch a break because, the next thing we know, we literally got a thing in the mail that said Steve owed something like a half-million dollars in tax and the accountant or the lawyer said you've got to get out of England, they're going to come and arrest you.

**Christine Lore:** The stress after that letter came, boy. I suggested to Steve if you just leave and go into tax exile like the Stones did, wait it out, it'll be okay; they expunge your debt [after three years of being a non-UK resident]. So, we decided to sell the house quickly and make this move quickly... he had ten days before they were going to put the screws on him, it was coming down fast. I got in touch with an agent and for ten and twelve hours a day Pam and I were cleaning up the house, making it as beautiful as possible and we sold it immediately for top dollar and I flew back over here [to Santa Cruz in California, on the northern edge of Monterey Bay, about seventy-five miles south of San Francisco]. I opened my soul up for Steve and Pam. I had to sign a document to vow they wouldn't take any money from the Government while they were in exile, and hoped they wouldn't.

**Pam Marriott Land:** We literally packed three bags and we fled England so Steve wouldn't be arrested. We had a friend in Santa Cruz [Lore] who said come stay here. Laurie [O'Leary] said, 'Leave everything in the house and I'll sell up everything to try to pay this debt.' I was American so it was easy for us to come to America. We were able to ship just a few things... I loved Laurie O'Leary... he was there for us.

**Christine Lore:** Laurie was a character. He took me out for dinner. Steve often talked about him. Steve loved the Krays, anything gangster he loved. Steve's drummer Dave Hynes was in love with me and wanted me to marry him. And there was Jim Leverton and [his wife] Dawn, they wanted to come to America too. Dave and I actually almost did get married and then I came to my senses, stopped drinking.

*O'Leary recalled the tax bill being for £100,000 and it was he who offered Marriott the option of 'leave England or go to jail'. He also claimed, as Pam concurred, that it was he who arranged the sale of the Golders Green home. Arriving to evaluate the property, once Marriott had left the UK, he said he found the front door open, all the electric fires fully turned on and the place empty apart from a rented TV. 'Some of Steve's friends, knowing it was empty, had been partying in there,' he said.*

**Jim Leverton:** When Steve cleared off to Santa Cruz, Laurie took care of business for him. Laurie was in the picture because he was looking after all of us at that point.

**John Skinner:** Laurie was a very nice man. All right, we all know his background, who he was and who he associated with but he always treated me fair. I liked him a great deal. I never saw him have a row with Steve. He'd tell us stories about when he worked with the Krays, little snippets, make us laugh. He was in charge of Steve's financial matters and [was] doing the best for Steve he could. I took Steve to the airport when he left for America, he ran away. He left everything in the hands of Laurie. Laurie took the Aston and sold it to pay the Inland Revenue.

# CHAPTER 14

# Big Train Stops At Memphis

*Santa Cruz, California. August 1978.*

**Christine Lore:** I had a farm fifteen miles from the beach at Santa Cruz, in Corralitos. It was a one-horse town, had a gas pump station with a little post office inside and a general store where they cured bacon all night long. The house was in this beautiful canyon, middle of nowhere, a creek ran through the property, magic, idyllic. I wanted Steve to meet the [local] musicians as soon as possible. He wanted to get started right away. I called Dale [Ockerman, who had played keyboards in a version of sixties San Francisco psych-rock band Quicksilver Messenger Service] and had him get in touch with a lot of our friends, and the next thing there are 120 people all down my lawn, in the vegetable garden, picking fruit from my trees, in the trout pond. It was a beautiful day and we had a concert for the neighbours.

**Dale Ockerman:** [Concert promoter] Bill Graham once lived in Corralitos, and Carlos Santana too. I'd known Chrissie since the early seventies, she was a blonde-haired sweetie, a music fan – her family was pretty wealthy. She would come and go. She'd be real broke and raising her son by herself and then all of a sudden jet-setting it. She had been with Chris Squire from Yes, not a groupie but somebody to be with when they were not with their wife, and she was also with John Paul Jones so she would hang out with Zeppelin. Chrissie wanted Steve to meet Jerry Miller, the guitar player in Moby Grape. They jammed a little but they both liked to drink and snort so much I don't think they ever got serious. At the party at Chrissie's Steve was playing his black Les

285

Paul, we did some blues stuff... I had set up a little keyboard. He said, 'Okay let's do [Ray Charles's] "I Believe In My Soul"'... we had a great time. I switched from keyboard to lead guitar and, after I did a lead, Steve comes over and said, 'Oh, you're a clever little cunt, aren't you?'

*Ockerman was enrolled in the band Marriott started to put together.*

**Dale Ockerman:** We made some commercials for radio at a big house in Felton [six miles from Santa Cruz] that belonged to John Chesleigh, who had financed some of the Moby Grape reunions [and had produced the 1978 *Live Grape* album]. Steve brought in [UK engineer] John Wright [who had engineered on both Small Faces reunion albums] and there was a nice 24-track board and system set-up in the living room. It was a complete mess, wires everywhere, but he was recording. John [Chesleigh] was a guy that had some money and he had a big, eight-car garage that was made into a rehearsal room with a big PA, stacks of Marshalls. John had been in prison because of his illegalities [drug dealing]. There was a lot of partying in Santa Cruz, lot of toot...

**Pam Marriott Land:** We all drank and we all liked to party – we were all insane back then, it wasn't just Steve. Snorting coke and having a ball every day – that was the thing to do. We didn't want to go out unless we had a gramme of coke. None of us knew it was bad for you, that was the era. I had an alcohol problem too.

**Christine Lore:** One time I babysat [Toby] and Pam and Steve went with this guy, took off in his Mercedes, and two hours later I get a call. Pam was sitting on the desk of Monterey police department. She said, 'I'm taking care of the desk, cleaning it with my butt.' She'd taken over the entire cop station. The guy they were with had thrown his pot out the window when they were pulled over for speeding and they'd taken the boys back out looking for it and left the girls in the station. Pam asked, 'Can you come get me down in Monterey?' I had to load the kids in the car, get down there, and there she was with all these cops loving her.

**Pam Marriott Land:** Santa Cruz was a hippy town [there were forty clubs and two colleges, almost half the 40,000 residents were students] and there were plenty of musicians but he was afraid to do anything without his mates. When Laurie got the money for the house [in Golders Green], Jim Leverton and his girlfriend came out, Dave Hynes came out, Johnny [Wright] came and Steve took care of them, and money runs out really quickly when you're supporting six people, so that was very frustrating. It put a strain on everything because we were broke again.

*Despite the fact he had no driving licence, Marriott also bought his dream car, a '59 Cadillac with giant fins and chrome wheels. He had to sit on a pillow so he could see over the steering wheel. He also started wearing American bib overalls [dungarees].*

**Christine Lore:** It was the end of August, so we could be outdoors a lot because this house was only 1,000 square foot and we had Dawn and Jim, Dave, Pam, Steve, their son, my 10-year-old son, their collie, my dog, my cat had just given birth to eight kittens and Steve's macaw parrot – all in three bedrooms and one bathroom. They stayed about a month. Steve realised it was too much of an imposition. When he left he owed me all this money for phone calls so he gave me this Gibson and his Marshall Tweed amps… one from Small Faces and one from Humble Pie. They ended up getting a place not too far from me, in Soquel, a totally middle-class tract home [multiple similar houses on an estate], three bedroom, two bathroom, linoleum floor, avocado ranges, tangerine refrigerator… they didn't have any furniture, Steve bought one chair for himself, a big easy chair that nobody else was allowed to sit in.

I had an invite to go see Blondie at the Coconut Grove [in San Francisco] one night and Pam and I went with this friend in his limo. Steve was so happy to be babysitting, sitting home watching the telly, that was all he needed but we brought everybody home. Debbie Harry sat on the floor and she took a look [at the interior] and said, 'All that's missing is the miniature poodle.' Chris Stein and Steve got on really well. It was great because there was no alcohol, the stores were closed and nobody had drugs. Debbie was pretty down on drugs. We stayed up all night talking and the sun was coming up and Steve said he was going to make a fry-up for everybody, farm-fresh eggs from the little chicken stand down the road, and he cracked one open and there's a half formed chick in there… there goes breakfast, I couldn't eat eggs for years.

They only stayed in that tract house about a month… then they moved up to another house in Ben Lomond built by [eighteenth-century explorer and general Zebulon] Pike [a mountaintop in Colorado is named after him, Pikes Peak]. It was a lovely cabin, very unique, and that's when Steve started drinking too much and I would get hysterical calls from Pam in the middle of the night and she'd show up with Toby and she'd have a black eye, not in good shape, crying. Steve could be cruel.

**Pam Marriott Land:** Steve's drinking got out of control. It was a miserable time for me, we fought a lot, and he got very violent physically, to the point where he cracked my cheekbone. And then it was always, when he was sober, he was going to be okay, let's just give it one more try, blah, blah, blah. He was an alcoholic and it was alcohol when he turned violent with me. He was so remorseful after it had happened, half the time he wouldn't even remember. He would cry and go, 'What happened to you?' and I'd go, 'Well, you hit me.'

**Christine Lore:** The last house they had [in Santa Cruz] was in Boulder Creek [where Moby Grape also had houses, fourteen miles from Santa Cruz beach, up in the mountains, redwood trees, isolated, lots of rednecks, loggers and bikers]. That's where Leslie [West] came. It got worse when Leslie came. Steve's bird died too… they think it was the gas, someone had turned on the valve and the gas was leaking. He adored that bird. Leslie brought a very bad, intense ugly vibe to the house. All of a sudden he was a permanent guest… he was eating them out of house and home. He was so enormous, so obese, it was gross. I would go over there and clean up after them: Steve and Leslie were just like little piggies. There was food things all around them. I was sweeping up and Leslie wanted to see the [American football] game [on TV], and Steve said, 'Hey Chrissie, Leslie wants to see the game,' and I offered Leslie the brush and asked if he wanted to clean. Steve didn't think I should speak to his guest like that. He said, 'Why don't you just take the broom and fly away?' and I said, 'You know what? I am going to do that.'

*Leslie West, guitarist, vocalist and songwriter, was 33, two years older than Marriott. He was renowned for his heavy drug use, chiefly cocaine and heroin, and was famously overweight – his 1975 solo album, which featured Mick Jagger on rhythm guitar, was called* The Great Fatsby *(peaking at US No 168). In the sixties he had fronted an R&B-influenced band, The Vagrants, before forming hard rock band Mountain with former Cream producer Felix Pappalardi. Mountain played Woodstock and scored two gold albums in the early seventies and a big hit single with their best-remembered song, 'Mississippi Queen'. After the band split, West formed a band with Cream bassist and singer Jack Bruce before reforming Mountain in 1973. Humble Pie and Mountain had frequently played gigs together. Humble Pie's tour manager Mick Brigden had worked for Mountain. He was now running Bill Graham's huge concert promotion business and a friend of his was interested in managing the project between West and Marriott. West's most recent solo album,* The Leslie West Band, *featuring ex-Johnny Hallyday sidekick Mick Jones, now of Foreigner, had been a flop.*

**Jim Leverton:** We recruited Leslie West and had this group called The Firm. The name was Marriott's idea [The Krays referred to themselves as 'the firm']. Leslie came in with guns blazing. He wanted me and Dave [Hynes] put on wages and for him and Steve to be the main deal. Marriott wasn't having any of that; he said, 'No, they're my mates.' There was a stand-off for several months. Leslie moved out of the house and the only communication between the pair was by written notes; some of them were quite vicious.

**Pam Marriott Land:** It was a great idea [The Firm]. When Leslie came to live with us we had to hide Toby's sweets from him. It was at a point where I was trying to maintain and take care of my son and I butted out of all that because I didn't know anything about the music business. All I knew was every time I turned around there was a call from some dude who Steve had pissed off or something was going on. He would never give me a straight answer, every time I asked what's going on, what are we doing, Steve always had another answer... he was never straight up with me.

**Jim Leverton:** Leslie went to Milwaukee and when he came back Steve asked me to pick him up from San Francisco [airport]. When we were driving back, he said, 'I've been checking you out, you've played on quite a few records, you're bona fide man, you're in.' I thought to myself, I was in before fucking you! Then he said, 'But Dave ain't got the same track record, we're going to keep him on wages.' I said, 'Steve's never going to go for that, it's a four-way split or not at all.' There was another stand-off. Leslie finally had to concede because Steve said to him, 'What do you want, a quarter of something of 100 per cent of fuck all?' There was a party held at Steve's house to celebrate our new understanding, our unity, and at the party Leslie and Dave had a massive row. Dave was really horrible to Leslie... it was pretty vicious. Steve ran off into his bedroom and hid. As Leslie was going out the door, he shouted back to Marriott, 'Steve, for you the Red Sea... but I can't work with this sick fuck.' That's the way it went down.

*Hynes returned to England. B. J. Wilson (1947–1990) of Procol Harum and the Joe Cocker band briefly played drums with The Firm before Marriott's pal and former All Stars band member, Ian Wallace, joined.*

**Jim Leverton:** It was starting to sound pretty good in the studio. Steve and I had written some really nice numbers: 'Big Train Stops At Memphis', 'Be The One' and 'Take It From Here'. The group had carved out nigh on twelve tunes and CBS were very keen. Negotiations were taking place. Barry Rothman, a high-flying LA lawyer, got involved. He came to Santa Cruz to talk about what we were going to do. I was in America on a visitor's visa that was about to expire. I really needed a working visa. Rothman suggested I go to Canada for two or three days and come back in and apply for an extension on my visitor's visa and then we would apply for a work visa. So I flew to Canada but they wouldn't let me back in...

*The Firm fizzled out.*

**Dale Ockerman:** Leslie West and Steve brought out the worst in each other. They did some recording and it didn't sound like either of them. They recorded at FANE studios in Santa Cruz... definitely no Abbey Road [the material has not surfaced]. It was just party time, lots of toot. Steve started to show up in town [in Santa Cruz] and jam with people, he jammed with some country and western bands. He would just show up at a bar, grab the mic and start singing and he could whip a crappy band into something decent. Everyone would go, 'Jesus Christ, have you heard this guy?' He was a like a whirlwind, a Tasmanian devil when he came into town. He liked to drink; he liked to jam. One of the times he jams it's with Dallas Hodge, who was the leader of The Deluxe Band, who were all from Detroit [originally], big guys playing Les Pauls through Marshalls, a little bit like Lynyrd Skynyrd, really good blues, funky, Southern-sounding stuff. Dallas reminded me of the Bear in Canned Heat, a big furry guy in his bib overalls who made the Les Paul look small. They used to hire me sometimes to play with them because they didn't have a full-time keyboard player.

**Dallas Hodge:** We were doing stuff in the vein of Bob Seger and the Ohio Players, some good old foot-stompin' rock'n'roll but more on the R&B style. Columbia was interested in the band, but we had some personal issues and the deal went away. I was the singer, frontman, guitar player. We had run The Deluxe Band for several years before we ran into Steve in 1979, and then things changed immediately.

**Gary 'Diz' Putnam:** One night I got a call from a friend of ours who was out playing bass with Ted Nugent [managed by future Marriott management team, Leber-Krebs]. They were doing a gig in San Francisco and he said, 'Hey, me and the drummer,' English guy, Cliff Davies, 'are going to come down and see your band play, and he's going to bring a friend who lives in Boulder Creek.' I had no idea who was coming. The night we met I'd been listening to [Humble Pie album] *Rock On* before I went out. Steve was one of my heroes. So we were sitting in the club and this little guy walks through, spitting and cussing and I made a mental note to stay away from him. He was wearing bib overalls, looked like he combed his hair with an eggbeater, four days' growth. He went swaggering up to this guy he knew and he said, 'Ah, you're a fucking cunt,' and hawked a wallop on the floor. I thought, this guy is mad. I didn't recognise him but then the friend of ours said they were going to sit in with us on stage and I see that little arsehole get up on stage with them, and the minute he opened his mouth I dropped to the floor. Holy shit! After the gig I got a call about four in the morning from Steve who wanted to talk to our leader Dallas and he offered Dallas a gig. Dallas said, 'No, I'm committed to my band but if you don't have a band'... Dallas was a few years younger than Steve and I was a few years older.

*Marriott sat in with the group at one of their regular gigs, Scopazzi's Restaurant in Boulder Creek.*

**Gary 'Diz' Putnam:** He had forgotten to bring a guitar strap, so someone got a bar towel and a length of clothing line... the stage was a little corner of the room where they threw a rug down.

**Jim Hannibal:** It was a small community so anywhere Steve would go it was a big event, word would get around and the place would fill up. Before he came along we had bit of notoriety but when he joined we were like local rock stars. One time the band was going to go down to Big Sur, south of Monterey, a ninety-minute drive. We were playing this little place and we went by his house and he was in a squabble with Pam and we convinced him to jump in the truck with us and go down to Big Sur. He just grabbed his guitar and jumped in the big-panel step van. Big Sur was very remote back then, just mostly hippies, but they were well aware of who Steve was. We had a great time and after we played he stayed up and was entertaining the campers on the campground. He was quite a wild man. He was still energised by doing our performance. We were younger guys but we were worn out, up in the rooms, and I could hear him down in the campgrounds singing, everybody loved it.

**Gary 'Diz' Putnam:** They still talk about when Humble Pie played Big Sur. We weren't Humble Pie. He went down with us, to Fernwood Resort, they have little log cabins you can rent. We used to literally just set up on the floor. Steve really liked Dallas's playing and it turned out he really like the band too. We had our own thing going on but we said we'd love to be part of his project and all of a sudden we were rehearsing.

**Dallas Hodge:** When we started rehearsing he comes in one day and puts a bucket on the floor. He said whenever we make a mistake we throw a quarter in the pot. We're all individually making mistakes and reaching into our pockets and throwing the quarters in, until it got to one song and we all screwed up and there was a ton of coins hitting the pot at one time and we busted out laughing. I said, 'Hey Steve, what are you going to do with all this money?' He said, 'Ale, mate, ale… we're going to go down the liquor store and get some Elephant Ale.' He made it fun, he made it relaxing… we had a ball. We had a great band with Steve. We had three guitar players but both George [Lindberg] and I knew when not to play so we didn't get in Steve's way or each other's way. We had Jim [Hannibal] on sax, Drew [Charles Herb] on bass, a great keyboard player in Dale Ockerman. It was a really rocking good band.

**Dale Ockerman:** They bring me in to rehearse in Felton [at John Chesleigh's home] and there was a lot of drinking and carousing going on. We'd hang out between rehearsals, watch videos. Steve was respectful to my wife, to all our ladies, all the guys in The Deluxe Band were married. He wasn't really chasing tail.

**Dallas Hodge:** First place I ever had shepherd's pie was up at his house in Boulder Creek. He made the pie and my wife and I sat down with Pam and Steve and Toby, and John Wright was there too. He and Pam loved each other immensely. They could also fight like cats and dogs. To get up to Boulder Creek [from Santa Cruz] you had to drive up a little country mountain road, lots of curves, sheer drop-offs, places you couldn't go over twenty miles an hour, a thirty-minute drive, and that may have been to his advantage because the readily available shit [drugs] that was around [in Santa Cruz], he had to bust his arse to go get it and then he had to drive up a road on the way back that if he was loaded you never knew what was going to happen. Did he still do drugs? Yeah. Did you sometimes think it was a little far out? Yeah. But it wasn't like the days of old where he was loaded twenty out of twenty-four hours a day.

**Gary 'Diz' Putnam:** If we wanted him to do anything we had to go get him and we had to take him home. I was the only one in the band that had a passenger vehicle and so after rehearsals I would be the guy to drive him home. He always talked me into coming in and he would play records until the sun came up and when I would start making for the door he would pull out this box that contained dozens of tapes of him with all kinds of musicians, some of it was reel-to-reel, some cassettes… one was the Steve Marriott All Stars…

*Marriott would later expound on the material in the box. Forty reels of stuff, he said, cut at Beehive, mentioning contributions from musicians such as Mick Jagger, Keith Richards, Paul Rodgers and Elkie Brooks. 'Hundreds of people came to my studio, and I cut them all there,' he said.*

**Gary 'Diz' Putnam:** His house in Boulder Creek was run-down, a big place, kind of beat up, in the middle of the woods. There was a screened-in porch with a sofa, and numerous nights John [Wright] would sleep out there. There was nothing real fancy in the house other than his fantastic record collection. At the time Steve was taking glass bottles back to the grocery store to get smokes or to get something to put on the table. Things were pretty tight for him, he wasn't buying fancy clothes, or guitars, I don't think the family even had a car. When you bought a beverage you paid two to five cents a bottle extra that was refunded when you returned those bottles to help with litter [it was a Government-led initiative].

**Steve Marriott:** I was taking the fucking 7 Up bottles back. I lived up on the top of a mountain, and I'd put all these bottles in a sack and I'd drag the sack down and it would split regularly all the way down. I rarely had enough money to take the bus to take them into town. Then I used to have to buy more bottles so I had more to take back. I'd get some eggs, steal some margarine…

**Dallas Hodge:** It wasn't until Steve met up with a guy who was a drug dealer in town who wanted to back Steve [that he had money]. It was kind of a double-edged sword: the guy had money but he also had drugs. I think being that broke was a very humbling experience for Steve, in his soul. It was a point where he said I really don't want to get down here ever again. I never saw him go too crazy but he had some warm discussions with the guy who was trying to buy him.

**Pam Marriott Land:** Michael Scott [RIP] was a guy who was a fan that had a bit of money. He became his so-called manager but all he did was end up losing all his money. That's when he contacted Jerry to reform Humble Pie to get out of Santa Cruz. Steve and Jerry hadn't spoken for a long time. There had been a lot of animosity between those two.

**Jerry Shirley:** The phone rang one day and it was Steve. The band I had, Magnet, was falling apart at the seams. And the management we had, which was somewhat connected to Leber-Krebs, Aerosmith's management, got wind that Steve had called me and said, 'Well, great! Fuck Magnet, it's not going anywhere. Get Humble Pie back together. We'll manage it and get you a record deal.'

*Shirley's post-Humble Pie band, Natural Gas, with Badfinger guitarist Joey Molland and former members of Colosseum and The Sutherland Brothers, had cut one album and toured with Peter Frampton before transmogrifying into Magnet around 1977. Magnet, featuring ex-Montrose singer Bob James (James had replaced Sammy Hagar in Montrose), released one album in 1979.*

*As Marriott put the wheels in motion on a Humble Pie reunion, he also recorded material with The Deluxe Band.*

**Gary 'Diz' Putnam:** John [Wright] was rewiring a studio in Santa Cruz [the same FANE studio where Marriott had recorded with Leslie West] and while he did that the studio was closed so he invited us down there to rehearse. While we were rehearsing John started setting up equipment and then he said, 'Hey, you guys want to come in and have a listen?' It was like a work tape that turned into a demo tape that Steve used to go to Leber-Krebs with. We did five songs [including a cover of Elvis's 'All Shook Up' and three Marriott originals, 'Big Train Stops At Memphis', 'Infatuation' and 'Wasname' – a reggae tune on which Marriott played organ]. Through our contacts we sent that tape to Punch Andrews [Bob Seger's manager] and he went nuts for it and he set up a showcase for us [in Detroit] that he planned to bring some record people to.

*Marriott was a Seger fan, had included a cover of his, 'The Fire Down Below', in the Small Faces reunion live set. The well-respected Detroit singer-songwriter had scored a Top 20 hit in 1968 with the single 'Ramblin' Gamblin' Man', and then struggled commercially while recording music that gained him widespread respect. Now, however, he was at the peak of his success, having scored a major breakthrough with his 1976 album* Night Moves, *a six-times-platinum monster that spawned a Top 5 single. His most recent album,* Stranger In Town, *had also gone six times platinum, peaking at US No 4.*

**Gary 'Diz' Putnam:** It then gets into a 'he said, she said'-type situation. Marriott went to New York when he was playing with us to talk to Leber-Krebs, and Jerry Shirley was at the meeting. According to Steve, however, he was pitching The Deluxe Band [to Leber-Krebs], he really wanted to do it with us but the Humble Pie thing was instant money. When he was [first] dealing with Leber-Krebs, Steve somehow found out they had already said to Atlantic they had Steve Marriott but at that time he hadn't actually signed. He would get on the phone and he would be brutal with them and then he'd get off the phone and be singing, 'Whatever Stevie wants, Stevie gets.'

*David Krebs (who had seen Marriott with the reformed Small Faces in Germany in 1977 and been impressed) and Steve Leber were the men behind influential management and production firm Leber-Krebs. They represented not just Aerosmith (1979 saw the band score their sixth multi-platinum album) but also Ted Nugent (on a run of five huge platinum and gold US albums), AC/DC, Joan Jett, Bobby Womack, Funkadelic, Parliament, Scorpions, and a host of lesser names.*

**Steve Marriott:** David Krebs sent Jerry out to get me. He said, 'Will you come and talk about getting back?' I said, 'Okay, as long as you pay the airfare.' I went to New York and sat there, it's going nowhere, quite frankly. A friend from Santa Cruz who is used to me being arrogant signalled to me to tell them to fuck off. At the end of this meeting we said, 'We'll write a hit song over the weekend and record it ten o'clock Monday morning in a shoebox [small studio].' The best way to tell them to fuck off is to do it. So we went – bang! – wrote 'Fool For A Pretty Face' over the weekend. We recorded it Monday morning, waited for a reaction, it freaked, and then I split, went back to California and thought no more of it.

**Jerry Shirley:** He was not happy about being up at nine in the morning to record. But I managed to talk him into it. We went in and cut a great track and that one song got us a record deal. I went to Italy to record with Francesco De Gregori, who Andrew Oldham was producing, and when I came back Steve had disappeared. We tracked him down and I went to visit him of my own volition. He just wanted to do a few reunion gigs. I wanted to do it properly. I wanted to help my mate. Pam has always told me how grateful she was I rescued them from the situation in Santa Cruz.

*Marriott played more games: he used the Deluxe Band demo tape to attract interest from a Los Angeles management firm who organised to video a showcase Steve Marriott & The Deluxe Band gig in Santa Cruz.*

**Gary 'Diz' Putnam:** We did a showcase gig [September 1979] and Marriott said the place was packed with record [industry] people. John Wright did the sound, gave me the biggest, fattest drum sound. Everything was as loud as you could get it.

**Dale Ockerman:** It was really triumphant: Steve Marriott & The Deluxe band at the High Country, second storey, could fit about 400 people in. It was packed. Three lead guitar players, all playing Les Pauls through Marshall stacks, they're cranked... we're doing 'Big Train Stops At Memphis' and Steve came over and looked at me, guitar round his neck, drops the microphone and starts singing, and he was louder than the whole band. Good God, what amazing pipes.

*The local papers gave the forty-five-minute show glowing reviews, despite the 'obnoxiously loud volume'. The band opened with 'Infatuation', played covers of Chuck Berry's 'Route 66', Rufus Thomas's 1965 'Walking The Dog', Edgar Winters' 'Keep Playin' That Rock 'N' Roll' and Brenton Wood's 1967 'Two-Time Loser'. They also gave a debut to 'Fool For A Pretty Face', closing with Ray Charles's 'Hallelujah, I Love Her So', familiar to Humble Pie fans.*

**Dallas Hodge:** Bill Blackwell, Punch Andrews' right-hand man, came out to the gig. The band was smoking but it was over the next few months that whole thing came down.

**Jim Hannibal:** After this debut concert, the Bob Seger agency set up a concert for us on the southside of Detroit and that was going to be where producers from Capricorn Records and people with the Bob Seger band would come down. They were going to take Steve Marriott & The Deluxe Band out on tour with Bob Seger. We didn't know about the plans to reform Humble Pie but they made him a big offer and he had a wife and young son and no money, so he took the money on the table...

**Steve Marriott:** We got such a violent reaction on it ['Fool For A Pretty Face'] – airplay in New York, stuff like that – that we said, 'Okay, let's make a go of it.'

**Dallas Hodge:** He gave us a going-away present of some cash. It was nice as a thought, but not necessary because we all understood, but by the same token he felt obliged to do something for us. I told him, 'If that's what you got to do for your career and your family, you have our blessings 100 per cent,' and you could kind of hear him getting emotional... we loved him.

*Marriott also produced, as a thank you, a demo for The Deluxe Band.*

**Gary 'Diz' Putnam:** Two weeks later he called us. He had got a block of studio time at Villa Recorders in Modesto [on an eighty-acre ranch, one and half hours from San Francisco] for Humble Pie. He said pack your shit and get over here. It was a live-in studio in the middle of nowhere, big bunkhouse, stove, refrigerator, bunch of mattresses. He gave us a block of Humble Pie time and stayed up for seventy-two hours straight to produce. He had a scraggy beard, crazy hair... walking around in his shorts with a smoking jacket, work shoes with the socks rolled down. He looked a wreck and of course there were stimulants. After three days he got kind of crazy. The studio was in the middle of an almond orchard and the owner lived on the property. Steve said when he'd arrived there was just this little tiny dish with almonds in it. Steve said, 'What is it with this tightwad? We're paying all this money to come to the studio and he gives us a little handful of nuts in the middle of an orchard.' So this one night, I think it was a little taste of Melvin, he started pacing up and down, up and down, building up some steam for something... and he disappears and comes back half an hour later laughing his arse off. He'd gone up to the house at 3 a.m., beat on the door, and when the owner came to the door asking, 'What do you want?' he said, 'Got an axe, mate?' 'What do you want an axe for?' 'Almonds, mate...' He wanted to chop the tree down. While we were there he was trying to rent motorhomes so they could bring them to the studio. The bunkhouse was clean and neat but if you're going to reunite with your old bandmates you probably don't want to do it all together in one big room with mattresses on the floor. He looked into it and called the rep for Leber-Krebs and the guy asked, 'Oh, for that price does it come with food?' Steve went ballistic and every time he talked to them after that he would end up getting that phrase into the conversation, 'Oh, does it come with food, mate?' We stayed a week and left with a real high-quality Deluxe Band demo tape. I thought that was real cool of him.

**Jim Hannibal:** He produced the whole thing along with John Wright. It was a beautiful studio, all brand new, with a swimming pool. He seemed like he never slept during that period. He would sing the harmonies he wanted me to play. He would say, 'Jim, trust me on this, this is what Ray Charles would do. I know how he does arrangements.' He cooked for the guys, made shepherd's pie, and he liked to pull pranks. He wanted me to wake up the guys by blowing my sax in their ear. Pam brought the wives and girlfriends of the band out. My girlfriend, now wife, rode with Pam and she said they stopped to get milkshakes and she had a bottle of liquor and was spiking the milkshakes, so by the time they got to the studio they were in good shape.

*Dallas Hodge later spent six years playing with Canned Heat. It is tantalising to think what path Marriott's career and life might have taken had he pursued the Southern rock/deep soul musical direction he was taking with The Deluxe Band, especially had they secured the guidance of Bob Seger's management. Instead...*

# CHAPTER 15

# Fool For A Pretty Face

**David Krebs:** Steve was rather damaged by his old management. Don and Dee… what a one-two punch that is. But he was one of the most heavenly singers I've come across in my career. I put him in the same sentence with Bon Scott [of AC/DC], Steven Tyler and Klaus Meine [Scorpions], all the great singers I've worked with. He was a star but when you have that much talent and you see how much bigger you could have been it must be amazingly frustrating. I think that's part of what Steve went through. I had a great relationship with him but we had a big management company, a very big roster, so I was as hands-on but to a limited degree. The only band I was really hands-on with and close to was Aerosmith – I managed them for twelve years. Phil De Havilland brought us Steve initially. I made the record deal [for the reformed Humble Pie] with Doug Morris [then president of Atlantic Records, currently chairman of Sony Music Entertainment Group] one on one. We gave them a great shot. Doug loved Humble Pie. People in the business knew Steve and knew how talented he was.

**Phil De Havilland:** I managed Magnet. They were with A&M and after they got dropped we recreated Humble Pie. Clem flew in from England and we were doing a recording out in Modesto, and after a couple of sessions he flew back home, he wanted no part of it. Peter Frampton considered it but after a meeting he had with Steve he decided he couldn't go through it again. As talented as he was Steve was just a bad guy. We never talked about Peter being in the band [when pitching the Humble Pie reformation idea to Leber-Krebs] but we did say Clem. Leber and Krebs were partners, with Aerosmith, in the [New York] nightclub I owned, Privates. David called Doug Morris and he signed Humble Pie over the phone. It wasn't a super big deal but it was okay, a decent deal...

**Dave Clempson:** Steve and Jerry called me. I was actually making plans with Bobby Tench to put together a project. I said I was working with Bobby and I was reluctant to just blow him out. And they decided it would be great to have Bobby in the band as well. So Bobby and I flew out to meet with the rest of guys in San Francisco. The whole thing was a nightmare. We got into the studio [in Modesto] and it was still kind of where we left off years before. I'd been told that Steve had left his old recklessness behind. There was still too much indulgence and not enough music. I couldn't get excited about it. I stayed for two or three days and decided I didn't want to be involved and I just came home and Bobby stayed.

**Jerry Shirley:** As soon as Clem got back into Steve's company, he couldn't handle it. They all went home for Christmas and Clem decided he didn't want to go on with it. I called Bobby and said, 'Where does that leave you?' And he said, 'Aw, fuck Clem, I'll have a go at it.' So we had our line-up, which was Bobby, Anthony Jones, me and Steve. Anthony Jones was a friend of mine through my days in New York. He was in a great late punk/early new wave band called The Planets. He helped out when Steve and I needed a bass player to do 'Fool For A Pretty Face' and as a result of that session he got the job in the band. Steve told me he had contacted Greg [Ridley] and he wasn't interested but I found out later that Steve never even contacted him... I couldn't figure out why.

**Steve Marriott:** I rang Greg Ridley. He's selling antiques in Gloucester – retired, officially. He said, 'My old lady won't let me do that stuff no more. I'm quite happy in the antiques business.'

**Pam Marriott Land:** Steve was upset that Greg didn't want anything to do with it, neither did Clem but it was very hopeful, especially with Leber-Krebs representing them. So we were really happy for about three months. We were [leaving Santa Cruz and] on our way to [living in] New York. It was the best Christmas [1979] we had. We went to

England. I thought this would change him and he would really embrace it and do well. It seemed like everything was going to be okay.

**Jerry Shirley:** Toby recently thanked me again for engineering their exit from Santa Cruz. He told me that Steve was definitely at his worst in Santa Cruz and that once they had arrived in NYC and got settled their lives had a complete 360 turn around. They had money again as Steve was now playing in a great working band once more. David Krebs even arranged a visit home to the UK for them that Christmas. I was thrilled to be able to help my old friend get his life back on track.

*Tench, who Shirley had wanted to replace Marriott in Humble Pie circa 1974, would play guitar and sing in the new line-up. After his rock/soul band Hummingbird had broken up he'd hopped around a few other outfits including Streetwalkers, the Laurie O'Leary-managed Widowmaker and played with Eric Burdon before becoming an integral part of Van Morrison's band as guitarist and singer.*

**Phil De Havilland:** We did the first album in Modesto and that's where I got a real good taste of Steve. He was a really, really bad drunk. He hated everybody in the music business because he felt he got fucked over by everyone in the music business. David Krebs treated Steve much better than he treated the rest of the band. He took care of him on the side a little bit, always gave him whatever he wanted. Any problems that arose Steve didn't come to me, he went to David. It was more like I managed the rest of the band and David managed Steve, who was a very selfish guy. This is typical Steve Marriott. When we first got to Modesto I didn't really know him that well and his lawyer was flying up from LA to talk to Steve and me about what was going on and for two days before the guy got here he told me he how much he hates this guy, he's the worst, he can't believe he's his lawyer, he's so typical LA – 'I don't know what I'm doing with him.' And then the guy walked in the door and Steve throws his arms around him and starts kissing him, 'Great to see you, you're the best, I love you, thanks for coming.' I just kind of shook my head but he actually was right about the lawyer.

**Elliot Saltzman:** Phil De Havilland was a weird scenario. Privates was a big building, five floors, there was a restaurant, a 1,200-seater rock club. Phil was running that. He was not really a rock'n'roll manager. The story goes that Phil found Steve in the middle of San Francisco taking empty bottles to the grocery store to cash in for the money. Phil was almost a silent partner [in the Humble Pie reformation]. I took over Humble Pie's day-to-day [management]. I worked for Leber-Krebs. I stayed with Steve until the end of 1981 when I moved over to Joan Jett. I had a history of handling acts that were a little bit difficult but Steve broke the mould. He was something. Steve and the boys needed a lot of minding. Steve was obviously very talented but almost his own worst enemy.

*The reformed Humble Pie had spent two weeks recording material for an album, with John Wright engineering, at Villa Recorders in Modesto. The album was finished at the Soundworks studios in New York, which was next door to Studio 54. Marriott had christened Anthony Jones, who was black, 'Sooty'. It seemed a clearly pejorative nickname but was essentially the language Marriott had grown up around. His mother, in late 1999, was still using terms such as 'darkies' and 'Negroid'.*

**Elliot Saltzman:** We had sent a photographer to the studio in Modesto while they were recording. He arrived way too early and woke the band up to take a press photo for the record and the band were not impressed. Finally at about 5 p.m. they start doing the shoot. They wanted to do it in front of a pool table and figured it'd be cool to put a little packet, a wrap, of blow, cocaine, racket as they called it, on the table, which they did and the photographer tried for two and a half hours to get a photo of all of them that would work and he could not do it. The closest thing they had was one where Bobby Tench's eyes were closed... so we had an artist airbrush eyes into Bobby Tench. If you looked at the press photo closely Bobby looks like a zombie. This shot ended up on the back cover of *On To Victory*. They smashed great holes in the photographer's grey back-screen and then taped them back together to try and show their disdain in being woken up at 9 a.m. The photographer was fine – he just said, 'Go ahead, Leber-Krebs are picking up the bill.'

Everybody's feeling was if they could just keep Steve on the straight and narrow we could get something going, everybody wanted to create another big band. Leber-Krebs found them a band house in Lake Mahopac [near the town of Carmel in Putnam County, New York – fifty miles from Manhattan] a beautiful area, beautiful six-bedroom house and they all lived there except Jerry, who lived with his pregnant wife Lottie about ten miles away. The person who owned it was a doctor. Steve would take Toby and go fishing on the lake but he wouldn't touch the fish or the hook or the bait but he brought a big mallet with him. He would get the fish, wouldn't even take the hook out of them and he would smash it over the head until it was dead and then he'd put it in the freezer. Pam was living in Lake Mahopac, she was kind of isolated out there.

**Pam Marriott Land:** He'd go to the city and I'd be left in the house. It was in the middle of nowhere. And Steve always had a terrible habit of forgetting to give me money. He'd give me $40 and say, 'I'll see you later,' disappear to the city and I'd be calling him, saying, 'Me and my son haven't eaten in a day or two.' Eventually I said, 'I can't do this, I can't even get a job or do anything out here'… so we moved to the city [an apartment in Greenwich Village].

**Elliot Saltzman:** I saw her a little more when they moved into town but I got the feeling if nobody had to know nobody would know he had a wife and child. It wasn't something he talked about like most people do. My first week working for him, Steve called me and he wanted me to get him a record player, he said he was staying downtown at a friend's place in the East Village, an English bird. I go there, the girl's in the bathroom, she walks out and she was married to another very, very, very famous musician at the time, one that we [Leber-Krebs] managed.

**Andrew Loog Oldham:** In the 1979 of New York, a year by which, unbeknownst to a lot of us, she and that other lady in our lives, the white one, was starting to exact every ounce left in us – the creative and physical ebbing away of the last grand reserve – Steve called to tell me he had everything under control. Atlantic was paying him $120,000 [over $400,000 today] for a finished product and Steve assured me he could bring it in for a fast forty-five grand. At the time Steve looked like he could bring the gig in. He wasn't that out of it and seemed to be looking forward to the money. Next thing I heard was that as usual America or at least Steve's vision of it had driven the old boy off the deep end again. He'd got his $120,000 all right but had spent north of 160 bringing it in.

*Atlantic chose 'Fool For A Pretty Face', credited to Shirley and Marriott, as the band's comeback single. It fell just short of the American Top 40, peaking at US No 52, but was a promising start, gaining the group significant airplay and media attention. The band prepared themselves for a long slog on the road beginning with a hard rock package tour, Rock N' Roll Marathon, featuring a glut of Leber-Krebs acts such as Frank Marino & Mahogany Rush, Angel and Mother's Finest, that ran for eight weeks from late March 1980. Elliot Saltzman was tour director.*

**Elliot Saltzman:** We were all based in New York and we'd be doing a gig and Steve would call and say, 'Hey El, I'm in Virginia Beach [a six hour drive from New York] at a friend's house, I'll fly from here'... but invariably I could never wake him up. He'd tell me the house he was at, give me the address, I'd get that out of him. What I had to do is find a taxi service and say, 'Hey, my name's Steve and I'm staying at this address, do me a favour – the doorbell doesn't work, I can't hear, I'm working on something, when you get there just really pound on the door and I'll come, I'll give you a good tip.' Sometimes he'd just tell the guy to fuck off but we made most of the gigs. On the road he chased women but not very well. He'd say something really stupid or do something really rude and even these [type of] girls [hanging around the tour] would go, 'What is this?' He made them nervous and that would frustrate him and he would drink more. If he was chatting up a girl for two hours and all of sudden she went home with her boyfriend, forget it, that night was a bender. Jerry had a wife, he had started a family, he wanted this [Humble Pie reunion] to be a success, he was more business but he would relapse as well, so we'd have Jerry Shirley situations too.

*Humble Pie's comeback album, titled* On To Victory, *was released in April 1980. It peaked at No 60 on the American charts. It featured, alongside the single, two more songs that had their genesis in Santa Cruz, 'Infatuation' and 'Take It From Here' (both credited to Marriott). There were two songs credited to Shirley, Marriott and Jones, a group effort and a Tench/Marriott collaboration. None of these songs were accredited to a publisher, Marriott's song-publishing arrangements remaining something of a mystery. There were three covers on the album: 'Baby, Don't Do it' – Marvin Gaye's 1964 single that the Small Faces had recorded, 'My Lover's Prayer' by Otis Redding (1966) and 'Over You', first cut by Aaron Neville in 1960.*

**David Krebs:** On that album there was one brilliant song, 'Fool For A Pretty Face'. If there had been a second great song, it would have been like one and one equals ten and that album would have gone gold or platinum and given them a whole new lease of life but, the fact is, it was one song deep in the opinion of everyone… it never got beyond 'Fool for A Pretty Face'. And at that time way too many drugs were being used. If they had made a lot of money who was going to control what was spent on drugs? These guys had habits at that time. Elliot [Saltzman] must have had his hands full.

**Elliot Saltzman:** Steve met a girl who was a friend of mine. He said, 'El, she's coming with us [on tour].' Next day we're taking a flight out of Atlanta and Steve's wearing his canary yellow jacket, almost as big as he is, drunk out of his mind. I had to take the bottle away from him, you can't walk around the airport with a bottle. Steve walked up to the counter and as soon as the woman said something, he said, 'Fuck you, I'll buy your fucking aeroplane.' The cops came, they escort us out. What can I do? I get rid of the girl, take the yellow jacket off Steve, push down the spiked up rooster hair – a style which he told us – and he said he got this from Rod Stewart – was created by putting mayonnaise on his hair and rubbing a towel on his head really fast. I gave him my jacket and I got a wheelchair and I put him in that and booked on another flight. Then I had to push him past all the gates where he'd just caused a commotion. I gave him one of those 'Steve, don't fucking say a word' looks, and he wouldn't because he knew the next thing I was going to say was, 'or I'll knock you the fuck out.' We were going to lose the gig, lot of money that me, everybody, was depending on. He goes, 'Right El, I get it,' and then the wheelchair starts making a noise and at the top of his lungs he kicks the wheelchair and shouts, 'Fucking cunt!' But we made the plane, first class, he's still in the wheelchair, I have to make up another story. 'Oh yeah, he's just had an operation, he's heavily medicated.' I went to the bathroom for two seconds and when I came back, he's ordering double whiskeys. I had to tell the air stewardess just to tell him they had run out and that's what my life with Steve was like continuously. The band gave me a piece of advice: when you're at a restaurant make sure you're the last one there. It was because Steve stole the tips. We eat, leave tips, all go out, and all of sudden Steve said I've left my cigarettes and goes back to the table and takes everybody's tip.

**Phil De Havilland:** I can give you one more typical Marriott story. We were on the road, somewhere in Texas, San Antonio maybe, and after the gig Marriott got to the promoter before Elliot and took all the band's money and bought a whole bunch of coke and locked himself in a room with some chick he met and wouldn't come out, wouldn't share the band's money. He spent it all and didn't make the plane the next day to make the next gig. Steve was a real pain in the arse. It's funny now but I didn't think it was funny that day, that night, and the band didn't think so either but Steve was the frontman and he got on that stage and he'd put on a show and a half, he was a performer. I appreciated his talent but his character was out of whack, as a human being it was hard for me to like him.

**Bobby Tench:** This goes without saying: you've got to rest sometime. Have an early night. But Steve thought he had endless amounts of energy. He didn't understand what it was doing to him. It never bothered him to have to sing the next day. It would bother me. If we were up too late and had a show the next day, my voice would be shot. Jerry and Steve were always arguing but they couldn't do without one another. They needed to do that sort of stuff to be on the edge.

*Leber-Krebs continued to support the band as best they could, booking them on high-profile support slots with the company's biggest acts – Ted Nugent, AC/DC and Aerosmith, taking Marriott and Shirley back to the 10,000– 20,000-capacity venues they had once headlined such as the Cobo Hall in Detroit, Long Beach Arena, San Diego Sports Arena and the Spectrum in Philadelphia. There were also headline gigs across the country at smaller 2,000–3,000-capacity theatres and big clubs. The AC/DC gigs were potentially huge for Humble Pie. The headliners were touring their* Back In Black *album, a worldwide hit selling over 50 million copies, peaking at No 4 in America and going twenty-two-times platinum.*

**Elliot Saltzman:** 'Fool For A Pretty Face' did well on radio and that gave us some momentum so there was a resurgence and then you get booked on an AC/DC tour... it looks good. AC/DC worshipped Steve Marriott. They were doing the Back In Black tour and our first gig with them was in Philadelphia, the [17,000-capacity] Spectrum [31 July 1980] and after that we were going to do the whole [American] tour to sold-out arenas [a further fifty-plus dates over three months]. It was going to be marvelous. The rumour was AC/DC had been contemplating having Steve replace [their singer] Bon Scott [who died in February 1980 of acute alcohol poisoning – his first band, Valentines, had covered the Marriott/Lane Small Faces song, 'I Can't Dance With You']. At the Spectrum, AC/DC were running late and Humble Pie didn't get to soundcheck and the show was a disaster. Our dressing room was right next to theirs; it was the same room but separated by an air wall. I was coming backstage after the show and from the hallway, I could hear Steve shouting, 'Those motherfucking poxy bullshit arseholes... those little ungrateful midgets have no respect... this is the worst show.' I went in and I could see all of AC/DC listening to this with looks on their faces like I'd never seen before. Needless to say that was the first and last show we did with AC/DC and then all of a sudden you're scrambling for gigs... gigs which aren't very high profile.

On To Victory *was released in the UK on Don Arden's Jet Records. His main act ELO were at the peak of their popularity with a recent No 1 UK album,* Discovery *(their fourth Top 10 America album on the bounce), and American No 2 hit single 'Xanadu' from the soundtrack album to the film of the same name.*

**David Arden:** Humble Pie II, the deal was done with me and David Krebs and Steve, just a deal with Jet for the UK and few territories in Europe. I was thrilled, the Old Man was thrilled but could we get them to do any promotion? No, as hard as we tried. Steve could say things to people and get them pissed off and wound up. I was out with John Bonham at the Rainbow and Ritchie Blackmore [Deep Purple] invites us up to his house for a party. Stevie was there. I'm talking to someone else and could see there was a bit of talk between Steve and John and then the next thing there's Steve pulling himself up off the ground. Bonham had flattened him... threw him on the floor and jumped on him. Steve got up, 'Eh man, that wasn't cool, that wasn't cool at all, man.' I went up, 'Eh, John, what's gone on?' 'He drives me fucking mad... fucking idiot.'

*The Humble pie reunion material sold poorly in the UK.*

**Elliot Saltzman:** David Krebs said, 'We're putting him in the studio again, we've got Gary Lyons, he's this big producer, he's English, he'll know how to handle Steve.' Gary Lyons ended up being worse than Steve. The first day, Steve starts his business and Gary Lyons walks in with a fire extinguisher and douses Steve and the whole recording studio with dry dust.

*Lyons recorded the second Humble Pie reformation album at Mediasound studios in New York, where Stevie Wonder and Blondie had recently cut albums. He had used the studio to produce the most recent Aerosmith album, 1979's* Night In The Ruts, *which peaked at No 14 in America.*

**Gary Lyons:** At the beginning of the recording process he was pushing me as far as he could but I wouldn't stand for it. We had a clash pretty early on and one session ended abruptly. He was drinking brandy and threw the bottle at me and it smashed. He loved to see how far he could push the envelope. He was like a kid but I wasn't standing for any nonsense. The [album track] 'The Driver' [written by Marriott] was great and so was the Elvis song, 'All Shook Up' [which he'd also cut with the Deluxe Band]; that was one of my favourites. There was one [song on the album] he had a hard job singing, the ballad, and we were always playing tricks on one another and on that one I told him that I'd got a phone call and his dog had died and he was gutted and I said, 'Well, we've still got to sing this track,' and he did it really depressed. Afterwards I said I was only joking about the dog.

*The album was completed at Soundworks in New York with a young in-house engineer, Craig Goetsch, then in his early 20s. Goetsch had met the band when they finished* On To Victory *at Soundworks. He recalled engineering 'Fool For A Pretty Face' there with Marriott informing him that he'd written the song while on the toilet.*

**Craig Goetsch:** I was doing the second album at Soundworks. They had to bring in a big name, Gary Lyons, but I did most of the recording. I was working with Steely Dan and Harry Belafonte in the day [at Soundworks] and Humble Pie at night and we'd go on until the wee hours of the morning. John Lennon was doing his album [*Double Fantasy*] a few blocks away at the Hit Factory and his whole gang used to come up after their sessions finished, Andy Newmark [drums], the engineers, some of the players... not John because apparently his wife said no. [Lennon was murdered in New York, December 1980, three weeks after *Double Fantasy* was released. Marriott wrote a song, 'Teenage Anxiety', for the new album in tribute.]

*Tensions within the band were growing as Marriott's smoking, drinking and drugging grew worse, his vocals now suffering badly. There were days when his voice was so wrecked he struggled to sing and would storm out, leaving a frustrated band behind.*

**Elliot Saltzman:** Gary [Lyons] told me when Steve wanted his bottle of Courvoisier I should empty half of it out and fill the rest with water to make sure he could at least last for a certain amount of time in the studio before getting totally inebriated.

*Bobby Tench was also keen to include more of his own material on the album but Marriott was dismissive, despite the fact he and Tench had collaborated on what would be the album's title track 'Go For The Throat'. The album would include two Marriott/Shirley collaborations, including 'Lottie And The Charcoal Queen', a song in part about Pam, but Shirley was growing increasingly dismayed with Marriott's behaviour. He had heard about Marriott's recent visit to a New York studio to see his old pal Rick Wills recording a new Foreigner album. The band's lead singer Lou Gramm was a lifelong admirer of Marriott but Marriott was horribly rude in return. He was becoming a liability.*

**Elliot Saltzman:** He always made these remarks, often about Rod Stewart because he'd become more famous than he had, but he would do it in front of people too. We were in the studio one time and Peter Frampton was coming in to record and he found out Steve was there and he didn't show up. He was afraid because he would get tormented.

**Craig Goetsch:** He was Steve. He could get on people's nerves if he got out of control. There were one time when we were recording at Soundworks where he demanded money [from management] or he was going to walk out the studio. He was ordering bottles of champagne from the Sheraton down the street. A guy came down [from the record company] with a cheque and he said, 'I don't want a cheque, I want cash,' and he spat all over the cheque with the champagne. The kid who came down with the cheque was an upcoming guy and as these kids grow older they don't forget. Next thing you know here comes David Krebs with the cash... 'Inkrebable', Steve would say, 'Inkrebable' and 'Unbeleberable' was what he called Leber and Krebs.

**Elliot Saltzman:** With the record label, he was rude to everybody. It was something to behold. It always seemed that in the back of his mind whoever he was talking to or dealing with were either going to or already were taking advantage of him... managers weren't giving him the money, tour managers were not getting the right hotels or flights or they were getting the blow and not giving it to him. He was always suspicious, questioning people about everything that was going on very quietly, 'See that [conversation happening] over there, what do you think that's about?' In his mind he thought he should have been as big as everybody else and it was everybody else's fault that he wasn't as big.

*A single emerged from the album sessions, a new version of 'Tin Soldier'. It picked up a good response, peaking at No 58 on the Billboard charts. The album sessions went on as Marriott continued to party, often at Privates. As the night wore on he'd become verbally abusive and try to start fights.*

**Gary Lyons:** Privates had live bands on and it was a regular hang-out of a lot of people in the music business. It was a bit like Tramp in London. When I finished work, ten/eleven at night, I'd go there for an hour or two, have a drink, and there'd be a gang of us: Richie Supa, who was very close with Phil De Havilland and David Krebs; the Aerosmith guys; myself; Steve Marriott and his guys. We all socialised a lot. At that time there was a bunch of us around the Aerosmith project and Richie Supa was one of those guys hanging around helping Steven Tyler with some of his writing. Steve felt he'd been financially ripped off. He never had a good word to say [about anyone in the music business]... he tended to make light of it, joke about it but it was a constant thing [a favourite tale Marriott told was how he had once caught a tour manager rubbing the tops off of sevens, changing T-shirt revenue from $1700 to $1100 and pocketing the difference – an entertaining story but one with questionable veracity].

*Marriott cut two Richie Supa songs for the* Go For The Throat *album – one, 'Chip Away The Stone', had already been recorded by Aerosmith.*

**Craig Goetsch:** We used to go up Richie Supa's apartment and we ended up at Ronnie Wood's place downtown in the village a couple of nights. We'd go down Electric Lady Studio when Free were recording… be there all night, Steve singing, everybody loving it. We'd be up Privates most nights. We always put everything on the slate. Humble Pie had to [eventually] play a gig there [broadcast live on the radio] in order to pay off their bar bill. Michael Bolton was sitting next to me while I was mixing sound at that gig. The guys from KISS would be up there. When the doors shut everybody would be sitting around having a sing, carrying on. Steven Tyler loved Steve. We'd go up to his apartment carrying on and Steve used to call him Tylenol [after a sleep aid tablet] and he hated that. When we did the show at Privates, Steve said, 'Hey, maybe we can get our friend Tylenol out here and he can bang his cane [following a motorcycle accident Tyler was walking with the aid of cane],' and Steven walked out.

**Phil De Havilland:** Steve was at Privates every night and as the night went on he got drunker and drunker and more fucked up. It was just not fun. Pam used to come in [to the club] a lot. Pam was a really nice person. I don't know how he ever ended up with her. I never saw him be not nice to Pam but I never could understand the relationship, were they together, splitting up, I don't know. Pam was a sweetheart.

**Christine Lore:** I got a call from Pam having a nervous breakdown basically. They had this giant dog, huge, and she had just had six puppies that were five weeks old and they couldn't contain them so they were taking over the house, pooping everywhere. I went over. It was total chaos. I built a little pen for them and got them all happy. Craig [Goetsch] took us out to Studio 54 and Pam goes, 'Look over there', and

312

it was this guy from her favourite soap [*Another World*], Ray Liotta, and he was staring over at Pam. He went nuts for her. She was worn out by Steve. It'd be easier to get a full-time job and a normal life. You didn't know what chaos was coming round the corner, who Steve was going to find to bring along to the party.

**Pam Marriott Land:** He was out and about screwing any dog he could find and came home with crabs and all that stuff. It got to the point where I just couldn't deal with him. We split up and I told him I didn't want to reconcile and I was seeing Ray Liotta and of course Steve was always, 'Well, let's get back, it's going to be better.'

*Craig Goetsch got to see a more homely side of Marriott when he lost his apartment and Marriott invited him to rent a spare room at the home in Greenwich Village he shared with Pam and Toby.*

**Craig Goetsch:** It was a walk-up, second floor, had a living room with a fireplace, down the hall there were the three bedrooms, a dining room and a really big kitchen where we spent 90 per cent of our time. It was odd because I was a big fan of Humble Pie and now I'm living with this big rock star but Steve became like my older brother. I'd have a night out and be in my room and I'd hear a knock on the door, 'Craig, you getting up? Come on, Craig, wake up, here's your coffee,' and he'd put the coffee down by my bedside, 'come on, son, I've made up some eggs, fried tomatoes, beans… we're having breakfast.' There was a better side to him. He had a crock-pot that he made soup in; he had soup going all the time. It'd start out as one type and turn into another but always soup on: slow cooked, he'd say, 'You know, mate, you've got to slow cook it, that's the best.' It was a big thing to go to Jefferson Market [grocery store] and shop [for food]. We were also big movie guys; we watched a lot of comedy, lot of Richard Pryor…

The money wasn't always flowing and some nights he'd say, 'Come on, mate, let's go have a drink somewhere.' We'd go down to Bleecker Street to [legendary rock club] Kenny's Castaways and as soon as we'd go in, right from the stage, 'Oh my God, I think Steve Marriott just walked in the door, can we get him up here to do a song?' Steve would head to the stage, I'd head to the soundboard, he'd do a song, the place would go crazy, do another song and before you know it, all night, we're having great fun. We'd get home and he'd make up what he called the 'bit tray', some sliced tomatoes, cut salami, good cheeses and we'd call up a name from the phone book and prank people, pretend to be other people and record it. He had a 4-track at home and was constantly writing songs. A lot of rock stars would come by, Keith Richards, Ronnie Wood... I was going to work with Keith's band, X-Pensive Winos.

Go For The Throat *was released in June 1981 (again there appeared to be no publisher attached to the songs). At Marriott's insistence Goetsch posed (alongside a female model) for the cover.*

**Jerry Shirley:** *Go For The Throat* was a pretty decent record but the record company chose to drop it at birth because Steve was particularly rude to the senior vice president of Atco [Atlantic Records] at a party to celebrate its release! And this guy sent a memo around his office on Monday morning which basically said, 'Dump this record, don't work it.' The two things Steve was the best in the world at were singing the blues and pissing people off.

**Steve Marriott:** I'm very proud of the new album. Gary Lyons is a great producer. I want to use him forever. He says it's his best album and he's worked on a few. The drive on it is insane and there's not one cut I can point to as weak. *On To Victory* was groping for ideas like *As Safe As Yesterday* but Gary sifted through all our songs and chose some things that maybe I wouldn't have picked and they all turned out to be spot on. It took us almost a year to get this out but no complaints at all.

*The album stalled at No 154. Phil De Havilland quit. The band went back out on the road.*

**Craig Goetsch:** They took me on the road. I'd never been on the road. He said, 'C'mon, don't be a cunt, come on the road, mate: sex, drugs and rock'n'roll'. I'd had none of that because I was in the studio. He taught me a lot of stuff, moulded me into what I am today [vice president Live Nation Production, New York]. He put me on the straight and narrow, believe it or not. In the studio you watched your meters, on the road Steve came and put a piece of cardboard across the meters. 'I want you to shut your eyes and open your ears,' he said, 'and that's the way you mix.'

*Marriott, with his personal life in disarray and his finances fragile, enjoyed life on the road, the highs and the parties, and wanted to stay out as long as possible, happy to jump on dates at short notice, supporting acts such as Judas Priest, Ted Nugent, Iron Maiden or Blue Oyster Cult. Tour manager Saltzman and the band had to cope with his often outrageous behaviour as best they could. At most gigs they would collude in a variety of charades to delay Marriott getting to the bottle of Courvoisier on the rider until as close to show time as possible. He was often dishevelled, in purple OshKosh dungarees and a banana-yellow drape jacket with black velvet lapels and stack heels that caused him to teeter forwards, hair spiked up but unable to hide the onset of balding. The audience welcomed old hits such as '30 Days In The Hole' and 'I Don't Need No Doctor' while also, to the band's utter joy, cheering newer material such as 'Fool For A Pretty Face' and 'Infatuation'.*

**Elliot Saltzman:** He was arrested in Texas, El Paso. The bus was stopped to check for illegal immigrants and when the customs officer walked on, Steve screamed at them, 'Oi, Gestapo's on board'... they took him right away, he didn't have his papers. We had to get our immigration lawyers to fax them his papers and then I had to get Craig to drive fifty miles to pick him up, and then they had to drive 400 miles to the gig. There was always consequences for his actions that everybody else had to deal with and that's why everybody got fed up. There's three other guys in the band and a road crew and everybody's depending on this person to do the right thing but he would drink and take whatever drugs... he would take Quaaludes from people in the audience while the show was on, hoping the show would be over before it hit him really bad. On a plane, I was sitting next to him and the guy in front had a comb-over and Steve got up and spat on to the guy's head. That was his thing. He would spit on the stage. He wouldn't care, he would spit at the bass player [Jones] all the time, there's pictures with spit hanging down from the bass player. He was uncontrollable.

*Shirley recalled Marriott referring to band members as 'bitch' or nigger' on stage. It was this that sparked a fight between Marriott and Tench. The upshot was a broken rib for Marriott that necessitated the cancellation of several gigs.*

**Jerry Shirley:** They got into a fistfight because of something Steve said on stage. 'Aw, I couldn't understand why Bobby got uptight about it,' Steve said. Whereas everybody else, including the 18,000 people who were witnessing it, could well understand why Bobby wasn't too pleased. In the hotel after the show Steve used derogatory racist language towards Anthony and Bobby took offence. Suddenly Steve lunged at Bob with a brandy bottle, threw it at him. The roadies were holding Bobby back as they knew Bobby could hurt him. Steve saw Bob was restrained and went for him so all Bob could do was use his feet and karate kick him in the ribs. Steve and Bob got on fine [in general]. Bobby is a kind and lovely but tough and proud man.

**Craig Goetsch:** Fight night... sometimes he spat out at the audience and all of a sudden the audience would spit back and the band was pissed off. We all got spat on. There were three phases of Steve: Steve the guy I lived with was a great home guy; when we hit the road he turned into Mel; and then there was Mega-Mel and Mega-Mel would go up to a seven-foot guy and curse him out. It was our way of describing Steve when someone asked how he was – 'He's Mel,' 'He's getting Mel,' and then maybe later at night, 'Ah he's Mega-Mel,' out of control. I tried to steer him, that was a lot of what I did on the road, kind of talk him out of things but he had his moments with us when he was too much. But it was fun too. There was always play fights in the hallways, people coming out with shaving cream or I'd go in Sooty's room and take the bolts off the door, take the phone apart, put all the furniture on the bed and unscrew all the light bulbs... and then when he'd come in with a chick, he always had a chick, he opens the door, it falls in, there's no lights, trips over the furniture... We were in Beverly Hills one time, all sitting by the pool and Steve passed out in one of the lounge chairs and we had a photo shoot the next day and so me and Bobby took a towel and covered half his face, diagonal, and when he woke up he had burned his face on one side... he was pissed about that, real pissed.

**Elliot Saltzman:** They were relentless. It wasn't camaraderie. It was any way they could find to get one up on the other. Steve had a higher place [in the pecking order] and, as a result, was spending way more money, over and above his fair share, and it bothered Jerry and Bobby. They would always be looking out to see what the other guy had going on, waiting about in the hotel corridors, looking through the peephole. They got into the habit of, if there was a girl two of them was interested in, one of them would hide a Quaalude in the other's food. Bobby once crumbled up a couple of Quaaludes in Craig's salad because he wanted to be with a girl and Craig didn't even make it through the meal, he went bam down on the table. Bobby moves right in, 'You want to come to my room to listen to some music?'

**Craig Goetsch:** True. We were both out with this chick and he wanted the chick. I was sharing a room with Bobby and I woke up in the morning, where the hell am I? He put a lampshade on my head and was in the bed with the girl. When we hit the road Steve said, 'We're going to give them who they think we are,' and if he didn't want to become that person, off to the bar and become that person. We had names for everybody. Steve was Mel and Jerry was the Turk Mosquito. The word for coke was racket. Steve had a saying, 'I got a packet in my pocket, it's full of racket, let's go and rock it.' In Chicago, we had this party, room full of people, and Steve was standing there with his fingers round the bathroom door jam talking... and someone ran in the bathroom and slammed the door and Steve screamed bloody murder and the person inside is afraid. Steve's screaming, 'Open the door, you fucking cunt,' going mad. We got laid off for ten days in a hotel and we ruined that hotel.

*In hospital, doctors drilled holes in the base of Marriott's fingernails to reduce the swelling and less than two weeks later he was on stage again.*

**Craig Goetsch:** We were always on the road, we'd come home for a bit and then be back out, and when we travelled, because Steve knew so many people and so many people knew him, the entourage used to grow. We'd run into The Blackberries in Detroit or Chicago and Steve would say, 'Come on,' and everybody would be up to the rooms and they'd be having a sing, drinking, partying after the show. Bumble Bee

Bob [Novak, well-respected blues musician who played with Muddy Waters and B. B. King] used to be there all the time. When we were down South, Steve and I would go to gospel shows, churches. If we were in Chicago we'd go to Chicago Blues [bar] and when they recognised him he'd get up there and sing 'When A Man Loves A Woman'. One night we ended up at my Italian–Sicilian mother's house in New Jersey, we'd been driving all night, in a rental truck. I crashed out and when I woke up Steve was in the kitchen frying tomatoes, cooking breakfast for everyone. My [younger] brothers and sisters know he's a big rock star, seen him on TV and they tell their friends and at the end of my driveway there's fifty or sixty kids coming to see this big rock star. He went out there and talked to them all.

**Elliot Saltzman:** We were in Salt Lake City [majority Mormon population, very conservative, massively anti-alcohol] and when I got to the hotel there was a chair with its leg sticking about three feet into the tar in the car park and police officers looking on. 'What happened?' 'It seems like one of your people threw a chair out of the window.' They'd been up to Steve's room several times but he wouldn't answer the door. So with the police and the hotel manager we go up to Steve's room and he answers for me and says, 'I don't know how it happened, someone must have broken into my room.' I jumped on that: I said, 'Oh my God, Steve where's your guitar?' He looks at me as if I'm out of my mind. I said, 'Your guitar, it was in your room. Mel must have broken in and dumped the chair out the window and then stolen your guitar.' The cops started to feel a little sorry for us. I explained that there was this guy, a bald-headed wrestler named Mel who followed the band around who does this kind of thing.

I then had to make out this police report for a guitar that wasn't lost, what's the serial number? I went back into the truck and get a serial number and it was fine. The situation was diffused so I go get a burger. When I got back to the hotel, twenty minutes later, there are thirty police cars outside, more furniture in the car park. I get up to Steve's room and there are eight cops at the door and the hotel manager banging on the door. Steve just thought it was the band pounding on the door. He had a couple of girls in the room and to impress what he thought was the band he had them go, 'Stop it, you're killing me, you're hurting me.' The police draw their guns, they say we're going in. I said, 'Give me a minute,' I said 'Steve, it's Elliot, you must open the door now'... he opened the door in a Humble Pie tour jacket, bare-chested. The police said, 'Okay, you're out of here; we're not going to spend our whole night coming back here.' Steve looks at them, like, okay, fuck you and he goes to pull his suspenders [braces] which he always wore but which you couldn't see under the jacket, and one of the cops screams 'Gun!' Eight cops pull their guns on Steve. 'No! No!' I'm pushing their guns away. 'Okay,' I say to Steve, 'go get your bag; you're out of here.' He had this little suitcase, tweed, looked like it was from the 1920s and he stuffs his clothes in, closes it, and it's like a movie, clothes are sticking out the sides and little Stevie, bare-chested with his jacket on, and his suitcase, eight cops behind him, 'Keep moving, keep moving.' They took us to the city limits and they said, 'Don't come back,' and I don't think we ever did. Those were the kind of things Steve would get us into all the time. It was non-stop.

**Craig Goetsch:** One time we were doing a big coliseum show with Judas Priest and we're running late. So we're walking through the kitchen and there's this big giant spoon and a flour bag. I go, 'Now wouldn't you like to have a spoon like that, Steve?' He goes, 'Hey mate, I've got an idea. I'm going to call for that.' On stage he goes, 'I hope you don't mind but I think I need a snort,' the crowd go mad, 'you don't mind if I have a snort now do you?' The place went mad. 'C'mon Craig, mate, give us a bit of snort.' I walk out with this giant spoon with flour on it, the whole place is erupting, stamping. He takes the spoon, throws half the shit all over his face. That was all funny but with the sweat and the hot lights, the flour stuck to his face and he looked about 90 years old up there.

**Elliot Saltzman:** I'd get a knock on the door backstage. 'You Elliot?' 'Yeah.' 'You owe me 300 dollars.' 'What?' 'Steve took a quarter ounce from me and said Elliot would pay for it.' What am I supposed to do? Someone would come in with a big bag of cocaine and Steve would take a look, take three, four sniffs and hand it round and all the band would do the same and then Steve would take three or four more... get through three grammes of coke and give it back to the guy and go, 'Nah, don't like it.' Most of the time because it was Steve Marriott they'd leave scratching their heads but with the bikers, it became a little more tense. 'No, you'll pay for that.' You had to be on your toes all the time.

*Marriott was winning few friends. When Judas Priest's guitarist Glenn Tipton told Marriott he was a hero to him, he threw it back in his face. 'You were never a hero of mine,' he spat. Leber-Krebs were also growing wary. Marriott had hired a former member of Humble Pie's seventies road crew as an assistant, a heavy biker. In New York Leber-Krebs used Studio Instrument Rentals to store equipment for Aerosmith, Joan Jett and Humble Pie. When Marriott's biker pal lost the key to the band's lock-up he pulled out a .357 Magnum and shot the lock off. All of Leber-Krebs acts were banned from using the facility. In July 1981, prior to a gig in Dallas, Texas, the inevitable happened and Marriott collapsed. He was rushed to hospital.*

**Pam Marriott Land:** Steve would spit up blood all the time. He had some serious health issues.

*It was reported in the press Marriott had collapsed with 'bleeding ulcers'. Gigs were cancelled in Houston and New York.*

**Steve Marriott:** I was really ill. I was in fucking intensive care. It wasn't an ulcer, it was duodenitis. The way they termed it on the paper was 'acute duodenitis with bleeding'. What that means is internal bleeding through a split in your intestine. I would've rather had an ulcer than duodenitis because you can't do nothing for it. It has to clear itself up. But the one thing you don't do is a lot of drugs and a lot of booze. I came out of it thinking a lot. I curbed everything.

**Craig Goetsch:** Then the [band's equipment] truck got stolen. One of our crew parked the truck outside his apartment in New York for the night. We were supposed to take off the next day. He got up and the truck's gone. Some of Steve's famous guitars were in there. We had nothing...

**Jerry Shirley:** By this time Leber-Krebs were pretty much supporting us financially and they could only put up with doing that for so long. So when the truck was stolen that pretty much ended it. We couldn't survive. It was done by the summer of 1981. We stayed together until Leber-Krebs pulled the plug. Bobby and I were going to put a band together but it never went anywhere. I got a job refinishing old pine furniture and painting houses, then I got a job offer from Fastway [with Motörhead's Eddie Clarke and UFO's Pete Way] in late 1982. I felt for Leber-Krebs as they put so much trust in Steve and a lot of money yet all Steve did in return was make up all these awful anti-Semitic songs and call them derogatory names of that nature.

**Steve Marriott:** I had no income at all. They [Leber-Krebs] just stopped my income right there, like they can do.

**David Krebs:** This is funny. I was told after he left us he was talking about how we had not been fair with his money. I never questioned him about it but I laughed to myself. I think we invested $150,000 or $200,000 [about $400,000 or $500,000 today] in Humble Pie [and never asked for it back]. We always invested in our artists to help them develop. When I look back on Steve, I wish I had been his manager before Dee Anthony; it would have been a different turnout in my opinion. I only met Dee once in my life and we were at some convention and we got into some discussion about who was the bigger star, Steven Tyler or Peter Frampton, and this so angered Dee Anthony that I would say it was Steven Tyler he threatened to get physical. I couldn't believe it. What does everybody say about the relationship between Steve and Dee Anthony… that this was not a good relationship when it came to finding out where the money went? Isn't that correct?

321

# CHAPTER 16

# Ain't You Glad New York Can't Talk About You

*As he recuperated in New York, broke and without a band, one of the things Marriott ruminated on was his friendship with Ronnie Lane, whose multiple sclerosis had been diagnosed shortly after he had walked out of the Small Faces reunion. Lane had since cut a solo album for Atlantic – said to be under the umbrella of the deal that had taken the Small Faces to the label – that did little to improve his financial situation. Eric Clapton had subsequently supported him in the making of one further album, 1979's* See Me, *but Lane was now living, essentially, hand to mouth.*

**Pam Marriott Lane:** Steve and Ronnie [Lane] met up again in New York. I'll never forget that night. Ronnie said come on over to the flat and Steve was so excited, he couldn't wait, he ran upstairs to the apartment and when he opened the door Ronnie was in a wheelchair. Steve just burst out crying. It was so emotional and Ronnie said, 'Look, I just didn't want you to know,' and Steve just kept saying, 'Oh mate, oh mate.' That's when they started doing some work together.

**Craig Goetsch:** Ronnie lived with us [at Marriott's Greenwich Village apartment] for a while. He had a hard time sitting up. Keith [Richards] started helping Ronnie with some supposed cure for his MS, snake venom shots down in Florida. He'd fly him down there.

*The Miami Venom Institute was a dubious business venture. The man behind it was Arden Frederick 'Freddie' Sessler, brother of London restaurateur and*

*Mayfair club owner Siegi Sessler. Freddie was a well-known party animal and drug user/supplier and a close friend of Keith Richards and Ronnie Wood. Marriott stayed with Lane in Florida and injected him with this snake venom.*

**Christine Lore:** Steve helped pay for it with the last of his money. He got back penniless. The 'cure' was bogus. Pam was broke and Steve took off, left her with no money and she didn't know when he was coming back. Keith Richards found out Steve had left her high and dry with no money, no groceries, and Keith gave her $5,000 to get by and said, 'Don't tell Steve about this but I can't stand what he's doing, I'm really angry.'

**Pam Marriott Land:** When he came back from Florida, we tried for a couple of weeks and then that's when I said I'm leaving. I wanted to go back to Atlanta.

*Marriott had plans now for a benefit gig with Lane in London. He wanted to record the show and release it as an album with all profits going to Ronnie. He put the gig together himself. It took place on 1 September 1981 at the Bridge House pub in east London. Marriott recruited Joe Brown, Jim Leverton, Dave Hynes and Zoot Money to play in the band. The set list included: 'Tin Soldier', 'All Or Nothing' and 'Whatcha Gonna Do About It'.*

**Zoot Money:** It was Steve asking people to come along, 'We're doing it for Plonk [Lane].' Plonk did play a couple of tunes with Steve but for the most part it was us being led by Steve. The crowd was very rough and ready, a seething mass of very drunk Londoners, very spirited. We weren't what you would call rehearsed and we were fuelled by various substances. Backstage afterwards Steve was singing old cockney songs, he had hundreds of them – some he made up himself.

**Eddie Piller:** Ronnie had to be carried on stage. He managed a few numbers and was then carried off. I went up and introduced myself to Marriott afterwards. I told him I was Fran Piller's son and I'd been one of the boys carrying the 'Itchycoo Park' sign for the adverts and he said, 'Fuck me, that means you're Ronnie Lane's child,' which I thought was a most amusing way to greet me. He had an irrepressible and rather violently rude sense of humour. The gig was pretty empty; I'd say there was about eighty people there. Joe Brown's daughter, Sam, did some singing.

*It was decided that the show, recorded with Ronnie's mobile studio, was not of a high enough quality to be released. Marriott approached Laurie O'Leary with an idea to fund a studio album of new songs from Lane and Marriott. He agreed. O'Leary had recently attending the 1980 Royal Command Performance at the London Palladium as tour manager to Miss Peggy Lee. Marriott assembled a band. Alongside Hynes and Leverton he hired session keyboardist Mick Weaver, whose band Wynder K. Frog had been popular in the sixties, to replace the busy Zoot Money, and one of his idols, former Johnny Kidd & The Pirates guitarist Mick Green (1944–2010), to play guitar. Marriott also wanted money for someone called Charlie. 'Who the fuck is Charlie?' asked O'Leary. The recordings took place over two weeks at Corbett Drama Theatre in Loughton, Essex. Again, Lane's mobile studio was used.*

**Jim Leverton:** Laurie O'Leary financed the album. He used to come down and check to see if we were all working. I think Steve was staying with his mother at the time. It was great to work with Mick Green: he was very rock'n'roll and his guitar playing always had a bite to it, he'd just plug in and go for it. He was everyone's hero really, someone we all looked up to when we were kids. It was a big buzz in that respect. The whole of the fortnight was really pretty much a drinking situation and I also remember daily pilgrimages to the local pie and mash shop in Loughton. Ronnie loved the stewed eels and Steve just had to have his daily intake of pie and mash. Then, of course, there would be mercy dashes into Notting Hill to get certain substances! Me and Steve carried Ronnie most places.

We recorded 'Toe Rag' [a song written by Marriott about his son Toby, now 5] in the students' bar and it was packed with students at the time. Mick Weaver went missing for a couple of days and Steve took over on keyboards. I've always liked [Marriott's] 'Lonely No More' and 'Bombers Moon' [by Lane] but the one everyone seemed to pick up on [from these recordings, first released in 2000 under the title *The Legendary Majik Mijits*] was 'That's The Way It Goes (Two Black Eyes And A Broken Nose)' credited to Ronnie Lane. It was a typical Marriott/Lane cockney carry-on with the accent accentuated. At the end of the two weeks we had a big party at a pub called the Grapes in Islington. Everyone that played on the album and their other halves were at the party. It was quite a flash restaurant and they had a grand piano there. Marriott got on the piano with Ronnie sat on a stool beside him and they knocked out a few songs. I remember carrying Ronnie out at the end of the evening.

*Both Marriott and Lane were pleased with the album and Marriott flew back to New York, accompanied by Jim Leverton, with the intention of trying to attract a record label to the project. Craig Goetsch had moved out of the apartment, was working on the road with Ian Hunter and Mick Ronson. Pam was heading back to Atlanta, Georgia. She had started working again as a flight attendant.*

**Jim Leverton:** Steve said, 'Why don't you come back to America with me?' I said, 'I can't, I've got an immigration problem.' He said, 'Come with me, it'll be all right.' We turned up at the immigration at Kennedy airport and he said, 'All right mate, me and my mate here, we've come to clean the windows,' and the immigration guys said, 'Get out of here, you're crazy,' and we were in! The front of Marriott got me in. We spent three weeks [at his apartment] in Greenwich Village writing songs – 'Poor Man's Rich Man', 'Be The One', a beautiful little song. He was absolutely broke. We were taking bottles back to get the deposits.

*There was obvious commercial potential in the concept of Marriott and Lane's reunion but it was countered by Lane's health and Marriott's poor reputation.*

**Steve Marriott:** We took the tape to everybody: Arista, CBS, Virgin, A&M, Atco… if one person passes on it it's like a chain reaction. We thought Keith Richards was going to buy it but at the last minute he said no as well. I don't think he wanted to be responsible for anything. Don Arden might have taken it on at Jet but I don't think any of us wanted to go down that route.

*Marriott and Lane now fell out again. Lane claimed that Keith Richards had loaned Marriott money to work further on the material but that Marriott had kept it for himself. They were never reconciled. In 1983, Lane would corral musicians such as Eric Clapton, Jeff Beck, Jimmy Page, Bill Wyman, Charlie Watts, Ronnie Wood, Kenney Jones, Steve Winwood, Joe Cocker and Paul Rodgers into performing a number of high-profile concerts in the UK and America for the Action for Research into Multiple Sclerosis (ARMS) charity. Marriott would not be invited to take part.*

**Kenney Jones:** It never crossed my mind to invite him. Steve's reputation was poor because of the way he was behaving. It's the way he conducted himself. He let himself down. He became rude, obnoxious. No one denied the fact he was a great vocalist – couldn't give him enough praise for that, but they didn't particularly like him. That's what happens when you take drugs. He went down this long road of no return. He had ample opportunity to turn it around and he didn't take the bait. He was just one of those guys that went down the wrong road. He ended up with a chip on his shoulder. I can never forgive Steve for leaving the band. I'm still angry and upset that he walked out on three of his greatest mates, who ended up being three of the greatest musicians around. I would have thought he would have realised that at some point too, which probably ate away at him a little bit more.

*Marriott was now desperate to restart his career. He had chanced upon a young lawyer from the Bronx, fresh out of law school, Martin Druyan, who wanted to manage bands and, crucially, had a credit card to pay expenses.*

**Martin Druyan:** I met him when no one was his friend in New York pretty much and he had no money. We went to Leber-Krebs: 'Please give him another chance.' Leber-Krebs told me they didn't want anything to do with him. He went to Dee Anthony, 'Take me back'... 'No.' No one wanted anything to do with him. He was unreliable, a pain in the arse. People who were trying to do business would not deal with him after he had one of his episodes or after he took money and did not deliver songs and then became manic and uncooperative. He had a bad reputation. Freddy Bienstock had given him publishing money, hundreds of thousands of dollars, and he never gave Freddy any songs. Everybody was mad at Steve. He had a reputation for not delivering songs and not delivering tours because he would get out of control. All of this stuff spelled no money. Success was eluding him but only because he would walk away from it. If he didn't walk away from it he'd spit in its face. He didn't care. I met Keith Richards and said, 'Hi, I'm Martin, Steve's buddy.' He said, 'Steve's a bit daft, right?' His wife Pam was supporting him. It costs money to live in New York. Keith [Richards] would give him a cheque. Steve would say, 'I don't want to be cap in hand.' Why is he begging Keith Richards for money? It's bullshit. My idea was I'd help Steve, Steve would be happy, and then I'd make money on the next band. I wasn't really looking to make money out of Steve.

*Marriott planned now to leave New York and follow Pam to Atlanta as he tentatively began putting a new band together. He knew he could count on Jim Leverton and he had his eye on a young Chicago drummer he had met during the last days of the Humble Pie reformation. 'Brilliant drummer, a negro chap,' said Marriott.*

**Fallon Williams:** I met Anthony Jones at a gig in Chicago on the South Side, and he introduced me to Steve. I was in a cabaret cover band playing at a hotel six nights a week. Everyone went back to the hotel after the gig and Steve said he wanted to come back to my house to talk. The Hells Angels were at the Humble Pie gig and when we left Steve and I got in my car and the Hells Angels escorted us back to my house. I think the neighbours were a bit surprised, there was about sixteen or seventeen motorcycles going down the street waking everybody up. We had an upright piano in the lounge so we had a good night. Then he called and said, 'I'm going to have two tickets for you to fly to Atlanta in two weeks and we'll meet you at the airport with a Rolls-Royce.' Unbeknownst to me the manager at the time owned a Rolls-Royce. Steve said we're going to do two weeks' rehearsal and then we're off touring. Pam was off and on when I got to Atlanta, lots of verbals going on.

**Steve Marriott:** I borrowed some money from Keith Richards to do it. Otherwise I don't know what I would have done. Guess run home to England with my tail between my legs, which I didn't want to do.

*Pam recalled Keith Richards giving Marriott $5,000 to help her and Toby relocate.*

**Pam Marriott Land:** Then at the last minute Steve booked himself a ticket too. I wasn't particularly happy with that. But he promised me things would be different and he would get his act together. It was an apartment in Stone Mountain we moved to, so I could be close to my sister. I was happy to be flying again. My friends were always flight attendants. I had my friend base, was back making money, back in aviation. Steve was being promiscuous to a point of no return. It was just time for it to be over but I knew him better than anyone, I would sit for hours consoling him, talking to him, I knew the reason behind his demons; that's why I didn't leave for a long time.

**Christine Lore:** Steve liked Atlanta but Pam was on her home turf, she had more confidence, he couldn't beat on her. She was safe at home and he was floundering. Pam had to look out for number one, she had Toby to look after. Steve never felt like that, he was never a nurturer. Everybody else had to do these things and he was like, 'You can do my share.'

*In April 1982, Marriott began touring the band, advertised as Humble Pie, under the aegis of an odd character named Steve Green who had introduced Goldy McJohn (1945–2017), Steppenwolf's original keyboardist, to the line-up. Steppenwolf had scored huge success in the late sixties with four gold albums and the classic hit single 'Born To Be Wild'. More recently, McJohn, in conjunction with Green, had been touring with his own version of Steppenwolf. The new Marriott band travelled on a tour bus with a four-man road crew: Bill Hibbler, who had worked on the road for the reformed Humble Pie; a bodyguard, Frank Pastrano from New Orleans; a bus driver named Paul Grant who was an ex-Hells Angel; and Mark Ballew.*

**Mark Ballew:** I saw Steve punch Frank right in the mouth and knock one of his teeth out, and he was the bodyguard! Frank spit the tooth out and said, 'You feel better now?' Frank was a bad motherfucker, a security blanket for Steve who felt like he'd pissed off enough people that somebody would always come round to start a fight. I did the same thing for him. You didn't fuck with Steve or you'd get your arse kicked. We were that way. We were nice people but we didn't put up with any bullshit. We all would have killed for Steve. I'd take a bullet for him.

*The crew quickly grew suspicious of Steve Green.*

**Mark Ballew:** We were in San Antonio doing a show and this sheriff's department came in and was holding our equipment hostage. Steve Green had booked a date for some other act, taken the deposit and the act never showed up and the promoter wanted his money. We had to pay him. All the money we made on the date went to this guy. As time went on we found out more about Steve Green.

**Bill Hibbler:** He ended up going to jail. He was double-, triple-booking the band. He'd collect a 50 per cent deposit from three different venues and then pick which one was most convenient for him. So Steve was getting a bad reputation as a con artist. Green had all these aliases. Marriott called him 'Clayface', he always had this tanning make-up on, and he wore a wig. He was on the tour but kind of in hiding. There were people out looking for him and a lot of times he would never come off the bus. I found out his real name was Steve Greenberg, and sometimes he went by the name Ken Scott, but he was the guy behind every bogus act on the road you ever heard of, the fake Steppenwolf, fake Grass Roots... I told Steve about it and we ended up pulling a runner in the middle of the night.

**Mark Ballew:** One night after a show in Pennsylvania we were in a cool hotel off in the woods, beautiful bar and restaurant. Steve Green and his girlfriend went back to Pittsburgh where we were due to play. We ran up quite a bill and Steve [Marriott] came to my room at midnight and said, 'We're getting out of here, can you drive the bus?' We got all our stuff on the bus ready to do a runner from this hotel... but we couldn't get the bus started. Everybody got out to push and I had to jump-start the bus. We drove back to Atlanta.

**Bill Hibbler:** For a while the whole band was living in this cheap motel down the road from Steve's place in Stone Mountain, just outside of Atlanta. It's a gateway to Stone Mountain Park, a beautiful place. Steve knew a guy who was managing Johnny Van Zant [the younger brother of Lynyrd Skynyrd founder Ronnie Van Zant, who took over on vocal duties with the band after his brother and other members died in a 1977 plane crash] and he was going to get him to be the manager. That didn't work out but that manager turned us on to Alex Hodges, who ran the Empire Agency in Marietta, a city fifteen miles northwest of Atlanta, who we went with. Empire was born out of Capricorn Records [the Southern rock and soul label whose best-known act was The Allman Brothers Band], and they booked all the Southern rock bands, Stevie Ray Vaughan and Charlie Daniels, Atlanta Rhythm Section, Wishbone Ash. Alex Hodges managed Gregg Allman at the time.

**Mark Ballew:** Alex was a big timer. When he picked us up we started moving forward. Steve wanted to change the name but a lot of promoters didn't want to book the show because they wanted to use [the name] Humble Pie. In time Steve came back around and came to his senses and we went out as Humble Pie. We did everything from 200-capacity clubs to 5,000-seaters to the Electronic Music Festival in Nashville to 100,000 people. We opened for Alvin Lee, Krokus – our biggest market was the Midwest and the East Coast. When we played Detroit we could sell out two nights in a row, 4,500 seats. The West Coast was pretty good too.

**Steve Marriott:** I couldn't stop the club owners putting it up [the name Humble Pie]. Then I got threatened. I was amazed people would even think I wanted the name, and annoyed as well. After all, I had thought up the name. If anybody had a right to use it, it should have been me. I wanted to call us The Official Receivers but as soon as we went out, we were billed as Humble Pie.

*In 1982 A&M released a Humble Pie compilation album,* The Best of Humble Pie, *indicating there was still some purchase to be had from using the band name in America.*

**Bill Hibbler:** There was a whole thing about this wasn't really Humble Pie. Steve would have preferred to just be Steve Marriott and sometimes it was Steve Marriott & The Pie. It was a question of [getting] gigs. They could get booked as Humble Pie. Live, the opening song was always 'Whatcha Gonna Do About It'. If Jim was there they did 'All Or Nothing'. We did 'Tin Soldier' maybe a couple of times but Small Faces were not as well known over here so it was 'Fool For A Pretty Face', 'The Fixer', which wasn't a hit but he always did that. He never did 'Hot 'N' Nasty', it was a tough note for him to hit.

*It was not ideal but at least Marriott was making money again. With a couple he had met in Stone Mountain, his neighbours, he rented a new home – a house – in downtown Atlanta, on Peachtree Circle, close to the Buckhead area, where the city's rock bars were located. Pam moved in with him.*

**Pam Marriott Land:** A really nice house. That's when Steve was going out a lot to this nightclub, Hedgen's, with Rick Richards and The Georgia Satellites and all of them.

**Fallon Williams:** We'd gig and come back to Atlanta and party at the weekend at Hedgen's with the Satellites and play on stage, sit and jam on open-mic night. Sammy Hagar might come in. One night the percussion player from Chick Corea's band came in and sat in.

**Keith Christopher:** Me and Rick Richards had a band called Keith & The Satellites. I left the band and joined The Brains but we still got together under the Satellites name and would play at Hedgen's. We were all huge Humble Pie fans. Steve started showing up and he was in the audience one night and was going to sit in with us and, as a wind-up, I introduced him as Peter Frampton. 'We've got a rock star coming up on stage. Ladies and gentlemen, Peter Frampton.' He loved that – 'Fuck off, you stupid cunt.' We got along right off the bat. He started coming down more often and sitting in. Steve was an angry man. I saw him slap the shit out of Ricky Byrd, guitar player for Joan Jett. We were in Hedgen's sitting at the table and Ricky came up just trying to be nice and Steve said, 'Oh, just fuck off, you cunt,' and slapped him. 'Fuck off, you cunt,' that was a big one with Steve. It was pre-Olympics time [in Atlanta] and there was still a noticeable rock'n'roll scene and Steve was one of the lads.

**Steve Marriott:** I think some of them like the idea that I'm living there, I get around the clubs in town, occasionally get up and play with somebody when I've had a few. It's nice to be part of a place that's growing and maturing, rather than somewhere fully developed and static. I'm working for a living – literally. Paying the bills, paying the rent, buying food, buying the old lady a new ring. There's something good about working for a living. You know exactly what you're getting and you know exactly where it's going. For me, that works. I'm very happy like that, and I wish it would carry on like that forever. I don't want to get too much money again and not know what I'm doing. And I never want to have so little that I have to take the fucking bottles back again.

*Marriott was upbeat for the press but the situation he found himself in – essentially touring a knock-off version of Humble Pie – was frustrating and, as well as displaying anger, he began to succumb to bouts of depression.*

**Pam Marriott Land:** It was just very difficult for him. Constantly he always said that he was going to die young because he said the only way he would ever be popular again was if he was dead. He always made jokes about himself being a has-been or whatever. But he truly believed he wasn't going to live a long life. I think he would probably have committed suicide at some point anyway [if he had not died in the fire], because he was just dead set that he wasn't going to live to be an old man.

**Martin Druyan:** After Steve Green, I started supporting him. The idea was to make a little bit of money touring but the key was to get him a record deal. He needed a record deal, needed to be on the radio, but he wasn't writing songs. He needed to collaborate with another writer. Sting called him up wanting to collaborate and he hung up the phone on Sting, telling him to sing like himself – 'Don't sing like me.' Pete Townshend wanted to collaborate. Keith Richards tried to help him. It was difficult for him because he had played million-dollar gigs when he was on the radio and now we were playing $1,000 gigs, or $3,000 or $4,000 or $5,000 gigs. It was all small money and it made him unhappy and because he was unhappy he wasn't writing songs. There's a lot of detail to this but that was the basic problem. There was also a part of Steve that resented everybody making money off him. He had to pay everybody [the band and crew], and after expenses he was making $500 or $1,000 or $2,000 a week, shit money. He wanted $20,000 a week. He got pissed off, he'd get angry with me because we couldn't be successful and I couldn't get him a record deal.

*While Druyan tried to get Marriott a deal, he also began to look into Marriott's business affairs.*

**Martin Druyan:** I said it didn't make sense that he had no money. 'Where's your publishing?' He didn't know, so I tracked it down – every hit has a different story to it. So I'd pick a hit and look for royalties. There was no [record] royalties. He didn't have any paper… no one knew what was going on [with that] but the publishing was traceable. I got him his royalties from music publishing, which somebody named Laurie O'Leary in the East End of London was taking. It wasn't a lot – remember the big Humble Pie song was 'I Don't Need No Doctor', he didn't write that, so there was no publishing on that. But at least now, every month he'd get a cheque, a couple of thousand dollars from his publishing. That's why we were friends. I didn't steal his money, I gave him his money. There were no PRS royalties until I got involved. I did it. He got that PRS cheque the rest of his life. I don't know about Laurie. Everyone becomes a benefactor for Steve but then are they benefiting Steve or are they benefiting themselves? Laurie may have claimed that Steve took his money, I don't know. But here's the thing, when Steve got money he would start drinking and carousing. The money didn't help. There were times when we had money and the entire band were acting like arseholes. The money made it worse.

**Jim Leverton:** I liked Martin Druyan. He was good and he toured with us sometimes. Steve was frustrated that we had gone out in America as Humble Pie. He didn't like that at all. But on another tour in Australia, the promoter wanted to call it the Small Faces. So there we were, 'Whatcha Gonna Do About It' [and 'Itchycoo Park'] and Goldy was getting more out of his head at this point. It was a bit of a mess the whole thing. Steve didn't even have enough money to get home. I got me and him an air ticket back to Atlanta from LA. He had nothing at all.

**Steve Marriott:** They expected us to play 'Itchycoo Park'… it was awful.

*That tour added to Marriott's frustrations. Even when he had performed as the Small Faces and played his old hits, many shows were still poorly attended. He went back to touring Humble Pie in America, arranging with John Wright, who was now working at Villa Recorders in Modesto, to record some new material in the hope of attracting record company interest.*

**Fallon Williams:** We played at the Fillmore in San Francisco and we went across the bridge to Santa Cruz and played a show there and Peter Frampton showed up. Pete was trying to get along with Steve but I could see from Steve's mindset he seemed jealous somehow of Peter. There was this undertone of rivalry but they sort of got along. Peter was trying to get Steve to cross over and be a bit more commercial. After we did the gig, we went down and did some recording with John Wright. We stayed in the house next to the recording studio and in the morning we went in the tour bus and there's Goldy passed out, naked, with the TV rolling. You can imagine what was on TV. We were just flabbergasted. That was the start of the end for Goldy. In his moments, Goldy was a very good player but there was a bit of racial tension going on between Goldy and myself and he had a bit of a substance problem.

**Mark Ballew:** All night long Goldy had been coming round beating on people's windows, raising hell, keeping everybody up. Goldy's former manager when he was with Steppenwolf had called me when we were doing dates in Southern California and he said, 'Keep your eye on Goldy, he has a thing for these certain type of downers.' When Goldy did them he would stay up and do all kinds of goofy shit. We get to LA and check into the Hyatt on Sunset and the front desk called, 'Do you have a gentleman with you, tall, curly hair, beard.' 'Yeah.' 'Well, he is in the foyer among the Hollywood memorabilia display, sitting in the director's chair, with the megaphone, directing people when they walk by.' I go down, he is laughing his arse off, thinks this is the funniest thing in the world. I took him up to my room and took my eye off him for a minute and he was hanging off the balcony, thirteen floors up. He was getting fucked up on stage too, falling down. Second day at Modesto, Steve told me: 'Goldy's out. Get him out of here. He's done.' Goldy busted in while Steve was telling me this. He said, 'You've got my pills, if I don't get my pills I'm on the first plane out of here.' Steve said, 'I've got your pills and you're on the first bus out of here.' I drove Goldy to the bus station and sent him on a Greyhound bus to Seattle, Washington.

**Jim Leverton:** Goldy was a very strange chap. He was taking these barbiturates, Placidyl [also popular with Elvis and Steven Tyler], and you're just totally incoherent on them. The two road crew, Hibbler and Ballew, used to spend the whole set standing him up because he couldn't

Marrying Pam at Chelsea and Kensington Register Office, March 1977. Their son, Toby, had just turned 1. 'You couldn't help but love Steve,' says Pam. 'But he had his demons.' MIRRORPIX

Reformed Small Faces with Rick Wills (second left) replacing Ronnie Lane and P. P. Arnold along for the ride, 1977. 'Things got out of hand,' says Kenney Jones. IAN DICKSON/SHUTTERSTOCK

'Steve literally had a different personality when he drank,' says Pam. 'He'd tear up everything and anybody around him.' 1977.
MICHAEL PUTLAND/GETTY IMAGES

Marriott persuaded Wings guitarist Jimmy McCulloch to join the reformed Small Faces.'They'd get completely out of their minds together,' said Rick Wills.
ANDRE CSILLAG/SHUTTERSTOCK

Marriott left London for Santa Cruz, California, joining forces with local outfit The Deluxe Band.'He made it fun – we had a ball,' says the band's leader, Dallas Hodge (third from left), 1978. MICHÈLE BENSON

On stage with Steve Marriott & The Deluxe Band, 1978. 'Everything was as loud as you can get it,'says drummer Gary 'Diz' Putnam. 'Obnoxiously loud,' said one review. MICHÈLE BENSON

Showcase Santa Cruz gig at the 400-capacity High Country for The Deluxe Band (Marriott, far right), 1978. 'The band was smoking but over the next few months it all came down,' says Dallas Hodge. MICHÈLE BENSON

On the beach, Pam and Toby with Marriott in background, others unknown, Santa Cruz, 1979. 'Steve's drinking got out of control in Santa Cruz,' says Pam. COURTESY MICK BRIGDEN

Reformed Humble Pie, (from left) Marriott, Jerry Shirley, Dave Clempson, Bobby Tench and Anthony Jones, recording in Modesto, California, 1980. 'As soon as Clem got back into Steve's company, he couldn't handle it and quit,' says Jerry Shirley. COURTESY FRED EICHEL

Outtake from a cocaine-fuelled record company promotional photo shoot, 1980. 'We gave them a great shot at it,' says band manager David Krebs. 'But way too many drugs were being used.' COURTESY PAM MARRIOTT LAND

Brief period of domesticity with childhood sweetheart Manon Piercey and their child, Mollie, at their Essex home, 1986. 'She kept him off the drink and the drugs,' says long-time pal John Skinner.

With son Toby, 1988. 'Steve was not really built for the parenting role,' says Toby. 'He was never really there.'

Posing in his trademark dungarees, 1989. 'Steve was a full-blown alcoholic,' says Jerry Shirley. MIRRORPIX

With Peter Frampton on stage at the Half Moon in Putney, 1990. 'He jumped at the chance of recording with me again in LA,' says Frampton.

The aftermath of the fatal fire at Marriott's Essex home, 1991. The coroner said Marriott had consumed a 'lethal' amount of Valium, cocaine and alcohol. MIRRORPIX

Marriott's third wife, Toni Poulton, at his funeral, 30 April 1991. They had married in July 1989. 'No one is particularly enamoured with Toni as she never shared her financial good fortune after his death with his true heirs.' says Jerry Shirley.

MICHAEL FRESCO/EVENING STANDARD/SHUTTERSTOCK

Performing with Humble Pie at the Miami baseball stadium, 1974. 'Anybody who witnessed Steve on stage, God almighty, he put his whole heart into it,' says Pam Marriott Land.

even stand up on his own he was so out of his head. Steve played all the keyboards when we recorded in Modesto.

*Marriott recorded a new song, 'Ain't You Glad New York Can't Talk About You'. It was a popular live number, Marriott singing while playing his Fender Rhodes electric piano. Saxophonist Cornelius Bumpus (1945–2004) from Santa Cruz, who played with Moby Grape, The Doobie Brothers and, later, Steely Dan, guested on the track. With McJohn gone, Marriott determined to carry on as a three-piece, quit bringing keyboards on the road, with an idea to call the band The Three Trojans (Trojan being American's No 1 brand of condom). 'The birth of [future band] Packet of Three,' said Jim Leverton. Marriott's drinking and cocaine use again started to spiral out of control. It was a familiar pattern – after staying up partying, Melvin took over. One night he demanded $1,000 from an exhausted Mark Ballew for drugs. When he finally sobered up he had forgotten taking the money and accused Ballew of stealing.*

**Bill Hibbler:** Another time with me, it was the end of the tour, in Chicago, and he's got a girl back to the room and he comes to see me and he's drunk and he said, 'Give me $500, I'm going to get some blow and don't give me any of your Jewish crap.' It's his money so I handed him 500 bucks and he said, 'Bill, you did a great job on this tour,' and he turns and, he's so out of it, all the money falls out of his hand and he leaves. I could show you pictures – this is Steve and this is Melvin. Melvin looked pretty evil. Steve almost broke my nose once over a girl, or Melvin did. Steve was very divided on what he wanted: he wanted to be a big star but he was also terrified of being a big star so a lot of times he would sabotage important meetings. He'd go back and forth between 'Yeah, I'm going to get signed, going to do this deal,' to 'Oh, I don't want nothing to do with it, it's all bullshit, I'm just here for the music.' So that was something going on within him. And, the on/off situation with Pam also took its toll.

**Jim Leverton:** He was a very overwhelming character. I avoided Melvin like the plague. When we were on the road in America you'd see him coming down the corridor and you could hear he was Melvin from what was being said. You could see a change in his face, his hair went all spiky, his eyes changed, the pupils became very large and black. I used to hide. It was a number of things: alcohol, not enough sleep and cocaine. He did like a drink and he did like a line and then he'd be up for three days on the trot. I once I stayed up with him for forty-eight hours doing drugs and I said, 'Steve, I've got to go and lie down, have some rest,' and he said, 'You boring cunt!'

*Back in Atlanta, spitting up blood again, and crippled with stomach pains, Marriott was forced to visit a doctor.*

**Fallon Williams:** The doctor said, 'If you don't stop drinking it's going to be your demise.' He had an ulcer, I reckon from drinking and bad eating and the rest, worrying, the stress took its toll as well. He was having a tough time personally. I think he really cared about Pam and Toby. Pam said it the best when she said he didn't know how to be a good father, although he wanted to be. But, for the record, he was pretty much a father to me because I didn't have one. We toured across America, which I probably never would have done growing up in the ghetto, worst part of Chicago, Altgeld Gardens [public housing project], education wasn't very good.

*Martin Druyan continued to try and get Marriott a record deal. In January 1983 he organised for him to undertake a recording session in Macon, Georgia, for Capricorn Records, the label that had links with Atlanta booking agency Empire. They were said to be interested in signing Marriott. Unfortunately, Capricorn was in as poor shape as Marriott. Having lost its distribution deal with PolyGram, the label had gone bankrupt in 1979 and was now just operating on a wing and a prayer. Marriott said he had nine new songs to record and he intended to cut a version of Brenda Lee's 1959 hit, 'Sweet Nothin's'.*

**Jim Leverton:** Steve was in a mess but Capricorn Records were keen on working with us. They had big plans. I went back to England for Christmas. [My wife] Dawn was in prison, she got involved in dealing cocaine, silly girl, and got three years in prison. I went back to visit her in prison and then we were going to make some recordings for Capricorn. I had a song called 'A Fool In Love' that Capricorn loved and were earmarking it for Steve's new single but when I tried to get back into America Customs wouldn't let me in. For a second time I got turned away at the door. Steve and Fallon had to go down on their own. Steve played the bass.

**Fallon Williams:** I did whatever I could, drums, backing vocals, bit of keyboards, and Steve did the rest.

**Bill Hibbler:** I have a 2-track mix of the Capricorn songs that hasn't been touched since. A lot of the time Steve would record the same songs. 'Heartbreaker' was one, 'Teenage Anxiety' was on that, a funny song called 'Convent Girl' that I know was new.

*On the session, Marriott also cut 'Sweet Nothin's' and 'Birthday Girl', a track he had already cut on the 1981 album he recorded with Ronnie Lane.*

**Martin Druyan:** At that time the Allman Brothers couldn't get a deal so I was going to help the Allman Brothers get signed in New York. That's why Capricorn were interested in Steve – they thought his name might help get a deal. It was the same old problem. Steve didn't have the songs. Steve had given me some songs and they were really pieces of older songs he had written so they weren't fresh songs. I got along very well with him but trying to do business with him was a problem. How do you do business with someone who really doesn't want to do business? This is the down period for Steve. We're all trying for Steve, believe me, Jim Leverton tried, we all gave it our heart and soul, we gave him our money but Steve would have had to cooperate and write songs and he couldn't do it. He needed to show up for gigs, not be drinking, not be resentful... it's the end of his star. I was a nice guy, I used to say, 'Oh, you don't want to go to the gig? Don't go,' I'd go along with him, never opposed him. I knew him pretty well. He wasn't one for commercial success as he got older. It wasn't easy anymore, it was hard, and he was hanging on. That was the heartbreaking part. Everybody wished Steve would meet his potential. At some point I said, 'Steve, we're not getting anyplace.' It was too much shit to make no money.

**Steve Marriott:** I must admit, I don't write as much as I used to. Now if something good comes along, I'll work on it, but usually I don't bother. I've got a surfeit of stuff but I have to realise only X amount of it is what I would consider really good, and the rest is really nice bullshit on a stoned evening or something. Trouble is, I write a lot on piano, and it doesn't really transpose that well to two-guitar rock'n'roll. I did a lot of stuff in the Capricorn studios in Macon, but it's mainly keyboard stuff. It's in the can, but people don't expect that stuff from me. I'll give you Krebs' line: 'Why can't you do a whole album of "Fool For A Pretty Face"?' Because it's called *progress*, arsehole! They've got no idea. They don't see it. They see a formula, they want you to stick by it. And, even if they release it, they have the power to bury it, which is even worse because you're pissing in the wind. The business has changed that much. The best days for me were with Immediate [Records], because we could do whatever we fucking wanted and laugh and get away with it.

*Pam had now left Marriott.*

**Pam Marriott Land:** It just started to become *The War of the Roses*. It was who can be meanest and he taught me well about being vicious. I told him, 'I'm going to take all your shit until the day I wake up and look at you and don't love you anymore,' and one day that happened. It wasn't that I just didn't like him anymore – it was like a contest of who could hurt who the most. I was flying. I was busy, and I no longer gave a shit who he was screwing. Basically the only time he called was if he was having sex with an underage kid and I had to go get her out of his house. He did some despicable things.

**Rick Richards:** The [Buckhead] mansion in Atlanta became a swinging bachelor pad. On Sundays in Atlanta you couldn't buy any booze, so one Sunday we'd been partying and he said, 'We're all out of booze, what are we going to do?' He said, 'Take me to the 7-Eleven and I'll buy some NyQuil,' this cough medicine that had a tiny percentage of alcohol in it, and he bought a shit load of NyQuil… that was hardcore.

**Bill Hibbler:** We were all living in this mansion, totally broke but every night there was a party, all kinds of crazy shit was going on. The neighbour moved out and Michael 'Mo' Martin [RIP] and his wife Debra moved in. Mo started managing the band. He was a former independent record promo guy, worked radio stations. He had some drug issues and had been knocked down the a ladder a bit… but he had worked for a bunch of different labels, Casablanca for a long time, he worked with Clapton and KISS, and he had gold records for the Osmond Brothers. Walking into the house there was like 150 gold and platinum albums on the wall and only two of them were Steve's and the rest were Mo's. People would ring up the house, a lot of times a drug dealer, some guy with money that wanted to impress his girlfriend, and Steve would be on the phone and he'd say, 'Oh, can you do us a favour, mate? Can you stop by the liquor store on your way over and get a couple of bottles of Jack Daniel's, maybe some ice?' and then, the next person, vodka…

*Marriott let it all hang out.*

**Bill Hibbler:** He'd say, you're a Jew, all Jews steal but you never take too much, you just skim off the top. He wouldn't move from that but there was no malice.

**Fallon Williams:** He would sing these anti-Semitic songs about the gas chambers and make up derogatory things. I was living with him in Buckhead and we had no money, and Mo was complaining about me and Steve said, 'That's all right, make the nigger pump gas.' He'd say silly things but he didn't mean it. He wasn't anti-Semitic or racist really. He could be aggressive with just about anyone if he was drinking and someone said the wrong thing but then totally sober he could get along fine with just about anyone.

**Toby Marriott:** His sense of humour was intact. While living in Atlanta he would often go down one of its major roads called Ponce De Leon Avenue. He would often see a hobo walking up and down the street badgering people for money. Steve nicknamed him Leon De Ponce.

*A replacement for Leverton, who could not get back into America, was needed.*

**Keith Christopher:** I went for an audition. It was set up on a stage in a big club in Atlanta. Mo and Bill [Hibbler] were there. After the first song Steve said, 'Ah, that's it, you got it,' and sent everybody else home. He asked how much I wanted, I told him $600 a week. 'Fuck off,' he said, but finally he agreed.

**Bill Hibbler:** Keith Christopher played a lot with Rick Richards at Hedgen's. We all hung out there. If you needed a roadie or anything, you went to Hedgen's Monday night. With Keith, the band got younger, Fallon was young – and Steve got younger, dressing a little better on stage, and the band got leaner and started to get some attention. We did a thing in the studio [in Atlanta] with Eddy Offord, who had produced Yes. The demos were being shopped. We probably did four or five [recording] sessions like that in three years trying to get record deals.

**Fallon Williams:** Mo was supposed to be the manager but Steve had gotten, in his words, burned so many times he didn't want to adhere to what the record companies wanted. Steve wanted to do what he wanted to do, play R&B, and the record companies wanted him to be a pop star, play more commercial music.

*As well Christopher on bass, Marriott added a guitarist, Tommy Johnson, who owned a music store in Chattanooga that supplied the band's amps.*

**Keith Christopher:** He was in the band because that's where Steve got his Marshalls. He was very excitable. Steve was always ragging him about putting ankle weights on him. We went to Chattanooga to record. We went up in a bus that was being finished and it was just plywood interior with lounge chairs set up in the back. It was a weird studio [Pyramid's Eye]. This guy had a glass eye in some kind of necklace and there were hands and pyramids all over the studio, weird voodoo stuff. The guy wanted Steve to sign some kind of a contract and Steve said follow my lead, Keith. We go in and the guy puts out all his blow on the table and he has the contract to sign. So Steve took the straw and snorted two big lines off the table and handed the straw to me, I did the same thing, and then Steve stood up, took the contract and wiped his arse with it, said 'Fuck off,' and left. He was pure rock'n'roll.

**Bill Hibbler:** He recorded 'Sweet Nothin's' again…

*The new line-up was rehearsed and ready to go out on tour again but Marriott now broke his ankle.*

**Keith Christopher:** He was doing something he shouldn't have been doing, as usual. He was carrying on with some neighbour's wife or girlfriend and he's hightailing it home and he jumped over a fence and his foot went in a hole. He broke his ankle but he still ran home. We thought the tour was going to be cancelled and he went, 'No, fuck no,' and he hobbled out on crutches, went out and sat on a stool. On the tour bus he gave Fallon shit all the time, wouldn't even let him sit in the back lounge. There was this rule, no chicks on the bus. Steve wrote these rules on the door of the bus… another rule was no whining. We travelled on an old bus but it was perfectly fine. Anyway, Fallon met a girl and he was telling Steve, 'No, this is different, we're going to get married,' all this stuff. Steve was going, 'All right Fallon, okay Fallon.' Next thing she's in the back of the bus with Steve and Fallon is knocking on the door, 'Steve, I know she's in there.' He's like, 'Go away Fallon, you won't like it.' 'C'mon Steve, let me in.' 'Go away Fallon, you won't like it.' We're all dying. Finally he opens the door and both Steve and the girl are naked. Oh my god, Fallon came and got in Steve's face and Steve headbutted him, gave him a black eye. Then they sat down on the bus and Fallon's crying, 'Oh, I'm sorry man, I thought she was the one.' Steve gave him a fatherly talking to and then he dumps the girl out at truck stop and tells the driver, drive on. Bill must have called someone to come pick her up. Steve was the one of the funniest guys I ever met, a comedian most of the time. A lot of drunk times he reminded me of the movie *Arthur*, he reminded me of Dudley Moore, and he was a big fan of Peter Cook and Dudley Moore. We would watch those things on the bus.

**Bill Hibbler:** Bryan Adams came to a show at the Agora, Houston [July 1983, Marriott wearing a sleeveless Union Jack T-shirt]. They had changed the name [of the band to] the Faces and the club owner said, 'Hey, Bryan Adams is in town, he's a huge fan and would like to meet Steve.' He was touring and *Cuts Like A Knife* [his 1983 breakthrough album, a Top 10 in America] was out. Steve had a cast on so he's sat on a stool and he can't move around much. Basically Bryan and his guitar player sat in the front row jumping up and down the whole show and for '30 Days In The Hole' Keith waves Bryan up on stage and I don't think Steve even knew he was there. He didn't say anything and they both, Bryan and his guitar player, played on 'I Don't Need No Doctor', the encore.

341

**Bryan Adams:** I saw Steve only once in Houston, Texas, with a mock Humble Pie line-up. He had a broken leg and hobbled on to the stage, sat down on a stool and propped his manky leg up on another stool and then proceeded to sing one of the most amazing concerts I'd ever seen. I jumped on stage at the end of the night with him. I can't remember which song I jammed with him on but it didn't matter. I'd sung with one of my heroes.

**Mel Collins:** I was playing with the Stray Cats in America, they were touring on the back of a double platinum album, it was huge, and I was on the road with them for about six months. Steve was playing in one of the halls down the road from where we were playing and I went to see him afterwards and he was in a terrible state. He'd broken his ankle. He was on stage in a wheelchair and not very well. I felt sorry for him because things weren't going very well at all, it was a ropey old band, and he was being wheeled around by a dodgy boiler. He wasn't so friendly. I turned up with a girl on my arm, it was all going on, and he said, 'I used to be like you.' It was all very sad.

**Steve Marriott:** The only people I keep in touch with are Keith Richards and people like that, because they're the only people I want to talk to. He'll be on my next album. He loves me. He's always been on my side. He got me out of the hole. So he'll be around whatever happens. Whether he plays guitar, whether he pushes knobs, who cares? I'll write on the back of the album in big black letters, 'Thank you, Keith, for bailing me out!' My manager Mo says to me, 'Ring Keith, ring Keith!' and I said, 'Fuck it' – for once in my life I'd like to ring Keith and just go, 'How are you?' Instead of 'Keith, help me do this, Keith, help me do that.'

**Keith Christopher:** Everyone knew he drank too much, he'd wake up and have cocktails in the morning, and then he would go into a blackout. That was what Melvin was, a blackout. He never got mean with me but when he got really nasty, he'd turn into a different person, totally belligerent, and you stayed clear. Basically it was too much booze and being up late, and there was a lot of blow around. We'd get paid for gigs sometimes with money and a certain amount of blow. I never saw any heroin, just blow and a couple of the Mandrax [the name Quaaludes

342

were sold under in the UK] type stuff, the downer scene. But he started having stomach problems. He had to go to the hospital one time while we were on the road. He had to calm down; I think he started mixing Scotch with milk.

*Tommy Johnson lasted one tour. Christopher hoped to get friends of his in the band: Rick Richards of The Georgia Satellites or Jerry Riggs of popular Atlanta band Riggs.*

**Keith Christopher:** Jerry was a great guitar player, great vocalist, cool down-to-earth guy, not a big party guy, which was probably part of the problem. We had a great rehearsal at Steve's house jamming in the garage, sounding great, but Jerry had a pimple on his nose and Steve didn't like the pimple on his nose.

*Riggs joined the hard rock Pat Travers Band, who like Marriott were now coasting on past glories. Marriott hired a guitar player called Phil Dix, who he nicknamed 'Duck Dix'. He moved out of the Buckhead mansion and, with his manager Mo and Mo's wife Debra, rented a ranch out in the country, close to the small city of Griffin, Atlanta.*

**Bill Hibbler:** It was the final place he lived in Atlanta. It was a weird deal. These people had a lot of acres and the husband had been busted for pot and they leased out the house. It was surrounded by land and cattle, it had a swimming pool and there was a lake behind it. Griffin was better for him. It was always alcohol but it was less and less of the drugs. He seemed happier. There weren't parties every night and he would go fish on the lake and he'd lay out in the sun, he lost some weight. He turned me on to Philip K. Dick, he was always reading. Musically it was always Motown, Ray Charles, but he started playing Chas & Dave.

**Toby Marriott:** That was a strange era when he was living in Atlanta, especially when he and my mother split up and he moved to a ranch house in Pike County, which is about forty minutes south of Atlanta. He lived there with an 18-year-old stripper… Bunny. Even at age 8, I remember thinking that she didn't seem that much older than me. One morning I woke up and they were riding this horse in the field behind the house and they had a teepee up. Because he was so short, he looked like a jockey. After Steve returned to the UK, Bunny's mother sent Steve's mother a picture of a baby that he had supposedly fathered. Then a few months later wrote to say that the baby had died. Who knows what happened there?

**Keith Christopher:** Griffin was way out in the sticks. The reason he was out there was something to do with the sheriff's daughter.

**Bill Hibbler:** Bunny was a girl who ended up coming backstage. She was hanging out with one of the guys and then she ended up hooking up with Steve. They started calling her Bunny. There were lots of girls on the road. We were sitting on the floor watching TV [at the ranch] and this Save the Children TV thing came on, Steve looks at me and says, 'Save the Midget, won't you please help?' and that became the next tour, the Save the Midget Tour. We didn't do many long tours, we did a lot of two weeks, three weeks. For a lot of us we would live a lot better out on the road than we would at home in those days.

**Keith Christopher:** Steve and I used to be called the Fewari Brothers, somebody gave us these hats and they had a Ferrari on them, we had these satin robes. I had a blast. Yes, he would sometimes take the gig money and buy drugs with it but I was always welcome to do them too and the gigs were great. We were being billed as Steve Marriott's Humble Pie. There were some arena gigs, we did a little tour with Quiet Riot, their lead singer [Kevin DuBrow] was a big, big Steve fan, so we got on that tour when they had that big hit 'Cum On Feel The Noize' [November 1983, a Slade cover version from their US No 1 album *Metal Health*; Quiet Riot had covered 'Tin Soldier' and 'Afterglow' on their first two late seventies albums].

**Bill Hibbler:** 30 November 1983 opening for Quiet Riot, it was the El Paso Civic Centre [8,000 capacity] and I watched Steve go off the mic and cup his hands and get the audience going, singing back to him on 'I Don't Need No Doctor'. Kevin DuBrow was a huge fan and they'd asked for us. We also opened for [heavy metal band] Dio [whose first album went platinum].

**Keith Christopher:** He would just go out there and give it 100 per cent every night. It was amazing. A lot of times Bill would wake us up after taking Mandrax to go to sleep or some kind of pills, and we'd get our clothes on, take a couple bites of apple or banana, then a couple bottle caps would blow, then grab a Heineken, shot of brandy – this is still walking toward the front of the bus putting on our clothes. Then more bottle caps, more drinks and then, 'Hello, motherfuckers,' and away we go. There was always something funny going on. When we played with Foghat they went over on the soundcheck intentionally so we wouldn't get a proper soundcheck and everyone was losing their mind but Steve was being really calm. He gave me his pyjamas and a silk robe and we all went out in our pyjamas and silk robes with kazoos and did 'I Don't Need No Doctor' with kazoos as a soundcheck, thank you very much, then went to get dressed, came out and tore the stage up. Okay, follow that.

**Bill Hibbler:** Harpos in Detroit [notorious 2,000-capacity metal club] was probably our biggest gig in America. They always paid us well. I used to walk out front with passes before the show and look for pretty girls. Steve hooked up with Terri [Elias] at Harpos. Her family owned the Big Boy [burger restaurant] franchise, they were a pretty successful family. With her it wasn't like a groupie thing, we played Detroit twice a year, so she'd show up and at some point she and Steve got together.

**Mark Ballew:** Terri was a Lebanese chick. She lived in Windsor, Canada. I met her in the lobby at Harpos and she was drop-dead, leave-your-wife beautiful. She and I had a thing for a while and then the next thing I know Steve and her hooked up and the next thing was she was having a baby.

**Keith Christopher:** He knocked up a girl in Chicago and there was some kind of Mafia guy involved. Steve had to sneak in through a back door [at the gig], he didn't come in on the bus, because the girl's brothers were looking for him. We were supposed to come back on for an encore but he'd snuck out, gone.

*Despite these extramarital liaisons, Marriott was still hopeful he could rekindle his relationship with Pam.*

**Bill Hibbler:** I took Steve to this breakfast place to meet with Pam and he thought they were going to get back together and she was dating some guy and Steve realised it just wasn't going to happen and it wasn't long after that he left [to go back to the UK].

*Duck Dix was out and Christopher again suggested getting Rick Richards in the band. Marriott had recently sat in with The Georgia Satellites when they played a show for* Night Flight, *a TV arts show.*

**Bill Hibbler:** Rick Richards was perfect for the band. He and Steve were made for each other. The Georgia Satellites were always breaking up and getting back together.

**Rick Richards:** Keith Christopher and I and Fallon all met at a house forty or fifty miles outside of Atlanta where he was staying [the ranch in Griffin]. We drive down early in the morning and Steve's still in bed. We say to Mo, 'Go wake him.' He says, 'Fuck, no way. You go wake him.' Nobody had the balls to go wake up Steve. We sat there until mid-afternoon and he finally comes out and we play a few songs and that was my one day in Humble Pie and he fired me after that. He told me, 'Why don't you go back to Hedgen's and sing "Keep Your Hands To Yourself" for the rest of your fucking life?'

**Keith Christopher:** That was unfortunate. We did the rehearsal and it was the best it ever sounded, sounded like a real band, so good. Steve loved it, everyone loved it, a lot of potential, and then me and Rick went out to a bar, some chicks got involved and we got coked up. It was afternoon when we woke up and we'd missed a recording session. I thought something like that Steve would have understood, 'Been there, done that, I'll reschedule, don't do that again,' but that didn't happen. He just said fuck them and he got a couple of wankers to go in the studio with him, kind of sad. Steve had a thing where if things were going too good he'd bite the hand that feeds him. It was almost like he didn't want to succeed, like he was almost glad that happened. It wasn't long after that he went back home.

**Bill Hibbler:** Steve fired everyone. Mo and Debra had been carrying a lot of the bills with their savings, which were running out. Now Debra was pregnant and it was Steve paying the bills. Suddenly Steve said his father was sick, maybe dying, and he was going home. I talked to Mo and said, 'He's not coming back.' He just wanted to get out from under that responsibility.

**Keith Christopher:** When he left I recall he was just going away to visit and then come back but they took his visa away for tax reasons and he couldn't fly back to the States anymore, that's what I heard. I also heard he ran up a bunch of debt [in Atlanta] and then all of a sudden had to go home to see his son… all of a sudden British tax evasion didn't sound so bad.

*Christopher now plays guitar with Lynyrd Skynyrd.*

**Bill Hibbler:** When Steve was living in Griffin, I was hanging out there once and we were in the back office of this grocery with these guys who owned the store. Mo and Debra had been running up bills on the tab. These guys were big old rednecks and some alcohol had been consumed and I realised they were Klan guys. Griffin was a big home of KKK [Ku Klux Klan, white supremacist hate group]. Steve had said something about Fallon being black, just joking, and they were like, 'We'll take care of him for you.' At some point Steve was saying, 'Yeah, Bill will take care of it, he's a third-degree black belt,' which I'm not, or any other belt, and it was like, what the hell are we doing here? I know he owed these guys money and some of the equipment got sold in town [Atlanta]. Mo brought it to town. When Steve left them, the rent was due.

*Beside him on the plane, flying back to London, remarkably, was Pam.*

**Pam Marriott Land:** We had separated but he persuaded me to go to England. On the plane he told me had gotten a girl pregnant and that was Tonya's mother [Terri Elias] and by the time we got to England I said this isn't going to work, I can't do anymore of this and so I flew back home. And when I got back to our house, it was empty. There was not a stitch of furniture, nothing, and I found out Steve owed the cocaine dealer $5,000 and that was why he was in such a hurry to go to England. I had no money so I was homeless for about two weeks living in my car. I tried to reach him and he told me something different but

347

the people said, 'Nah, he owed the cocaine dealer and so they came and just took everything out of your house.'

*Terri Elias gave birth to Tonya, Marriott's second known daughter, on 16 February 1984.*

# CHAPTER 17

# Five Long Years

**Fallon Williams:** He got out of Atlanta and left everybody behind. Steve thought about himself first and foremost, let's not be silly about that. The reason he left was the UK tax department had pardoned him from his UK tax evasion. That's what he told me. And there I was in Atlanta without a paddle. Steve could be really hard-faced, just up and go, or tell you to fuck off, or slap you in the face.

*Marriott arrived back in the UK with not much more than the clothes he stood up in. He did not even have a guitar. He went initially to his mum and dad's house at Stoneleigh in Sawbridgeworth. Bill was now 71 and Kath, 57. Their son had been away five years. The house was one of the few things he had managed to make sure was secure before fleeing for Santa Cruz. Back then he had told his mum the reason he was leaving the UK was because Pam was missing the warm weather of America.*

**Kath Marriott:** Bill used to worry. He'd say, 'How could you let this happen to you? You're right on the floor with nothing.' He said, 'That's what I like, Dad. I enjoy being broke.' Bill said, 'Don't be stupid.' Steve said, 'I do, I enjoy coming up when I've got it again.' He said, 'As long as I've got these hands, I'll never want for anything. I can always walk into a pub, sit down at the piano and earn a few bob.'

**Steve Marriott:** I came back because my dad was ill and he turned out to be all right and then I sort of got sidetracked into staying here by Jim Leverton and a couple of other people. 'Why don't you hang about and play a bit over here again?' I thought about it, found myself a new old lady, she was my girlfriend when I was 16 and it all felt good. So I decided to stay. There was talk of Jimmy Page wanting me to sing with his new band but I don't think I could do it...

*Jimmy Page formed a band called The Firm in 1984 with Paul Rodgers of Free and Bad Company on vocals. Marriott lodged with his sister, Kay, in her council house in Sawbridgeworth, close to their parents' home. Kay was 31, married, and working part-time in a local pub. The spare room Marriott stayed in had no windows and he referred to it as 'the cupboard'. His behaviour caused Kay concern: she had seen cocaine psychosis and alcohol abuse so often sour what was good about her volatile brother. Now she found him in the house crawling on his hands and knees so as not to be seen through the windows from the outside. He told her he had been issued with a tax summons and the bailiff had followed him back to the house. It is likely he was hiding from someone but probably not the Inland Revenue. He read, went to the cinema, and started to put his life back together, which meant getting a band back together – recruiting Jim Leverton and drummer Dave Hynes, last seen in Santa Cruz. Kay's husband, John, let Marriott use a warehouse that was part of his glass manufacturing business to rehearse in. Marriott called the band Packet of Three, a reference to condoms.*

**Jim Leverton:** I was given the story that he left Atlanta when his dad wasn't very well and he had to come back to see about it. I think there's probably more to it than that. The UK tax problem being cleared makes more sense. He always wanted to come back here. He wasn't very happy with the band in America. He used to call me from Chicago or Memphis and complain about a shitty gig he had just done. America was never good for Steve, everything was too readily available. In England things were a lot more down to earth.

*Joe Brown lent Marriott a guitar for a first gig back in Sawbridgeworth Memorial Hall. He'd invited the 'new old lady', Manon Piercey, to the gig and they were now dating. She was a friend of Kay's and his old childhood sweetheart from the flat in the block opposite.*

**Manon Piercey:** He wasn't in great shape. He'd only come over for a fortnight. He had an American tour booked when we got together and he didn't want to go back. He cancelled the tour. We stayed with his parents for a month, which was interesting. He loved his mother but I don't think he liked her very much, and then we got somewhere to live.

*Piercey and Marriott found a two-bed house in a village, Stanstead St Margarets, in East Hertfordshire, about six miles away. Marriott's son Toby, now 8, who had been living with Kath and Bill (Kay and John had also been looking after Toby), moved in with them briefly. It meant a change of school. Piercey said she felt incredibly sorry for the child, 'forever being taken from one home to another overnight'.*

**Toby Marriott:** Steve was not really built for the parenting role. When we were together it was fine and I always looked forward to seeing him but it was not really a possibility living with him long-term given that he was touring nine or ten months out of the year. Kay and John helped out with me a lot when I was a kid. Kay and Nan both always worked at pubs, they cooked at the local pub in Sawbridgeworth. That's where Kay met John and he was a diamond. They couldn't have kids, which was a tragedy, but I'd usually spend every weekend if not days in the week with them – they only lived about a mile away from Nan and Grandad, whose house was in a very nice area.

*Piercey bought Marriott a guitar, a Gibson ES-335 blonde Dot. 'The only blonde you're allowed to cuddle,' she told him.*

**Eddie Piller:** I tried to help [get Marriott gigs] but he didn't really want help, to be honest. I put him on a few times, including at Benny's in Harlow. We did double-headers with the band I managed, Fast Eddie. I put him on at the Three Pigeons in Glasgow. He would get about £80 [about £250 today] for the gigs. He would never compromise, he would play heavy metal blues versions of his Small Faces hits when, of course, the audience was a gang of Mods aged 18–20… and they want to hear uptempo R&B and Small Faces tunes. He's playing 'Whatcha Gonna Do About It' at half-speed, like a Jimi Hendrix version. It didn't go down well. I was thinking, fucking hell, Steve, why don't you do a little bit of compromising? But he didn't give a fuck. He seemed genuinely happy; he seemed to enjoy everything he did, regardless of whether there were eight people there or 800.

*Gigs continued. John Skinner was brought back into the fold and Fallon Williams replaced Hynes.*

**Fallon Williams:** When I finally got back to Chicago, I got a call from Steve saying, 'Look, my drummer's ill, I'd like you to come to the UK and let's do a couple of tours of the UK.' He put me up with Jimmy [Leverton] at Jimmy's flat in Wembley. Jimmy was a really passive sort of guy.

**John Skinner:** The fact he was away for five years meant I think he got away with the tax. I think if the Inland Revenue had really wanted him when he came back they would have got him. I never heard anything. He was totally skint. Manon rescued him and saved him. Kay absolutely adored him. Terri was a darling. You could see why he fell for her. She brought Tonya over here to show Steve when Tonya was six months old. It was a lot more than a one-night stand.

I was the driver, I was the roadie, I was road manager, I got the money, set the gear up, got them drinks, set up the dressing room… broke all the gear down, put it in the van, got the money, paid them, got in the van and drove off to the next gig… or every so often had to sit there until three in the morning while they all got pissed. Fallon would be off the stage, changed, brushed up and back out in the audience looking for some tart that night within two minutes of finishing the gig. He was a serial shagger. Steve and Jim shared a room. I shared a room with Fallon. I'd come back and Fallon would be in there humping some bird… I'd tape my wallet to my arm and leave them to it and in the morning she'd be gone.

*Marriott had begun to get regular live work through booking agent Mick Eve, a saxophonist who had been around the Soho scene since the early sixties playing with Georgie Fame & The Blue Flames and Herbie Goins & The Night-Timers before finding success in the seventies and eighties with Gonzalez. He was working from an office above Ronnie Scott's in Soho, booking out high-class jazz players such as James Moody and Dizzy Gillespie.*

**Mick Eve:** Laurie O'Leary brought Steve to me. It was an unlikely match-up but Steve was such a good performer that everyone saw the wisdom in it. Laurie was a guiding light for Steve, like a big brother.

He was the one to say, 'You can make a living doing what you do, follow this path and you'll make money.' From day one Steve was the easiest person to book out. He said, 'Just let me go out and play the guitar and sing and earn some money and life goes on...' Very simple outlook on things.

*Eve had known O'Leary since the sixties – they met when he had played Sibylla's club. As well as introducing Marriott to Eve, O'Leary took him to meet Ronnie Kray in Broadmoor high-security psychiatric hospital. Ronnie had been certified insane, suffering from paranoid schizophrenia, and been transferred to Broadmoor in 1979. It was said that he and his brothers, Reg and Charlie, continued to run Krayleigh Enterprises, a lucrative bodyguard and protection business for Hollywood stars, Frank Sinatra among them.*

**Mick Eve:** Laurie would have known the Krays better than anybody. They always took a shine to Steve for some reason and he'd rehearsed early in his career at their club Esmeralda's Barn. Laurie was lovely; straight as they came as far as I was concerned. The only strange thing was when he was upset that a photograph had been taken of him carrying Ronnie Kray's coffin at Chingford Mount [Ronnie's funeral was in 1995]. Laurie's wife was really concerned: 'Oh, what will all the neighbours think?' Laurie was such a sweet guy, had a lot of a class.

**Jim Leverton:** Was Laurie good for him? How can I put it? It wasn't really a bona fide thing in the same way as if you were being looked after by Miles Copeland or someone... it was all a bit shady.

*Eve put Marriott to work – four or five nights a week – on the London pub circuit, 250-capacity venues such as the Half Moon in Putney, the Royal Standard in Walthamstow, Nashville Rooms in West Kensington and the Torrington in Finchley. In their first year Packet of Three played around 200 gigs. 'A hard slog by anyone's standard,' said Eve. The money was £500 a gig (about £1,500 today), cash in hand.*

**Mick Eve:** He travelled all over the UK, he had a following in the far north, in Wales. He was the one act you could guarantee to the person who was pledging to pay him a deposit or fee that would always pull the business in for them – no one lost money. And Steve was enjoying doing it. It's a different world, a real world, where 200 people pay a fiver on the door, come in and have a really good time and see and appreciate what he was doing up close as opposed to him being a distant superstar. The pubs were delighted because they did good trade [on drinks] and it was always a happy sort of experience. I can't remember a miserable night ever. He was happy and he was making a good living. He wasn't a star-struck kid who thought he was going to hit the big time.

*In March 1984 Marriott was a panellist on popular prime-time BBC 1 TV show* Pop Quiz, *hosted by Mike Read. He featured on a team with Holly Johnson and Bob Geldof pitched against Paul Jones, P. P. Arnold and Tom Robinson. 'Available for bookings!' he quipped when introduced.*

**Kay Marriott:** Mike Read was one of the top DJs in England. My husband and I were in there watching and Steve had the audience in hysterics! They kept breaking down [during the shoot] and my brother kept filling in, making them laugh quite naturally. And, out of the blue, he said to the host of the show, 'You should employ a comedian. So when things go wrong they can entertain the audience.' And Read said, 'I think I have!' He was just being Steve. He had that charisma, that presence.

*Fallon Williams moved in with Marriott and Piercey, but it couldn't last as he soon fell foul of Piercey after bringing a girl back to the house.*

**Fallon Williams:** Manon was a commanding woman but really sweet. I found her to be a real lady. I moved into St Margarets with them. I was really friendly with this girl, Trisha, and Manon didn't really like her. Trisha was a bit of a wild character, I have to admit. Trisha had a friend who was also a bit of a wild character. I met Trisha [doing a gig] at the Half Moon, Putney. The house was part of a big manor. We were staying in the cottage next to the manor house that was owned by a couple of South Africans. Dutch white South Africans. They tolerated me being black, if you know what I mean. Once I started hanging out with Trisha it made Steve start to want to be young again and go out flirting. Steve didn't drink at home; so on the weekends, Friday night, we would go to a pub round the corner and have a couple of ales but everything was really kept in check when he was with Manon.

**Manon Piercey:** Fallon came home with two girls one day and he said, 'I'm just taking them upstairs,' and Steve said, 'No, you're not. Absolutely not.' He had to go. Steve seemed to calm down quickly. People would come round with cocaine and that and he would say, 'I don't need it, I'm happy.' I didn't drink, or do drugs and he liked that, the fact I was on an even keel. If he went to a gig and came back I'd still be the same state as when he left.

**John Skinner:** It was possibly the best period for Steve but it may also have been the worst. Manon is lovely, beautiful, and she did the best for Steve but she turned him into a little fat middle-aged man – he wasn't a pop star anymore – she fed him so well, kept him off the drink, she kept him off the drugs. We'd go round, 'Oh, bloody hell, Manon hoovered up my stash; you haven't got a bit of smoke?' She'd say, 'Steve, are you smoking that stuff? Don't make a habit of it.' She loved him and looked after him. He was fat, happy, content, there were plenty of gigs, money coming in. They were very happy together. He began to call himself the little fat midget on stage; he was only in his 30s. They were like a beautiful old married couple.

*Some felt Piercey attempted to exert too much control over Marriott and his life and was overbearing – she was, for instance, keen that he bring in a regular wage. A Packet of Three show was recorded at the 500-capacity Dingwalls in Camden, north London, and broadcast live on Capital Radio. The set included 'All Or Nothing', 'Fool For A Pretty Face', 'The Fixer', '30 Days In The Hole', 'I Don't Need No Doctor' plus covers of roots material, Jimmy Reed's 'Shame Shame Shame', Robert Johnson's 'Love In Vain', Buddy Guy's 'Five Long Years', Rufus Thomas's 'Walking The Dog', and Elvis's 'All Shook Up'. There were also originals: the throwaway 'The Cockney Rhyme', plus 'Big Train Stops At Memphis'.*

**Steve Marriott:** I don't think you can escape your history and I don't even want to. But I didn't want to get sunk in nostalgia either. The respect we get from punters is enough, I can't see us appealing en masse. We want a nice little niche for ourselves. We aren't exactly image bound, not old tossers like us [Marriott was 37]. But it's true, I am happy and it shows. You get the fucking long-haired Humble Pie freaks with Steve tattooed across their chest, bless their hearts. You get all these

Mods, bless their hearts. Then you get, like, punks that have come because their big brother said so – great. It's a right interesting cross section. It seems to work.

*Packet of Three also toured Europe in 1984 – dubbed the 'European Earner' – Marriott finding strong support in Germany and the Netherlands. Again, on tour, Marriott tested the patience of his band and road crew, namely John Skinner.*

**John Skinner:** He was a lovable rogue. I loved him. But he could be obnoxious. There were times I hated him but the good times far outweighed the bad times. We were in Norway and I'd try and wake him up in the morning at eight for a long six-hour drive. 'Ah, fuck off, give us half [an] hour.' He wanders out at eleven. We'd been in the van ten minutes, and he said, 'Here, shall we stop for breakfast?' Total disregard. If he wanted to be awkward he could be awkward; sometimes he'd be awkward just out of spite, if he didn't like a promoter, others times he'd be so funny you fell about laughing at him. He had a wicked, twisted sense of humour – he really took the piss out of Jewish people. We visited Dachau and Belsen and it didn't subdue his humour because he came out singing more songs. The ulcer he reckoned he had meant he had to be careful what he ate but he was a bugger really – he loved curries and he liked the Louisiana Hot Sauce on everything. And on the rider was the bottle of brandy and he consumed most of it so that didn't do his stomach any good. With Steve it seemed to be periods of excess and periods of nothing.

*The Dingwalls show was released as an album in late 1984 by the small independent Aura label run by former photographer Aaron Sixx. Aura had recently put out a live album by Alex Chilton, former lead singer with The Box Tops and Big Star. A single from the Packet of Three album, a live version of 'Whatcha Gonna Do About It', was also released by Aura.*

**Fallon Williams:** I fought over the phone with Aaron Sixx, who helped produce that album. We did the live recording and then we spent time in a studio in London and did overdubs and the album came out. I helped with the arrangements on the songs. I got nothing and I was pissed off with Steve.

*Williams recalled attending the funeral of Kay's husband, John, run over at night by a train while drunk, a tragedy that destabilised the Marriott family.*

**Toby Marriott:** John died in 1985, another tragic, suspicious, death. They said it was suicide but anyone who knew him was, like, no way... but like Steve there was not much of an investigation. John got run over by a train at six in the morning. No one knows what he was doing or why he was down there, he'd gotten into a fight with Kay and stormed out of the house and then died that morning. He did a lot of things with me that a father would. He taught me how to swim, how to ride a bike... things I didn't get from my real dad. Kay's fiancé before John had died as well. He got electrocuted on a job site. That was when my mother was pregnant with me. Kay had a real tough time. She had children later in life, two kids [one named Steve, said to be a chip off the old block].

**Chris Welch:** I was driving through Blackwall Tunnel and I passed this club, the Tunnel club, and it had this sign saying Steve Marriott's Packet of Three. I stopped, pulled over and walked in and there was Steve. I thought, my God, it didn't seem that long ago he was playing Hyde Park, the Hollywood Bowl and big stadiums across America and it had come to this, this little tiny pub gig. We arranged to meet at the Gioconda café and we did an interview and he was back in his old ways, relaxed, very friendly, laughing about things. He was laughing about a really bad review he'd had for Packet of Three [*Sounds* had panned the Aura live album] and he said, 'What do they want me to do, slash my wrists?' brushing it all off. Then we started talking about the Small Faces and he was almost in tears... he was a little guy, very vulnerable, despite all the bravura, all the shouting and swearing, he was at heart quite a sensitive guy. He needed looking after.

*On 3 May 1985, Piercey gave birth to Marriott's fourth known child, a third daughter, Mollie Mae. The three moved to a modern property in the Essex village of Aythorpe Roding, about a fifteen-minute drive from Sawbridgeworth, and Piercey recalls a brief period of domestic stability. They holidayed as a family in Clacton, revisiting the bungalow Marriott had holidayed in as a child, and at home Marriott enjoyed cooking and reading.*

357

**Mollie Marriott:** He was clean, wasn't drinking and had stopped cocaine. When you listen to Packet of Three in that period his voice is back again. He was teetotal when he was with Mum.

**Manon Piercey:** Steve adored Mollie. He was content, as long as we had enough money to pay the bills and we had lovely food, and if we saw something we liked we could buy it... we didn't want that much... we weren't materialist. We had a nice little comfy home. I liked decorating. He was an amazing cook and he loved cooking and shopping for food. There was no one on earth who could cook like Steve. His food was out of this world. He never had a cookery book, just made it up. The downside was, he'd make something incredible and then I'd say, 'Can we have that again?' and he'd say, 'Oh, I don't remember what I did,' so you'd never have it again.

**Toby Marriott:** I tried to live with him when Mollie was born and it didn't really work out. He was never really there and Mollie's mother had to look after me, which wasn't really fair on her given she'd just had a child so I went back to live with my grandparents. My resentment toward Steve came later on when I had kids and I started to think, how could someone turn their back on their kids... but I've let it go.

*Marriott toured America with Packet of Three in the early part of 1985, a long stretch of dates booked by the Empire Agency.*

**Bill Hibbler:** We had a six-week tour and the idea was keep filling in dates as we went but the band wasn't drawing that well. At a gig in Washington, DC, there was only thirty-two people there. The word gets out and suddenly we had more days off. We played New Orleans for 500 bucks. Steve was wearing his old funky overcoat on stage and it was like the old men tour. Steve would say stuff like thanks for coming out and seeing a bunch of old farts. It was like when I would see Lightnin' Hopkins or Muddy Waters on tour, that's how Steve was acting. On the bus there was a big difference: my first tour with Steve the curtains on the bus were always drawn so it was like this seedy little pub, and in 1985 it was like we actually got to ride around with the curtains open during the daytime and we could actually see America as we drove through it.

**Dale Ockerman:** The last time I saw Steve was in 1985 when he came to Santa Cruz with Packet of Three, played a small club, the Albatross. Only fifteen or twenty people came to the show. He had a joint of some really average Mexican kind of weed and he said, 'I always hated that thing in Santa Cruz, you guys had such good pot, it was like heroin, and I'd do a joint and be on the floor.' He was saying, 'I don't do that shit anymore, I don't sniff coke, don't do junk, I just have a couple of beers and do this light weed.'

**John Skinner:** On that tour, Fallon turns to Steve and says, 'Eh, what's Jerry doing now?' I looked at Steve and said, 'Your fucking job, if you're not careful.' Steve done a little chuckle and gave me a wink and I thought, oh dear, I know that wink, you're not long in this band, Fallon. Steve did exactly what he wanted to do, you couldn't tell him anything. If you wanted Steve to do something you had to use reverse psychology, you had to suggest something that you might do yourself and a couple of days later he'd come up with this brilliant idea.

*After the tour, following a few dates in the UK, Marriott sacked Williams. He called Jerry Shirley, now 33. They hadn't spoken in two years. Shirley had recently left Fastway after two albums with CBS, the first of which broke the US Top 40, and several tours, including with acts such as Rush, Iron Maiden and the Scorpions. 'What are you up to? Do you fancy playing a bit of rock'n'roll?' Marriott asked. Shirley did, debuting with Packet of Three in July 1985.*

**Dave Clarke:** 'I've spanished the Sooty.' That's what he said on stage at the Half Moon after sacking Fallon. He was wearing a boiler suit, playing a Gibson 335, he joked he was hiding behind it because, 'Well, I've got a bit fat now, I suppose it'll be a big Gretsch next.' He was always a bit conscious about how he looked.

**Jerry Shirley:** We were touring a lot in Scandinavia. The first year when I was with him was great; we were selling out places all over the place. I wanted Steve to be doing what Eric Clapton was doing in terms of putting his life back together but he really wasn't interested in the mainstream at all. He positively kicked against it. He was happy as a clam playing in pubs around England and Europe and I have to say not only was it a lot of fun but he was making a nice living too.

**Jim Leverton:** The Packet of Three was quite a good little group, especially when Jerry came in. It became quite a punchy little outfit but he never would record [a studio album], he didn't want to do it, I'm not sure why, maybe he was scared it would not be as well received as his previous stuff. He just wanted to tick over and play the blues. Drugs were a secondary thing at the time and he had more focus...

*In good health, Marriott guested on several projects. Inspired by July's Live Aid concert, he sang on a cover version of 'All Or Nothing', released as a charity single, under the banner of 'Mod Aid', with profits donated to the Band Aid Trust and Ronnie Lane's ARMS trust. Chris Farlowe, P. P. Arnold, Kenny Lynch, Eddie Piller and Mod revival band Purple Hearts were also involved. Marriott also appeared on an album by Illusion (an Atlanta heavy metal band signed to Geffen) and solo efforts by Jim Capaldi (Traffic drummer and prolific songwriter) and Herman Rarebell (Scorpions drummer).*

*Marriott was no angel, however. Some of his wildness began to resurface on the road, especially in Europe. He was arrested and jailed in Sweden for drunkenly blasting his guitar through an amplifier on a hotel rooftop at 4 a.m. He recorded a duet with famous Swedish rocker Monica Törnell, who had performed in the Eurovision Song Contest that year, on a version of Willie Dixon's 'I Just Wanna Make Love To You'. In London, Lesley Ashcroft, his daughter with Sally Foulger, now in her early 20s, went to see Packet of Three play. Her boyfriend approached Steve and told him Lesley was there. 'What do you want me to do, mind me fucking language?' he said.*

**Don Arden:** I had dinner with David Gilmour and [hugely successful music producer] Bob Ezrin [Alice Cooper, Pink Floyd and Lou Reed, to name a fraction of his work], and Dave said, 'I went down to see Stevie Marriott six months ago and his front door was all smashed in, shot to pieces.' Dave said Steve had told him, 'Oh, Don Arden came round the other week and he was pissed off with me and he blew the door off its hinges.'

**David Arden:** Bob Ezrin was working with Pink Floyd [on the 1987 album *A Momentary Lapse Of Reason*] and he said, 'Don, David Gilmour would love to meet you.' So off he goes, and when he came back he said, 'I can't fucking believe it, fucking Steve Marriott'... the Old Man was genuinely upset. 'I haven't even seen him, why would he say these terrible things about me?' I tried to get him to understand that for Steve that wasn't him being insulting and wicked about the Old Man, that was him showing off he knew big guys.

*In 1986 Packet of Three were back touring America. Mark Ballew was acting as road manager.*

**Mark Ballew:** He said, 'I'm bringing Jerry with me.' He also brought [roadie] John Skinner. When Jerry came back in, the gigs were billed as Humble Pie and we did great business. The tour was booked by Ruth Miller Agency in Los Angeles and the band made decent money, not through-the-roof money but good living money. I think there was a little tension between Jerry and Steve because of a certain bass player in the band. Steve would make jokes about Jerry with his briefcase but the tour was pretty good. I could tell there was respect between Jerry and Steve but there was also a little bit of caution. Jerry would get a little bit flustered at times because behind the scenes him and Steve might have had a word here and there.

**Jim Leverton:** Jerry said to me, 'Check shirts and waistcoats, you look like a farmer.' I said, 'I'm just comfortable in these clothes.' He wanted us to smarten up a bit. He wanted the heyday back but once that's gone you can never grab that back. There was a lot of trouble between him and Steve. When it got down to finances they had very different ways of looking at things.

**Jerry Shirley:** The briefcase was used by me specifically to piss Steve off as he was such a smart-arse; taking the piss behind your back. So I did it to wind him up. Jim was increasingly frustrated by Steve's reluctance to get back into recording an album and pull himself out of the pub circuit. That band was a great three-piece and they were both writing some strong songs. Jim consistently used Steve Winwood's return to the top, with his ironically titled album *Back In The High Life* [1986], as a perfect example. He wanted us to encourage Steve to do what Winwood had done, clean up his act and go in to make a top-class album. Nothing wrong with that, but he tended to leave it up to me to push this approach on Steve. Sadly, I went about it in the wrong way. Steve's main problem with me was I would not put up with his nonsense and the more he wanted to get away with his nonsense the more he realised that I would stand up to him, which no one else would do. Mind you, when he was clean and sober he told Pam and Manon that the one thing he always loved about me is that I always gave it to him straight. So you're damned if you do and damned if you don't I guess. Jim was always Steve's go-to guy, a yes man would be too cruel a description; he just didn't like confrontation and knew what Steve was capable of. I think it's called protecting your job. He didn't want to rock the boat but behind Steve's back he was happy to agree with me and encourage me to try and get Steve to smarten up. He did nothing to try and prevent Steve from drinking and drugging; in fact, he would be his willing drinking partner a lot of the time and moan to me and John Skinner and Mark Ballew about how Steve needs to smarten up and record a proper album. He was also very possessive of Steve's friendship – if he saw it being threatened by a third party, he wouldn't think twice about stabbing you in the back.

**John Skinner:** We called Jim Leverton 'Two Hats'. Whoever he was standing with, he would slag off the other person. If he was standing with me, he'd slag off Steve and Jerry; if he was standing with Jerry, he'd slag off me and Steve. It was just the way Jim was. I loved old Jim, he was a lovely old boy, very good friend, but he had this annoying habit of talking about you behind your back. Steve knew about it. 'Oh Jim,' he said, 'I'm surprised he's not got splinters up her arse, he sits on that fence. He tells you one thing and he tells me another. I know he's a bullshitter but the trouble is he's a fucking good bass player.' Jerry suggested things the band should do or try and maybe Steve and Jim misinterpreted that into thinking Jerry was trying to take over, but Jerry was looking out for the band as a whole; everything Jerry did was for the good of the band.

*Marriott was again now acting something close to his worst, especially when he began freebasing cocaine. There were more dates in America booked by an agency called Risky Business. Some of the more lucrative dates were earning the band around $4,000 (almost $9,000 today).*

**Mark Ballew:** Steve was getting pretty messed up and there was this chick he was hanging with, she looked like she might have been Asian, Hawaiian, he was dragging her everywhere we went and staying pretty fucked up, hard to deal with. Pam Cross, who had worked with Alex Hodges [at the Empire Agency], was booking us gigs.

**Pam Cross:** I gave him Valium to send him to sleep disguised as vitamins. He would drive me crazy. The opening acts would try and pay homage by bringing him blow. He smoked non-filtered Camels but he smoked pot more than anything. And there had to be a bottle of brandy at all times. His problem was more drinking than anything else. After the show he would get into Steve mode and do the little entertainer for a while then get bored. If he hadn't pulled a girl by then he was done and ready to go. When he'd get really drunk you never knew what was going to happen, if Melvin was going to come out or not. One time he tried to headbutt me and he missed and hit the wall. He loved to headbutt people. If you were Jewish he would start talking about Hitler. He had one of those Hitler tour T-shirts, Hitler's invasion 1944. It had all the places that he bombed. He would wear this on stage. And he would tease Bill Hibbler all the time because Bill was Jewish. He was always saying Bill was stealing his money because Bill was a Jew. There was no money to steal. He was making about $1,000 a night and playing real crappy clubs. When he had Jim Leverton he always had an ally and they would pick on everybody. Everybody was fair game.

**John Skinner:** When Melvin was on the loose, everyone kept their doors locked. I've got a friend now who suffers from bipolar disease and the similarities between him and Steve, as he was, is almost uncanny... it's almost as if Steve was bipolar. He could be as nice as pie and another day he could be as miserable as sin and a bastard, a complete bastard and then he'd be all right again. He was a notorious womaniser – if there was a woman at the gig Steve would grab her and take her to the back of the bus. He got webbed up with this Asian girl and she came on the bus with about an ounce of cocaine. About a week later they came out and we dumped her at a truck stop in the middle of nowhere... and left her there... 'What's happened, Steve?' 'Oh, the blow's run out.'

**Jerry Shirley:** It was exhausting being around Steve but what it must have been like to be Steve, God only knows. He had to put up with Steve twenty-four hours a day, seven days a week. Ian McLagan said Steve was useless at understanding the human condition – he just wasn't hard wired to understand the other man's point of view at any level. He was often accused of being overwhelming and he'd go, 'I'm not overwhelming, am I? Am I? I'm not overwhelming... what do they mean?' And in an overwhelming way he'd tell you he wasn't overwhelming. It was always the same with Steve. He was so full-on, so exhausting and infuriating to be around but so indispensable at the same time that most people wouldn't dare confront him about anything, let alone the big stuff that could lead to him saying, 'Fuck you, I'm off.' Jim was very much that way. He would moan about him for hours behind his back but when it came to getting Steve to see his point of view about recording a great record, etc., he wouldn't do it for fear of his job. So he would get me to do it and look what happened, I lost my job. Steve always played people off against one another.

**Mark Ballew:** Dates kept getting cancelled and Jim said, 'We ought to call this tour the World Spend Spend Spend tour'... we were spending more money than we were making.

**Jim Leverton:** The schedule was ridiculous. We had to criss-cross the States in long, gruesome night journeys that sometimes took more than fourteen hours. I was ready to go home after just two weeks. The bus they gave us was pure luxury but the driver was a nutcase. After five weeks we realised Risky Business were losing money, our money, Steve had had enough.

*What happened next does not reflect well on Marriott. There was a shortfall in the band's accounts and Marriott blamed the road crew. He had, in fact, spent the money on cocaine and crack.*

**Jerry Shirley:** For John Skinner and the rest of the road crew to be accused of anything dishonest was so disgraceful as they were all such devoted, stand-up guys.

**John Skinner:** Steve said to Jerry one day, 'Do you reckon you could help John out with the money?' I was so busy, it was a great help. Jerry would get the money, give it me, I would take my money, the expenses, and everything was a three-way split. It morphed into something like, 'Jerry's been nicking all this money off us,' but that wasn't true. Jerry wouldn't do that. Then Jim made some ludicrous statement about the road crew taking liberties… it's not true, none of it.

**Mark Ballew:** Jim and Steve kind of walked out on Jerry. Steve loved Jerry. And Jerry loved Steve but there was a wedge here because of Jim. I didn't know all the details but they had left and gone back to England. That hurt Jerry.

**Jim Leverton:** We just fucked off back to England in the middle of the night.

*It was the end of 1986, December in Ontario, close to Toronto. Shirley was left with the crew and the band equipment. Returning home, Marriott was questioned by Piercey, who had expected him to bring back his share of the American tour profit. It seems he implicated Shirley and she insisted he be fired – all based on lies.*

**Jerry Shirley:** My long friendship with Steve hit one of its many bumpy patches, which ended up with him having someone else tell me that he no longer wanted me in his band. I was devastated. Hurt. He told lies about the money being stolen by the crew. The implication I was involved was pure fantasy. It wasn't one of Steve's finer moments as he used me as a scapegoat to get himself off the hook in a set of circumstances… it doesn't matter anymore. I was not the first close friend that Steve dumped on for his own benefit but I chose to let it go.

*Marriott cancelled a German tour and then quickly assembled a new band, The Official Receivers, with Leverton and a new drummer, Richard Newman, Joe Brown's 19-year-old foster son. Newman's father, Tony Newman, who was only four years older than Marriott, was an infamously wayward drummer who had played with Eric Clapton, Jeff Beck, George Harrison and many more. Marriott had known Richard since he was a youngster, always encouraging him to play on his visits to Brown's Chigwell home.*

**Richard Newman:** He said, 'Me and Jim have been talking and we think it's about time you came to work with the big boys.'

**Jim Leverton:** In my time with Marriott, The Official Receivers was the best thing. He wanted Mick Green in on the guitar and I said, 'If you're going to add anyone let's add a keyboard player because it opens the door to so much more.' I was surprised when he said, 'I think you're right, mate.'

*The keyboard player was Mick Weaver, the keyboardist who had played with Marriott on the aborted Ronnie Lane collaboration recordings in 1981.*

**Richard Newman:** We went down to the rehearsal room in Putney and Mick Weaver turned up in a black outfit on his moped and we called him 'Darth Weaver' and that was our name for him for the whole time we were together. We did our first gig at the Tramshed [1,000 capacity, Cardiff] and then I spent a year on the road with him. We were out all the time. Steve wasn't afraid of working. We used to go away for months. He'd had it with America, didn't want to go back there, so we did mainly the UK, Germany, the Netherlands and Austria. We were in the Chevy van forever, me, Jim, Steve, Mick and the two Johns [Skinner and new roadie Poulton]. It was great. I loved it. We played some place in the mountains in Austria, didn't look like anyone would be there, they all turned up and went berserk. Steve had calmed down but he could still go out and get right out of it and you'd think, I don't know where the fucking hell he's been. He'd turn up absolutely pissed as arseholes but actually in the year I did it he only got up about three times where he wasn't great, which is pretty good for the amount of gigs we did. We didn't half do some dives as well. The dressing room at the [250-capacity] George Robey in Finsbury Park was just a toilet. We did the George once every month or every six weeks and he always filled it and we always blew the roof off. Most gigs we did were full. There were a couple in the Netherlands that were empty but they were just gas fillers, petrol money gigs.

**John Skinner:** When the American tour fizzled out, I stayed in America to sort the equipment, came home a week later and I was told he was rehearsing in Putney. I turned up to a rehearsal of The Official Receivers and little Johnny [Poulton] was their roadie. Johnny was there to help me. Because of his connection with [his sister and Marriott's future wife] Toni [Poulton] and Nipper [soundman for Chas & Dave], he became a bit of a gofer. When Steve first met Toni he said to me, 'You want to come out this afternoon? I'm going to see a tart; apparently she's got some good gear.' 'What? Smoke?' 'No, good blow.' I said, 'I'll come with you for a ride out,' and we left Manon and rocked up at North Weald, where Toni was living with Nipper. I walked in and said, ''Ello, Toni.' Steve's face was a picture of astonishment...

*Skinner had known the Poultons as a child.*

**John Skinner:** Toni's mum, Viola, and Dad, Johnny, ran the local greengrocer's shop on the estate in Shelley, Essex, where I lived as a kid. He was our Del Boy, he always seemed to have money, always had a flash car, usually a Jag. When she had the kids, Alfred John [who became known as Johnny], Joanna, Toni, I saw them growing up. Toni was an obnoxious child... you'd walk past her and she'd call you a long streak of piss and she was only little... ''Ello Skinny Skinner'. Then they bought a house in Ongar but Johnny divorced Viola and then she went back to live above the greengrocer's with the kids.

*The Official Receivers' set list was more soul/R&B influenced, smoother, more laidback than Packet of Three and included 'Some Kind Of Wonderful' by The Drifters, 'Can I Get A Witness' by Marvin Gaye, 'Don't You Lie To Me' (a forties song popularised by Fats Domino and Chuck Berry), 'All Or Nothing', 'Whatcha Gonna Do About It', 'Talking 'Bout You' by Ray Charles (which Leverton sang), 'My Girl' by The Temptations, 'Fool For A Pretty Face', Buddy Guy's 'Five Long Years', 'Tin Soldier', 'Run Rudolph Run' (Chuck Berry's 1958 Christmas song), 'I Know (You Don't Love Me No More)' by Barbara George and 'Slow Down' by Larry Williams.*

**Richard Newman:** We started recording a new album in London but Steve walked out halfway through. Jim tried to recover the tracks... what happened to them I don't know. That was new, original material. One was 'Say The Word' that Jim had written, there was a couple Steve had written ['If You Find What You're Looking For', 'Be The One', 'Phone Call Away']. We got offered two huge deals.

**Jim Leverton:** I was going to go to Cologne with him because EMI in Germany wanted to sign the group [for a reputed £100,000, about £250,000 today] and Steve said, 'I'll come to Cologne if I can bring my bass player with me because he's my best mate,' so we went out to Heathrow and stayed the night in a hotel for an early flight and when we got up in the morning he just said, 'I'm not going'… and we didn't go. You can't make somebody do what they don't want to. He said once you make a record and sign a deal it's out of your hands, someone else is in control of it. He didn't want to know about the business side of the music business, he was very suspicious, and he wouldn't work for cheques.

**Richard Newman:** I don't think Steve wanted to get into the big wheel again. He'd had enough of that. But at 19 you're thinking, you've just turned a record deal down, what are you doing? We got paid all right on the road though. He was very fair: everything we earned was split four ways. The Half Moon in Putney could be a grand a night so after he paid the crew [John Skinner and one other] he split the rest. We'd go home with between £300 and £350 each from gigs – in 1987 that was good money. Everything had to be in cash, but Steve wasn't the only one. I preferred it in cash as well. We had socks full of it. Steve always had cash flying about. I'm not sure if his taxes were sorted but, like us all at that time, if you can keep a bob in your pocket you're not going to give it to them, are you?

**John Skinner:** In Germany, some guy wanted to make a record, offered him a good advance. He said, 'No, fuck off, you Kraut. Don't want to know, go on, fuck off.' The poor man was insulted. Steve didn't seem to have any ambition to be famous again. He'd say, 'Nah mate, I just like playing in pubs, getting a bit of cash in my pocket, I love it… that's all I want to do.' That was Steve's attitude, every time someone came up and said, 'Steve, we got a chance of making money but you've got to commit yourself to doing this': 'Fuck off, don't want to know. I play in pubs, mate, that's what I do.' Jim's sitting there and it would have meant a good earner for Jim… the alcoholism in his [Marriott's] later years led to his downfall. He'd become an alcoholic and that was sad to see but what did we do? Every night we'd do a show, have four of five pints and a few brandies and then he'd go home... we'd always be in a pub somewhere drinking. He was a social animal, he loved to talk. He'd think nothing of walking up to the biggest bloke in the pub and go, 'All right, you cunt, what do you fucking want, then? Can I get you a drink, mate?'... almost like small man syndrome.

*Everyone around Marriott was becoming concerned with the amount of alcohol he was drinking. He would binge, be seen banging on pub doors at 11 a.m. opening time.*

**Manon Piercey:** Steve was straight for a long time with me and it was pure bliss. But towards the end of our relationship the drink and cocaine came back with a vengeance. Because I didn't drink, he felt guilty about drinking himself and then he would go on binges. I didn't want Mollie growing up with that. He was very Jekyll and Hyde.

**Jim Leverton:** Could well be an alcoholic. He was looking for a drink at lunchtime, which is a sure sign.

**Richard Newman:** Yeah, he was drinking heavy. It upset me. I couldn't understand it. He had another side to him called Melvin and when Melvin came out you knew not to go near him for a bit. Jim was laidback about it. He knew there was nothing you could do about it. I just wanted Steve to survive. The heavy drugs had gone. The dealers came around every now and again but it wasn't a full-time thing for him. He'd be sober for a lot of the time and then he'd go on another bender, that's the nature of the disorder. You can't do anything about it. I wanted to go on working and he'd get ill. Unequivocally, did I think he was an alcoholic? I think he probably was, yeah. He was famous from the minute he stepped out of school. That's a lot for any man to take.

**Jerry Shirley:** Wondering if Steve was an alcoholic was like saying I wonder if Muhammad Ali was black. Steve was a full-blown alcoholic who never got the chance to get help, like so many of his contemporaries have. Add to that his awful habit of pissing people off for no particular reason when he was drunk or high and you have a long litany of disastrous setbacks in his career. The only quote I ever heard from Toni [Poulton] that made sense was in a local Essex paper, many years after he died and she had been in jail. It said, 'he was a genius in music but he was crap at life,' and that struck me as being so spot on. Manon was the last shining light in his life but he didn't realise it until it was too late. She had class. Had he stayed with her he would still be here. She and I almost had him admit he needed help with his drinking. She believed in him so much. No matter how bad he became, as a result of his drinking, he was not a bad man, he was just a bad drunk. So was I, which is why I stopped. I just wish he had done so too; he may well still be with us had he done so.

*The final years of Marriott's life would be spent with another heavy drinker, Toni Poulton. She was 26, fourteen years younger than Marriott, the girlfriend of Chas & Dave roadie Nipper and on the surface a potty-mouthed party girl from Essex. She had met Marriott via her brother John Poulton, who had acted as roadie for The Official Receivers. She said Marriott christened her 'the little hippy' because she was always stoned.*

**Jim Leverton:** She was into cocaine when Steve met her. That was the attraction really. It was always a pitfall for him; you can't perform or be creative on cocaine. We supported Chuck Berry later on and all took cocaine, and we played the set way too fast. It was all over in twenty-five minutes.

**Richard Newman:** His new girlfriend, Toni, didn't help. He'd been with Manon at the start of The Official Receivers. All I knew was he got on the bus and he's got a new girlfriend. Toni wasn't good for him. She liked to party, she could drink and do just as much as he could. I didn't mind her but she couldn't half get on my nerves with her obsessive talking, and he used to tell her to get back in her hutch. If we were in a dressing room he'd go, 'Hutch, get in the hutch,' and she would!

*Poulton had a young daughter, Leanne, and a troubled, traumatic, background. In 1983 she was behind the wheel of a Renault 5 in Epping, near her Essex family home in the small village of North Weald, when the car veered off the road and scaffolding construction decapitated her elder sister, Joanna, in the passenger seat. Both sisters had been drinking. Toni had volunteered to drive to protect Joanna, who already had a caution for drink driving. Joanna worked as a PA for an entertainment agency owned by Brian Shaw, who handled concert tours for acts such as Freddie Starr, Jim Davidson, Les Dawson, Cannon & Ball and Bruce Forsyth. Poulton was convicted of drink driving and banned for eighteen months and fined £250. Remarkably, with Toni's cooperation, Joanna's horrific death had been used as the subject matter for an anti-drink-drive play by Mark Wheeller called* Too Much Punch For Judy. *Toni was Judy and when she met Marriott the play was becoming increasingly popular, often acted out at schools and various educational establishments as a powerful, sometimes controversial, campaigning piece. Wheeller had interviewed Poulton and her mother, Viola, at length for the play. He said Viola had suggested he speak to Joanna through a medium, one of Brian Shaw's clients – Doris Stokes.*

**Mark Wheeller:** Toni spoke openly and honestly. The play is so powerful because she was so honest. She was really amazing. The accident was horrific. She said, 'This is my only opportunity to have something good come out of something dreadful.' I said I'd like to give her some money from it. She never asked but she took the little bits of money that came. It was only tens or hundreds of pounds. She seemed quite affluent anyway. This was 1987 and at her house she had a CD player and I'd never seen one before. When the play was first performed, she did the interviews. She was on breakfast TV [ITV's *TV-am*] and on *Thames News*. She was a tough cookie, no doubt about that. She lived a rock'n'roll life. She started to go out with Steve after the play was written but while I was still in contact with her and he was interested in the play, which was strange because it was this propaganda play about do not drink and drive. Toni's brother, Johnny, was a bit of a naughty boy, that's how the policeman [featured in the play] knew the family.

**Manon Piercey:** Toni's mum was very beautiful and very kind. We were round there once and Toni was going out and Toni said something about getting drunk and she was driving. Her mum said, 'Please be careful,' and she said, 'Well, I'm not going out sober – you can't go out sober and enjoy yourself.' I felt so sorry for her mum. Toni was a very troubled girl and she was a terrible mother. Leanne [Toni's daughter] was such a beautiful girl. I was upset, hurt [when Steve left me], but I was more worried about Mollie. I knew he loved her but I couldn't understand why he never saw her but then I didn't want him to if he was with Toni. I didn't want her looking after Mollie.

371

*Manon and Mollie moved out of Marriott's home in Aythorpe Roding and Poulton moved in.*

**Toby Marriott:** When he was with Manon, I recall them getting in a row over at my grandmother's house and she left with Mollie and a week later I went over to my dad's house and there was another woman there. Toni. I'd go over there maybe one weekend a month. I didn't live with them. Toni's daughter was there at the start, for three months, and then I guess she moved back in with her dad.

**Pam Marriott Land:** I was not a good mother back then, always sending him to his grandparents and Kay, God bless them. And when he was staying with Steve and Toni, it was because I let him go back to England for the summer and, once there, Steve called me and said I'd never see my son again if I asked for child support or involved lawyers in a divorce. So I totally backed off. I didn't need nor want a thing from him.

**Mick Eve:** When he introduced me to Toni he said, 'This is the love of my life.' I thought, oh, I hope it lasts. She didn't have the class that Manon did. Manon was a very nice lady but then again Steve was a real 'cor blimey' type of geezer, so maybe Toni suited him.

**Manon Piercey:** With her Steve could do everything with ease. It was a shame he got into the drugs and drink because when he was himself he was a great, great guy, wonderful personality. It was when Toni came into the picture he changed. She said to me once she didn't like the way he sang. She showed that side to him when everyone else thought he was so amazing. He would have wanted to win her over. She got him that way. She was out to get him; I loved him so much I thought, if she's going to make you happier, go. She used to come to gigs with her brother who was his roadie. She got in his ear. She would say to him, 'Have another drink,' and she'd try and get me to drink and if he said, 'No, I won't have one,' she'd say things to him like, 'You're like an old man.' To someone like him that was the worst thing, he didn't want to be old or get old. And he always knew he would die young, he always told me that. He said, 'I will die young, I know that.' And I knew it.

**Mollie Marriott:** My mum said the she tried to ask Kath for help [as Marriott careened off the rails] but the response wasn't very positive. Kath decided she didn't want anything to do with me anymore. My mum stopped me going over so much [to see Steve]. She didn't mind me being around my dad, she just didn't want me around Toni. My brother [Toby] was also living with them on and off and he said, 'I'm so glad you weren't there.'

**Manon Piercey:** Kath treated Mollie appallingly, disgraceful. His mother was the worst grandmother I've ever met. How she could turn on a 2-year-old is beyond me... no matter what she thought of me, you'd think she'd say, 'Right, it's my granddaughter, I will look after her.' She used to look after Toby and if he did something wrong she'd turn on him instead of being the loving grandma... he never knew where he was. When I split from Steve, Laurie [O'Leary] always said he would protect me. He rang me when Mollie was about 5 or 6, and said, 'I'll always help you if you need it.'

**John Skinner:** Toni was another Steve. They were so alike that they shouldn't have been together. Whatever he'd do, she would do more, so he'd do more, so she'd do more and it just spiralled out of control. They had very good periods together but they also had very bad periods. It wasn't long after she came on the scene that I decided I wanted out of it. I began to hear little snippets that I didn't like: whispers between Steve and Toni – it wasn't him because he wasn't like that. She'd say, 'Here, if you paid them blokes £50 a night, if we do the Half Moon, Putney, we could come out of there with 900 between us.' 'Oh, I suppose we could, doll, but it's a four-way split.' 'Yeah mate, but if it wasn't, that'd be 900 in your bin.' Then it'd be, 'Shame you had to come up here in this van, if you had a little amplifier that'd fit in the car I could carry it.' I thought I'll have a break. In June 1987, I said, 'Come Christmas, I want a few months off, I'm telling you now so you can organise something.' It was 22 December, Royal Standard, Walthamstow, packed the gear, and I said, 'Steve, you haven't forgotten that this was my last gig for a couple of months?' 'Oh no, mate, no.' Steve stands up. 'Excuse me, I just want to tell you something, I'm splitting this band up, I'm going to do something else.' And I came home thinking, well, I wonder how long this has been going on, Toni saying if you hook up with this other band, all you got to do is take your guitar and amp and we can get all the money.

**Jim Leverton:** It was getting unpleasant to be a part of. My nerves were on edge. When it finally blew apart I thought, thank God for that. I needed a break. Steve, I loved him, and one on one he was great but you put another person in the equation he was a nightmare, it was almost like you open the fridge door and go into your act.

**Richard Newman:** The DTs were dying to work with him, they couldn't wait, and it was the cheapest band he could get. And they were shit. Absolute shit. He was at the worst of his alcoholism and everything at that point. The DTs was Steve going backwards.

# CHAPTER 18

# Gypsy Woman

*The DTs – delirium tremens – severe mental and nervous effects caused by withdrawal from alcohol. The DTs – the band – were a popular Midlands pub R&B outfit appearing regularly at the 250-capacity JB's in Dudley. It was here where they had first run into Marriott at a Packet of Three gig. The band's singer and harmonica player Simon 'Honeyboy' Hickling became a regular at Marriott's Midlands shows and had helped get the band gigs in the area. The DTs had supported The Official Receivers in Northampton at the Old Five Bells, and at the gig Marriott had surprised the band by joining them on stage. Afterwards they had asked if he would be a special guest at another of their shows in Leicester.*

**Simon Hickling:** We arranged a date with Steve and he didn't turn up. He got in touch and apologised, he'd split up from Manon. He rescheduled and arrived with Toni. I asked him what numbers he'd like to do and he went, 'No mate, fuck that, no, no, I'm coming up as a member of the band. I'm not just coming up for a couple of numbers.' He came up for the start of the show and he was there at the end. We had a drink back at the Holiday Inn and he went on his way. I thought that would be it but I got a call and he said, 'Would you like to be my band for three weeks for dates around London? It'll get you into London and people will get to see you, could do you some good and it'll help me out.' We rehearsed for a couple of days at our local pub in Lutterworth [in Leicestershire]. I booked Steve and Toni in at a local hotel. He asked how much do we go out for and we agreed a fee and that's what he paid us and we started gigging. He was going home with £400 or £500 [over £1,000 in today's money] in his pocket every gig.

375

**Craig Rhind:** We would just turn up at a gig in our own van and he wouldn't have to worry about organising people. He just had to turn up: him and Toni in the car. We even started carrying Steve's amp around in the back of the van – seemed easier than him humping it in and out of his car all the time. He wanted to get away from doing the Small Faces and Humble Pie songs all the time. 'All Or Nothing' was the only one we did. People would call out for stuff and he'd say, 'No I don't do that stuff anymore. This is The DTs, a blues band, and I love it.' He just wanted to knock out some blues.

**Simon Hickling:** He and Toni used to smoke a lot of dope. If we had more high-profile gigs then perhaps people would turn up [with cocaine] and they'd have a bit of that, but it was very detrimental to his vocal performance. We did the three weeks, places like the Half Moon, and he said he'd really enjoyed it and how did we feel about carrying on? The drummer didn't want to do it but the rest of us did. Steve went away to Portugal to visit his sister [who had remarried a Portuguese man and emigrated there] and I had to find a new drummer. I got [Alan] 'Sticky' Wicket who I knew really well but I wondered what Steve would make of him. He's a character. We did a gig at the Corn Exchange in Cambridge [1988] and Sticky turned up in a Safari suit and a cravat and a trilby...

**Alan Wicket:**... and his first words to me were, 'Blimey mate, where's the spaniels?' I said 'Hello, Steve,' and he said, 'Fucking hell, you're in the dome club? Yeah, you're in.' In other words he had a receding hairline and I had a slightly more receding one. We had a beer and set up and he said, 'Let's just play a shuffle'... and he said, 'Fucking great, mate, lovely shuffle.' It turned out to be a great night and Simon said, 'Oh, Steve loves your drumming, wants you in the band.' We never rehearsed anything, we played a lot of blues standards, just twelve-bar blues and shuffles.

**Simon Hickling:** Steve chose the tunes and there was a lot of chuggers in there [including 'Five Long Years' and 'Crosscut Saw' by Albert King].

**Alan Wicket:** After a show he liked to have chats, talk, tell jokes, he was a great conversationalist. He'd do impressions, he could do a great Richard Burton, he'd hardly stop. He loved that personal contact with people, he'd chat for ages with fans. He was comfortable with that – sometimes he said they were a fucking nuisance, people he didn't feel were genuine, he always had a thing about people being genuine. He liked Mick Eve, felt he was genuine, could trust him.

*Poulton and Marriott moved to a sixteenth-century listed cottage house, Sextons, in the village of Arkesden in Essex. It was an expensive house to rent. Arkesden was upmarket, conservative, pretty, with a population of less than 400. To the residents, Marriott was 'the pop star'. The village had enjoyed a degree of notoriety itself as a location for long-running British prime-time BBC 1 comedy-mystery-drama series Lovejoy. Sextons, one of the oldest houses in the village, was used in a pan shot and the local pub was often used for filming. It is unclear what arrangements were made for the couple's children. The DTs said Marriott never talked about his kids. Poulton's daughter did not live there permanently but was often seen playing in the village, especially during school holidays. Toby sometimes visited at weekends, spending the majority of his time with Kath and Bill (who Steve had nicknamed 'the lizard').*

**Toby Marriott:** Dad's relationship with his dad was domineering. He'd shout at him a lot, especially when he had been drinking. I only ever heard him shout at his mum once. He knew with her he'd met his match. He owed them a lot really. I mean, they raised me. A few times when we went out to eat, Steve had too much to drink and would yell stuff. Bill would try to calm him down. Bill didn't like swearing or obnoxiousness. Steve wound Bill up and sometimes Bill trying to reason with Steve made him even worse. But Steve would take care of his parents, give them money for double glazing, give them money for me when I was staying there. They were living off their pensions so needed help.

**Mollie Marriott:** Toby spent the most time with Dad. Tonya didn't really know Dad that well and I was very young when he died. Dad wasn't a great dad. I don't think he really knew how to be. His dad wasn't very present in his life; although he was there, he didn't say much. Bill was quiet, just sat in a chair and said nothing, with his glass eye.

**Simon Hickling:** The house was beautiful, idyllic, with a little stream in front and you went across a little bridge and into the pub. I went to stay with Steve quite a lot. He was having his meals without potatoes trying to lose weight. He and Toni would have Perrier water and a bottle of white wine and that's all they drank. Toni had said, 'I don't want to go to gigs if you're going to be pissed up and making a fool of yourself.' He'd invite me and my wife down and ask if we wanted to borrow the bikes. He'd bought these two matching bikes with saddlebags and he and Toni would go off cycling around the villages together. He'd have two or three gigs a week with The DTs and then he'd have the life of Riley. Toni was a really good cook and he told me all areas of their relationship were very good, which he was happy about. She really looked after him. At gigs, he'd walk in carrying his guitar and she'd struggle in carrying three bags and she'd say, 'You all right with that guitar, Steve? Just leave me fucking struggling with all this.' They were a real comedy team. We'd go on these away weekends and he used to like planning where we'd stay, like a little adventure. They were happy, there's no getting away from it.

*Marriott and Poulton were also frequently drunk and there were rows. Poulton recalled having a huge fight with Marriott the week after moving into Sextons, climaxing with him throwing all her possessions in the front garden. When they rowed and Marriott's temper flared, she would flee to the pub opposite to escape. One time, after another drunk row, she returned to find the doors locked. Screaming for him to let her in, Marriott appeared in the window, in his dressing gown, smoking a spliff, holding a piece of paper with the words 'fuck off' written on it. They became well known at the pub, the Axe and Compass, especially for their colourful language.*

**Jeff Edmans:** She probably swore louder than he did. She had a terrible foul mouth on her. When they would talk to each other in the pub it would sound like they were having a row but it was just their usual way of communicating. The landlord, Gerry Roberts, who Steve called 'Gel-Boy', used to have a go at Steve for his swearing and he used to say, 'Sorry Gel, I won't swear no more.' And then he'd go, 'What the fucking hell are we drinking then?' It was a nice pub with a restaurant the other side. Gerry would say, 'If you keep swearing I'll have to ban you.' 'Ah, you can't afford to ban me.' It was banter all the time. Drink killed Gerry, he died within a year of Steve. I was 'the nuisance', that's what Steve called me, I was in my 20s, lived in the village all my life. We'd have a few beers, go back to his place, and have a few more beers. You can imagine, he's living opposite the pub, come back to mine. We rarely spoke about music, I wound him up once about Rod Stewart and he threw a bottle of Pils at me. We used to bite the tops off the bottles with our teeth in the pub, we hid them under the table. Toni would moan that he was going to hurt his mouth and wouldn't be able to sing... she was always moaning.

*The DTs drummer Alan Wicket was another frequent visitor at Sextons.*

**Alan Wicket:** First time I stayed over I was looking at his books and he had these volumes of Noël Coward's *Diaries* and Steve said, 'Oh, he's my fucking favourite,' started telling me things he knew and liked about Coward, the plays and stories. That was the first time I thought, well, there's obviously a lot more to Steve. Toni liked me. I was one of the family, so to speak. I wasn't any threat and we just got on well. He liked his home life. He loved Sunday dinner and to watch a film in the afternoon. He loved old movies. *Blazing Saddles* and *The Producers* [both directed by Mel Brooks] were up his street, sense of humour wise. Toni said he was starting to get what he deserved from royalties [a healthy PRS cheque]. He seemed content.

*Visitors noted he had an impressive record collection and often listened to Randy Newman, Dr Hook, Willie Nelson, Little Walter, B. B. King, Howlin' Wolf, Taj Mahal. There was still mischief in his heart.*

**Jeff Edmans:** There was a Jewish lad who worked as a stockbroker in London called Ben who lived in the village and his partner had these mock life-size sheep in the garden. Steve used to say we need to do those sheep. One night we'd had a few in the pub and gone back to his place and carried on drinking and the lamb had overcooked, it was cremated, but we still sat down to dinner and over a few bottles of Pils he said, 'C'mon, let's do the Jew boy's sheep.' He knocked off a great big jar of mint sauce and we got in my Jeep, we shouldn't have done but we were only going a mile up the road, and I turned round to shine my lights on the sheep, this is two in the morning, and Steve put mint sauce all over these sheep... that was the only time I was with Steve without Toni. She was always there, she never left his side, even when we got drunk late at night back at his, she'd go to bed but she'd always be about. It was very rare he was ever on his own.

*Marriott took The DTs on a tour of Germany. They travelled over by boat, Marriott hiring himself and Toni a suite while the band were in cabins. It was their first insight for the band into what Marriott could be like on tour.*

**Simon Hickling:** The one thing we found difficult to get used to was the volume he played at: that was horrendous. We spent all our time trying to persuade him to turn down. In Germany, in Hannover, we did the first number and the crowd was going berserk, and then as the clapping subsides the soundman goes, 'Steve, you are too loud, you must turn down.' He goes, over the microphone, 'That's it, everybody's enjoying themselves, there's always one cunt.' We do another song. The voice again: 'Steve, you are still too loud, you must turn down.' He goes, 'Who won the fucking war, mate?'

**John Skinner:** Steve played at his volume. He played his amplifier at a set volume, and we were not allowed to alter it, usually loud, wherever he was – at Shea Stadium or someone's front room. It got to be known as Steve's volume. The last time I saw him was in the Axe. Me and the missus went to visit and they were in the pub and he was paralytic and Toni was sat next to him talking to him as if he was a baby – 'Come on, mate, you'll be all right, c'mon you're okay.' He said, 'Toni, I feel sick.' And she cupped her hands and said, 'Go on then, mate, sick into my hands,' and he spewed up in her hands and she emptied it into the ashtray. 'Feel better now, dear? Feel better now, babe?' 'I'm going home.' 'Oh, all right then.' He went home and went to bed and that was the last time I saw him. They were good together but, unfortunately, they were bad together.

**Toby Marriott:** Toni was a lot younger than Steve, very fiery, which I think he liked at first. She was a lot of fun, always wanted to do stuff, definitely stood up to him more than anyone I'd ever seen, apart from his mother. But after a few years it seemed like it wasn't doing either of them any good. I was in and out of their environment from the summer of 1987. They seemed to get along but they had a lot of fights – some were physical, it almost seemed like she enjoyed it sometimes.

**Alan Wicket:** Toni was bit of a party animal herself. In Hamburg Toni kept asking Steve to take her around the red-light district. He was really worried about her.

**Craig Rhind:** Toni was not a stable character. Toward the tail end of the German tour he announced he was going home, we had three or four more gigs to do, he just announced he was going home. He said Toni's mum had died.

*A tour of Scotland was abandoned at short notice and then a tour of Japan was cancelled.*

**Mick Eve:** In 1971 Steve got his one and only conviction for drugs: smoking a joint on a park bench, for which he got a £20 fine. In 1989 I set up a nice little tour for him in Japan knowing he'd already been in and out of Japan with Humble Pie. All of a sudden, the day before he was due to go he was refused entry due to his conviction. The promoter in Japan was devastated, as he'd got a beer company to promote the gigs.

*There was evidence of Marriott's drinking taking increasing control of his life.*

**Simon Hickling:** He turned up pissed once, we had to do the first set without him. There was a phone call and he said his fan belt had broken, and it just so happened the car he and Toni had didn't have a fan belt. Toward the end of his time he was with The DTs, he said, 'I'm going to be straight with you, Si. I've had an approach from Bad Company' – Simon Kirke, Boz Burrell and Mick Ralphs – 'they want me to join and they've offered me a huge amount of money... I've got to look at it.' He told me they came to watch us to see if Steve had still got it and they arranged for him to go to Simon Kirke's house.

**Simon Kirke:** Steve Marriott was one of the most amazing vocalists I ever heard. And it seemed only natural that when Paul Rodgers opted out of Bad Company for an indefinite period of time our management would consider him as a replacement. I went to see him and his band at a pub in London and was blown away with his singing and guitar playing, he was pitch perfect and so soulful. We arranged for him to come to my house in Chiswick, where I had a studio, so he could jam. On the appointed day he arrived but he was really late, like a couple of hours. I'm a stickler for punctuality so this really got me off to a bad start with him. He was very much worse the wear for drink and God knows what other substances. He wanted to go down the pub straight away but I had another appointment after this one and we were already late, so I sent out to the off-licence for a dozen cans of lager. Pretty much from the beginning I could see this wasn't going to work. He was so scatterbrained and jumpy, either coke or speed was coursing through his veins. And he kept draining one lager after another. After the years of dealing with dear Paul Kossoff and his addiction I certainly didn't want to go down that road again, and after an hour or so we bade Steve and his girlfriend [Toni] goodbye.

**Simon Hickling:** Steve came in after and said, 'Nah, fuck that... Si, if I want to sing somebody's old hits, I'll sing my own.'

*Jerry Shirley got in touch with Marriott about putting together a new version of Humble Pie in 1988 – but without Marriott. He wanted consent to use the name. Marriott told Shirley, 'I would rather see you doing that than driving a van for a living.' Shirley was working as a courier driver at the time to feed the family.*

**Jerry Shirley:** He also said, 'Just make sure you always put a great band together,' and I always did.

*The 1988 version of Humble Pie had former Ted Nugent guitarist Charlie Huhn on vocals, and Anthony Jones on bass. They recorded a 1989 single, 'Still Rockin'', and played at the twentieth-anniversary celebration of the Woodstock Festival. Anthony Jones's life would spiral out of control over the next decade: he became addicted to crack, was jailed, and died in 1999, aged 46. There was talk in this period of American rockers Bon Jovi and Guns N' Roses being interested in collaborations with Marriott, who continued to keep the surprises coming for The DTs. Although unclear how he got the job – it had not come through Mick Eve – Marriott had supplied vocals for a sixty-second TV advert for sportswear manufacturers Puma. Over pounding jungle drums, Marriott essentially repeated the line 'It's the law, the law of the jungle'.*

**Craig Rhind:** One Saturday afternoon Toni rang up. She said, 'Steve's done an advert for Puma today and we got paid loads of money... cash. Why don't you and Barb come over to the hotel suite?'

**Simon Hickling:** He'd been paid something like £5,000 in cash and we had a gig that night in Birmingham and he booked the top penthouse suite at the Rotunda Hotel in the centre of the city. He said, 'We used to book all this when we were with the Small Faces.' He'd got about three bedrooms up there. He phoned Craig and his wife, and I went and he ordered the Dom Pérignon.

*There was another TV advert – this time for Nescafé Blend 37 and a reputed £15,000 payday (around £40,000 in today's money). Marriott sang on a new version of 'Black Coffee'. Dave Clempson was also hired to play guitar. The TV ad would win a Best of the Year advertising award in 1989.*

**Dave Clempson:** It was the first time I'd seen him in a couple of years and he was in really good shape. We did it in one take, with Steve singing his heart out as he always did. I loved it. And that was the last time I saw him.

*Marriott also cut an unlikely solo album in 1989, his first since 1976. It was produced by Stephen Parsons, former lead singer with seventies Island Records act Sharks. Parsons had gone on to work with Ginger Baker, recorded solo material with producer Steve Lillywhite and was involved in the early career of Adam & The Ants. He was now composing music for films.*

**Stephen Parsons:** I was working for America company Filmtrax, doing horror films, and there was one called *Food Of The Gods II*, terrible picture. The music supervisor rang me up and said we've got [rights to] the song 'Shakin' All Over' and they wanted to use that over the end titles. I thought of Steve Marriott, I got his number and cold-called him. I think it was £1,000 he got for singing the track. It had to be in cash. I agreed the key with him and I did the music, largely programmed –

samplers and synthesizer – with real instruments blended in here and there. He just tore the thing up.

*Parsons recorded from his home studio close to Alexandra Palace in north London. Filmtrax suggested that if Marriott would record other songs they had acquired they would fund the recording of an album. It would be made in the same way, with Parsons providing the music. Marriott wondered if the album might include some of his own songs.*

**Stephen Parsons:** He gave me a cassette that had four songs on it and I did not think he had anything that great. The problem was some of the songs we were doing were really classy songs and I'm not sure he even thought the songs he'd written were great; he didn't make a big deal about that.

*The album would include one Marriott original, 'Phone Call Away'. The cover versions included: 'Knockin' On Your Door', from a recent solo album by Creedence Clearwater Revival's John Fogerty; 'One More Heartache', cut by Marvin Gaye in 1966; 'Um, Um, Um, Um, Um, Um', a 1963 single for Major Lance written by Curtis Mayfield; late sixties Donovan album track 'Superlungs My Supergirl'; the 1929-penned 'You Rascal You (I'll Be Glad When You're Dead)', cut by many acts including Fats Waller, Dr John and Taj Mahal; and 'The Clapping Song', originally sung by Shirley Ellis in 1965.*

**Stephen Parsons:** He got paid £10,000 – again, cash in a paper bag. £5,000 at the start and £5,000 at the end. I had heard he could be problematic in the studio but we never worked at night so the drinking didn't start. Plus it was my house and my kid was there and my missus and it was a nice atmosphere. To liven things up a bit, I'm a half-decent singer and I did guide vocals on the track, did them well and it was hysterical because I said to the guys working with me, you watch his face when he comes in. The first one we put on was the Bob Marley one, 'Get Up, Stand Up', and you could just see him thinking, I'll fucking top that, and that's exactly what he did. I love him singing 'Gypsy Woman' [The Impressions, 1961, written by then band member Curtis Mayfield]. We did 'Life During Wartime', the Talking Heads song, and he reconstructed it. 'All Or Nothing' was a mistake, it was the one track I'd rather not have done. Filmtrax wanted it. They hoped when somebody wanted to use 'All Or Nothing' for film or TV they could offer a cheaper version than the original. We put some brass on a couple of tracks, got Pat Arnold to come in and do a duet.

*As well as providing vocals, Marriott played guitar on the album. He was only in the studio for three days.*

**Stephen Parsons:** He'd come with his girlfriend and they'd just bicker in a good way – 'Yeah, fuck you, fuck this,' and this would be going on while you were playing the tracks. They were very funny people. I think they knew it in a way. Things would spark off it. Some people bring a wife or girlfriend and she sits there. I'd rather have had Toni as lively as she was. He was tubby at the time, little tubby guy with thinning hair. I said to my wife after the first time he came round, 'I don't think Steve's got long for this world. I think he's done everything he needed to do and that's why the album's called *30 Seconds To Midnite*.' When we released the album it didn't do much [in terms of sales or critical acclaim]. It was kind of an oddity, I guess, in the Steve Marriott canon. People are divided about it because it's largely programmed but he didn't have a problem with that at all, he was into things like B-52's and Prince. We kind of modelled the way we went about on the way Prince was making records at that time. He was very, very happy with the album.

*Marriott invested some of the* 30 Seconds To Midnite *cash in a longboat that he kept on the River Stort by the Maltings, in Sawbridgeworth.*

**Jeff Edmans:** He had a downstairs toilet in the cloakroom at Sextons and above the toilet was a calendar with longboats on it and his boat was one of the ones pictured. He was proud of that and a bloke in the village was going to repaint it. Steve had this thing where if you were looking at the calendar while you had a pee he'd come up behind you and go, 'Don't move,' and he'd pee between your legs... and he'd think that was hilarious, while he'd tell you about his longboat.

**Craig Rhind:** His dad went to the boat and fell in the canal, which Steve found very funny. He never took it out. One time he had to call the AA because he'd started it up but he didn't know how to turn the engine off. He'd tell stories about having £70,000 [about £175,000 in today's money] in a biscuit tin under the bed on the boat. He was not so much in hiding from the Inland Revenue as looking over his shoulder for them. He revelled a little bit in his outlaw status. He told some risqué stories about a mate of his that had a car showroom [Ray Newbrook, who ran a second-hand car sales business in North Weald, Toni's territory, twenty miles south of Arkesden, between Epping and Ongar] who they used to hang out with. Toni liked to tell stories about her father's connections... I put it down to East End bravado.

**Simon Hickling:** Ray [Newbrook] was a mate of Toni's. Ray used to get cars for Steve and Toni. They changed cars a lot. Toni's brother used to come to many London gigs and her dad came to the Half Moon once. He and Toni's brother were both greengrocers as far as I knew.

*Marriott was driving a flash, blue XJS Jaguar that he nicknamed Big Nose. Filmtrax released 'Um, Um, Um, Um, Um, Um' as a single from the 30 Seconds To Midnite album. Like the album, it didn't do much. Marriott kept a stack of them in the fireplace at Sextons. Jeff Edmans took an Italian musician friend round to meet Marriott at the time.*

**Jeff Edmans:** Toni's exact words were: 'Who's the wop?' Steve and a couple of other men were sat around watching a film, *Texas Chainsaw Massacre*, and Steve turned round and he also said, 'Who's the wop?' In the end Steve said to him, 'So you play guitar in a band? Show me how you move? Not how you play guitar but how you move.' He always had a Spanish guitar in the inglenook [fireplace]. Steve goes, 'You're doing it wrong, you're doing it wrong.' Steve's showing him how to move. The pair of them pretending to be on stage, larking about. Giorgio had a fantastic night.

*Such nights were increasingly rare. Poulton began to complain to his pals that Marriott had days when he was low, 'hardly spoke'. He missed Jim Leverton, watched a lot of TV, complained of pains in his kidney, liver and stomach. He was seen in the village walking his big Irish wolfhound or lying asleep on the bench.*

**Jeff Edmans:** He'd look like a garden gnome: blue dungarees, belly stuck up, his hair would all be spiky. We called him 'Spiky', not Steve. If you woke him up, he wasn't drunk, he was just having a kip. Apparently, he did it when he was younger as well.

*In 1989 Alan Wicket left The DTs for a financially lucrative job drumming with Chris Barber OBE, a well-known trombonist and bandleader who had been instrumental in starting the career of Lonnie Donegan and Alexis Korner. Marriott replaced him with Les Sampson (RIP) who was best known for playing with Noel Redding. The DTs then lost their guitarist Steve Walwyn to Dr Feelgood and Marriott replaced him with a friend, Phil Anthony.*

**Simon Hickling:** We did a big festival in Denmark, Rory Gallagher was on the bill and Phil went up to him and said, 'All right Rory, how ya doing? Putting on the pork, ain't ya?' Steve said, 'Do you have to? You fucking embarrass me,' and they had a bit of a fall out. At the gig I asked the promoter if he was coming back for a drink with Steve and he said no, the last time he had done that Steve had got drunk and pulled a knife on him.

**Craig Rhind:** We were having a meal afterwards and the rest of the band had cleared off and there was just me and Steve sitting there and he said, 'Right, I'm calling this a day, this is it, we ain't doing anymore gigs.' He wanted to get back with Jim. I took it on the chin, 'No problem, good luck, we've had a good time, we'll just crack on with The DTs.' Simon, however, was pretty upset about it.

**Simon Hickling:** On the plane home he asked if I was all right. I said, 'Yeah, it was only supposed to last for three weeks and it's been two and half years and I've had a great time, I can only say thanks.' He went, 'Well, you don't have to leave, mate. If you're happy playing harmonica and singing a few songs, I'll give you a ring.'

*Marriott had a name for his next band, The Next Band. Leverton hated the name, felt it disrespectful to himself and the musicians who were asked to join. Hinkling was invited to rehearsals. Toni, rather than Marriott, called Richard Newman.*

**Richard Newman:** I said I've got six weeks before I've got to go on this tour with Sam Brown because we had a huge album [Brown's debut 1988 solo album *Stop!* had peaked at UK No 4].

*In July 1989, Marriott married Poulton at Epping registry office.*

**Richard Newman:** I think they got blitzed and decided to get married. Next thing they turn up, 'We've got married,' like a fucking pair of teenage kids. We're all sitting there thinking, oh, you haven't, have you? I don't think Toni was trying to get her hands on his money. I don't think she was a gold-digger. I don't think they even thought about it when they got married.

**Simon Hickling:** After Richard went off to play with Sam Brown, Kofi Baker [estranged son of Ginger Baker] came in. He was recommended by Mick Eve and that line-up lasted for about six or seven months. We did a tour of Germany. Steve bought two small Marshall amps, a valve and a transistor, and he linked them and got a really good fierce powerful sound but the reason he got them was because Toni could carry them. They weren't too heavy. She'd carry the amps in and take them to the stage for him. She'd look after him, she'd take the money after gigs [everything was still cash but, like The DTs, the band were now on a wage, no more four-way split]. Jim asked me had I met Melvin yet. I knew exactly what he meant. I said, 'Ahhh, Dr Jekyll and Mr Hyde.' You could see when it was coming and I just used to go back to my room. You could be having the best night and he was being really entertaining and then you could start to feel something changing in his mood and he could be very obnoxious.

**Kofi Baker:** He had some kind of drinking problem, something to do with his stomach, so he had to stop the drinking, wasn't drinking very much. It was more the pot and he was doing coke. He said he'd calmed down a lot. He was still pretty wild. I've got a picture of him hanging out of a window in Germany doing the Hitler 'Sieg Heil' thing, finger across his top lip, he burned the cork of a wine bottle and made everybody have a Hitler moustache and he was walking around Germany going, 'Sieg Heil'. I was like, oh my God, he's going to get us killed, but he got away with it.

*Marriott could command around £1,000 per gig in the UK (almost £2,500 today), often playing smaller venues two nights consecutively rather than play bigger venues. Baker was 18 and Marriott, now 42, became a surrogate father figure. He also continued to keep an eye on Toni.*

**Kofi Baker:** Steve was a bit protective toward Toni. They got me a little bit tipsy one gig and Toni said she'd take me to my hotel room. Steve said, 'No you won't! Take some young drunk guy to his room.' She was drunk too. With Steve every second word was a 'fucking'. Toni was exactly the same. Jim was great, Uncle Jim, as we used to call him. But that Simon guy was an arsehole. Steve paid him less than everybody else and he had a complex about it. He was always trying to put me down. Steve would tell him to fuck off, leave him alone. It was a very energetic set, Steve had a lot of energy and he gave me a drum solo too, full drum solo going into '30 Days In The Hole'. He always used to say before the gig, 'Keep it simple, Baker,' because I was into jazz and fusion. I was a heavy drummer but I also had the jazz touch and that's what he told me he liked, that I had the intricacies but I also had the power. We toured England, Germany and the Netherlands. I learned a lot from Steve about stage performances and being professional.

*Marriott cut a new version of 'Itchycoo Park' for a Kleenex toilet paper British TV ad in a deal handled by Laurie O'Leary. Ultimately the original Small Faces version was used but with the song back in the public ear, he was persuaded to include it in The Next Band's live set. He also hooked up with Rick Richards of The Georgia Satellites to record a single, 'Poll Tax Blues', in 1990 under the name The Pollcats. The Georgia Satellites had broken out of Atlanta and become nationwide stars in 1986, when their song 'Keep Your Hands To Yourself' hit No 2 in America and their debut album went Top 5.*

**Rick Richards:** We played the Town and Country. It was a big night. I stayed up all night and then we went to [Jethro Tull drummer] Barrie Barlow's little studio [the Doghouse in Shiplake, Oxfordshire]. I was feeling like shit but when we got there it just went like butter, so smooth and so much fun. I was really proud of the record but it was kind of a novelty song. In that time there was the poll tax riots [March 1990]. It got a little bit of notoriety, couple of blurbs, but didn't really set the world on fire. It was great to see him, he was in a great mood, and he seemed to be at peace almost. He wasn't as edgy and pissed off.

*Kofi Baker left The Next Band to pursue his career in Los Angeles. Marriott and Toni took a three-month holiday in Barbados. Marriott's parents went with them but after what was described as 'vicious' argument Bill and Kath cut their stay short. When Marriott returned to the UK, he put Packet of Three back together with Leverton and Alan Wicket, who had now left Chris Barber. There were more gigs in the UK – cash, same circuit, Marriott still in his dungarees.*

**Alan Wicket:** We had a rehearsal and started working. It was an entertaining mixture of blues, Humble Pie and Small Faces tunes, couple of original things, him and Jim used to do this cockney number together. He'd give me big drum solos he called 'the Sticky show'. Jim used to sing as well. It was a three-piece we could all be a part of and shine, rather than Steve upfront and the band. It was the three of us and Toni, a cosy little family. Steve and Toni were two peas in a pod but they were always swearing and arguing with one another – and sometimes it would turn into fisticuffs. They had a big fight one night in a hotel, you could hear it, big shout-up, and Toni comes down with Steve next day for breakfast, arm in arm, all lovey-dovey but Toni had a black eye. She said it was a freak accident, she'd asked Steve to hand her this bottle of water and he'd hit her. It was explosions that calmed down. We did a gig on the Old Kent Road [in south London] at the Thomas A Becket pub, Steve had been on the brandy the night before with [tennis player] Vitas Gerulaitis, he was wrecked and Toni wasn't much better. Toni was spark out in the training room upstairs at the pub, it used to be Henry Cooper's training room, and Steve said, 'Fucking hell, look at her, she could have been a contender.' The gig was not that sharp.

**Christine Lore:** I ran into him in London in 1990. He was playing at this Mexican restaurant as Packet of Three. I went to the soundcheck in the afternoon and there's Dawn and Jim and Steve. His jaw dropped and he was so happy to see me. He invited me to come stay with him and Toni in the house in the countryside. He was doing okay. We'd take these long walks in the countryside. There was nothing for miles, but across the street was a pub, but we only went for one pint and that was it in the four days I was there. I was very proud of him. Toni provided something Pam didn't but I didn't think he was in love with Toni. He was stuck with her. They didn't seem like a couple to me. Trust seemed to be missing. He told me he had borrowed a lot of money from Toni's dad and was worried about paying him back.

*Peter Frampton now re-entered Marriott's life.*

**Alan Wicket:** Peter Frampton came down to the Half Moon and jammed on a couple of numbers [with Packet of Three]. We did 'Natural Born Bugie'. He was pushing Steve to do some stuff. Steve had a nickname for him: he used call him 'The Blouse' [as in 'big girl's blouse' – a wimp, sissy] because he was a bit airy-fairy or something. He was a nice bloke actually but Steve had a nickname for everybody. He used to call me 'The Wallet' sometimes because I used to say, 'Can I get my petrol money, Steve?' so I was 'always after the wallet'.

*After the very public failure of the musical fantasy feature film* Sgt. Pepper's, *in which he starred alongside the Bee Gees, Frampton's post-Dee Anthony career went into a tailspin. He recovered from his car crash in Nassau but his credibility was permanently damaged and he was soon dropped by A&M. He had recorded a well-received comeback album on Atlantic Records in 1986 but commercial success of the sort he'd enjoyed in the late seventies was long gone. His old pal David Bowie had given him a huge boost when he used him as lead guitarist on his 1987 album,* Never Let Me Down, *and the massive Glass Spider tour that followed. A second Atlantic album, released in 1989, had, however, peaked at US No 152, and he was currently without a label.*

**Peter Frampton:** So I put a band together. But something was always missing. My girlfriend said, 'You're looking for Steve Marriott. Why don't you give him a call?'

*After the Putney gig, Frampton visited Marriott at home in Arkesden and the pair tried writing songs together. Marriott played Frampton various demos of songs he'd written.*

**Peter Frampton:** One was called 'Itch You Can't Scratch'. I was a fan of that track. I loved it. It might have been me who said we should work on that one. My fave was 'Phone Call Away'. I loved those demos. 'I

Know Better Than That' was another one we worked on a little bit. It was like a flashback to when we first worked together. We wrote something that first day ['Out Of The Blue'] and we both got very excited. He seemed happy enough but I didn't understand the logic of it [the career path Marriott had chosen]. Put it this way, I know he jumped at the chance of recording with me again in LA.

*There was talk of the pair recording a one-off album and doing an American tour. Marriott said Frampton assured him they would not need to resurrect the name Humble Pie. In early 1991 Packet of Three toured Germany and Switzerland. In Hannover, famed UFO, Scorpions and Michael Schenker Group guitarist, Michael Schenker, came to pay his respects. Marriott threw him out of the dressing room.*

**Jim Leverton:** That was a very, very difficult tour for me. Up until a few days before we went I was inclined on not doing it. All he'd say when I asked him about the future of the band was 'What do you mean?'

*There was talk of a $3 million advance ($5.5 million today) for the Frampton/Marriott project.*

**Alan Wicket:** Jim didn't want Steve to go to the States because Steve had had such a bad time before. Jim said it'd be a disaster. Steve kept saying he didn't want to do it, he was happy doing what he was doing. But something persuaded Steve to go over. Jim was really upset. They almost fell out. Steve was going on his own, him and Toni. Jim had toured with Steve in America and he knew. He'd seen all the temptations and problems, alcohol and the drugs, that were thrown his way.

*Toni claimed he had committed to the Frampton project for her, to secure the couple's future and so she could have 'what the others [wives] have had'. Leverton said Marriott told him that he had to get back to the big time so he could start to help people.*

**Jim Leverton:** It was a complete turnaround. I think Toni had a lot of sway.

*After the Packet of Three dates, Marriott flew to Los Angeles after a gig in Switzerland on 3 February 1991, staying in a rented beachfront house in Santa Monica with Toni.*

**Mick Eve:** Steve was lured out to the US by Peter Frampton and, although he is a nice man, he's a different animal altogether to Steve. He wanted to get Steve involved in a film theme he was working on, which he could earn a substantial amount by doing. However, the lawyers and record company then started talking about a three-year recording contract.

# CHAPTER 19

# The Bigger They Come

*According to Frampton, the recording started well.*

**Peter Frampton:** There was a huge deal waiting for us. There was this one song, 'Shine On', we wrote absolutely 50/50. We were triple-tracking the chorus together around one mic and on the multi-track you can hear us laughing between each take because we knew it sounded great. We were having the time of our lives that day. I was back with my idol. It was my chance to work with the greatest British singer of all time. He rented a place in Santa Monica, and I had a room in LA where I eventually built a studio. So Steve and I would hang out there in the day during the week, and we started working, writing together and we came up with the first four [songs], and then rehearsed with the other two guys, and it was sounding really good.

*The album they planned to record was given the working title* Chalk And Cheese. *Other tracks from these sessions included: 'I Won't Let You Down', 'Out Of The Blue' and 'So Hard To Believe'. 'I Won't Let You Down' was released by A&M in 1992 as one of four songs on a CD single under the name 'Peter Frampton with Steve Marriott'. Frampton was credited with guitars, bass synth, drum programming and vocals. Marriott was credited with vocals and 'third lead guitar break'. The lead track from the CD, which was padded with a couple of Frampton's seventies songs, was called 'The Bigger They Come'. Marriott sang and played harmonica. Frampton sang and played guitar. Both songs involving Marriott on the CD were credited as being produced by Frampton. Session drummer Anton Fig, who had worked with Frampton before, as well as with a host of big names such as Bob Dylan, Paul Simon and KISS, was credited as playing drums on 'The Bigger They Come'.*

**Anton Fig:** I never was actually in the studio with Steve. I would have remembered if I had recorded with Steve live – so Peter must have added him later. I do remember Steve coming over to my apartment in New York. He played acoustic and sang full voice late at night – it was fantastic. He did not seem inebriated at the time but he did appear to be in a great mood! I wish I had recorded that. How he got there is also a mystery.

*'The Bigger They Come' was the film song Frampton had been commissioned to record for the 1991 MGM studio action/biker flick starring Mickey Rourke and Don Johnson,* Harley Davidson And the Marlboro Man. *John Regan, who played bass on the track, was credited as co-writer of the song alongside Marriott and Frampton. Regan played with Frampton in the early eighties and has since played with The Rolling Stones, Billy Idol and David Bowie. 'The Bigger They Come' would be included on the film's accompanying 1991 soundtrack album, released by Mercury Records. Other acts on the album include Waylon Jennings, Kentucky Headhunters and The Screaming Jets. The film was a financial and commercial flop.*

**Peter Frampton:** We went to see different record labels [with the new material] and I was the one selling the project. People would say, 'How is it?' and I would say, 'Well I think it's better than ever, Steve and I are working together better than ever before.' And Steve would say, 'Oh really!' He would always play it down in front of these people. And he knew I was telling the truth, that's the thing. He would say to me, 'You really want this to work, don't you?' And I would say, 'We've got a project – why wouldn't we want it to work?' We had the top lawyer talking to us about different deals and stuff. The only thing was we weren't going to call it Humble Pie. They all wanted us to call it Humble Pie. That was not going to happen. This was a different project. You know Marriott/Frampton or Frampton/Marriott, whichever one of us you spoke to, and it would have been a kind of duo with a band.

*In total, Marriott stayed in America for almost two and a half months, his final two and a half months, his unravelling. This is what is known. He visited*

*English nightclub owner Peter Stringfellow at his newly opened club in Los Angeles, Stringfellow's. Stringfellow had run the famous Stringfellow's in London since the early eighties, and his franchise had spread to America, first New York (where the club had recently introduced 'table dancing', erotic dancing on punters' tables rather than the stage), then Miami and now LA. The two men were familiar with one another. One of the first Small Faces gigs in early 1965 had been at Stringfellow's Mojo club in his hometown of Sheffield. Both had travelled a long way since.*

**Peter Stringfellow:** He wasn't pissed, he wasn't drugged. He was raving about the songs he had done with Frampton. I was so pleased for him.

*Marriott also contacted Kofi Baker, who was back in London.*

**Kofi Baker:** Steve told me to send Peter a tape of me playing because Steve really wanted me to play on the recordings. I sent him a more progressive tape and Frampton said I was too progressive. That was what Steve told me, 'You sent him a tape of you playing all these fills and everything. Frampton thought it was too much.'

*He often called Jim Leverton back in London.*

**Jim Leverton:** He was ringing me constantly from LA, all the time. He said, 'I'm going to get you over here, mate, no matter what. Peter keeps going on about his Italian bass player but I want you here.' I said, 'Don't rock the boat, mate, do what you got to do, don't worry about me, I'm doing okay.' He said, 'No, it's me, I'm worried about me, I want my mates with me.'

*He also contacted his old road manager Mark Ballew.*

**Mark Ballew:** He called me from Santa Monica and asked if I wanted to do the tour with him and Peter.

*And his old manager Martin Druyan.*

**Martin Druyan:** They were supposed to open for Nelson, Ricky Nelson's kids, the band of that year. They were like The Monkees. [Nelson had scored a massive American No 1 single in 1990 '(Can't Live Without Your) Love And Affection' and a follow-up single, 'After The Rain', was in the US Top 10]. He was close to having another shot. I was going to fly out, do contracts.

*Druyan had dropped out of the music business after managing Marriott and was building a practice representing accident, malpractice and misconduct victims. Frampton, understandably, preferred that they use a major music business attorney, one who was said to be also representing Michael Jackson. This was likely either Allen Grubman or John Branca. Jackson had recently left his long-time entertainment lawyer, Branca, who was now representing The Rolling Stones and Aerosmith, for Grubman, whose clients included Bruce Springsteen and U2. Grubman was considered by* Businessweek *to be 'the most powerful lawyer in the music business'.*

**Peter Frampton:** We had people lining up for record deals and publishing and everything. So it was just a case of when and where, really. And then we had a little set-to, as we always did. We didn't necessarily come from the same tree. We were different people and that's why it worked so well creatively, and this time was no different. I'd completely stopped drinking and doing anything, and Steve hadn't.

*Marriott tried to contact his Small Faces bandmate Ian McLagan.*

**Ian McLagan:** I was doing a gig at the Cocoanut Grove nightclub and a geezer popped a bit of paper in my hand in between songs and said, 'Steve's in town and wants you to call him.' I thought, oh great, file under I won't use this number, and I never called him. God bless him! If he was in town today, I'd change my name three times at this hotel, I'd still be avoiding him. I could only imagine how exhausting it would be to spend time with him.

*Marriott took a call from producer Gary Lyons, the Englishman who had produced Humble Pie's 1981 album,* Go For The Throat. *Lyons was still on top, having produced albums with UFO, Saxon and Aerosmith in the eighties, among others. He was currently recording a new Aerosmith album,* Pandora's Box.

**Gary Lyons:** I had an aunt who owned a large furniture warehouse store and she was talking about doing a little radio ad, and she wanted someone to record a jingle, and I mentioned it to Steve when he was out in LA. I asked was it something he wanted to do, just for fun, bang something together? And he said, 'Yeah, I'll do that.'

*He was seen at the famous celebrity and rock star (and groupie) hang-out, the Rainbow Bar & Grill on Sunset Boulevard, close to Beverly Hills. He bumped into Ozzy Osbourne in the exclusive upstairs club.*

**Ozzy Osbourne:** I hadn't seen him for six or seven years. He told me he was going to form another band with Peter Frampton to go on the road. The next day he went on a drinking tour.

*Frampton (who was in recovery from his own substance abuse issues) asked Marriott to refrain from drinking or doing drugs while they worked. He was not keen on having Toni around in the studio either. And he insisted Marriott stay sober for business meetings.*

**Peter Frampton:** The thing was he agreed. 'Look,' I said, 'it's during the day. I don't care what you do when you go home. Why don't we just try?' If one person has a drink and the other one hasn't during the day, it's difficult to work. And we were working so well until he started doing that again. Steve would short-circuit when things were close to working out. I'd noticed it even before he left the Small Faces. Maybe he was nervous of being too famous. There was a bit of sabotage going on. He was the most talented person I've ever known but there was something in his psyche. Some huge problem.

**Jim Leverton:** He rang me and said, 'I'm meeting The Blouse on the beach later.' They had a photo session to promote the pair of them and he told me that he'd had a word with the photographer to give him a sign when he was about to click the shot. He said, 'I'm going to jump out the picture,' and that's what he did. He jumped out the picture and so there was just a picture of Frampton. That's pretty offensive.

**Jerry Shirley:** Steve resented the fact he was being watched so closely and he was also scared to death of the idea of going out there into the big time again. The idea might have seemed like a good one at the time, but once reality set in, oh dear, I'm going to have to go and do it all again. He was getting twitchy, out of his comfort zone. It was not where Steve wanted to be. He was happy going into bars, playing with his three-piece blues band. What Peter cared about, rightfully so, was being real straight about it, we're going to do it right – no drinking, no drugging. Steve sees the business people offering him all kinds of money and he sees Peter siding with them. And then, when it came down to a screaming match, Peter just let Steve go on his merry way and the next thing he knows, from what I understand, after having this row, Steve went on a bender for two or three weeks in LA.

**Peter Frampton:** Things started to crumble. Steve was getting high. I didn't want that to be the basis of our working day – our first few weeks together had been stupendous. Then things just started to drift off. There was that mistrust again. He had this Perrier water bottle with him, in fact two bottles – and I realised it wasn't water in those bottles. It was white wine. It pissed me off.

**Martin Druyan:** Steve told me he had a fist fight with Peter and beat him up and then he started drinking, just couldn't cooperate. His wife was a drinker. She was a drunk, it was a negative, didn't help.

**Jerry Shirley:** I do not believe that Steve would have hit Peter no matter what. Plus, Peter had all his people there who would have stopped it. Steve was famous for saying he had decked someone when he had not done so. He would have screamed at the top of his voice. Peter has never mentioned it to me. That doesn't mean it did not happen but Steve, you've seen how Steve could elaborate and tell tales. Pam always used to say, 'Steve would tell people what he thought they wanted to hear, which was not always the truth.'

**Peter Frampton:** Steve beating me up? Mentally maybe – lol – but never had any violence between me and Steve. The reason I said I couldn't continue was because we had agreed to work straight and he started to bring alcohol in a Perrier bottle so as to hide it from me. Made my decision very simple. Then he went on a ten-day bender, staying with a supposed coke dealer until the day they flew home. That's all I know about that period before they went back.

*On 20 March, Eric Clapton's 4-year-old son fell to his death from a fifty-third-floor balcony in New York. The tragedy hit an already fragile Marriott hard. The last time he had seen Mollie he'd had a huge argument with Manon and declared, halfway into a bottle of brandy, he wanted nothing more to do with her or his daughter. She would be 6 in a few weeks. He desperately wanted to reconcile with her. His son Toby had turned 15 in February. He had missed the celebrations but would catch up with him in the summer. Toby had been practising guitar and was keen to show his dad that he could play. Tonya, he barely knew. She had turned 7 while he was in LA. Perhaps he thought of Lesley as a sixties mishap. But he grew melancholy thinking of his children, of his life, and his wife, who was not fit to be a mother to her own young child, never mind Marriott's children. He tried to discuss these things with Toni. He drank. She drank.*

**Toby Marriott:** Seemed like when Steve and Toni were in LA the marriage might have hit the end of the road. From what I heard it was lucky someone didn't die in LA – a lot of bad stuff was going down. I spoke to him about two weeks before he died. He called one morning before I went to school. I hadn't heard from him since I'd moved back to America [to live with Pam], in five, maybe six months. He was pissed out of his head... he told me he was going back to England. Then he put Toni on the phone and she didn't sound well at all either. I was only 15 but I could tell something bad was going on. Later, when Toni used to tell me stories about them living in LA, it was always more that Steve was the aggressor not her – that he was acting the role of Melvin.

*At one music industry meeting Frampton arranged, it was said that Marriott turned up drunk, dishevelled, grabbed an executive (Frampton was close to John Kalodner, the Geffen A&R executive who had signed Nelson and worked with Aerosmith, Jimmy Page and Sammy Hagar) by the tie and screamed in his face: 'You can't bend the midget with a contract that lasts bloody years.' In Toni's words, he 'went on the turn'. Marriott, she said, hit the bottle harder still, growing increasingly out of control. 'He was scared,' she said. He told her he didn't want to front the band and felt Frampton should take the lead. In an unsent letter, dated 23 March 1991, Marriott wrote, 'I always had my doubts about living a pressurised lifestyle for money again. Now I know I don't want or need it.' There was some talk of crack cocaine being involved. Marriott had a limo on call and was seen on the town with Toni. He was drinking Courvoisier, popping Valium and snorting cocaine. It would later be stated that Marriott and Toni's home in Arkesden was burgled while they were in LA, the TV and some guitars removed. It seems inconceivable Marriott would have been unaware of this, one further agitation, burden, problem, trauma.*

**Jim Leverton:** I got a call, 'I'm coming back and I want to put the group back together.' I said, 'I don't want to do that.' I said, 'I want to make a record, we've written those lovely songs, "Phone Call Away" being one of them, and we've never done them. It's madness. I want to do that.' He said, 'Don't you want to go on the road?' I said, 'No, I've had enough of playing dingy little clubs for £100 in my pocket. I just said I don't want to do it that way anymore. I want to make a record with you.' And he agreed. That was the plan. He was coming back to make a record.

**Kofi Baker:** I was about to rejoin Steve's band just before he died. I'd cancelled all my work to be with Steve for six months. I was going to go to his house on the Saturday, we were going to rehearse, and I was going to stay the night and we were going to leave for Germany on the Sunday. He had a lot of European gigs lined up. It seemed like he was on a comeback. He died Friday night. The thing I was doing in LA had collapsed, I'd lost all my money, my van was on its last legs and Steve said come back to work for me and make some money.

**Mark Ballew:** I get a call from Steve, 'I'm going home, fuck this. I'm drinking too much.' Steve got around the wrong people, he was easily dragged along if there was a good time to be had. That's how he lost himself.

**Mollie Marriott:** Peter [Frampton] said, 'I know Steve was flying back to see you.'

**Peter Frampton:** Before he left to go to England, he called me, and he said, 'Did you just call me?' And of course I didn't. 'Oh, I was just seeing how you were,' he said. I think he was fishing, it was too good.

If he'd had a clear moment there, or when his next clear moment would have been, I think that we would have finished it. With his talent, which was supreme, came a lot of baggage. And Steve had his share of pain and for whatever reason he was the way he was and he couldn't change that. And God alone knows people tried. I figured I'd call him up later and say, 'C'mon, let's finish this thing.'

**Gary Lyons:** I almost asked him to stop off in New York [to record the jingle] on the way back to London and if I had I'm almost certain he would have, but I never did because I thought it was a bit of an imposition and I thought, well, if we ever get around to it, fine.

*It seemed, however, as if Marriott had a change of plan. He called Christine Lore, who now lived amid the beautiful scenery of Lake Tahoe, the upmarket tourist hot spot in the Sierra Nevada mountain range on the Californian border.*

**Christine Lore:** He asked if he could stay with me for a couple of weeks up at the lake and unwind. I said perfect. My parents had this beautiful place right on the lake and nobody was there. So Steve and Toni were coming to stay. I got the house ready, all Steve's favourite things in the fridge and the next day I was waiting for Steve to call from LA to let me know what time to pick them up at Reno Airport. But then I got a call, had I heard what had happened to Steve? I said, 'But how is that even possible; I just talked to him last night?' It just did not make any sense at first. Two hours later Toni phoned from England.

Do you want to hear what really happened in LA? Why they had to fly back? I'll tell you, because Toni has done several things since, regarding the family, to Toby in particular, that I don't like. So, I'm going to tell you the truth, and the truth is they were driving back from dinner and she got a DUI [driving under the influence] and because of her record back in England, where she had accidentally killed her sister, she was really scared about this DUI, about being in America, a very volatile place. So she ran, said, 'Let's get on the next plane,' and they did. They just grabbed their shit and went straight to the airport.

**Toby Marriott:** The DUI? Toni told me that they were both drunk, that she hadn't drank a lot but she'd had some. They were pulled over and they hauled Toni off to jail and Steve just left her to sit in jail. She was in a cell a few hours and the guy who was looking after them – Howie, I think his name was – came and got her out. They went and searched for Steve and found him at the Rainbow with a woman on his lap. Toni walked up and punched him in front of everyone and that was the end of that night.

*Toni would later claim that Marriott was pressured to stay (by whom is unclear) in America, asked not to return to England, but that he wanted to. She said both of them did. They were unhappy. Marriott and Toni arrived at Heathrow on 19 April 1991. It was midday. Marriott was 44. Toni was 30. They were both hungover and jet-lagged. She said the flight – which if it were non-stop from LA would have taken just under twelve hours – had been 'total hell' and that fellow passengers had complained about the couple's loud arguments. Both, she says, were downing 'drink after drink'.*

**Simon Hinkling:** He called Jim Leverton to pick him up from the airport, he tried everybody and they didn't want to know. Phil Anthony went and got him. Steve could ring Phil up when nobody else would help and Phil would be straight round there. If he wanted something doing on his boat Phil would go do it.

*Phil Anthony had been tasked with keeping an eye on Marriott's Arkesden home while he and Toni had been in LA, so presumably he would have been the one to call Marriott about the purported burglary.*

**Toby Marriott:** Nan said she and Bill were never told about the burglary [at the time]. I don't think she believed there was one. She thought maybe his stuff got sold and a burglary was used as a cover story. It wasn't reported in the paper or reported to the police anyway. Phil passed away but he stopped talking to Toni long before. I'm not sure why.

*Anthony said that when he collected the couple from the airport Marriott was agitated. Every time Toni said something he'd shout her down.*

**Jim Leverton:** I know he and Toni were not getting along at all well in LA. Phil Anthony told me it was all over between them when they got back. They'd finished with one another.

*They stopped off at Anthony's home in Old Harlow, Essex, for a cup of tea. Old Harlow was en route from Heathrow Airport to Arkesden, which was just twenty miles further up the A1184. After the cup of tea, they drove five miles up the road to Sawbridgeworth and stopped again, to check on Marriott's narrowboat. Then they drove on to the house, presumably keen to know what exactly had been stolen in the burglary. Toni said Anthony dropped them off and left. Anthony said both Marriott and Tony were 'pissed', drunk. According to Toni, once Anthony was gone, Marriott went 'berserk', smashing up the house, telephone and anything else to hand. His behaviour, she said, was frightening. At this point, in all written versions, Toni's car dealer friend, Ray Newbrook, 47, called in at the house, having already been notified the couple was due back from LA that day. The drive from Heathrow to Arkesden non-stop takes approximately one and a half hours. If baggage and customs took an hour and the stops en route ate up another hour, then it was 4 or 5 p.m.*

**Jeff Edmans:** Steve was down the Axe briefly on the night before he died with a bloke who looked like a skinny Elton John, in a suit with glasses. It wasn't Ray. I'd seen him in the pub with Ray. I'd never seen this guy around Steve before and Steve had a suit on. I'd never seen Steve in a suit ever. I said, 'Christ, what's happened here?' He'd just come back from Frampton, so I said, 'Must have been good,' and he groaned and said, 'Don't give me that,' and he told me he'd been flying and hated it and he was jet-lagged. I said, 'We need to have a beer.' He said, 'If the lights are on later, come round.' He used to have a lamp in his window and of course the lamp was always on. He was going out for dinner. Toni was with him and this bloke. It was about 8 p.m. on the 19th.

*According to Ray Newbrook, he, Toni and Marriott went out to dinner that evening at the Straw Hat in Sawbridgeworth, a well-known restaurant. Newbrook said Marriott was being aggressive towards Toni all evening and the staff intervened several times, asking them to keep the noise down. Newbrook recalls that after the meal (the restaurant likely closed at 11 p.m.) he drove the couple to the home of top showbiz concert promoter Brian Shaw, the man who had employed Toni's sister Joanna. This was a secluded, four-bed detached property, Kings Ridden, in Ongar, a twenty-five-minute drive away. They are said to have arrived at the house at 12.30 a.m.*

**Brian Shaw:** I don't recall anyone bringing Steve and Toni to the house. I thought they arrived by taxi but it is a long time ago and I may be wrong. Ray was just someone I got to know socially around the area and we became friendly. He stayed at my house from time to time.

*There have been several reasons posited for the visit to Brian Shaw. In one retelling, Newbrook even claimed he took the pair back to his own house. He told the* News of the World: *'We were celebrating his trip. Steve had been working on a record deal with Peter Frampton. At the end of the evening the pair were dead on their feet from jet lag. They came back to my house and I put them both to bed. But a few minutes later Steve got up and said he wanted to sleep in his own bed. I called him a cab and he went home alone. Toni stayed where she was.' Elsewhere Newbrook has claimed he did not drive the couple back to their own home after their meal together, as he was fearful of leaving them alone, suggesting Marriott's foul mood was worrying Toni. He said he told Marriott, potentially to placate him, there could be 'stimulants' at Shaw's property. Once there, he showed them to the spare bedroom. He said Marriott was heard shouting in the bedroom. It is possible the couple was arguing about Marriott's desire to reconcile with Mollie. Toni was said to be against the idea of bringing the girl and Manon back into their life, and there is a story of how she took off and threw her wedding ring at Marriott. In this version, Newbrook recalled having to wait 'an absolute age' for the taxi that came for Marriott.*

**Brian Shaw:** I was living in Kings Ridden with my girlfriend at the time, Lisa (now my wife). She knew Steve and Toni from before she and I met. On the night in question they had flown back from recording in America and unexpectedly called to see us. Toni stayed the night and Steve got a cab home late on. There were certainly no "stimulants" at my house. My 3-year-old daughter was also staying with us at the time. So it was just Lisa, myself and my daughter at home.

*Both Newbrook and Shaw stated that Toni slept through the entire episode of Marriott's departure. Shaw said he did not try to stop Marriott. 'Quite simply, Steve Marriott was his own man,' he said. 'Nobody told him what to do. Whatever he wanted to do, he did it.'*

**Brian Shaw:** I feel sure you will understand that I am, and always have been, loath to comment further on a period and sequence of events that were tragic in the extreme. I further note that, whilst you have clearly spoken to a great many people on the subject, Toni herself does not appear to be amongst them. This being the case, I would be disinclined to contribute anything that might prove hurtful or upsetting.

*And there is another version of events, or at least an alternative location for the events. This time Marriott is not in Ongar but Clavering, a village two miles away.*

**Jeff Edmans:** They went back to Ray's after the meal, he lived in Clavering, the village next door, and that's where Steve came back from in a cab and was dropped off in the early hours. I was coming back from a party with my friend and the light was on [at Marriott's home] and I was actually going to knock him up but I didn't bother. It was probably about three in the morning. Apparently, he'd come back on his own from Clavering in the cab and was in the house on his own. Don't get me wrong, that sounds a bit of an unusual thing for Steve to do but then again we all do these things. It was common knowledge that the cab driver was local and that he'd dropped Steve off. He'd have been from Bishop's Stortford.

*The home address most often mentioned for Ray Newbrook is Little Hallingbury, ten miles from Arkesden. But it has been suggested Newbrook had a car sales pitch in Clavering. Marriott certainly did know someone in Clavering.*

**Brian Shaw:** Viola [Toni's mum] and her partner Les were close friends of mine. Joanna [Toni's sister] worked for me from around 1979 until her death, and of course I knew Toni. Les was living in Clavering after Viola died a couple of years earlier.

*Brian Shaw maintains Marriott left his home in Ongar in a cab at around 1.30 a.m. Years later, circa 2013, a then 51-year-old Marriott fan, Gary Kent, a singer in a punk/Mod pop covers band who also runs a fan site dedicated to punk band The Stranglers, declared he had been Marriott's taxi driver that night. Kent would have been 27 in April 1991. Although he was a Mod, punk, new wave music fan, he said he failed to recognise Marriott when he picked him up. The rest of his story is beguiling. He claimed the owner of the cab firm he worked for at the time was called Wally Taylor, a wiry old man, a heavy drinker and smoker, who had scars on his arms, legs and back from a fall-out with a former business associate involving a burning warehouse. The cab office was based just outside London, and Kent said he had just dropped his previous fare in central London at 1 a.m. and that he was ready to knock off when Wally called to book the ride for Marriott. Kent said Taylor told him Marriott had already been waiting ages (this does throw the timings of other accounts out of whack). Taylor added that he'd had a 'nice chat' with Marriott and described him as a 'bit pissed' but all right, and although it was way out of 'our area' and 'he's going further afield' (i.e. further out of London from Ongar) the client had got money. It's approximately an hour's drive from central London to Ongar. So perhaps in this version Kent arrived to pick Marriott up at 2 a.m. And then it's a further forty-minute drive from Ongar to Arkesden. Kent said Marriott gave him directions but was otherwise silent.*

**Jeff Edmans:** I would find it a bit far-fetched [if anyone said] that a driver had come from London to pick him up. Maybe Stortford or Harlow… they are also London [black] cabs. With the airport [Stansted] being so close someone might be getting crossed wires. Perhaps what they're saying is the cab didn't come from Saffron Walden, which is where the cabs came from when you ordered one where we lived. You can't get one of them after nine at night.

*Another striking feature of Kent's story was what he said happened to cab firm owner Wally Taylor. Kent claimed Taylor was found dead on 21 April, the day after Marriott perished. As a culmination it makes Kent's telling difficult to believe.*

**Brian Shaw:** It's funny, we never thought of tracking down the cab driver at the time. It just never occurred to any of us.

**Jeff Edmans:** I was woken a few hours later to flashing lights around out village, which is pretty rare. It was the fire brigade. I knew them [the firemen] so I was straight down there. They didn't say much. I asked, 'Was anyone in there?' and they wouldn't say anything but it became clear there was someone in there, and I was very surprised at the time, between you, me and the wall, that Toni wasn't in there with him.

407

*It was 6.30 a.m. when it was claimed a passing motorist noticed Sextons was on fire. A neighbour of Marriott's said she had called the fire brigade. 'I smelled smoke and looked out to see the roof of next door on fire, just feet away,' she said. 'The operator told me that they can't send a fire engine right away but they will as soon as they can.' Assistant Divisional Officer, Keith Dunatis, described entering the house to the* News of the World.

**Keith Dunatis:** When we arrived there was smoking pouring out of the building and the flames were really fierce. We had to break in through the back door. There was memorabilia everywhere. When we got in the house we could see pictures of rock stars on the wall. I especially noticed a print of guitarist Ronnie Wood. I deal with many fires but this one was like walking down memory lane. You knew you were in a pop star's house immediately. It was a tough fight getting upstairs. We searched the bedroom areas and it was very hot – we knew immediately that no one could have survived the fire. We began to feel our way around the walls and discovered him lying on the floor in between the bed and the wall. I would say he had been in bed and tried to escape. As soon as I saw the body clearly, I knew who it was. I used to be a fan. The scene was horrific in that corner of the room. It was lucky he was still a person and we could preserve his dignity. We managed to salvage all his guitars and musical equipment.

*Given the above statement, it is safe to assume that if Marriott's home was burgled while he was away in Los Angeles, the thief or thieves left behind many valuable items. The* Sun *said that the police had revealed to them that the 'charred body was found in an airing cupboard'. They believed Marriott had dived through the wrong door attempting to escape the blaze. A police inspector, Martin Reed, said: 'There were doors on either side of the bed. He opened the cupboard by mistake.' The identity of the body was confirmed by dental records and fingerprints. Reed issued a statement from Toni, that said, 'we will miss him very much, and we will all be playing his records and thinking of his music'. PC Ian O'Sullivan said the cause of fire was a lit cigarette end or possibly a candle. Marriott had a habit of using candles, sometimes lighting two together. He had already set himself alight with a candle one night, in bed with Pam after drinking wine. 'Set his whole head of hair on fire,' she said.*

**Jeff Edmans:** His mattress burned right through the floor, must have been so hot. It was a tiled roof [there were persistent statements made to this author by interviewees that Marriott's rented home had a thatched roof – it didn't]. The house opposite, next door to the pub, had a thatched roof and that was burned down just before his. It was very odd – two fires in the middle of the village in the space of a few months. Apparently that one was a gas bottle and it ignited under the thatch… and that was burned down virtually to the ground. The cause of the fire at Steve's was a cigarette. They told me he'd gone to sleep with a cigarette still lit and set the mattress on fire. That's what the fire brigade told me. I knew them because they were local.

**Christine Lore:** Steve had to stop and get some Old Holborn [on the way back from the airport] for his roll-ups and they didn't have any, so he bought a pack of cigarettes. The Old Holborn will go out and the cigarettes will keep burning.

**Jeff Edmans:** I did go in after the fire and it'd burned the roof off his bedroom, and the shape of the bed had burned through the floor. It was an old cottage with really old beams so it just shows you the heat of the mattress. In that room [downstairs] the only thing that was damaged was a rectangle hole where the bed had come through from the room above. I was told he was face down in the airing cupboard. When you got up from Steve's bed there was an airing cupboard to the left and the bathroom to the right. If he'd got out of bed the other side he'd have fallen down the staircase. It's what you hear from the firemen. I saw him, carried out in a wooden box, he was put in a little Rascal Bedford van, on the way, in Steve's words, to be recooked. If that had been Steve standing there with me, he'd have said, 'There you go, they've got to recook that one.' It's the kind of joke he'd have come out with.

*Marriott's death made the front page of the* News of the World *the next day, 21 April. The headline read 'Ciggie Blaze Kills Rock Legend'. Inside, Rod Stewart, Peter Frampton and Kenney Jones paid tribute. The following day, there was an interview with a sobbing Toni in* The Star *newspaper. She stated that the reason Marriott had slipped out of their friend's home was so he could tidy up Sextons before she got home. 'Steve wanted to check because we'd had a burglary,' she said. 'But how I wish he'd woken me. I can't imagine life without him. If I had been with him, he'd be alive. The fire was caused by a lit cigarette. He must have fallen asleep with it in his hand. Steve was always doing that… but at least I'd be there to put it out. It was one of our rare times apart in four years. Normally I was with him every minute.' She added: 'He had kicked his drink and drug habit.' Ray Newbrook was quoted in the same article. He said he was with the couple at the friend's house and revealed how police and firemen thought Sextons was empty at first. 'When they phoned about the blaze, I told them, "For Christ's sake go back. Steve's inside."'*

**Kofi Baker:** The house wouldn't have caught fire if Toni had come back. Toni wasn't there to take the cigarette and put him to bed and it was an old house, the floor leaned to the left, and he had two doors in his bedroom, one to the right was the door out and one to the left was the closet, and they found him in the closet, so he'd obviously got up and with the smoke couldn't find his way out, and with the room leaning to the left… and collapsed in the closet. This is what Toni told me. Right after he died Toni gave me a pair of purple Converse shoes Steve had bought for me in America… I had purple hair at the time and Steve used to call me Purple Baker. They didn't get burned in the fire.

*Toni recounted one version of the events the day after the fire. Ray Newbrook left Shaw's house in Ongar early on Saturday morning to attend to his car showroom. He drove past the fire engines and went to investigate. Newbrook phoned Shaw at the house in Ongar and broke the news to Shaw, who woke Toni and drove her to the showroom, where Newbrook told her what had happened. Toni said she went berserk, 'kicking the shit out of motors', and that it took three people to hold her down before she was taken to a local doctor to be sedated. In one printed version, Shaw told it slightly differently, said he drove Toni to a friend's house to break the news. He gave this author the following account.*

**Brian Shaw:** I got a frantic call from Les [Viola's partner] at around 7.30 a.m. asking were Steve and Toni with us because the house was on fire. The phone was passed to a police officer and the story unfolded. A short while later, my driver took Toni and, as I recall, dropped her at Ray's garage, from where he drove her to Clavering.

*Marriott's mum, Kath, readying for a shift at the local pub, said Toni called her at home around 9.30 a.m. Kath recalled Newbrook then driving Toni over to*

410

*their house. Toni's brother John Poulton phoned Jim Leverton to let him know. The recriminations began immediately.*

**Pam Marriott Land:** Steve could never be alone. I have a problem trying to understand how he was in a cab by himself. I've never seen Steve call a cab or be alone in my life. I used to have to go with him to the store. He couldn't do anything alone. I just found it very odd, very odd, that he went to the house on his own. He did always fall asleep with a cigarette. It must have been American cigarettes because he always rolled his own and they never stay lit. Steve was forever setting cigarettes down on the edge of a table. He never used an ashtray. There were constant burn marks on everything we had. That's one of the reasons he started rolling his own cigarettes. But I could never understand how he didn't wake up anybody in the house because if Steve woke up, Holy God, he wasn't a quiet man. When I heard he was dead, the very next day there was this postcard from LA, from Steve, and all it said was 'I want my family back.' I also thought that was odd. I'd just got back from Kuwait, I was in the Civil Guard. From what I was told, by someone in California, he wanted a divorce that night on the aeroplane. There's no love lost between any of the family and Toni.

*The incident of the house opposite burning down, in addition to the mention of robbery at Marriott's home and the seemingly violent atmosphere between Marriott and Toni and their often self-mythologising stories about their contacts with 'shady' characters, plus the conflicting accounts on the exact detail of Marriott's final day on earth, have allowed room for much speculation and suspicion to creep into this deeply upsetting and tragic story. There were, for example, persistent rumours that Marriott had been at a party the night he died. Several people this author spoke to mentioned it, including Kenney Jones.*

**Kenney Jones:** I've always found his death very suspicious. I often think it. Steve was known for upsetting a few people.

**Christine Lore:** They went to some friend's house and there was a welcome home party for them. There was probably a lot of things there that you shouldn't do, but one does… a lot of them when you're Steve Marriott and he got tired and went to bed and Toni stayed downstairs. When the party was over she went up and Steve wasn't there, and she fell asleep.

*Others felt Marriott's death was simply an accident waiting to happen.*

**Alan Wicket:** When Phil picked them up at the airport, he said, 'Fuck me, you two, you're wrecked, just go home and get loads of sleep,' and he dropped them back home. Steve had taken Valium because he didn't like flying and he'd been on brandy. They had loads of messages on their answerphone, and one said, 'Steve, we hear you're coming back, we've got a party locally,' this friend of his, 'we'd love to see you if you get back on time.' Despite all Phil's attempts to dissuade them from going, they went to this party in a complete state. I hear Toni completely collapsed at the party, which she was known to do when she'd had too many, she'd just fallen sleep and you couldn't get her up. Steve decided to go home. He was home alone, could have been a candle, they liked to light candles, could have been smoking in bed, or a joint.

**John Skinner:** Me and my missus, Jill, and Toni went and stood outside looking at the burned-out house. It was horrible. We got in touch with her and picked her up from Ray Newbrook's car dealership in Clavering. There was a flight case in the showroom, which I assume had the blonde 335 in, and there was another guitar case. It was always going to be fire that would take Steve's life. He blew himself up trying to light his oven. Pam rang up and said, 'Steve's nearly dead, blew all his hair off, eyebrows, eyelashes, burned his face.' We were in a restaurant and he was drunk and he said, 'Is there any wine in that bottle?' 'No, it's got a candle in,' but he picked it up to take a swig and he jabbed a candle in his face. We were in a Greek restaurant having fiery Sambuca and he knocked his drink over and set his coat on fire. He nearly set fire to my house one time. He was so drunk I wouldn't let him drive home, he'd been up a couple of days, and so I put him to bed. Jill went up and he was fast asleep with a cig in his mouth; when he breathed in, the end would glow, my wife took it out and the response was, 'Oi, you cunt, I'm smoking that.' Oh Christ, Steve Marriott, usual routine, holes in the sheets, covers burned... luckily it was a roll-up. I managed to gently pluck it out of his mouth without him waking up... he was a terrible smoker in bed. So when the news broke, we just went, 'Well, it had to happen.'

*A funeral service took place on 30 April at Harlow Crematorium. Aside from family, those present included: P. P. Arnold, Laurie O'Leary, Terence Stamp,*

*Jerry Shirley, Greg Ridley, Jenny Dearden, Peter Frampton, Manon Piercey, Joe Brown and Kenney Jones. Pam Marriott Land and Marriott's son Toby were noticeably absent. Toni chose the music for the service, 'Saylarvee' from the Small Faces reunion album* Playmates, *'Drown In My Own Tears' by Ray Charles and 'All Or Nothing'.*

**Greg Ridley:** It was real sad. We were all thinking, how the hell could he fall asleep one night with a fag and end up like that after he'd done it a million times.

**Jerry Shirley:** It was an accident. I'd taken a cigarette out of his hand when he fell asleep hundreds of times. He did smoke roll-ups but when they ran out he'd smoke cigarettes. The only consolation is, and the authorities told me this, when you go like that, the smoke inhalation literally knocks you out long before being burned up. His funeral was sold out. Standing room only! And the amazing thing was, out of nowhere, between fifty and a hundred Mods showed up on scooters, literally right out of Quadrophenia. They lined up in the back of the church, very respectful with their heads hung.

**Jeff Edmans:** At his funeral I was talking to Beaky from Dave Dee, Dozy, Beaky, Mick & Tich, and Kenney Jones was sitting in the pew in front and they played 'All Or Nothing' and Kenney was drumming along with his fingers. Not a lot of people spoke to Toni. I spoke to Brian [Shaw], who introduced me to Peter Frampton. Joe Brown was giving loads of interviews.

*A small group of funeral goers – Laurie O'Leary and Bobby Tench among them – refused to go back to the house where Toni was having the wake. They felt she was already showing signs of becoming proprietorial over Marriott's estate.*

*In July 1991, at an inquest into his death, held in Epping, it was recorded that Marriott had enough cocaine, Valium and alcohol in his system to put him in a coma. He had then breathed in lethal fumes from the fire that was probably started by a cigarette. The inquest was told he may have taken Valium to offset the effects of cocaine and misjudged the dose because he had drunk so much. The verdict: accident. Essex coroner Dr Malcolm Weir said the effect of the Valium and alcohol would have put Marriott into a deep sleep and that the Valium,*

413

alcohol and cocaine together 'probably would have been lethal on its own'. Toni said he had taken Valium that day because he was 'terrified of flying'. She added that he was not into drugs in a big way and that he liked to drink more than anything. The Guardian reported on the death at Marriott's 'sixteenth century thatched cottage' [sic]. The article suggested he had taken 'a large quantity of Valium as well as alcohol and there were traces of cocaine in his system'. There was no evidence he had tried to take his own life. The cause of death was carbon monoxide poisoning due to smoke inhalation.

Sextons was boarded up, repaired and rented out. Toni moved to nearby Hatfield Broad Oak. For years, fans of Marriott visited the house in Arkesden to pay their respects, leaving flowers and pictures.

# CHAPTER 20
# Afterglow

**Jim Leverton:** Toni? I mean, what can you say about that? Backstreet abortion time, really. All the substandard records [CDs chiefly] that have been released since Steve's demise have been put out by Toni and a lot of them are cassette recordings from the desk. It's fucking cheeky and she made quite a lot of dough doing that. It was unforgivable really, especially as she doesn't hand any of the dependants any money whatsoever, the children. She hasn't taken care of things that should have been taken care of. She hasn't got a clue what she's doing but you've only got to ask, girl, ask someone who knows and they'll tell you, 'No, don't do that, that's wrong.' All the backstreet abortion deals cheapen everything. It's small time.

*It is close to impossible to give full details of posthumous Marriott releases that relate to his career post Humble Pie. Musicians who played with him from the mid-seventies at Beehive, through Santa Cruz, Atlanta and beyond have all spoken to this author about their disappointment or confusion over a whole swathe of dubious recordings, complaining of a lack of clarity, accuracy, quality and accreditation. This would apply to live recordings, live DVDs, solo compilations, sometimes even releases claiming to be by Humble Pie. It seems almost certain Marriott's box of reel-to-reel demo recordings ended up in the hands of amateurs, charlatans and enthusiasts. The veracity of all recordings, often copies of copies of cassette tapes, not officially sanctioned by the Small Faces or Humble Pie is highly questionable, amplified by frequent mis-listings as to musicians involved and studio locations. It has been, to coin a phrase, a shitshow. And that's being kind. Criminal activity regarding stolen tapes, broken promises or lies are commonplace.*

**Stephen Parsons:** There were some extra tracks [from the *30 Seconds To Midnite* album] released on a CD single: 'Oh Well' [a Fleetwood Mac song, written by Peter Green], [Lorraine Ellison's] 'Stay With Me (Baby)', which is... my God... I almost break up every time I hear it. They were leftovers and I stuck them out and immediately a load of people just copied them and started putting them on albums. The problem with all this low-level stuff is it's not worth your while to chase it and they know that. Filmtrax eventually sold the [*30 Seconds To Midnite*] album to Castle and Castle put it out. It floats around now on different labels. I don't get anything from anybody.

**Jim Leverton:** Toni gave me her blessing to do a legacy record [of his solo years]. I got the recordings from Capricorn, recordings from Modesto and I was arranging a really nice tribute to my mate and we were bringing in players like Robbie McIntosh [session guitarist who has played with Paul McCartney and The Pretenders] and Paul Beavis [session drummer with Andy Fairweather Low, Robert Fripp and countless others] and P. P. Arnold and [Joe Brown's daughter and solo star] Sam Brown [to augment the work]. It was real classy. Toni wanted a copy of it. We sent her snippets of each track, because we were wise; don't give her the whole thing, because she'll put it out. But she did end up with an unfinished copy, don't know how, but she put it out. The people financing me to do the record, Rory Gallagher's brother, Donal, pulled out, said it's already come out on backstreet abortion records. He said, 'I don't want anything to do with the Steve Marriott situation.' It's just a mess.

**John Skinner:** Pam gave me some of Steve's ashes. Toni had sent her some. I got a couple of teaspoons. Toni used to drive around with them in the back of her car. I heard a story they'd been interred with his mum and dad at the graveyard at Sawbridgeworth.

**Jerry Shirley:** No one is particularly enamoured with Steve's widow Toni as she never shared her financial good fortune after his death with his true heirs, i.e. his children. A shameful thing to do. She only knew him for five minutes, relatively speaking, and, by her own admission, on the very night he died, she told him to shove his marriage up his arse. Nice lady.

*Things would get worse. In October 1993, Toni Marriott, 33, was involved in a second fatal car accident. It happened on the same stretch of road in Epping where the crash that killed her sister had occurred. It was reported that she had spent the previous evening partying until 5 a.m. and had 'topped up' in a number of pubs throughout the following day prior to driving her Vauxhall Astra GTE on the wrong side of the road, at least ten miles over the 40 mph speed limit, head-on into 21-year-old Penny Jessup's Seat Marbella car. Jessup died instantly. One witness said he was 'surprised' at Toni's driving speed in the wet conditions. He believed she was travelling at between 50 and 60 mph in a 40 mph area and saw Toni's car hit the nearside kerb, then veer to the other side of the road. Toni suffered minor injuries. A blood sample showed she was two and a half times over the legal limit. Traces of cannabis were also found in her blood. In July 1994, after pleading guilty to driving without due care and attention when over the alcohol limit, she was jailed for five years and disqualified from driving for ten years. The judge labelled her as a 'menace and a danger to the public'. She was sent to Holloway, where she discontinued the alcohol counselling she had undertaken post-crash, pre-sentencing.*

**Mark Wheeller:** I saw her after her second car accident before she went to prison. That affected us, because we had a little cottage industry around *Too Much Punch For Judy*. The play had been doing well and the ending was her saying, 'I'll never do anything like this again, I'll never drink-drive again.' Then she had this second accident – 100 metres down the road. I thought the play would have to stop. She greeted me at the door and just burst into tears. Her words were, 'I've dropped a bollock.' She said she was really proud of the play, it was a good thing and she wanted it to continue and she offered to talk about the second accident so we could use it in the play. She said the first half of my life has been seriously bad, the second half needs to be better. I added the second accident to the play. Then the issue was raised around the fact Toni was earning money from a crime [the play's royalties Wheeller had agreed to give her]. Very quickly I said, 'Well, let Leanne have it, her daughter.' [The parents of Penny Jessup, however, protested about this arrangement]. Now the money goes to an alcohol and drug advisory service [somewhere in Harlow] who were the people who supported Toni in the months after the second accident, and they still receive a proportion of the money that comes from the play. At that point it hadn't been anywhere near as successful as it now is.

**Toby Marriott:** The first few years after Steve died, I felt the need to be around Toni – felt I would get some answers to my questions. Then after a while of being around her I realised she didn't really have anything to give me in terms of finality. Trouble seemed to follow her around. Any time I was out with her and a group, something bad would happen. She got attacked on an escalator at Victoria station – just some random guy who started yelling at her. I remember a woman collapsing on her on a train... I met her and her boyfriend in New York once. When I arrived, they had been fighting so bad that he had headbutted the hotel room window and broke it. Then the next day while we were walking through Greenwich Village a gypsy-looking woman on the side of the road started screaming at her. It was really strange.

*While Toni was in prison, the bootlegging of Marriott's post-Humble Pie material grew exponentially. Almost every cassette that could be found was considered ripe for exploitation. But Marriott's legacy, fortunately, did not rest on his solo work, his multitude of haphazard late night collaborations, or his work with The Firm, Packet of Three, Official Receivers or indeed The Next Band – although undoubtedly there were gems there to discovered. In 1996 the veneration of the Small Faces began in earnest when the band was handed a prestigious Ivor Novello Award for Outstanding Contribution to Music. Ray Davies of The Kinks did the honours at a ceremony at the Grosvenor hotel on Park Lane. His mum, Kath, represented Marriott. 'Steve would have hated to grow old,' she said. Marriott's father, Bill, died in 1996, aged 83. Kath said he had been going 'downhill' since Marriott's death. 'He was so proud of Steve,' she said. The same year, 1996, there was a BBC radio documentary about the band and a tribute album,* Long Ago And Worlds Apart, *with contemporary bands covering Small Faces songs, with profits intended to go Ronnie Lane. Eddie Piller, the boy holding the 'Itchycoo Park' sign, the early eighties Marriott acolyte who was now running the hugely successful Acid Jazz record label, who had hits with Galliano and Brand New Heavies, was behind the project. It became clear that it was not just the Marriott estate in some desperate sort of turmoil.*

**Eddie Piller:** Acid Jazz was going through Warner's at the time. We hatched a plot that I'd get an advance of $200,000 that would go direct from Warner's to Ronnie in Texas. I got Oasis, Blur, Primal Scream, [Paul] Weller, most of the main Britpop bands, and I got M People to do a version of 'Itchycoo Park' and then somebody realised this money wouldn't be going through the Trust Fund [Ronnie Lane's Estate] that was administered by a lawyer. They started a misinformation campaign about me among the acts. It got to be disgusting. I'm still heartbroken because Ronnie died a year and half later in absolute penury. I walked away, half of the groups walked away. They released the album and I think it raised about £5,000 and, worse, they turned down M People, saying we don't want this kind of bollocks on our album and M People put the record out themselves and it got to No 1 [UK No 11]. It was one of the most embarrassing episodes of my career.

*Lane died in 1997, aged 51, in Trinidad, Colorado, from pneumonia in the progressive stages of multiple sclerosis. He was said to have been living in a mobile home, supported by little more than goodwill.*

*The first Small Faces Convention, which would become an annual event, also took place in 1996. It was held at the Ruskin Arms pub and organised by Steve Ellis and Dean Powell (1967–2013).*

**Steve Ellis:** It was a debt of honour to do the Ruskin Arms. If it wasn't for Steve I'd have never got into this in the first place. I was 15 [in 1965] when I saw the Small Faces doing 'Whatcha Gonna Do About It' on the TV and I went, 'Fucking hell, I can do that.' I was in a Mod gang and they put me forward for an audition. Next thing is we [Love Affair] are supporting them at the Albert Hall for the Aberfan disaster 1966, all these little Moddy girls down the front screaming at Steve. Dorothy Squires was on the same bill and she bent down and slapped one screaming girl around the face and they pulled her off stage and crucified her. When we had a No 1 [with 'Everlasting Love' in 1968] we were on *Top Of The Pops* and they were doing 'Tin Soldier' and Steve sent two bottles of champagne over. The first convention was primarily about Steve. I thought Steve had not had a proper acknowledgement. He'd been ignored. A couple of years later it morphed into the Small Faces Convention. Dean was a big-time boxing promoter/cut man, Frank Warren's right-hand man. It took us several months to put together. We had coachloads coming up from Brighton. Paul Weller put the PA on. I played the first one. My band was the house band. I got Kenney Jones to come down to rehearsals but he was a no-show. Dennis Greaves [from blues band Nine Below Zero] and [Steve] Cradock [from Ocean Colour

Scene] played. It was a wonderful night. It's where I met Kay [Marriott's mum Kath preferred to be called Kay in later life] and the family, Kay Jr, young little Steve [Kay Jr's son]. Kay, his mother, said the love of Steve's life was Jenny and he never got over that. She also said that Steve's downfall was the drink.

When Dean said we're thinking about turning this into some kind of convention, I wasn't sure but I was on the committee. Dean's my mate so I did the first couple [of annual conventions, also at the Ruskin Arms] and then I stopped. I didn't like the way it was rolling out: money was getting misappropriated. Dean wasn't taking it. Toni was out of prison and she turned up one time at the Ruskin Arms and she was really rude to me, very rude. I just walked away. I heard these stories where's she turned up saying, 'That's my money.' [This relates to an earlier aborted attempt at a convention.]

*The annual Small Faces convention continued. In 2009 it was held at the O2 Academy, in Islington, and attracted 1,000 fans from Japan, the US, Europe, willing to pay £20 a ticket. In 2001, on the tenth anniversary of Marriott's death, there was a memorial concert held at the 2,000-capacity Astoria Theatre in London. The event sold out and on the night the twelve-year bar record for the venue was broken. Guest performers, largely corralled by Ellis and Jerry Shirley, included Paul Weller, Noel Gallagher, Midge Ure and a reformed version of Humble Pie featuring Shirley, Dave Clempson, Peter Frampton and Greg Ridley, who died two years later of pneumonia and resulting complications.*

**Steve Ellis:** At the Astoria, Kay [Sr] heard me doing 'Afterglow' with The Mods [also featuring John 'Rhino' Edwards] at the soundcheck and she said, 'A shudder went through me.' Steve's mum became one of my best mates. I used to call her 'mum' in the end. Laurie [O'Leary] had motor neurone disease and he said to me, 'If I go, look after Kay Sr.' I used to keep, what me and Kay Sr called the vampires away, all these people out there bootlegging stuff. I got a bad reputation for doing the right thing. Jenny [Dearden] had some old tapes of Steve's and someone took them from her and put them out... these people make me sick. *All Too Beautiful* [Marriott biography, published 2004] seriously upset Kay and her family. [Co-author, John] Hellier took all Kay's personal pictures of Steve when he was a kid and whacked them in the book. I got hold of [the book's other co-author] Paolo [Hewitt] and said I want paying: he was trying to say it's public. I said I want £1,000 for Kay. They dished up £600. Hellier, in Mac's [Ian McLagan's] words, is a piece of shit. And I'll endorse that 100 per cent. [Hellier assisted in the making of a sixty-minute Marriott documentary circa 2002, *The Life & Times of Steve Marriott*. It was financed by American producers and went out on video and later on DVD. The official nature of the project was uncertain and participants complained to this author that their interview material was used elsewhere without permission.]

*The 2001 Astoria tribute concert brought together three of Marriott's children, Mollie, 15, Toby, 25, and Tonya, 17, for the first time. Mollie was in a popular girl band, D2M and had been since she was 12 – they regularly toured Europe. As a teenager Toby had been a promising footballer, trialling with several professional football clubs. After moving back to America in 1996 he began performing in bands, notably The Clinic.*

**Mollie Marriott:** The [Astoria] concert was great. It should have been in a bigger venue, it was scarily packed. It wasn't until that night that it hit me, everything about my dad. Not only was it the first time I'd met up with Toby and Tonya but it was the first time I'd seen my nan since I was young, seen my stepmother [Toni] since I used to stay there with Dad. It was such a difficult night in that respect. My brother [who performed on the night, as did Mollie] got wasted. I had to keep my mother [Manon Piercey had married Joe Brown in 2000; his wife Vicki died in 1991; George Harrison was their best man; Brown became Mollie's stepfather] away from my stepmother [Toni's daughter Leanne was also at the concert, she was a new mother]. It was all really stressful and emotional. I was working [singing backing vocals] with Oasis at the time so it was cool to have Noel there and it was great to see Zak Starkey [Ringo Starr's son was the drummer in the house band that night, led by former Bad Company guitarist Dave 'Bucket' Colwell, and also featuring Bobby Tench, Steve Ellis, Rick Wills, Billy Nicholls and Debbie Bonham], Humble Pie and Weller, but everyone was pissed off, grumpy, because it was so badly organised backstage with so many people and not enough dressing rooms. The name of the [concert release] CD was *One More Time For The Ol' Tosser* [a three-CD set released in 2005], so classless, made me so mad.

**Jerry Shirley:** Soon after the show was in place, we got wind of the most tasteless piece of merchandise we had ever heard of. John Hellier had arranged to have Steve Marriott ashtrays produced for sale at the show. When we found out, through the late great Dean Powell, we immediately put a stop to it. How tactless and untasteful, not to mention thoughtless and uncaring for the feelings of Steve's mother, sister, children, ex-wives and bandmates. Steve Ellis was really responsible for getting the concert organised. All Hellier did was interfere and cause unnecessary waves between the big name acts by trying to be their best mate. Of all the performers none of them came with lots of wardrobe changes, it wasn't that type of show. But Hellier changed his stupid shirts a total of twelve times during the show. He was supposed to be sorting out the backstage arrangements – which he fucked up royally – and was to act as the MC. We were all horrified by his crass approach. And when it came to doing the credits the only person who got a producers' credit for the concert was John Hellier; neither Steve Ellis nor I were even mentioned in that category when in fact we did all the work, along with Chris France who made sure that I was on board. It was basically Chris who had the idea in the first place and approached me to organise it for him. Steve Ellis was on board out of respect, plus he and I have been friends since we were in our early teens.

**Steve Ellis:** After the Astoria [Memorial Concert], which was a real stomping success, John Weller [Paul Weller's father] said to me, 'Steve, where's all this money going?' There's about three different versions of the Astoria gig. The first one was an official tribute [a 2002 CD, *Mustn't Grumble*, which preceded a more dubious 2004 DVD] and then someone put out *One More Time For The Ol' Tosser*. How gutter can you get?

**Chris France:** The Astoria gig in 2001 was laying down a marker, bringing Peter Frampton over, Noel Gallagher and Paul Weller turning up to pay respects. It was a really good show. It was going to be in aid of the Small Faces charity, Kenney's little baby, and it all became too difficult to deal with. It did get put out but I wish I'd never thought about recording it, just done the show.

*Chris France was now running the Marriott estate. He had been a music promoter in the early eighties before starting his own successful rap/dance record label Music Of Life in 1986. He'd also been involved in publishing and management. His hook-up with Toni came about via Kenney Jones, whose old accountant had been helping look after the Marriott estate.*

**Kenney Jones:** I gave Toni ample opportunity to give the kids some of the money she gets and she didn't do it. Toni's reputation precedes her everywhere she goes. She doesn't deserve a penny of the money. It's shocking. It should have gone to his kids. When she dies, where does the money go?

*Jones was introduced to Chris France by his new accountant and together they had spent two years in pursuit of monies Jones felt were owed the Small Faces (publishing monies relating to Avakak and record royalties which at the time were non-existent).*

**Kenney Jones:** Our band accountant Milton Marks never filed the accounts so the company Avakak got struck off. Chris and I weren't sure if the state, the UK Revenue, owned it. We called and they said they didn't so the door was wide open. Chris threatened legal action against EMI [who had taken over the Immediate Music publishing catalogue from United Artists], claiming the back money was millions. We thought there was a cover-up between UA and EMI. All these people need to inform directors of changes. The four of us owned Avakak and that's what we were trying to prove. In the band days, because I wasn't a principal songwriter, I would get a royalty cheque for one shilling and six pence, and three months later I would get a cheque for three and half grand, my share of the company profits. EMI had lots of money to spend on lawyers and we didn't.

*Soon after being hooked up with Toni, France stopped working with Jones and moved to live in the south of France, where he still resides.*

**Chris France:** I've been looking after his [Steve Marriott's] business [estate] for twenty years now. I took over the estate in 1998 after Toni had been released from prison. Steve died intestate [without a will] so the law says Toni, as his wife, automatically inherited the rights. That's the legal position. There was quite a long period where she tried to help the family, particularly his mum, and then they had a huge falling-out.

423

By the time I got to it, Toni was spitting feathers about Steve's mum and his mum was also spitting feathers about Toni: they'd got into a very deep, bitter row. There's very bad blood between Toni and the whole family. I think I'd be bitter in that situation, if my father had left his rights to a new wife and I didn't get anything from it, but that's not my job; my job is to look after the rights. I stay out of the personal. If he had made a will he could have looked after his kids. I saw the documentation quite early on and it was simply the probate office offered the guidance, it was the probate office's decision based on the intestacy. Toni was in the right place at the right time.

Toni was a heavy drinker before she went into prison and when she came out the whole estate was in complete mess. He was being bootlegged everywhere, particularly live tapes, and a few studio bits and pieces... nobody was taking care of business. Kenney persuaded me to meet up with Toni and try and help her out and that's what I did. She was chaotic. It took about three years of unravelling and suing people, reminding people of the rights, collecting royalties. It was a big ask. In the period Toni was in prison everybody knew nobody was taking care of business so lots of people were bootlegging and putting things out illegally, pretending to own rights they didn't have. It was a case of having to go round and perfect people's rights rather than having a nice open market-place and go, 'Who wants these [tapes]?' We sued a couple of people, [such as] Receiver Records... and the word got around that we can't abuse this anymore. John Hellier was chief culprit. He thinks he's Steve Marriott. Toni won't deal with him. Mac before he died would not deal with him. I kept him onside a little bit because I wanted to know what he was doing. We don't deal with him, we just keep an eye on what he is doing and stop him doing things he shouldn't be doing, like just this month [May 2019] he, with Easy Action, was going to put out an album of Humble Pie called *Illegal Smile* but we stopped him doing that. Tim Hinkley was another one we had to stop from ripping us off. He kept putting the 'Scrubbers' [1975 recordings] album out and getting an advance and not paying us anything.

**Alan Wicket:** I saw Toni again and she was on a mammoth bender and she said she was a professional waste of time. She was still reeling from Steve's death. She'd had tragedy in her life.

**Mollie Marriott:** Toby was staying with Toni not long after the Astoria and I think she did give him some money but there was a very toxic relationship. It's terrible what she did with Steve's music [after he died]. They were just demos and he would have been devastated they were released. They're demos for a reason. It was just another way of making money. It angers me. Us kids have nothing to do with the estate: me, Tonya, Lesley and Toby. We never have had anything. I got sent £200 when I was 17 and that's the only communication I've had from the estate. But it's not about the money: it's the principle. She [Toni] shouldn't have anything to do with my dad's estate. It should go to the kids. Toby should be managing it. It worries us now because when she dies what's going to happen to it? She's got his blonde Gibson 335 that my mum bought him [circa 1984] and she won't give that over, and my mum and [step]dad [Joe Brown] want that to go to Toby. I know it's the law but you would think any decent person would pass it over.

*It is worth noting here that the value in vintage guitars is high, especially those with heritage. For instance, when Marriott left Atlanta in 1983, he left behind a 1957 Les Paul. In good condition it would have been worth $3,000. As it was damaged it didn't fetch anything like that. A couple of years ago, the same guitar, refurbished, sold for $30,000.*

**Pam Marriott Land:** Toby went and spent a month with Toni and he will not talk about it. He said she's the most evil woman and these are evil people and that he doesn't want a dime from the estate ever. He will not even discuss it with me. I did send him to counselling so he could discuss it with someone.

*After his band The Clinic broke up, Toby formed The Strays, who released an album in 2005, and attained a level of celebrity in America. His final band, before he gave up on the music business, Black Drummer, released an EP in 2012.*

**Chris France:** Toni tried to help Toby for about a year, living with him, put him in the studio.

**Toby Marriott:** About five years after Steve died, she met Chris France through Kenney Jones. They set up what, at the time, was a licensing company to collect all of Steve's royalties that he hadn't received (or

425

cared to) over the years, going after record companies that had released any of his material. Toni also represented Steve in the Small Faces company/agreement called Avakak. When it was set up, Toni said I would be sent £500 a month and be part of the estate. I've never been quite sure what their true intentions were for this, since I was the only child of Steve's that had some sort of legal rights to his estate. At the time, £500 seemed like a fortune, so I shut my mouth and happily collected for several years. Eventually, we fell out and cut ties: a decision that I feel was the right one. I called and left a message that I didn't want the money anymore, and that was that. I felt then, as I do now, that she is a bad representation of Steve Marriott and I feel a lot of people will agree. With the contract with me, apparently Toni used to go around saying five years, if he doesn't do anything in five years he can't do anything. I didn't do anything. I just couldn't be bothered. All I can say is that if I was married to someone for twenty-four months and died knowing that that person, as well as their boyfriends, had lived off the fortune I had made (before meeting them) for thirty years without helping my children, I would roll in my grave, as most parents would. I'm not sure what Steve would have thought about this. He probably would just tell us that it's just money and to get on with our lives instead of getting involved with the mess he made. Which we all have. But to have these people represent him is very hard for myself and Steve's other kids to accept.

*Kath – estranged from Toni, a widow, still grieving for Marriott, with Kay, living in Portugal – wanted to get to know her grandkids. She had been visited by Lesley Ashcroft, Marriott's first daughter, who had flown over from her home in New Zealand. She took along her baby son.*

**Mollie Marriott:** Nan reached out when I was a teenager and said she wanted to see me. I was unsure because she'd never wanted to see me before. She'd pushed me away. I saw my aunt Kay and we got on really well and she said, 'Mum's here.' I walked in the kitchen and saw her face and I had to go out and stand in the garden. I couldn't see her. I thought, regardless what you've done to me, I know what you did to my dad as a child. She got upset and there was a huge traumatic drama. Kay said, 'I don't think I can see you anymore because you've really upset my mum,' and then my sister [Tonya, also a musician and singer, living in Canada] went to see her and Nan turned on her, and then Nan turned on Toby.

**Toby Marriott:** Tonya and I tried to put Mollie and her mum in contact when Nan was getting on, almost 90, to patch things up, but it just wasn't meant to be. Nan moved about five years before she died, moved in next to Steve's sister in Bishop's Stortford. She was in that house in Stoneleigh, Sawbridgeworth, for forty years.

*Chris France did the best he could with what he called the 'low-quality' releases relating to Marriott's post-Humble Pie material, the 'more marginal material'. He called it 'a collector's niche market'. He also, for his 20 per cent cut, straightened out what he could relating to the estate's income from the Small Faces and Humble Pie.*

**Chris France:** The estate now earns a very decent living wage for Toni out of Steve's royalties. It wouldn't be too hard to look up the accounts of Steve Marriott Licensing Limited.

*Turnover was £123,000 in 1999, worth about £200,000 today but more recent figures show income at a steady £20,000–£30,000.*

**Mollie Marriott:** They've always told us there is hardly anything coming into the estate.

*After Marriott's death, not including reissues of the original albums or re-mastered versions, there has been a steady flow of Humble Pie compilation packages, including:* Early Years *(1994),* Hot 'N' Nasty: The Anthology *(1994),* The Immediate Years: Natural Born Boogie *(1999),* The Best Of Humble Pie *(2000),* The Definitive Collection *(2006), and two volumes of a lavish box set package,* Official Bootleg Vol. 1 *and* Official Bootleg Vol. 2 *(2017/2018). Jerry Shirley curated the latter releases, as he does much of Humble Pie's legacy. He had been advised by Bob Dylan to take ownership of these live Humble Pie recordings, make them sound as good as possible and package them with care and class, to prevent bootleggers continuing to make money from them.*

**Jerry Shirley:** I now have control of almost all of it and I have managed to put a stop to a number of releases by folks who were stomping all over copyright controls that are mine. It was Steve's way of saying sorry by giving me the sole rights to the use of the name. Those bootlegs have made the bootleggers a fortune; at least I have put a stop to that. We have not made a lot of money from them but we spent a great deal making them as good as they can possibly be.

**Chris France:** Steve doesn't get record royalties from Humble Pie. He wanted to get out of his contract [with Dee Anthony] and basically Dee said to Steve, 'Okay, well, you hand over all your rights.' In those days the future rights were just not perceived as valuable so Steve happily signed away his rights to get out of his deal. I went through this [with lawyers], about undue influence, but they said he got value out of it because by freeing himself from Dee he could sign another deal, so it wasn't undue influence, it was a straightforward commercial decision that he made. We couldn't challenge that so the whole *Fillmore* [i.e. live album and peak period] section of Humble Pie [in terms of record royalties] we get nothing from. It goes to the Dee Anthony estate. We still get the publishing money but none of the money from record rights.

**Jerry Shirley:** When Humble Pie broke up we were only maybe a year or so away from paying back our debt to A&M; however, the contract that Dee had us sign meant they could take the loss from one record and deduct it from the profit of another one. Steve went off and recorded *Marriott* and something like half a million dollars later it didn't sell squat. It took the band fifteen years to pay off Steve's solo debt and start earning royalties.

*Where to start with the Small Faces reissues? In 1997, there was a substantial two-CD box set,* The Masters. *In 2003 the* Small Faces Ultimate Collection, *which sold 64,000 copies. The various vinyl and CD releases between 1976 and 1997, who knows?*

**Chris France:** For a time Castle Records were just licensing the hell out of stuff – they had a licensing deal with Tony Calder, who was in Antigua – and we [France and Kenney Jones] finally went there when the guy [Castle owner Terry Shand] was trying to sell Castle [1994] and he came up with a deal to pay the band a lump sum for past royalties [a figure paid in 1997, said to be circa £250,000, almost £450,000 today] and agreed to a percentage for future royalties [15 per cent].

**Kenney Jones:** I did a deal with Terry Shand. Castle was paying a peppercorn royalty, 1 per cent or 1.25 per cent. My old accountant fixed up a meeting. Shand said, 'I want to put things right, I'm selling Castle Communications.' I demanded 15 per cent for the royalties. Ever since then we've been doing really well.

*Castle had acquired the rights from NEMS in 1983 and exploited the Small Faces catalogue for over a decade. There were many complications, chiefly dating back to 1975, when Patrick Meehan Jr initially acquired UK rights to Immediate's back catalogue from the liquidator for NEMS, sparking the Small Faces reunion. At the same time Andrew Loog Oldham assigned various Immediate European rights to Charly Records for, he stated, a $10,000 advance. Oldham has retained – post-liquidation – control of the Immediate catalogue outside of the UK. It had been Oldham who had sold the rights to Humble Pie's first two albums to A&M for the 1973 American repackaging job. He had licensed other Immediate rights outside the UK to A&M and Sire Records, stating he had made close to $250,000 from such deals. In 1975, there had been heated arguments between Meehan Jr and Oldham, which Calder attempted to assuage by inviting Oldham on board with NEMS/Immediate as 'director of special projects'. This went badly when at the Midem Music festival Don Arden clashed violently with Patrick Meehan Jr over control of Black Sabbath and then put a gun in Calder's mouth. Arden was then attacked, headbutted and his daughter Sharon Osbourne flew at the assailant with a marble coffee table. Oldham sided with Arden. The issue between NEMS and Charly was never fully resolved.*

**Andrew Loog Oldham:** Between 1976 and 1983, Charly and NEMS carved up territories and stayed out of each other's way. In 1983, as CDs came along and jump-started the next twenty years, Meehan Jr, having parted with Calder, sold NEMS to Castle, who put out everything Immediate had ever recorded on CD for the next seventeen years. Castle kept to the UK. Charly continued to exploit the back catalogue worldwide.

429

*In 2000 the Castle catalogue was acquired by Sanctuary, who were taken over by Universal in 2007. BMG acquired the Sanctuary catalogue for $50 million in 2012.*

**Chris France:** We still get record royalties for the Immediate stuff that goes through Charly for the world and BMG for the UK. We all get paid. Some of the early recordings are with Decca now so they must have bought them from Don. Steve's not getting ripped off anymore and that's been the case for the past twelve, thirteen years.

*In terms of Marriott's music publishing from the Small Faces songs, his most significant body of work remains in Avakak, the company set up with Immediate Music in 1967. After Immediate went bust the company was taken over by United Artists, who in turn were taken over by EMI in the late seventies. No one this author spoke to was satisfied with EMI's handling of the Immediate catalogue, not least Kenney Jones, who continues to fight for his share in Avakak. EMI was subsequently taken over by Sony.*

**Chris France:** Sony sends regular publishing statements [to this day]. Marriott/Lane, who wrote nearly all the songs, receive a chunk of any publishing income, Kenney doesn't. Kenney feels he should share ownership of the copyrights and they would be worth a great deal of money, and of course he'd also get a share of the publishing.

*France also collects publishing monies on Marriott's songs post-Humble Pie and also on the Small Faces period under Don Arden's management.*

**Chris France:** Steve did sign a big money deal with [Freddy Bienstock at] Carlin and that is now recouped, we are now earning money from that, relating to material after Steve left Dee. It was an advance on songs to be written and there's nothing really big in there. Don [Arden] had the publishing for 'All Or Nothing'... and Aviation Music bought it from Don.

*There continued to be hiccups.*

**Eddie Piller:** In 2007 I licensed some material from Hellier for the Acid Jazz rare Mod series [*Steve Marriott's Moments* EP, released 2008]. He

430

implied to me it was on behalf of Marriott's wife's estate so I paid over my £750 and licensed a couple of tracks, as well as Steve Marriott & The Moments tracks from World Artists, 'You Really Got Me' and a track called 'Money'. We did particularly well on the EP, sold quite a few thousand and I got a call to say, 'Why have you bootlegged Steve Marriott? You of all people should have respected Steve's copyrights.' I said, 'I don't know what you're talking about, I've got a signed contract here on behalf of the Marriott estate,' but this was the real Marriott estate phoning me up.

*The family continued to feel locked out.*

**Steve Ellis:** I got in the middle of an email conversation a record label was having, patting each other on the back, Small Faces album's done so well, got yourself a gold disc. I said, 'What about his mother?' 'Oh, we'll get one made up.' 'You do that.' I took it up, she couldn't believe it, and she started crying.

*In 2012, the Small Faces were inducted (jointly alongside the Faces) into America's Rock & Roll Hall of Fame. Toni did not attend.*

**Chris France:** We found out the day before it was happening. Kenney knew months before. We'd definitely have gone over for it and enjoyed the moment but it was too short notice.

*A line-up of the Faces, including Ronnie Wood, Kenney Jones and Ian McLagan, with Mick Hucknall of Simply Red on vocals, played three songs including 'All Or Nothing'. Mollie provided back-up vocals.*

**Mollie Marriott:** I got dragged up [on stage]. Ronnie [Wood] grabbed one hand and Kenney grabbed the other. It was an incredible evening.

**Kenney Jones:** I asked Mollie to be there to receive the award for her dad.

*Steven Van Zandt, of the E Street Band and* The Sopranos, *inducted the band. 'Not too many bands get a second life,' he started. 'In this case I'm sure it helped having not just one, but miraculously two of the greatest white soul singers in the history of rock'n'roll, Steve Marriott and Rod Stewart. Steve was a child actor and walked away from a very promising acting career, deciding that music was a much better fit with his attention deficit disorder, long before it was fashionable…'*

**Toby Marriott:** At the Rock & Roll Hall of Fame, Chris called and asked us to send the award to Toni the next day. Me and Mollie decided to give it to Tonya, who hadn't received anything of Steve's and was rightfully due to get something. Toni has to have everything: his money, belongings, his awards. Total control. I think this whole role as acting director of Steve Marriott licensing, or whatever it is now, gives her this delusional sense of purpose and, more importantly, power; something she definitely wouldn't have achieved had she not met Steve.

*To coincide with the Rock & Roll Hall of Fame event, there were re-releases of what were billed as 'definitive newly expanded re-mastered editions' of four Small Faces albums,* From The Beginning, Small Faces, There Are But Four Small Faces *and* Ogdens'. *The albums were cut from the original masters and well reviewed. There was also freshly minted merchandise.*

*Toni, said to be remarried, suffered serious injury circa 2014/2015.*

**Chris France:** Toni had a very serious brain haemorrhage and, although she's made a good recovery, she's very tender. She's not as mentally robust as she was, she often repeats herself and when we speak every month she will ask about stuff we'd gone through the previous time. There was a year after the haemorrhage when she was not compos mentis. She's also an alcoholic in remission; she shouldn't really be talked to. I don't know if you've tried to talk to her but I'd prefer it if you didn't. I am concerned for her.

**Jim Leverton:** She took a fall at home and cracked her head on a stone fireplace and damaged her brain and she's never been the same since. I have seen her and she's not with you at all. She's not there.

**Manon Piercey:** I feel a bit mean knocking her now because she's not right. I don't know if she had a stroke or an aneurysm… she can't speak properly and she's still drinking, really drinking. I'm amazed she's alive. I wanted her to give Toby the 335 blonde Dot but she won't. She's got it under her bed. She remarried but I believe her husband died of drugs. Joe's [Joe Brown] upset [about her handling of his music] because there's stuff she put out that Steve would have been appalled with… anything to get money I suppose.

*Marriott's profile continued to rise. Val Weedon arranged for a green plaque to be put up outside Don Arden's offices on Carnaby Street in 2015. It read: 'Impresario Don Arden and Mod band "Small Faces" (Steve Marriott, Ronnie Lane, Kenney Jones, Ian McLagan and Jimmy Winston) worked here 1965– 1967.' Jones did the unveiling. 'Kenney is quite gracious about Don and he does recognise if it wasn't for Don they would not have got that break,' said Weedon.*

**Kenney Jones:** I've always had a soft spot for Don. We all did – deep down. He was a good man. He was fun to be with and he put us on the map. He was a big teddy bear, never the hood he wanted to be known for. I don't forgive him for ripping us off and selling us for £25,000 and all kinds of shit but, at the end of the day, the times we had in the beginning were good.

*There was also a short Steve Marriott biopic film shot in 2015. Well-known actor and long-time Marriott fan Martin Freeman, famed for TV roles in* The Office *and* Sherlock *and his film role in* The Hobbit, *took the role of an ageing, drunk, down-and-out Marriott arriving to play a tiny grubby pub gig in 1985 on the same day his contemporaries are playing Wembley Stadium as part of the Live Aid concert – shown on the pub's TV. Freeman, drinking heavily, talks bitterly to the few people in the pub about the irony in the situation. The climax has Freeman playing his heart out to a small crowd. Titled* Midnight Of My Life, *the film was directed by the veteran British actor Phil Davis, who starred in the film* Vera Drake, *the iconic 1979 Mod film* Quadrophenia, *as well as the BBC's* Whitechapel *TV series. It had been made with just £12,000, all crowdfunded, and screenwriter Nina Gerstenberger was hoping to attract interest in a feature film.*

**Eddie Piller:** The short film was Hellier, so I wouldn't have anything to do with it.

**Jerry Shirley:** I hated *Midnight Of My Life*. It was awful. I can also assure you that nobody who really knew Steve would have anything to do with Hellier. He just made money out of making people believe that he was close to Steve, when Steve disliked the guy immensely. The film is a lie from start to finish. He was not even in the country when Live Aid happened, let alone in a sleazy pub talking as if he were an embittered old man. He had many faults but I have seen him misrepresented so many times and I can say without a shadow of a doubt that 'bitter' is one word that does not describe him accurately. On the night of Live Aid we were on tour in Scandinavia, playing to packed houses, on a day off, watching Live Aid on the TV. It was me, Jim and our wonderful roadie John Skinner who were saying to him, 'You should be opening that show with "Whatcha Gonna Do About It", the place would have gone nuts.' He was his old sober self at the time and all he said was, 'Nah, God bless 'em, let them do the job, I am glad they are doing something about it.' For what it's worth, he and I donated on the phone lines a healthy part of the next night's proceeds.

*Through 2016–17 there was a 'Mod musical', All Or Nothing, touring the country. Loosely based on Marriott's life and featuring the Small Faces' songs, it was written, directed and produced by actress and writer Carol Harrison, best known for her TV roles in sitcom* Brush Strokes *and soap drama* EastEnders. *She was born in West Ham and was married at one point to Jamie Foreman, son of London gangster Freddie Foreman. 'My aunt lived two streets away from Steve's mum, my cousin knew him, and another cousin was in a band with him,' she said. 'He came round to our house when I was 8 years old and he was just this amazing bundle of effervescence and talent. I had a bit of a crush on him. I wanted to tell their story and explore how they were so ripped off.' The musical had been in the making since circa 2012.*

**Steve Ellis:** Carol called and asked if I could set up to meet Kay Sr. She [Kay] said, 'She can come and see me. I'll make my own mind up about her.' Carol went up there and Kay gave her blessing to Carol. Then she never got to see it because she was passed away [2015]. She was coming up to 90.

**Carol Harrison:** Steve's mother died before we opened. She was not very well, but I was hoping we'd get it on before she went. When I first met her to talk about writing the show, she was very pleased that I was going to play her. She'd liked me in *EastEnders* and she even said to me, 'You've got the right look. You're glamorous,' and I was very glamorous.

*Mollie Marriott acted as vocal coach on the musical, which transferred to London's West End for a short run in 2018.*

**Mollie Marriott:** It's been great to keep the spirit of the band alive… a really cool way to pass it on to another generation.

*Jerry Shirley and Jenny Dearden have all enjoyed the show. Kenney Jones less so.*

**Jerry Shirley:** It is a musical fantasy. When you have a guy talking to the audience from the grave, with a pint of beer in his hand, it is hardly based on factual correctness.

**Kenney Jones:** The musical portrayed him in a terrible way, as a drunken drug addict looking back on his life.

**Chris France:** The band has no rights in the stage play. They don't pay the guys [Small Faces and their estates] anything. We don't support that stage show. Marriott/Lane as songwriters get paid from performances [of their songs] in the theatres but Kenney is not getting anything.

*In 2017, for a 'BBC Music Day', forty-seven historic blue plaques were unveiled, celebrating iconic musicians and venues. Those honoured with a blue plaque include David Bowie, broadcaster John Peel, Delia Derbyshire (who composed the* Doctor Who *theme tune) and Steve Marriott. The plaque went up at Beehive Cottage.*

**Mollie Marriott:** I was invited down by the BBC, who were covering it, and I invited Jenny.

*Mollie was forging a career of her own as a solo artist. Her debut solo album featured a guest appearance from Paul Weller. Mollie and Jenny, however, did not ultimately appear at the unveiling. Mollie claimed John Hellier had told the BBC that she might cause problems and he would be the better person to represent Marriott. Mollie only learned this after the fact. The BBC apologised. On social media Mollie very publicly communicated her dislike of Hellier to fans of her father.*

**Toby Marriott:** All Steve's children were told that we couldn't attend a plaque showing at Beehive Cottage because the Marriott estate didn't want us there. This was messaged, by John Hellier, to the current owner of the cottage. This was the house I was literally born in.

**Jerry Shirley:** I found out that Hellier had wormed his way into the good graces of the current owners of Beehive Cottage and convinced them that he was the only close friend of Steve's that could and should represent Steve Marriott at this unveiling, because Mollie and Jenny, the love of his life, who had spent the best years at Beehive with Steve, had a legal dispute with the Marriott estate, which was total nonsense. In fact it was Mollie who the BBC came to in order to get advice on where the plaque should be placed. Hellier was going on vacation and didn't want any of us there who had disagreed with him. So he taped an interview and went on holiday. I got wind of it and went ballistic. He tried to pitch himself as the leading authority on all things Marriott but Steve hated him and told him all kinds of lies just to wind him up. I was contacted by the BBC and they asked me to tell them the truth, which I did. They erased Hellier's interview and used one from me as the representative of my dear friend and his family. Hellier was Steve's pet hate. He called him Engelbert Humperdinck [they looked similar].

**Mollie Marriott:** Every interview I do I always get asked that question: Steve Marriott being your dad, is it a help or hindrance? It's a help that I've got to know these people [such as Paul Weller] but it's a lot of pressure. And all the darkness that surrounds it... every interview you do it's brought up, and from the interviewers' point of view they just want to get a good story but they don't realise you then have to go through that mental pain again. That's why I've said I'm not talking about it anymore. This is the last time. I just want to move on.

*Mollie admits struggling to cope in her 20s. She is still estranged from her aunt, Kay.*

**Mollie Marriott:** If you look at everyone who was on a stage as a kid, they have a mental breakdown. It comes out at some point. My dad definitely used the stage as an escape: when you're on that stage it feels as if you're a completely different person and then you come off stage and you're hit with all the realities again.

*The Small Faces machine rolls on. In 2018, Rob Caiger, label manager and producer at Charly Records, and Kenney Jones, oversaw the release of a fiftieth-anniversary edition of* Ogdens'. *It received the best reviews of the band's career.*

**Rob Caiger:** Five star reviews all the way through, *Sunday Times* reissue of the week, *Mojo* – five stars, *Uncut* – massive feature article on it. And there's more to come, globally. We know the market's there: the [anniversary edition] box set [of *Ogdens'*] was around £50 or £60 for the vinyl and they've all gone. If I had known I would have tripled the initial pressing. Sainsbury wanted *Ogdens'* on red vinyl, 2,500 copies. They all sold out in six days. Timeless album, timeless artist…

**Pam Marriott Land:** I loved him in spite of who he was. If he were alive would we be friends today? I'm sure of it. We went through so much together and you cannot ask for a better man than his son. Toby is the opposite of Steve; he gave up his music career to raise his daughter. So now he's making great money in the software business and he plays with his friends on weekends. I'm very close to Steve's daughters, Tonya and Mollie. Since those years with Steve, I was able to reinvent my life. I've kept so much of my past quiet due to the fact I did not want my employers to know, especially since for the last twenty years I've flown the richest and most powerful people in the world. The last thing I needed is for them to know what a drug-addled loser I was. But I can't do this to Steve. I need to own my part.

**Christine Lore:** She commands a fleet of jets, NetJets, that is owned by one of the richest guys in the world [Warren Buffett] and he adores Pam, and Pam, all by herself, is in charge of his jet that takes the most famous and the richest people in the world from place to place. She's almost 67, still looks great and still can put on that smile and charm. Nothing has ever gone wrong on flight for her, she's always been in control and that was how she was in their lives – and if anybody needed that it was Steve Marriott.

*When Pam and I spoke in June 2019, Marriott's nephew, Kay's son Steve, was visiting Pam at her home in America. In subsequent email exchanges, she promised to try to be more truthful. I thought she had already been remarkably open. In October, she emailed.*

**Pam Marriott Land:** Seems I've outlived most of our friends from those years, and I guess that made it easier for me to spin my version of our life together to make me a victim and Steve the bad guy. That really wasn't the case. Truth is, what I should say most importantly is that Steve was the best mentor I could have ever hoped for. I've had an extraordinary life, and I wouldn't have done a third of the things I have if it wasn't for Steve's influence. I've never met anyone who loved life as much as he did. With money, without money, good times and scarier times, he never lost his sense of humour or ability to draw you in with him, even when you hated his guts. But I have to admit, I still can't wrap my head around Steve's continued popularity! He's a movie. That's for sure.

*The End*

# ACKNOWLEDGEMENTS

RIP: Dee Anthony, Don Arden, Benedetta Balistrieri, Frank Barsalona, Franklyn Boyd, Tony Brainsby, Vicki Brown, Tito Burns, Boz Burrell, Heinz Burt, Tony Calder, Jim Capaldi, Chas Chandler, Bill Corbett, Pauline Corcoran, Harold Davison, Terri Elias, Pete Erskine, Sally Foulger, Gil Friesen, Mick Green, Richard Green, Elliot Hoffman, Nicky Hopkins, Arthur Howes, Dave Hynes, Andy Johns, Anthony Jones, Clydie King, Maurice King, Terry Knight, Alexis Korner, Eric Kronfeld, Ronnie Lane, Alvin Lee, Phil Lynott, Bill Marriott, Kath Marriott, Steve Marriott, Sheena McCall, Jimmy McCulloch, Tony McIntyre, Goldy McJohn, Ian McLagan, Tony Meehan, Laurie O'Leary, Bert Padell, Fran Piller, Greg Ridley, Ian Samwell, Shepard Sherbell, Mort Shuman, Robert Stigwood, Dick Swettenham, Derek Taylor, Johnny Thunders, Doris Troy, Stanley Unwin, Penny Valentine, Robert Wace, Ian Wallace, Mickey Waller, Carlena Williams, B. J. Wilson.

THANKS: Dane Muise, Peter Rochford, the Joe Meek Society, Rudy Calvo, Jerry Brandt, Paul Francis, Honey B Mama, Joey Stann, Pete Mitchell (1958–2020), Randy 'Badazz' Alpert, John Reed, Fred Eichel, Len Brown, Andrew Loog Oldham, Jenny Dearden, Kevin Pocklington, David Barraclough, Imogen Gordon Clark, Alex Jaworzyn and Nikky Twyman.

SPECIAL THANKS: Jerry Shirley.

THOSE THAT GOT AWAY: John Wright, Derek Green, Bill Curbishley, Joe Brown, Doug Morris, Mick Weaver, Mick O'Sullivan, Adrienne Posta, Mick Jones, Dave Clark, John Hammel, Ray Newbrook, Jerry Moss, Doug Morris, Eddie Kramer, Cheryl Krebs, Phil Anthony.

# BIBLIOGRAPHY

Arden, Don: *Mr Big* (Robson, 2004)

Badman, Keith & Rawlings, Terry: *Small Faces: Quite Naturally* (Cherry Red, 2000)

Brooks, Elkie: *Finding My Voice* (Robson, 2012)

Brown, Joe: *Brown Sauce* (Willow, 1986)

Collins, Phil: *Not Dead Yet* (Century, 2016)

Daltrey, Roger: *Thanks a Lot Mr Kibblewhite* (Blink, 2018)

Dannen, Fredric: *Hit Men* (Vintage, 1991)

Faithfull, Marianne: *An Autobiography* (Little Brown, 1994)

Frith, Simon: *The History of Live Music in Britain, Volume 1: 1950–1967* (Ashgate, 2013)

Goodman, Fred: *Mansion on the Hill* (Pimlico, 2003)

Hagar, Sammy: *Red: My Uncensored Life in Rock* (It Books, 2011)

Hewitt, Paolo & Hellier, John: *Steve Marriott: All Too Beautiful* (Helter Skelter, 2004)

Hewitt, Paolo: *The Small Faces: The Young Mods' Forgotten Story* (Acid Jazz, 2010)

James, Billy: *An American Band: The Story of Grand Funk Railroad* (SAF, 2019)

Johns, Glyn: *Sound Man* (Plume, 2014)

Jones, Kenney: *Let the Good Times Roll* (Blink, 2018)

Matheson, Andrew: *Sick on You* (Ebury, 2015)

McLagan, Ian: *All the Rage* (Sidgwick & Jackson, 1998)

Muise, Dan: *Gallagher, Marriott, Derringer and Trower* (Hal Leonard, 2002)

Neill, Andy, *A Fortnight of Furore: The Who and the Small Faces Down Under* (Mutley Press, 1998)

Neill, Andy: *Faces* (Omnibus, 2011)

Neill, Andy & Kent, Matt: *Anyway Anyhow: The Complete Chronicle of The Who* (Virgin, 2007)

Oldham, Andrew Loog: *Stoned* (Vintage, 2001)

Oldham, Andrew Loog: *2Stoned* (Vintage, 2003)

Oldham, Andrew Loog: *Stoned Free* (Because, 2011)

O'Leary, Laurie: *Ronnie Kray: A Man Among Men* (Headline, 2001)

Paytress, Mark: *Marc Bolan: The Rise and Fall of a 20th Century Superstar* (Omnibus, 2009)

Pearson, John: *The Profession of Violence: The Rise and Fall of the Kray Twins* (HarperCollins 1985)

Pearson, John: *One of the Family: The Englishman and the Mafia* (Arrow, 2004)

Power, Martin: *No Quarter: The Three Lives of Jimmy Page* (Omnibus, 2016)

Reynolds, Anthony: *The Impossible Dream: The Story of Scott Walker and The Walker Brothers* (Jawbone, 2009)

Robinson, Tony: *No Cunning Plan* (Sidgwick & Jackson, 2016)

Roper, David: *Bart!* (Pavilion, 1994)

Rossi, Francis: *I Talk Too Much* (Constable, 2019)

Shirley, Jerry: *Best Seat in the House* (Rebeats, 2011)

Smith, Joe: *Off the Record* (Pan, 1989)

Spence, Simon: *Immediate Records: Lets You In* (Better, 2008)

Stafford, Caroline & Stafford, David: *Fings Ain't Wot They Used t'Be (Omnibus, 2011)*

Stewart, Rod: *Rod* (Century, 2012)

Tosches, Nick: *Save The Last Dance for Satan* (Kicks Books, 2011)

Townshend, Pete: *Who I Am* (HarperCollins, 2012)

Trynka, Paul: *Sympathy for the Devil* (Transworld, 2014)

Twelker, Uli & Schmitt, Roland: *Happy Boys Happy!* (Sanctuary, 1997)

Wheeller, Mark: *Too Much Punch for Judy* (Ten Alps, 2006)

Wheeller, Mark: *The Story Behind... Too Much Punch for Judy* (Pping Publishing, 2017)

Wood, Ronnie: *Ronnie* (Macmillan, 2007)

Articles

Arnhem, Andrew: 'Ogdens' newsletter (date unknown)

Cavanagh, Dean: 'The Small Faces', *Uncut* (July 2011)

Paytress, Mark: 'Lost Soul'. *Mojo* (May 2012)

# INDEX

442

# INDEX